VARIORUM COLLECTED STUDIES SERIES
Studies in East-Central Europe
General Editor: Ivan T. Berend

Baltic Commerce and
Urban Society, 1500–1700

Professor Maria Bogucka

Maria Bogucka

Baltic Commerce and Urban Society, 1500–1700

Gdańsk/Danzig and its Polish Context

Routledge
Taylor & Francis Group

LONDON AND NEW YORK

First published 2003 by Ashgate Publishing

Published 2016 by Routledge
2 Park Square, Milton Park, Abingdon, Oxon OX14 4RN
711 Third Avenue, New York, NY 10017, USA

Routledge is an imprint of the Taylor & Francis Group, an informa business

ISBN 9780860789093 (hbk)

British Library Cataloguing-in-Publication Data
Bogucka, Maria
   Baltic Commerce and Urban Society, 1500–1700: Gdańsk/Danzig and its Polish Context. (Variorum Collected Studies Series: CS760).
   1. Poland – History – 16th Century. 2. Poland – History – 17th Century. 3. Poland – Economic Conditions. 4. Poland – Social Conditions. 5. Baltic Sea Region – Commerce. 6. Gdansk (Poland) – History.
   I. Title.
   943.8'024

US Library of Congress Cataloging-in-Publication Data
Bogucka, Maria
   Baltic Commerce and Urban Society, 1500–1700: Gdańsk/Danzig and its Polish Context / Maria Bogucka.
      p.   cm. – (Variorum Collected Studies Series: CS760).
   Includes bibliographical references and index.
   1. Gdańsk (Poland) – Commerce – History. 2. Cities and Towns – Poland – History. 3. Sociology, Urban – Poland – History. 4. Poland – Commerce – History. 5. Poland – Social Conditions. 6. Poland – History – To 1795. 7. Baltic Sea Region – Commerce – History. I. Title. II. Collected Studies; CS760.
   HF3639.5.G35B64 2003
   943.8'22–dc21   2002032624

VARIORUM COLLECTED STUDIES SERIES CS760

CONTENTS

This volume contains x + 312 pages

PUBLISHER'S NOTE

The articles in this volume, as in all others in the Collected Studies Series, have not been given a new, continuous pagination. In order to avoid confusion, and to facilitate their use where these same studies have been referred to elsewhere, the original pagination has been maintained wherever possible.

Each article has been given a Roman numeral in order of appearance, as listed in the Contents. This number is repeated on each page and quoted in the index entries.

PREFACE

It is not an easy task to compile a long life's output in one volume. I have tried to collect those of my main studies which had been published in English, German and French. They reflect to an extent the evolution of my interests in the different spheres of early modern history: from the economy to social and cultural issues.

I started with studies on trade and credit (the first part of this book), then shifted to the social history of towns and townspeople (the second part); and in the last 25 years I have focused mostly on people's behaviour, customs and mentality (the third part). The choice presented in this book constitutes only a small part of my work; most publications are in Polish, a language not accessible to the wider audience of historians. There are, however, some books of mine published in English and German, which I would like to mention here: *Nicholas Copernicus. The Country and Times* (Wrocław 1973, pp. 201); *Das alte Danzig. Alltagsleben von 15. bis 17.Jahrhundert* (1st ed. Leipzig 1980, pp. 246), (2nd ed. Leipzig and München 1987 and 1988, pp. 246); *Das alte Polen* (Leipzig 1983, pp. 247); *Die preussische Huldingung* (Warsaw 1986, pp. 239); *The Lost World of the 'Sarmatians'. Customs as Regulator of Polish Social Life in Early Modern Times* (Warsaw 1996, pp. 202). My book *Women in the Polish Early Modern Society Against European Background* is forthcoming. My history of Polish culture up to 1918 (1st ed. Wrocław 1987, 2nd ed. 1991), the biographies of Queens Bona, Anna Jagiellon and Mary Stuart, as well as other books and numerous articles, are, however, published mainly in Polish. Therefore I am very happy to have the possibility to prepare the present book, which I hope may prove of use and of service to many historians. I am very grateful to the Editors for this opportunity.

MARIA BOGUCKA

Warsaw, August 2002

ACKNOWLEDGEMENTS

For permission to reprint these essays I am grateful to following publishers, institutions and individuals: Blackwells Publishers, Oxford (I); Luigi De Rosa on behalf of *The Journal of European Economic History*, Rome (II, IV, X); Giannini Editore, Naples (III); the Polish Academy of Sciences, Warsaw (V, VII, VIII, XIV, XV, XVII, XIX); Professor Dr J.S.A.M. van Koningsbrugge on behalf of INOS, Groningen (VI); Cambridge University Press (IX); Akademie Verlag GmbH, Berlin (XI); Böhlau Verlag GmbH & Cie, Cologne (XII); Ashgate Publishing Ltd., Aldershot (XIII); Franz Steiner Verlag, Stuttgart (XVIII); Verlag Paul Haupt, Bern (XX).

I

Amsterdam and the Baltic in the First Half of the Seventeenth Century

THE object of this article is to analyse the share, in the early seventeenth century, of certain Baltic ports in the great East–West trade which centred in Amsterdam and was so important in the world economy of the sixteenth and seventeenth centuries. The principal sources for the study are 1,784 freight contracts discovered whilst working on an inquiry into 124 notarial books in the Gemeente Archief in Amsterdam.[1] Because of the scarcity and fragmentary character of other data, these sources, although in some ways incomplete and one-sided, constitute a basis for certain conclusions and comparisons. Freight contracts, valuable for such research into the history of commerce, have already been discussed in the works of A. E. Christensen and J. Schreiner[2] and are of the greatest importance for the study of the Baltic trade. The existence in Amsterdam of over 2,000 notarial books with entries referring to the first half of the seventeenth century provides a rare mine of further valuable information on the subject. That they have not yet been sufficiently explored is due to lack of indexes as well as paleographic difficulties. Although the books studied by the present author came from those notarial offices whose main concern was the Baltic maritime trade,[3] a number of freight contracts could undoubtedly still be discovered in the wealth of material excluded from the inquiry. On the other hand, even the most thorough investigation of the 2,000 volumes would not furnish an exhaustive statistical picture of Amsterdam's sea-borne trade with the Baltic. Part of the notarial records has been lost; not all the agreements between ship's captains and merchants had to be certified in notarial offices; and when ships carried goods of the shipowners themselves there was no necessity to sign any such contracts. Moreover, some of the contracts may not have been realized; or may have been carried out with certain modifications. So we can never hope

---

[1] Gemeente Archief, Amsterdam (hereafter GAA), Notarielle Archiefen: Not. J. F. Bruyningh nos. 73, 78, 80, 84, 86, 88, 93, 94, 97, 100, 101, 103, 105–7, 110, 111, 113–27, 129, 131–4, 139, 140, 142, 150–4, 195–7, 199–201; Not. W. Benninck no. 335; Not. H. Bruyningh no. 741; Not. Pieter Capoen nos. 1567–75, 1587–9; Not. Siebrant Cornelis nos. 640, 641, 645; Not. W. Cluyt no. 343; Not. J. van Gieteren no. 1233; Not. Jan de Graeff no. 1623; Not. L. Heylinc no. 56; Not. Nic. Jacobs nos. 375, 377, 378, 381, 394; Not. Jacobs van Loosdrecht no. 1989; Not. Jacob Meerhout nos. 209, 210, 213, 215, 238, 253, 254; Not. Jan Volbr. Oli nos. 1525–35; Not. Evert Claesz Rooleau no. 856; Not. Gerrits Rooleau nos. 761, 763, 764, 781, 782; Not. J. Steur no. 1860; Not. J. Thielmans no. 2118; Not. Fr. Uytenborgaar no. 1821; Not. J. H. Vallengio no. 331; Not. Jan Warnaertz nos. 668–71, 673, 694–6; Not. Jan van Zweiten nos. 863, 869–75, 879.

[2] A. E. Christensen, *Dutch Trade to the Baltic about 1600. Studies in the Sound Toll Register and Dutch Shipping Records* (Copenhagen and The Hague, 1941); J. Schreiner, *Nederland og Norge 1625–1650. Trelast utforsel og handelspolitik* (Oslo, 1933).

[3] I am very grateful to Dr Simon Hart for his kindly help in my research work in the Gemeente Archief in Amsterdam.

to achieve a full statistical picture of Amsterdam's maritime trade from those notarial books, and the figures deduced on the basis of such records should be considered to represent a minimum. Nonetheless, notarial records supply valuable information concerning the trading orientation of Amsterdam's merchants. On the basis which they provide it is possible to draw conclusions concerning the intensity and frequency of certain actions occurring in particular periods, and make periodical comparisons of the intensity of contacts between particular ports or regions. The wealth of information contained in the sources enables one to develop hypothetical statistics which undoubtedly must be verified and checked with corresponding data obtained from other types of sources, including the Sound toll registers. The task of this study is to supply material for such a confrontation.

Table 1. *Amsterdam's Partners in the Baltic Trade, 1597–1651*

Port	Number of Freight Contracts	Percentage of Total	Ships' carrying capacity (lasts)	Percentage of Total	Average ships' carrying capacity (lasts)
Danzig	950	53·3	121,060	54·7	127·4
Riga	366	20·5	45,288	20·5	123·7
Königsberg	96	5·4	11,524	5·2	120
Revel	66	3·7	8,268	3·7	125·2
Windau	55	3·1	7,132	3·2	129·6
Wiborg	41	2·4	4,245	1·9	103·5
Abo	30	1·7	3,485	1·6	116·1
Stettin	29	1·6	2,624	1·2	90·4
Parnau	19	1·1	2,485	1·1	130·7
Lübeck	18	1	2,654	1·2	147·4
Libau	17	0·9	2,151	0·9	126·5
Narva	15	0·8	1,145	0·5	76·3
Memel	10	0·5	1,215	0·6	121·5
Elbing	7	0·4	870	0·4	124·2
Others	65	3·6	7,038	3·3	108·2
Total	1,784	100·0	221,184	100·0	123·9

A last, which was used as a measure of both capacity and weight, was roughly the equivalent of 2 tons.

Table 1 shows that nearly 2,000 vessels with a total carrying capacity of over 221,000 lasts and an average capacity of 123·9 lasts per ship were recorded in the notarial books of the early seventeenth century as having been sent to the Baltic. Over half of these ships were expected to call at Danzig which handled over 50 per cent, in terms of the number of vessels and their capacity, of Amsterdam's trade with the Baltic.

I. Danzig

In Table 2 the 950 contracts found for the Danzig voyages are broken down by decades. These figures cannot be taken as presenting a precise and conclusive picture of fluctuations in the intensity of Amsterdam's trade with Danzig since chance survivals may play a large role here. However, the tendency indicated by the table seems to be probable: increase in the frequency of trade exchanges in the first two decades; decrease in the 1620's, due largely to hostilities in the Baltic; and, finally, increase again in the 1630's and '40's.

Table 2. *Freight Contracts for Danzig voyages*

Years	Number	Years	Number
1597–1600	9	1622–1631	3
1601–1611	53	1632–1641	300
1612–1621	194	1642–1651	391

A separate but related question is that of establishing how many of the ships that had planned to call at Danzig (as set out in the contracts) actually did so. The possibility of bypassing Danzig and calling at some other Baltic port (Riga, Revel, Königsberg, or Memel), if this proved more advantageous, is envisaged in 90 per cent of the contracts. The percentage in practice of such irregularities in the Danzig trade cannot be conclusively established, but it could not have been high. Since similar reservations were also made in contracts having other ports of destination we can assume that to a large extent those deviations cancelled each other. The majority of freight contracts for shipment to Danzig were made by a single merchant (775 contracts, i.e. 81·6 per cent). Less frequent are contracts made by two persons (147 contracts, 15·5 per cent); and only a very small number (28 or 2·9 per cent) were made by more than two merchants. It is quite probable that some of the contracts into which individual merchants entered were in reality made by companies which, perhaps in order to simplify the notarial agreement, chose to remain unidentified. This was unlikely to have been general, however, so we can assume that a considerable part of the Danzig trade was carried on by individual firms: a feature undoubtedly connected with progress in shipbuilding, in navigation methods, and in the increase of safety at sea.[1] Most merchants who entered into contracts came from Amsterdam (76 per cent). Many, however, were from other Dutch cities or towns, for example, Oostzaan (15·4 per cent), Enckhuisen, Lantsmeer, Staveren, Hoorn, or Harlingen, thus attesting to the considerable interest in cultivating trade contacts with Danzig felt by Dutch merchants from the whole of the northern Netherlands. Contracts were also made by merchants from other countries, for example England,[2] Portugal,[3] France,[4] and Sweden.[5] This was undoubtedly due to the international character of the Baltic trade. Companies established for trade in the Baltic all bore the same international and inter-urban features: partnerships of Amsterdam and Danzig merchants were particuarly common.[6]

Table 3 shows that over 380 Dutch merchants were engaged in the trade between Amsterdam and Danzig. The attractiveness of the trade is therefore unquestionable. This can be confirmed by a study of merchants' profits: profits from the export of corn from Danzig to Amsterdam at the time were estimated to average over 40 per cent.[7] However, although many merchants were interested

[1] See L. A. Boiteaux, *La fortune de mer, le besoin de sécurité, et les débuts de l'assurance maritime* (Paris, 1968) and K. F. Olechnowitz, *Der Schiffbau der hansischen Spätzeit* (Weimar, 1960).
[2] GAA, Notarielle Archiefen, no. 869 fo. 142, no. 870 fos. 113–14, 202–4, no. 1589, fos. 273–4.
[3] GAA, Notarielle Archiefen, no. 153 fos. 123–5, no. 381 fo. 438.
[4] GAA, Notarielle Archiefen, no. 94 fo. 140.   [5] GAA, Notarielle Archiefen 1623 fos. 348–9.
[6] Cf. M. Bogucka, *Handel zagraniczny Gdańska w pierwszej połowie XVII wieku* (Wrocław [Breslau], 1970), pp. 106–9.
[7] M. Bogucka, 'Merchants' Profits in Gdańsk Foreign Trade in the First Half of the 17th Century', *Acta Poloniae Historica*, XXIII (1971), 82.

I

Table 3. *Number of freight contracts for Danzig signed by the same merchant (Dutch merchants only)*

Number of merchants	Number of freight contracts	Percentage
177	1	46·5
72	2	18·9
33	3	8·7
22	4	5·7
14	5	3·6
10	6	2·6
8	7	2·1
11	8	2·9
11	9	2·9
9	10	2·4
14	more than 10	3·7
Total 381		100·0

in the Danzig trade a small group carried it on with great intensity and on a large scale. Though such merchants as Aris Albertson Snoeck or Claes Cornelissen Melckpot (see Table 4) did not monopolize the whole of the Amsterdam–Danzig trade, they signed many contracts and sent a great number of ships, thus managing to collect a large percentage of the turnover. As Table 4 shows, Amsterdam merchants were foremost in this tendency towards concentration, and the second place was held by the inhabitants of Oostzaan.

Table 4. *The larger merchants in the Danzig Trade*

Name	Town	Number of freight contracts
Aris Albertson Snoeck	Amsterdam	46
Claes Cornelissen Melckpoet	Oostzaan	35
Cornelis Graefland	Amsterdam	29
Outgert Luytssen	Oostzaan	26
Claes Janssen Clopper	Amsterdam	23
Claes Andressen	Amsterdam	18
Egberth Dolingh	Amsterdam	17
Matheus Swellengrebel	Amsterdam	17
Symon Jacobsen Coppes	Oostzaan	15
Pieter Janssen	Oostzaan	14
Claes Jacobsen	Oostzaan	12
Dirck Rodenbergh	Amsterdam	12
Marten Cornelis van Hoorn	Amsterdam	11
Marten Crossen	Amsterdam	11

As a rule, each freight contract mentions not only the name of the ship but also its size. The data in Table 5 differ from the figures calculated by G. W. Kernkamp who divided the ships sailing through the Sound during the years 1601–43 into three classes: over 100 lasts (37 per cent), from 30 to 100 lasts (60 per cent), and below 30 lasts (3 per cent).[1] However, his classification included all the ships sailing through the Sound whereas our table includes only those ships which were to call at Danzig. Possibly the latter were larger either on account of the

[1] G. W. Kernkamp, *De Nederlandern op de Oostzee, Vragen des tijds*, deel 2 (The Hague, 1909), 65–96.

type of goods carried or because of the volume of business. The average tonnage nearly doubled from about 80 lasts in the first decade of the seventeenth century to about 140 lasts in 1640–50. This increase accords with Christensen's calcula-

Table 5. *Carrying capacity in the Amsterdam–Danzig Trade*

Carrying capacity in lasts	Number of ships	Percentage
0–15	0	0
16–80	92	9·7
81–120	202	21·3
121–190	574	60·4
191–220	47	4·9
unstated	35	3·7
Total	950	100·0

tions for 1594–1639.[1] This trend does not, however, seem to have lasted for long. In his examination of the grain trade in the second half of the seventeenth century A. J. Faber estimates the average carrying capacity of a Dutch ship going to Danzig to be only 80 lasts of grain,[2] which would mean a return to the average capacity at the starting-point for this study.

Freight contracts do not state clearly what kind of goods were to be shipped by the chartered ship. This may have been because considerable freedom was left to the ships' captains or agents in Danzig; or, it may be due to the fact that trade on certain routes proceeded along well-established lines and it seemed unnecessary to specify the kind of goods in the contract. Nearly 100, i.e. over 10 per cent, of the contracts discovered do not mention the kind of cargo at all. For those contracts which do specify cargoes, the relevant data are set out in Table 6. The miscellaneous cargoes probably included various industrial products: from time to time mention is also made of tar, potash, ashes, wax, fruit, flax-seed, as well as of coins and silver ore.

Table 6. *Types of cargo, where specified, in the Amsterdam–Danzig Trade*

Number of Contracts	Type of cargo	Percentage
719	salt	75·6
503	grain	52·0
329	ballast	34·6
83	timber or masts	8·7
81	wine	8·5
43	fish or herring	4·5
34	millstones	3·5
24	flax or hemp	2·4
48	miscellaneous	5·0

The routes mentioned in the contracts differed according to the dates on which the contracts were signed. During a first period running from 1597 to 1631 (259

[1] Christensen, *Dutch Trade*, p. 100. Cf. also P. Jeannin, 'Le tonnage des navires utilisés dans le Baltique de 1550 à 1640 d'après les sources prussiennes', *Le Navire et l'Economie Maritime du Nord de l'Europe du Moyen-Age au XVIIIᵉ siècle* (Paris, 1960).

[2] A. J. Faber, 'Het probleem van de dalende graanaanvoer uit de Oostzeelanden in de tweede helft van de zeventuende eeuw', *Afdeling Agrarische Geschiedenis Landbouwhogeschool*, Bijdragen IX (Wageningen, 1963), s. 7.

I

438

contracts) the simplest route stipulated was the passage from Amsterdam or another port in the Netherlands through the Baltic to Danzig or, when this was impossible or unprofitable for the merchant, to other ports such as Königsberg, Riga, Revel, or Memel. This route, however, appears in only a mere 11 per cent of the contracts. More common (27 per cent) were contracts concerning the voyage from the Netherlands to Portugal (loading salt at Setubal or wine at Faro), then to Danzig (unloading salt and taking on grain) and back to Amsterdam. About 6 per cent were contracts made for similar routes, though instead of Portuguese, French ports were mentioned, typically salt ports such as Brouage or, less frequently, ports in the north of France. A slightly modified version of this route was found in 18 per cent of the contracts: the ships instead of going back to Amsterdam from Danzig were to proceed directly to such Italian ports as Genoa, Spezia, Leghorn, Viareggia, Civita Vecchia, Naples, Bari, or Venice, or further, to Crete or Cyprus. In 13 per cent of the contracts the route was lengthened by calling at Portugal for the second time (mainly at Lisbon and the salt ports, sometimes at Faro or engaging in cabotage); in 12 per cent the ships were to proceed to Spain (Huelva, San Lucar de Barrameda, Cadiz, Malaga, Motril, Valencia, Barcelona, or Majorca); in 10 per cent, to France for the second time, usually to lade salt in salt ports in the vicinity of La Rochelle or wine in Nantes, Bordeaux, Bayonne, or Marseilles. In 93 per cent of the prolonged contracts the ships were to return to Amsterdam, thus terminating the complicated loop of the long voyage.

Deviations from the principal route were infrequent. Only very rarely do contracts envisage ships calling at Danish or English ports or at Ostend. On one occasion a ship sailing to Italy and to Mediterranean islands was to go as far as Africa and call at some ports in Palestine or Egypt;[1] one contract refers to a journey as far as the Canary islands, the freight being winepipes (casks).[2] The interest in maintaining close contacts between Danzig and the ports of the south is notable. It was due partly to the great demand for Baltic grain, so evident in the Mediterranean area at the time, and partly to the demand for Spanish and Italian wines, southern fruit, silk and similar goods in Danzig itself as Poland's main port.[3]

In the second period, 1632–51, the trade routes, as shown in the freight contracts, underwent considerable modifications. The direct contact between Danzig and the Mediterranean, which played such a big role at the turn of the sixteenth and seventeenth centuries, came to an end. In only one contract was mention made of sailing along the route: Amsterdam–Danzig–Marseilles–Genoa, Leghorn, or Naples–Sicily and back to Amsterdam.[4] Direct contacts with Spanish ports, so frequent before, are now missing: only three such contracts for the Danzig–Cadiz or S. Lucar–Amsterdam routes were found.[5] On the other hand, there was a small increase, to 12 per cent of the total, in contracts made for the simplest route, Netherlands–Danzig–Amsterdam. In this later period, most contracts were made for the route Netherlands–France (La Rochelle and the

[1] GAA, Notarielle Archiefen, no. 131 fos. 187–8.   [2] GAA, Notarielle Archiefen, no. 152 fos. 38–40.
[3] M. Bogucka, 'Handel Gdańska z Półwyspem Iberyjskim w pierwszej połowie XVII w.' Przegląd Historyczny, no. 1 (1969), 1–23.
[4] GAA, Notarielle Archiefen, no. 1525 fo. 153.
[5] Cf. also Bogucka, 'Handel Gdańska z Półwyspem Iberyjskim...' 16.

neighbourhood of Brouage, mainly in order to lade salt)—Danzig–Amsterdam. Such contracts totalled 373, or 54 per cent, if those in which there was a slight variation from the basic route pattern[1] are excluded, and 421, or 61 per cent, if they are included. Contracts for trade with Portugal take the second place (Netherlands–Setubal–Danzig–Amsterdam); about one-third of these contracts mention possible side-trips to Sweden (Nörrkoping or Stockholm) and to England (Dover or, less frequently, London). Altogether, this group amounts to 147 contracts, i.e. about 21 per cent. The rest comprise single contracts for trips Amsterdam–Danzig and then to Kalmar, Copenhagen, Stockholm, Bergen, Bremen, Hamburg, Rostock, London, Dover, etc.

Certain conclusions can be drawn from these data. The trade routes in the later period seem to have been shorter than in the previous period, though the traffic on these routes was apparently quite lively, in the sense that there were a considerable number of contracts. We may thus conclude that after a period of stagnation the trade was again intensified though at the same time its range became more limited and its specialization, in serving the shorter routes, increased. Baltic grain, or at any rate, Danzig grain, no longer held its dominant position in the markets of the Iberian peninsula and of the Mediterranean. There were several reasons for this change. Apart from demographic shifts and changes in the development of European agriculture occurring at that time, the most important factor was the relation between prices and profits. Intermediaries in the Danzig–Iberian peninsula trade could earn profits only when grain was exported. At the beginning of the seventeenth century the profits on that business, with the aid of low Dutch freight rates, often reached 100 per cent of the capital invested; and after a temporary and slight decrease in 1609–14 the profits increased still further.[2] Theoretically, taking into consideration the differences between the prices of grain on the Danzig and Spanish markets, in the 1640's the profits on the export of grain on that route should have amounted to over 200 per cent or even over 300 per cent.[3] In practice, however, further trade on that route became impossible. The import into Danzig of Spanish goods, of salt, or of such colonial goods as spices frequently became unprofitable because of high customs duties levied in Spain and of too small differences in prices.[4] The import of silver and coins to balance the grain exports—common at the beginning of the seventeenth century and profitable despite the risks arising from the prohibitions on the export of silver and coins, and the threat by the Spanish crown of severe penalties for those breaking the law—was discontinued in the 1630's and '40's. In the first two decades of the seventeenth century the *agio* on the Spanish ducat was very high, standing at over 50 per cent, but it later fell and even turned into a discount.[5] This was due to the shortage of silver that was beginning to be felt in Spain at the time, and which resulted in the disappearance of the considerable price differential between silver in the Iberian peninsula and in Danzig. Consequently, when profits derived from the import of silver and coins became doubtful the entire Danzig–Spain trade exchange came to a stop in spite of the high

---

[1] E.g. Netherlands–Nantes–Bordeaux–Danzig–Amsterdam; Netherlands–Danzig–Nantes–Bordeaux–La Rochelle; Netherlands–French ports–Sweden–Danzig; Netherlands–Bergen or Trondheim or Langesund–La Rochelle–Danzig–Amsterdam etc.
[2] Bogucka, 'Merchants' Profits...' 74–5.   [3] Ibid. 75–6.   [4] Ibid. 78–9.   [5] Ibid. 75.

grain prices in the Iberian peninsula. There was simply nothing that the merchants could profitably exchange for the imported grain.[1] The importance of France as the Baltic's trading partner grew as contacts with the Iberian and Italian ports decreased. In Danzig, French salt successfully competed with Iberian salt;[2] and French wines supplanted those imported in the early seventeenth century from the distant south.[3]

Certain data scattered in the notarial books give us an idea of the changes in trade organization occurring in this period. The merchants signing contracts now try to ensure maximum flexibility for their trade operations; most contracts say that during his journey the master should keep in touch with and follow the directions of the factors used by the merchants who chartered his ship. This was connected with the rapid development of the factorage system which at that time became the vital organizational basis for international exchange. On the basis of the information supplied by the factors, ships' masters were to decide at the last moment which ports to call at and what goods to lade. Two big information centres were established: one in the Sound, the other at La Rochelle. Together with Amsterdam these two places became disposition centres of the Baltic exchange whose organizers had already learned to respond quickly to market fluctuations. Another change worthy of note was the habit of sailing in whole fleets, very often under the convoy of warships. This system of transport protection had been known as early as the fifteenth and sixteenth centuries but it had been resorted to only periodically, during times of hostilities. In the second quarter of the seventeenth century, however, this mode of transportation became so much the custom that it was guaranteed to masters in 80 per cent of the contracts; when a ship was to sail alone, without the protection of a convoy, the freight charge was set correspondingly higher.

II. RIGA AND OTHER LIVONIAN PORTS

In the light of freight contracts Livonia (excluding Estonia and Courland) takes second place after Danzig as Amsterdam's Baltic trading partner. Livonia's share in Amsterdam Baltic trade in the first half of the seventeenth century can be illustrated by the following figures: 403 freight contracts, amounting to 22·6 per cent of Amsterdam's trade with the Baltic ports; the carrying capacity of ships calling at Livonian ports amounted to 49,263 lasts, thus accounting for 22·3 per cent of the total carrying capacity mentioned in the contracts. Large ships travelled on that route and although their average cargo capacity was slightly lower than that of ships sailing to Danzig, it was over 120 lasts (larger ships for the most part sailed on the Amsterdam–Parnau route, see Table 7).

Of all Livonian ports engaged in the trade with Amsterdam the most important was unquestionably Riga, whose turnover amounted to 90 per cent of the whole trade of the region and was equal to 20·5 per cent of Amsterdam's total trade with Baltic ports. Riga and Danzig were the most important exporting ports for

[1] Bogucka, 'Merchants' Profits . . .' 80.
[2] M. Bogucka, 'Sól w handlu bałtyckim w pierwszej połowie XVII w.' *Zapiski Historyczne*, xxxvi, (1971), no. 1, 101–10.
[3] Bogucka, *Handel zagraniczny* . . . n. 154.

Table 7. *Amsterdam's Trade with Livonian Ports*

Port	Number of freight contracts	Percentage	Total ships' carrying capacity (lasts)	Percentage	Average ships' carrying capacity (lasts)
Riga	366	90·8	45,288	91·7	123·7
Parnau	19	4·8	2,485	5·1	130·7
Narva	15	3·7	1,145	2·4	76·3
Osilien	3	0·7	345	0·8	115
Total	403	100·0	49,263	100·0	122·2

grain grown mainly in the boundaries of Poland at that time.[1] It would seem that the occupation of Riga by the Swedes in 1621 did not constitute a turning-point in the development of this trade. As can be inferred not only from freight contracts but also from other data in the notarial books, Amsterdam merchants maintained lively contacts with that port throughout the period.[2] Transactions with Russia were often also carried out through Riga, and this constituted an additional factor contributing to the importance of that port.[3] The notarial books also mention trading companies being established by merchants of Riga, Amsterdam, and Antwerp.[4] The exports of Riga to the West were made up of grain (rye, barley, and oats), considerable quantities of flax-seed and hemp-seed,[5] wax,[6] hemp, potash, ashes, sometimes timber. Large quantities of Portuguese and French salt, herrings, and wine flowed into Riga via Amsterdam; 22 per cent of freight contracts mention ballast. From Parnau, under Swedish control from 1617, and Narva, occupied by the Swedes in 1581, mainly grain (rye, wheat, oats, barley) and a considerable amount of wax were exported.[7]

The routes mentioned in the freight contracts connected with Livonia are for the most part fairly simple: 68 per cent of contracts concerned the Amsterdam–Livonia–Amsterdam route. Sometimes, before sailing to Livonia, the ship was to call at some salt ports in western France (14 per cent of contracts) or at Portuguese ports (8 per cent). In nearly 10 per cent of the contracts mention is made of a probable route from Amsterdam to Livonia, which included the lading of goods and shipment to France, mainly ports in Brittany, or Bordeaux, or salt ports, the lading of salt or wine, and then a return to Livonia, another unlading and lading, and finally return to Amsterdam.

In the Livonian trade in the first quarter of the seventeenth century an important role was played by Lambert van Tweenhuysen, as well as by the firm of Timmerman and Amelandt. Numerous freight contracts bear the signature of such Amsterdam merchants as Claes van Domselaer, Dirck Vlack,

[1] Cf. E. Dunsdorfs, 'The Riga Grain Trade in the Seventeenth Century', *Baltic and Scandinavian Countries*, III (1937), 26–35; G. Jensch, *Der Handel Rigas im XVII Jahrhundert* (Riga, 1930).
[2] Cf. GAA, Notarielle Archiefen, no. 94 fo. 145, no. 132 fos. 158–9.
[3] GAA, Notarielle Archiefen, no. 129 fos. 81–2. Cf. also G. Jensch, 'Rivalry between Riga and Tartu for the Trade with Pskov in the XVI and XVII Centuries', *Baltic and Scandinavian Countries*, IV (1938), 38–40.
[4] GAA, Notarielle Archiefen, no. 101 fos. 185–6, no. 132 fos. 150–9.
[5] GAA, Notarielle Archiefen, no. 152 fo. 60, no. 195 fo. 179, no. 254 fos. 46, 271–2.
[6] GAA, Notarielle Archiefen, no. 101 fos. 185–6.
[7] Cf. W. Kirchner, 'Die Bedeutung Narwas im XVI Jahrhundert', *Historische Zeitschrift*, CLXXII (1951), 265–84.

I

442

Guilliaume Bert, Dirck van Oostzaanen, Jacob Symessen Louw, Anthony van Beaumont, and Jacob Lucassen Rotgans. In the second quarter of the century the leading position in the trade was held by Selio Marselis, well known for his lively contacts with the Russian merchants,[1] the Goyke brothers and Aris Snoeck, Marten Carsten, Rutger Niederhoff, Hans Vlamingh, Marten Calschuyr, Cornelis Graefflandt, Egbert Dolingh, John de Gruyter, Cornelis van Cuyck, and John Calckbrenner. Many of them at the same time carried on active trade with Danzig.[2]

About 9 per cent of the freight contracts were made by merchants from Enckhuisen and Oostzaan, who conducted their business through Amsterdam. Amsterdam–Livonia trade remained almost entirely in the hands of Dutch merchants. There were, however, certain merchants of Riga, such as Jochem Crumhausen,[3] Jurgen Schraden,[4] and Lenert Huller,[5] who were active in Amsterdam. It is possible that they not only carried on their own business but also acted on behalf of other Riga merchants.

The organizational structure of the Amsterdam–Livonia trade shows considerable differences when compared with that between Amsterdam and Danzig. Almost half of the contracts indicate that the master was the owner of either part of the ship or of part of the freight—a phenomenon almost entirely unknown in the trade with Danzig where a very marked specialization, separating the functions of the merchant from those of a carrier, had taken place. As many as 37·5 per cent of the contracts were signed by more than two merchants; 18 per cent of the contracts which had Riga as the port of destination chartered not the whole ship but only ½, ⅓, or ¼ of the ship. This Amsterdam–Livonia trade had, therefore, a more scattered nature, was at a lower level of economic development, and was less monopolized than the Amsterdam–Danzig trade.

III. OTHER BALTIC PORTS[6]

Much has already been written about the role played by Estonia in the Baltic trade and the output of its manorial farms.[7] Revel, in Swedish hands since 1561, was the fourth largest trading partner of Amsterdam. The 66 freight contracts represented 3·7 per cent of the total; and the total carrying capacity of the ships named in those contracts totalled 8,268 lasts, i.e. 3·7 per cent. The route to Revel was served by large ships—the average carrying capacity was 125 lasts, only a little less than that of the ships sailing to Danzig (cf. Table 1).

Freight contracts signed for the journey to Revel mention first of all French and Portuguese salt among the goods imported from the West. Salt prices in Revel were much higher than in Danzig where the demand for salt was rather

---

[1] Cf. M. Bogucka, 'Zboże rosyjskie na rynku amsterdamskim w pierwszej połowie XVII w.' *Przegląd Historyczny*, No. 4 (1962), 621 ff.

[2] M. Bogucka, 'Handel niderlandzko-gdański w latach 1597–1651 w świetle amsterdamskich kontraktów frachtowych', *Zapiski Historyczne*, XXXIII (1968), no. 3, 174 ff.

[3] GAA, Notarielle Archiefen, no. 124 fos. 205–6, no. 196, fo. 392; DTB no. 674 fo 145, no. 675 fo. 117.

[4] GAA, Notarielle Archiefen, no. 152 fo. 60.   [5] GAA, Notarielle Archiefen, no. 132 fos. 158–9.

[6] This section deals with ports in Estonia, Courland, Ducal Prussia, Finland, Western Pomerania, Lübeck, Rostock, and Wismar.

[7] Cf. A. Soom, *Die Herrenhof in Estland im XVII Jahrhundert* (Lund, 1954). E. Blumenfeldt, 'Statistilisi lisandeit Tallina kaubalükluse ja meresoidu ajaloode am 1609–1629', *Ajalooline ajakiri*, XIV (1935), 1–18, 49–63.

limited since most of inland Poland consumed salt mined in Wieliczka-Bochnia and in Ruthenia—the Polish nobility purchased that salt at lower prices.[1] In return for the salt the merchants or ships' masters were to load grain at Revel (wheat, rye, and barley) as well as wax, hemp, and tar. Among those merchants a prominent role was played again by Lambert van Tweenhuysen, who employed factors in Revel[2] and advanced loans to merchants there.[3] Other Amsterdam merchants—Egbert Dolingh, Seger Cornelissen, John Calckbrenner, Melchior Crumhausen, the Cornelius brothers and Gisbert Hogenberg, Casper Brinckmann, Cornelius Graefflandt junior—also carried on a vigorous trade in Revel and had factors there.[4] The most striking feature of the trade carried on this route was the small quantities of goods shipped: individual merchants very often did not charter whole ships but arranged for the shipment of merely 50, 60, or 70 lasts of goods. Ship's captains and even ordinary sailors did a good deal of trading on their own or on behalf of shipowners. The contracts that had been signed generally involved the simplest route: Amsterdam–Revel–Amsterdam: only a small number of the contracts (10 per cent) mention plans of a direct voyage to France or Portugal.

The fifth largest trading partner of Amsterdam in the Baltic trade was Windau, the principal port of Courland, with 55 contracts (3·1 per cent of the total); the aggregate carrying capacity of 7,132 lasts represented a share of 3·2 per cent. The other major port of Courland was Libau which also carried on quite an important trade with Holland. In general, the Courland ports with 79 contracts accounted for 4·4 per cent of this Baltic trade, by number of contracts, or 4·4 per cent, by carrying capacity (see Table 8). The average carrying capacity of a ship travelling on this route was 129 lasts—bigger than that of ships calling at Danzig.

Table 8. *Amsterdam's Trade with Courland Ports*

Port	Number of freight contracts	percentage	Total ships' carrying capacity (lasts)	Percentage	Average ships' carrying capacity (lasts)
Windau	55	69·6	7,132	69·9	129·6
Libau	17	21·5	2,151	21·1	126·5
Unstated	7	8·9	910	9	130
Total	79	100·0	10,193	100·0	129·0

Amsterdam merchants carried salt, herring, and cheese to the Courland ports, bringing back in exchange grain (rye and barley), hemp, tar, wax, and timber. Many of the same merchants as were active in other regions of the Baltic, such as Lambert van Tweenhuysen, Anthony van Beaumont, Selio Marselis, Cornelis van Cuyck, Cornelis Claesen of Oostzaan, were to be found in this trade. Quantities shipped were small; shipowners and masters had a considerable share in the trade. Over 80 per cent of the voyages were made directly from the Netherlands to Courland and back, though occasionally the voyage was extended by calling at French or Portuguese ports or such German ports as Hamburg. Because of the substantial commerce of Königsberg the ports of Ducal Prussia

---

[1] Bogucka, 'Sól w handlu bałtyckim . . .' 108–9.   [2] GAA, Notarielle Archiefen, no. 196 fo. 320.
[3] Ibid.   [4] GAA, Notarielle Archiefen, no. 763, 5/XII–1634, 26/III–1635.

444

took next place in the Amsterdam–Baltic trade. Königsberg itself featured as the destination in 96 contracts (5·4 per cent of the total by numbers of contracts or 5·2 by carrying capacity). The other port, Memel, was of small consequence.

Table 9. *Amsterdam's Trade with Ports in Ducal Prussia*

Port	Number of freight contracts	Percentage	Total ships' carrying capacity (lasts)	Percentage	Average ships' carrying capacity (lasts)
Königsberg	96	90·5	11,524	90·4	120
Memel	10	9·5	1,215	9·6	121·5
Total	106	100·0	12,739	100·0	120·7

All in all the share of Ducal Prussia in the trade, both with regard to the number of ships and their cargo, probably did not exceed 6 per cent of the Amsterdam trade with the Baltic ports throughout the first half of the seventeenth century.

Imports into Ducal Prussia were French and Portuguese salt, tobacco, French and Spanish wines, herring, sometimes weapons,[1] and also considerable amounts of coin.[2] Exports from the area included the usual grains— rye and oats, as well as flax-seed, buckwheat and other cereals, hemp, wax, and timber. Lambert van Tweenhuysen was again busy in this trade, as also were Jonas Witsen, Dirck Rodenburg, John de Gruytter, Aris Albesten Snoeck, Gisbert Tiebbes Popta, and Heyndrick van Vecheln. Among the Oostzaan merchants concerned with this branch of commerce were Claes Cornelissen Melckpoet and the two brothers and business partners, Outger and Dirck Luytsen, known for their big transactions with Danzig (see Table 4). Some French merchants from La Rochelle also carried on business with Ducal Prussia via Amsterdam.[3]

The organization of the commerce on this route shows the same features as those observed in that with Livonia: scattered trade, small quantities, and a considerable participation of skippers. About 30 per cent of all contracts were made by more than two merchants, and in many cases the contracts stress that the signatories were acting on behalf of a company.[4] Very often factors acted on behalf of their principals.[5] The route most commonly mentioned (79 per cent) in the contracts is Amsterdam–Königsberg (or Memel) and return, though other voyages were extended to French ports, usually La Rochelle or the salt ports and sometimes to Portugal[6] or Norway.[7]

Trade with Finland accounted for 4·4 per cent of total contracts and about 4·0 per cent of carrying capacity. Contrary to the views of some historians,[8] the ships calling at Finnish ports with an average capacity of 108 lasts were probably somewhat smaller than those calling at other Baltic ports. As well as tar,[9] a little

[1] GAA, Notarielle Archiefen, no. 763, August 1635.
[2] GAA, Notarielle Archiefen, no. 215 fos. 147–8.
[3] GAA, Notarielle Archiefen, no. 100 fos. 151–2, no. 195 fo. 303.
[4] Cf. GAA, Notarielle Archiefen, no. 213 fos. 88–9, 164–6, no. 215 fos. 147–8, 163.
[5] Cf. GAA, Notarielle Archiefen, no. 150 fo. 155.   [6] GAA, Notarielle Archiefen, no. 150 fos. 87–8.
[7] GAA, Notarielle Archiefen, no. 763, September 1632.
[8] Cf. Möller Sylvi, *Suomen tapulikaupunkien valtaporvaristo ja sen kaupankäy ntimenetelmät 1600-luvum alku-puolella* (Helsinki, 1954), *passim.*
[9] Ibid.

Table 10. *Amsterdam's Trade with Finnish Ports*

Port	Number of freight contracts	Percentage	Total ships' carrying capacity (lasts)	Percentage	Average ships' carrying capacity (lasts)
Wiborg	41	51·3	4,245	49·0	103·5
Abo	30	37·5	3,485	40·2	116·1
Others	9	11·2	927	10·8	103
Total	80	100·0	8,657	100·0	108·2

rye and barley was exported mainly in exchange for salt from the West. Some familiar names were engaged in the trade: John Calckbrenner, the Cornelis brothers, Gysberg Hogenbergh, Anthony Benckmann, Jochem Crumhausen (a citizen both of Riga and Amsterdam), and the Oostzaan merchant, Jacob Claesz Slinger. The route of ships sailing to Finland was usually uncomplicated; none of the salt ports of France or Portugal were included in the voyage, perhaps because the cargoes of tar were intended mostly for the Netherlands.

There was a small trade with Western Pomerania: 41 freight contracts (2·3 per cent of the total) and a cargo capacity of 3,905 lasts (1·7 per cent of the total). The average capacity of ships sailing here was small, rarely reaching 100 lasts.

Table 11. *Amsterdam's Trade with Western Pomerania Ports*

Port	Number of freight contracts	Percentage	Total ships' carrying capacity (lasts)	Percentage	Average ships' carrying capacity (lasts)
Stettin	29	70·8	2,624	67·4	90·4
Others	12	29·2	1,281	32·6	106·7
Total	41	100·0	3,905	100·0	95·2

Stettin was of certain importance, other ports are seldom mentioned in contracts. It is likely that German merchants, rather than Dutch, and particularly those from the not too distant Lübeck, still played a major role in the trade with western Pomerania.

Lambert van Tweenhuysen was the principal Amsterdam merchant trading with Stettin; at the beginning of the seventeenth century he also acted as agent for Stettin's mayor, Simon Giesebrecht, and disposed of his commodities in Holland.[1] Other Amsterdam merchants who sent ships to Western Pomerania included Herman Dolingh, German Pouillie, Adrian van der Graeff, and Matthew Swellengrebel, as well as Pieter Cornelis of Lantsmeer, and Joris Labat, a French merchant, who carried on trade with Stettin through Amsterdam.

Wheat, rye, wool, and timber were the main goods carried from the area, in exchange for salt, herring, and wine. Again, the trade was carried on in small quantities; one merchant brought only 20 lasts of herring.[2] Some 60 per cent of the ships simply went from Amsterdam to Pomerania and back, though in about 10 per cent of the contracts the goods were simply to go to Pomerania and the master was then free to search for anyone willing to charter the ship. The remaining 30 per cent of the contracts involved longer routes, however, thus

---

[1] GAA, Notarielle Archiefen, no. 123 fo. 111.   [2] GAA, Notarielle Archiefen, no. 132 fo. 5.

showing that at the beginning of the seventeenth century there existed direct contacts with France, and even Portugal and Italy.[1]

Eighteen freight contracts mentioning Lübeck have been found: they amount to about 1 per cent of Amsterdam's total Baltic trade. That this share is so small is probably due to the fact that Lübeck's own shipping trade and merchant marine were well developed.[2] The ships sailing to Lübeck, however, were exceptionally large, averaging 147·4 lasts. It seems likely that business contacts between Amsterdam and Lübeck were quite active. Amsterdam merchants (Isaak, Carel, and Hans Wolff) consigned their commodities to a Lübeck merchant (Christopher Kus);[3] conversely, a merchant of Stavoren (Andries Pieters) was the Amsterdam agent for Lübeck merchants (John Vuchting and Henrick Breitefeldt).[4] Other Amsterdam merchants that kept constant contacts with Lübeck were John Calckbrenner, Gisbert van Raephorst, Rutger Niederhoff, and also the mayor of Edam, John Mieuwsen. Ships' masters from Lübeck are frequently mentioned as being in the service of Amsterdam merchants.[5] The usual cargoes in the Netherlands–Lübeck trade were wheat, barley, rye, and timber; with salt as the chief import. The direct route was varied in about 47 per cent of the voyages by a call at Portuguese ports.

Finally, mention must be made of three contracts involving Rostock and three for Wismar. All date from the beginning of the century; grain to be shipped to Portugal or Italy was the principal cargo.

IV

Amsterdam's Baltic trade in the first half of the seventeenth century, on the basis of the analysis of material contained in the notarial books, seems mostly to have been an exchange of two basic commodities, grain and salt, though silver or silver coin as well as ballast were also used in the exchange with the commodities from the east. Commodities such as wine and herring, from the West, and timber and forest products, from the East, were next on the list. For the Dutch merchants Danzig was the largest trading partner, commanding over half of the turnover, followed by Riga and other Livonian ports. The trade with Prussia, Estonia, and Finland testified to the wide area tapped by these Amsterdam merchants. Their volume of trade was smaller in Western Pomerania and in such Baltic ports as Lübeck, where trade exchange still remained in the hands of local merchants and sailors, successors of the Hanse.

The occurrence of the same names in the Baltic trade, regardless of a region or port, is striking. No doubt a certain group of merchants specialized in these contacts, and concentration of trade is most evident in Danzig. Contacts with other Baltic ports were looser and accordingly less specialized. However, even there most of the trade was in the hands of large Dutch firms geared almost exclusively to the trade between the Baltic and the salt ports of France and Portugal. These firms probably had a great deal of capital at their disposal;

---

[1] Cf. GAA, Notarielle Archiefen, no. 134 fos. 229–30.
[2] Cf. P. Jeannin, 'Contribution à l'étude du commerce de Lubeck aux environs de 1580', *Hansische Studien* (Berlin, 1961), 162–89.
[3] GAA, Notarielle Archiefen, no. 120 fos. 18–19.   [4] GAA, Notarielle Archiefen, no. 1526 fos. 54–6.
[5] Bogucka, 'Handel niderlandzko-gdański . . .'' 179.

they also made use of the ample credit facilities which Amsterdam offered; they employed numerous factors, and in turn frequently undertook factoring services in the West.

The material presented here also shows that the direct trade between the Baltic and the Mediterranean was fairly vigorous in the first twenty-five years of the seventeenth century, but halted in the years that followed. In the second quarter of the century there are few contracts involving the direct shipping of Baltic grain further than Portugal; on the Baltic markets, meanwhile, Iberian salt was being supplanted by French salt.[1] These phenomena, brought about to a large extent by changes in prices and merchants' profits, attest to an appreciable shrinking of the area of influence of the Baltic trade. In the notarial books we find at this time records showing that the Dutch attempted to purchase grain in ports other than those of the Baltic: in Russia,[2] in Denmark,[3] and even in France,[4] which had for many years been an importer of Baltic grain, rather than an exporter. Did these developments arise from the incredibly rapid growth of demand for grain on the Amsterdam market that occurred in the seventeenth century, or from the insufficient supply of grain in Baltic ports? Undoubtedly both played a part. In the final analysis, although the Baltic area still constituted Amsterdam's principal grain-base, the first symptoms of the approaching decline of what, in the sixteenth century, the Dutch had called their "mother trade", were already evident in the first half of the seventeenth century.

---

[1] Bogucka, 'Sól w handlu bałtyckim . . .', 105–9.   [2] Cf. Bogucka, 'Zboze rosyjskie . . .', *passim.*
[3] M. Bogucka, 'Handel baltycki Amsterdamu w pierwszej polowie XVII w'. *Zapiski Historyczne,* xxxiv (1969), no. 2, 22.
[4] Ibid.

II

The Monetary Crisis of the XVIIth Century and its Social and Psychological Consequences in Poland

Monetary troubles were characteristic of Europe as a whole in the XVIIth century, and were part of the general crisis which occurred in many countries from the beginning of the century and affected production and trade as well as demographic social, political and cultural relations. Although this crisis has been discussed by scholars for some years now,[1] its origin has not always been explained as fully as its development and consequences. One of the most controversial features of the crisis, which is also the most difficult to analyse, is undoubtedly the monetary perturbations which so greatly influenced the social and economic situation of various countries in the first decades of the XVIIth century. These perturbations took much the same form everywhere: there was a rapid deterioration in the silver content of the traditional currencies and a massive production of unsound copper coin which flooded the market (some historians, among them F. Braudel, have even spoken of an « age of copper ») and caused acute instability in prices, problems of trade and credit, and poverty for various groups of the population. They also exacerbated social conflicts, as is seen, for example, in the wave of riots in many German towns including Hamburg, Lübeck, Wismar, Stralsund and Frankfurt am Main, while in the mid-XVIIIth century a « copper revolt » broke out even in Moscow, a region that possesses an entirely different economic

---

[1] This problem has been studied in England by E. Hobsbawm, B.E. Supple, H. R. Trevor-Roper and others; in France by P. Jeannin, J. Meuvret and R. Mousnier; and in Italy by C. M. Cipolla, L. de Rosa and R. Romano. For analysis of this literature see J. TOPOLSKI, *Narodziny kapitalzmu w Europie XIV-XVII w.* (The birth of capitalism in Europe XIV-XVIIth centuries), Warsaw 1965, p. 141 *et seq.*

and social structure. It would appear that the causes and especially the consequences of the monetary problems had quite individual features as well as certain basic similarities. This was the case in Poland in particular, where from the XVIth century the general situation and trends of development took on forms that differed slightly from the development model adopted by the majority of countries of Western Europe.

There is not a great deal of literature available on the monetary crisis in Poland. Among early works we would mention the study by A. Szelagowski,[2] who identified the monetary crisis with the process of currency debasement and saw foreign speculation as its principal cause. This was also supported by other scholars, among them J. Rutkowski.[3] More recently, new studies have appeared which offer a new and more thorough account of events, among these being the works of Z. Sadowski.[4] This scholar rightly draws attention to the fact that the devaluation of the Polish penny (grossus) was preceded by an increase in the price of the crown (Thaler) and the ducat, and he concludes that the monetary crisis was a result of the great economic crisis and not vice versa. In Sadowski's view the problems did not arise from the debasement of the currency but rather from the rise in prices and their instability (in particular the relation of import-prices to export-prices). This had serious consequences in the redistribution of the national revenue and eventually also for social relations. The decline in the purchasing power of Polish exports forced the nobility to increase exports, which led to the increased exploitation of the peasants liable to enforced labour services. One of Sadowski's least convincing theses is, on the other hand, his assumption that crowns were being bought in bulk and paid for in gold.[5] The Gdansk sources, which provide information on the greatest monetary market in Poland at that time, refer rather to the purchase of crowns with debased foreign currency which increased their exchange rate and meant that good crowns

---

[2] A. SZELAGOWSKI, *Pieniadz i przewrot cen w Polsce w XVI i XVII w.* (Money and the price revolution in Poland in the XVIth and XVIIth centuries). Lwow 1902.

[3] Cf. J. RUTKOWSKI, *Historia gospodarcza Polski do 1864* (The economic history of Poland before 1864), Warsaw 1953, p. 156, and L. BABINSKI, *Upadek waluty w Polsce w polowie XVII w. na tle owczesnego przesilenia finansowego* (The fall of monetary values in Poland in the mid XVIIth century in the context of the financial crisis), Warsaw 1919.

[4] Z. SADOWSKI, *Rozprawy o pieniadzu w Polsce pierwszej polowy XVII w.* (Treatises on money in Poland in the first half of the XVIIth century), Warsaw 1959, and *Pieniadz a poczatki upadku Rzeczpospolitej w XVII w.* (Money and the beginning of the fall of the Republic in the XVIIth century), Warsaw 1964. Cf. also E. LIPINSKI, *Studia nad historia polskiej mysli ekonomicznej* (Studies on the history of Polish economic thought), Warsaw 1956, and J. GORSKI, *Poglady merkantylistyczne w polskiej mysli ekonomicznej XVI i XVII w.* (Mercantilist ideas in Polish economic thought in the XVIth and XVIIth centuries), Wroclaw 1958:

[5] Z. SADOWSKI, *Pieniadz a poczatki upadku Rzeczypospolitej* (Money and the beginning of the fall of the Republic), pp. 48-49.

(Reichsthalers) were being exchanged for « lion crowns » (Löwenthalers) or « crowns of the cross » (Kreuzthalers).[6] Similar methods were employed on a large scale in Cracow the second centre of monetary speculation after Gdansk.[7] The thesis that crowns were purchased with ducats is further weakened by the fact that the price of the ducat increased more rapidly than that of the crown. The tendencies to hoard do not by themselves explain this since, as we shall see later, ducats as well as crowns were hoarded and in fact the later were even more frequently mentioned in the inventories of accumulated treasure.

The origin and development of the Polish monetary crisis must be seen in the context of the period in which it took place. It would be wrong to speak of only one crisis — in fact there were two monetary crises in the XVIIth century which arose from different circumstances. The first began at the start of the XVIIth century and reached its climax between 1620 and 1623, that is at a time when monetary difficulties were arising throughout Europe. The main indication of this crisis was the rapid debasement of the Polish silver penny, although devaluation did not affect the more important silver and gold coins minted in Poland — the crown and the ducat. According to the monetary law of 1580 the penny contained 0.67 grammes of pure silver, in 1604 0.57 grammes, in 1616 0.51 grammes and in 1623 only 0.30 grammes. Between 1630 and 1662 the silver content of the penny was fixed at a level of 0.27 grammes of pure silver.[8] The devaluation of the penny was accompanied by a considerable rise in prices, especially in the price of manufactured luxury goods. This was not the- result of local devaluation alone, but also of a process that was taking place during those years in the markets of Western Europe which brought about a sudden deterioration in the terms of trade for Poland. These fluctuations and uncertainties in the Polish market in turn affected Western merchants and manufacturers, among them the English cloth merchants who saw a very sudden reduction in the demand for their goods which had become too expensive for the Polish consumer.[9] The fact that action and reaction, initiative and dependence, were bilaterally linked, then, is why the Polish crisis of the early XIIth century should be considered as one aspect of larges processes that were taking place in Europe as a whole. These were the result of demographic changes, the effects of the Thirty

---

6 Cf. M. Bogucka, *Zur Problematik der Münzkrise in Danzig in der ersten Hälfte des XVII Jh.*, Studia Historiae Oeconomicae, vol. 6, 1971, pp. 67-73.

7 Many examples are to be found in the study by W. N. Trepka, *Liber generationis plebeanorum*, ed. W. Dworzaczek, J. Bartys, Z. Kuchowicz, Wroclaw 1963, vol. 1, pp. 140, 251-252, 542-550, 601-602 etc.

8 Cf. « The laws on minting issued between 1580 and 1650 », published by Z. Sadowski, *Pieniadz a poczatki upadku Rzeczypospolitej* (Money and the beginning of the fall of the Republic), pp. 337-340.

9 B. E. Supple, *Commercial crisis and change in England 1600-1642*, Cambridge 1959, *passim*.

Years War, the decline of many of the traditional centres of production and also the reduction in the influx of precious metals from America which, together with the fall in output from European mines and the growing demands for circulating currency, brought in its wake a world shortage of metals.[10] The deterioration of the currency in the countries bordering on Poland — Brandenburg, Western Pomerania and Silesia — and in those countries, like the Low Countries, which had extensive commercial relations with Poland, resulted from the factors we have mentioned undoubtedly had some effect on the instability of the Polish currency.[11] But it is wrong to see, as scholars formerly did, the deterioration in foreign currency as the only factor responsible.

Deterioration in currency and inflation were characteristic of Europe as a whole, but their effects were exacerbated in Poland by secondary factors — above all by the disadvantageous price relations which developed in the XVIIth century, when Poland was exporting agricultural products and import-ing manufactured articles. The rapid rise in the price of corn, which was characteristic of the XVIth century, and which had made it a period of outstanding prosperity for landowners, had ceased at the beginning of the XVIIth. There followed a period of great instability on world markets, extreme fluctuations and sudden dramatic falls in prices.[12] Consequently the price of Polish export commodities rose little or not at all,[13] while the prices of imported goods, especially luxury articles, rose rapidly.[14] With its « debased » money the Polish nobility was able to buy fewer and fewer clothes, silks, furs, jewels and so forth from one year to the next. The complaints to be found in the writings of noble publicists in this period [15] and the uproar that took place in the Diets over the high cost of luxury

---

10 According to E. J. HAMILTON (*American Treasure and the Price Revolution in Spain 1501-1650*, Harvard, Economic Studies XIV, 1934) the influx of precious metals from America into Spain reached its height between 1591 and 1600 (2,707,626 kgs of silver); after 1600 a fall was recorded; between 1631 and 1640 only 1,396,759 kgs and between 1651 and 1660 only 433,256 kgs were imported.

11 On monetary problems in Gemany in this period cf. WIEBE, *Zur Geschichte der Preisrevolution des XVI und XVII Jhrs.*, Leipzig 1895. For more recent literature see V. A. DESPAUX, *Les dévaluations monétaires dans l'histoire*, Paris 1936.

12 Cf. J. MEUVRET, *Conjoncture et crise au XVIIe s.*, Annales, Economies, Sociétés, Civilisations, 1953, pp. 217-244.

13 Cf. M. BOGUCKA, *Handel zagraniczny· Gdanska w pierwszej polowie XVII w.* (Gdansk's foreign trade in the first half of the XVIIIth century), Wroclaw 1970, p. 124 et seq., and ST. HOSZOWSKI, *Rewolucja cen w srodkowej Europie w XVI i XVII w.* (The price revolution in Central Europe in the XVIth and XVIIth centuries). Kwartalnik Historyczny 1961, fasc. 2, p. 308 et seq.

14 *Ibidem.*

15 Cf. Z. SADOWSKI, *Rozprawy o pieniadzu ...* (Treatises on money ...) *passim.* J. GORSKI, E. LIPINSKI, *Merkantylistyczna mysl ekonomiczna w Polsce XVI i XVII w...* Wybor Pism (Mercantilist economic thought in Poland in the XVIth and XVIIth centuries). Selected texts. Warsaw 1958, *passim.*

goods,[16] clearly show how violently the Polish ruling class reacted to these events. Their complaints, however exaggerated, are confirmed by study of the Polish trade balance in the first half of the XVIIth century, which reveals a certain decline [17] that clearly explains the decrease in the flow of precious metals into Poland.[18] National silver production was of very slight importance,[19] and of necessity the unfavourable changes that occurred in Polish foreign trade sharpened the monetary crisis and forced the government to debase the currency.

The monetary crisis of the early XVIIth century was, then, a structural crisis which was connected with changes that were taking place in Europe, in the fields of production and international trade, and was exacerbated further by the particular characteristics of the Polish economy of the time. It was typical that in the 1630's and '40's minting almost entirely ceased in Poland and basically only large silver and gold coins (crown and ducats) with a fixed metal content were minted. So no attempt was made to emerge from the impasse by « improving » money, while at the same time it became impossible to put an adequate quantity of small coin into circulation to meet the country's needs. The Mint Commissions appointed by successive Diets [20] were unable to find a remedy and gradually the Polish market was flooded with foreign currency.

In the 1650's and '60's a new monetary crisis raged in Poland which seemed to contemporaries to be merely a continuation of the previous one, but which was in fact of a different nature. It was no longer, like the first, one element in a general European process but a local phenomenon brought about mainly by the destruction caused in Poland by the wars of the mid XVIIth century — the Cossack uprisings and the Swedish invasion. It had been caused in the first place by the necessity of finding the enormous sums of money with which to pay the mercenary armies. Revenue from duties was inadequate, and the problem was solved by debasing the currency, in the hope, it would increase the income of the Mints.[21] The pure silver

---

[16] Cf. The Diets of 1616, 1620, 1621, 1623, 1627, 1631, 1633, 1654, *Volumina Legum*, t. III, pp. 135, 179-180, 206, 217, 261-262, 320-321, 379, t. IV, p. 209.

[17] Cf. M. Bogucka, « Die Bedeutung des Ostseehandels für die Ausenhandelbilanz Polens in der ersten Hälfte des XVII Jhrs. », in: *Der Aussenhandel Ostmitteleuropas 1450-1650*, Köln 1971, pp. 47-55.

[18] Especially as some of this metal immediately left Gdansk, bought by merchant speculators, cf. M. Bogucka, *Zur Problematik der Münzkrise . . .*, p. 68 et seq.

[19] In the years between 1620 and 1640 2,900-3,400 tons of lead and 600-1,200 kgs. of silver were mined at Olkusz each year. See D. Molenda, *Kopalnie rud olowiu na terenie zloz slasko-krakowskich w XVI-XVII w.* (The lead mines of Silesia and Cracow in XVIth and XVIIth centuries), Wroclaw 1972, p. 272.

[20] In the years ·1616, 1621, 1623, 1631, 1633, 1649, 1659, *Volumina Legum*, t. III, pp. 135, 206, 217, 320-321, 379, t. IV, pp. 131, 279.

[21] In 1658 it was said at the Diet that « the Mint should give a profit of 150,000 every year », *Volumina Legum*, t. IV, p. 245.

content of the penny again fell, to 0.25 grammes in 1668, 0.24 in 1673, and 0.23 in 1685.[22] This was not a large devaluation and was not the main cause of the crisis, but rather the massive production of common copper coin, the farthing called « boratini » (Polish *boratynek*) from the name of the Italian Titus Livius Boratini who was the Farmer General of the Mint in 1659. Even worse consequences arose from the minting of bad *zlotys*, the circulation of which was obligatory. They were made by the brothers Andrzej and Tomasz Tymf, and bore the name « *tymf* » or « *tynf* ». While the Polish *zloty*, or the 30 pennies, according to the 1650 standard had to contain 8.10 grammes of pure silver, the new *zloty* contained only 3.36, equal in fact to only ⌈12 pennies.[23] As a result the market was flooded by the huge sum of 20 million *zlotys*, made up of farthings and *zlotys*, which created great speculation in the old currency, which was called *moneta bona* to distinguish it from the current debased coin, called *moneta currens*.[24] The two crises acted on each other and were aggravated by the rapid rise in the exchange rate of the larger coins, the crowns and ducats, used in international trade, or for hoarding. This rise is shown in the table in the Appendix. As one can see, the rise in the price of the ducat was greater (from 59-60 pennies in 1600 to 196-360 pennies in 1673) than that of the crown (from 36 pennies in 1600 to 102-180 in 1673). While in some cases the ducat had become six times dearer, the crown increased three to four times in value on average. This was due not only to hoarding, since all currencies were hoarded, and the crown in particular, but mainly to the variations in the relation of the prices of gold and silver on the world markets, which also affected Poland in particular way. The rise in the value of gold was sharper in Poland than in Western Europe, although there were some variations.[25]

As the table shows, the years between 1620 and 1623 were marked by great increases in the exchange rate of the crown and ducat, which the taxes introduced by successive Diets were unable to halt. The prices of the larger coins rose most slowly at Gdansk, where Dutch and other merchants bought Polish goods and left behind large quantities of them.[26] The consequences of the monetary troubles and the rise in the prices of the larger coins were more serious inland. These areas are represented in the table

---

[22] Cf. J. PELC, *Ceny w Gdansku w XVI i XVII w.* (Prices in Gdansk in the XVIth and XVIIth centuries), Lwow 1937, pp. 4-6.

[23] Cf. RUTKOWSKI, *Historia gospodarcza* (Economic history . . .), p. 194.

[24] In 1667 agio was 20%, in 1669 50%, and towards the end of the XVIIth century 100%, *ibidem*.

[25] The relationship between the prices of silver and gold in Poland was 13, 14 and 16 in the years 1601, 1611 and 1640, in France 11, 13 and 14 in the years 1602, 1636 and 1641, cf. Z. SADOWSKI, *Pieniadz a poczatki upadku Rzeczypospolitej . . .* (Money and the beginning of the fall of the Republic . . .), pp. 53-5......

[26] Cf. M. BOGUCKA, *Handel zagraniczny Gdanska . . .* (Gdansk's foreign trade . . .), p. 35.

by two important centres of trade and credit, Lublin and Lwow. As a result monetary speculation developed on a large scale throughout the Republic. The major centres were Gdansk and Cracow, the first because it was a great trading port which supplied the country with precious metal, the second because it was the centre for trade with Silesia and the Czech lands, to which Poland exported considerable amounts of coin. Then came Lwow, which was the centre for trade with the Levant, through which silver was exported from Poland to Asia, and where Ukrainian magnates purchased crowns and ducats,[27] and finally the towns where fairs were held, Poznan, Torun, and Lublin, which attracted merchants and nobles. All these centres were linked by complex commercial relations, involving the settlings of accounts and agreements. Little is known of the methods of monetary speculation, but it appears that at the beginning of the XVIIth century special trading companies operated in Gdansk composed of local and foreign merchants who bought « good » crowns and exported them to the Low Countries or to Silesia or Turkey, in which case they were sent via Cracow and Lwow.[28] In the Low Countries and Silesia these crowns were turned into coin of less value with a lower content of precious metal, which were then re-imported into Poland.[29] At the head of one of the companies which became particularly famous, and much hated by the merchants, were two Dutchmen, Isaac von Eicken and Jacob Jacobson von Embden (The Master of the King's Mint) and the wholesale merchant and well known Gdansk financier, Herman Wolf. The second was under the direction of two Gdansk merchants, Krzysztof Kanter and Hans von Coldun, in collaboration with the Jewish merchants Jacob Salomon and Aaron Vogel.[30] Two other citizens of Gdansk, the brothers Peter and Francis von Ende, also acquired dubious fame as great speculators at that time. They operated on the river Motlawa, at Cracow, and at Olkusz, and their activities brought them not only their fortunes but also ennoblement.[31] At Cracow the well known merchants Jerzy Wilderman and Stanislaw Szembek were the chief currency speculators.[32] However it was not only the burghers who speculated: the nobility and the magnates also gambled in

---

[27] We find a report by the town-councillor of Gdansk G. Schröder (died 1703) on the massive purchase in the town of the good old silver money and its export to the Ukraine and Turkey. Cf. *Library of the Polish Academy of Sciences in Gdansk*, manuscript department, Ms. 1254, p. 144.

[28] Cf. M. BOGUCKA, *Obrot wekslowo-kredytowy w Gdansku w pierwszej polowie XVII w.* (Letters of exchange and credit in Gdansk in the first half of the XVIIth century), Roczniki Dziejow Spolecznych i Gospodarczych 1972, vol. XXXIII, pp. 19-23. *Ibidem, Zur Problematik der Münzkrise...*, pp. 65-73. Much information on the organization of these companies in the first half of the XVIIth century is given in G. SCHRÖDER's notes, *Library of the P.A.S. in Gdansk*, Ms. 1256, pp. 16-23, 43 *et seq.*

[29] *Ibidem.*

[30] *Ibidem.*

[31] See W. N. TREPKA, *Liber generationis plebeanorum...*, Vol. I, pp. 140, 251-252.

[32] *Ibidem*, pp. 601-602.

this way, excited by the possibility of sudden, easily won gains, and were sometimes unaware of the risks they were running. « Almost all the lords and nobles began to get a taste for it. The ducat which he bought one day for 4 *zlotys*, or the crown for 75 pennies, he sold the next to someone else, the ducat for 85 groats, the crown for 90 », the noble publicist, Wojciech Gostkowski, wrote in 1622.[33] Another witness to these events, Walerian Nekanda Trepka, noted an interesting story which undoubtedly was well-known throughout Poland at the time. He wrote that in 1621 certain Cracow merchants, called Szembeks, persuaded several magnates, among them Prince Jerzy Zbaraski and the Bishop of Cracow Marcin Szyszkowski, to change ducats for Silesian *orts* at twice the current rate of exchange. They took the ducats to Silesia where they obtained an even higher rate and the Prince and the Bishop discovered, rather too late, that their « gain » was illusory, for they had become the owners of large quantities of a currency that was so weak that no one wanted to take it. In a rage the Prince of Zbaraz demanded that the merchant-speculator be imprisoned, but the latter killed himself fearing just vengeance.[34]

These astonishingly naive attempts made by the nobles and magnates to fill their pockets led to great losses (« we let ourselves be taken in », Gostkowski claimed bitterly)[35] but were only minor social effects of the crisis. In general the problems were regarded with incredulity and horror, which was intensified by the fact that the causes and the working of these events were not clearly understood. The sudden inflation which previous centuries had not witnessed, although there had been a certain drop in the currency standard, destroyed all sense of security and order, and shook the hitherto established ideas of property and the function of currency. An anonymous citizen of Gdansk wrote in 1604 in a treatise entitled *Brevis informatio de rei monetariae utilitate*: « Money which loses its original value not only ceases to be the correct measure for goods, but instead of bringing benefits to mankind it becomes an agent of numerous disasters and losses ».[36] Further on he wrote: « What a sovereign is to men, money is to all objects . . . and just as the sovereign must judge in the probity of his mind, money must measure the value of things through its natural probity, which it cannot do if this be lost, just as the sovereign who judges with a corrupt mind not only offers a judgement but destroys him, when he does not uphold the law or render justice, and also gives great office to all men ».[37] Noble publicists of the period

---

[33] WOJCIECH GOSTKOWSKI, *Sposob jakim gory zlote, srebrne, w przezacnym Krolestwie Polskim zepsowane naprawic* (1622), (How to restore the mountains of debased gold and silver in the illustrious Kingdom of Poland), in Z. SADOWSKI, *Rozprawy o pieniadzu . . .* (Treatises on mony . . .), p. 150.
[34] W. N. TREPKA, *Liber generationis plebeanorum . . .*, vol. I, pp. 542-550.
[35] W. GOSTKOWSKI, *op. cit.*, p. 147.
[36] Z. SADOWSKI, *Treatises on Money . . .*, p. 9-11.
[37] *Ibidem*, pp. 13-15.

The Monetary Crisis of the XVIIth Century and its Consequences in Poland

gave free rein to the surprise and indignation which « the money madness » produced and expressed their gloomy foreboding. « States perish very quickly as a result of bad money, anyone can see with his own eyes that our Realm is perishing in this way », lamented Gostkowski.[38]

Moreover these fears were not groundless, for the consequences of the crisis made themselves felt very quickly and painfully. The worst blow struck the nobility, which had grown accustomed to the lavish circumstances of the previous century and to a high standard of living. Almost overnight agricultural products fetched smaller returns because of the devaluation of the penny and the high cost of the larger coins. Added to this was the rapid rise in the cost of imported goods, so that the Polish nobleman's purchasing power was suddenly reduced. For the same quantity of corn he could now buy considerably less cloth, fewer furs, imported wines, and fruit from the South. The rapid rise in the price of gold resulted in the high cost of adornment, jewellery, plate, fancy goods etc. Opportunities for hoarding decreased in the same way, for not often ducats and crowns were now locked away in coffers. « Anyone in Gdansk or in any other town who will take 40 zlotys for his harvest or quit-rent will have no more than 20 zlotys when he wants to save them or buy something with them », Gostkowski complained.[39] « If a nobleman needs to buy anything in silver or gold for himself or his children, such as a jewel, spoon, chain, an inlaid sword or some article of clothing, he now has to cut twice as much corn than he had to a few years ago, when money was less costly » he lamented elsewhere.[40] In fact the noble was, generally paid in pennies or in foreign debased money for his corn, but when he wanted to buy imported goods he had to spend crowns or ducats, and when he bought them he was once again the victim of the agents, who demanded the highest rate of exchange.[41] The monetary problems also increased the losses suffered by the magnates, clergy and the Royal Treasury because of the fall in the real value of all quit-rents, incomes from leaseholds and taxes.[42] The nobles who farmed the magnates' lands should in theory have been able to enrich themselves in this situation but in practice their position was equally difficult, for the estate owners refused to draw up long term agreements which caused a state of uncertainty and a feeling of insecurity. Also the leaseholders were hit as much as the landowners by the disadvantageous terms of trade.[43]

It would appear that the peasants, who were the least involved with the market and the money economy, might have suffered least from the crisis.

---

[38] W. GOSTKOWSKI, op. cit., p. 153.
[39] *Ibidem*, p. 153.
[40] *Ibidem*, p. 165.
[41] Cf. M. BOGUCKA, *Letters of exchange and credit...*, pp. 22-23, and also W. GOSTKOWSKI, *op. cit.*, p. 146.
[42] Gostkowski's comment is characteristic, *op. cit.*, pp. 163-167.
[43] Cf. Z. SADOWSKI, *Money and the beginning of the fall of the Repubblic...*, p. 119.

However in practice the crisis rebounded very strongly on the situation in the countryside, because there was a tendency to suppress what remained of the quit-renting economy and to increase the degree of exploitation by the nobles. The income which the peasant derived from his farm, on which he continued to produce a certain amount of corn for the market, of course decreased as a result of the monetary problems and this reduced the peasant's opportunities to purchase goods from the towns. The acts of trickery to which he was subjected in the town, where he was virtually forced to take the debased currency for his goods and to pay sound coin when he wanted to buy anything himself, were very common, and added to his problems.[44]

But the town-dwellers themselves — with the exception of a small minority of lucky speculators — suffered from the crisis. The monetary problems were obviously most keenly felt in the lower strata of the towns, among the common people and the poor, the craftsmen and the wage-earners, since the real value of any wages began to fall with the depreciation of the currency and the rise in prices.[45] In 1630 complaints were made in Gdansk that because of the monetary problems the inhabitants had lost half of their possessions.[46] These complaints were undoubtedly exaggerated, but they show how acutely the crisis made itself felt even in such prosperous towns as Gdansk. Contemporaries even feared that the monetary problems would cause serious unrest in the towns.[47] In fact, in the most important centres strikes by journeymen protesting at the growing difficulty of living on their wages increased in the early XVII century.[48] In 1622-23, for example, a violent clash broke out in Cracow between the common people and the municipal council, mainly in the context of the monetary problems.[49] In Gdansk similar unrest developed later, in the middle of the century.

The poor and the working people were not the only victims of the crisis, however, for the well-to-do sections of the population of the towns,

---

[44] For examples see A. MACZAK, *Gospodarstwo chlopskie na Zulawach malborskich w poczatkach XVII w.* (Peasant farm in the Malbork Zulawy at the beginning of the XVIIth century), Warsaw 1962, p. 304 *et seq.* A. WAWRZYNCZYK, *Gospodarstwo chlopskie na Mazowszu w XVI i poczatkach XVII w.* (Peasant farm in Mazovia in the XVIth and early XVII th centuries), Warsaw 1962, p. 115 *et seq.*, 185 *et seq.*; J. TOPOLSKI, *Gospodarstwo wiejskie w dobrach arcybiskupa gnieznienskiego od XVI do XVIII w.* (Rural exploitation on the estates belonging to the archbishop of Gniezno from the XVIth to the XVIIIth centuries), Poznan 1958, p. 116 *et seq.*

[45] Even in a productive area as developed and rich as Gdansk, where manpower was in great demand, wages fell considerably and the wage-earners' conditions deteriorated, cf. M. BOGUCKA, *Gdansk jako osrodek produkcyjny w XIV-XVII w.* (Gdansk as a centre of production between the XIVth and XVIIth centuries), Warsaw 1962, p. 332 *et seq.*

[46] *The National Voivoide Archives*, Gdansk, no. 300, 10/153, pp. 219b-220.

[47] This was stressed by an anonymous writer from Gdansk in 1604, cf. Z. SADOWSKI, *Treatises on Money ...*, p. 21.

[48] For example in Gdansk, Cracow etc. cf. M. BOGUCKA, *Gdansk as a centre of production ...*, p. 350 *et seq.*, J. PACHONSKI, *Zmierzch slawetnych* (The decline of the notables), Cracow 1956, p. 283 etc.

including the patrician class, also suffered disastrous consequences. Large and small scale trade was seriously affected by the reduction of outlets on the Polish market, by the blow dealt to the well-being of the nobility and by the complete disappearance of the peasantry from the trading circuit. Unrestrained speculation and the considerable rise in prices, though sometimes bringing great profits, just as often, if not more often, brought considerable losses.[51] Also the merchant's tendency to compensate for the debasement of the currency by raising prices brought forth a reaction from the nobles, who fixed the price of goods, especially luxury goods, in an attempt to halt the rise in prices to some extent.[52] The insecurity and instability that threatened the burghers did not encourage business,[53] and credit which was so important for the growth of trade encountered great difficulties. The interests of creditors in particular suffered considerably, since debts were settled in a less sound currency than that which had originally been loaned. This caused difficulties in obtaining credit, especially on a long-term basis, or else led to a considerable rise in the interest rate [54] with which the creditors guarded themselves from possible losses. In practice this led to usury and blatant exploitation, and the victims included both the bourgeoisie (from the most well-to-do merchants down to journeymen and labourers) as well as nobles in need of loans which were often raised against future harvests [55] and even the peasants who were frequently forced to resort to the usurers.

Another no less serious consequence of the crisis appears to have been the psychologically understandable race to hoard goods as insurance against the insecurity of the monetary market. The valuables most often stowed away were precious metals and stones (jewellery, plate etc.), the larger coins, crowns and ducats, and probably also the common coin of earlier issues which had therefore a higher silver content than the current coin. Precious metals in the form of ingots, and bullion, were also hoarded. In the XVIIth century the magnates, nobility and well-to-do burghers sank increasing amounts of capital into jewelry and luxury plate, and amassed precious

---

49 J. BIENIAROWNA, *Mieszczanstwo krakowskie w XVII w.* (The burghers in Cracow in the XVIIth century), Cracow 1969, pp. 106-125.

50 E. CIESLAK, *Walki spoleczno-polityczne w Gdansku w drugiej polowie XVII w.* (Social and political unrest in Gdansk in the second half of the XVIIth century), Gdansk 1962, *passim*.

51 Cf. M. BOGUCKA, *Gdansk's foreign trade...*, p. 124 *et seq.*

52 Cf. the laws adopted by the Diets of 1620, 1621, 1627, etc., *Volumina Legum*, vol. III, pp. 179-180, 206, 217. See A. SZELAGOWSKI, *op. cit.*, p. 238.

53 Cf. M. BOGUCKA, *W kregu mentalnosci mieszczanina gdanskiego w XVII w.* (On the burghers mentality in Gdansk in the XVIIth century), in the press.

54 Cf. M. BOGUCKA, *Letters of exchange and credit...*, p. 28.

55 Cf. M. BOGUCKA, *Gdanskie kontrakty zbozowe w pierwszej polowie XVII w.* (Corn contracts in Gdansk in the first half of the XVIIth century). *Kwartalnik Historii Kultury Materialnej*, 1969, fasc. 4, pp. 711-719.

metals and solid coin by the ton.[56] The poor burghers and even the peasants also tried to lock away valuable ornaments in their chests, and sometimes a little of the old small coin which was greatly sought after in the XVIIth century.[57] This hoarding, which until then had attracted scant concern, undoubtedly had unfavourable consequences for the country's economy, since it froze considerable capital for many years. The purchase of landed property by the rich bourgeoisie also played a similar role. This increased rapidly, it seems, throughout the XVIIth century, and was not only a proof of the snobbish desire to rise to the status of the nobility, but was also a safe means of investing a newly amassed fortune which might otherwise easily be destroyed by devaluation.[58]

Hoarding as well as the investment of capital in landed property which has not been fully studied played a negative role in the whole Polish economy of the XVIIth century, by reducing productive investment and halting the growth of trade.[59] One might perhaps claim, then, that the monetary troubles had a number of serious consequences in different fields, ranging from a fall in the standard of living of various sector of the population, to the slowing down of growth in different sectors of economic life.

To conclude, then it is apparent that the whole of Polish society, with the exception only of very small groups of skilful speculators who succeeded

---

[56] Janusz, the Duke of Ostrog, left on his death in 1620 a sum of 600,000 ducats, 290,000 different coins, 400,000 crowns, 30 barrels of broken silver, cf. J. MACISZEWSKI, *Szlachta polska i jej panstwo* (The Polish nobility and their Estate), Warsaw 1969, p. 134. A similar treasure was left by Stanislaw Niemojewski the castellan of Chelm as the inventory made on 7-IV-1621 shows, *Voivoide archives of Torun*, register of the Torun assessors, IX-23, pp. 168b-184a. Information on hoarding by burghers of jewels, coin etc. is included in the Torun inventories of the 1620's, cf. *Voivoide archives of Torun*, registers of the assessors, IX-23, pp. 488b-497a, IX-38, pp. 275-277b, 327a-329a. Cf. also ST. WISLOCKI and J. NAWROCKI, *Inwentarze mieszczanskie z lat 1528-1635 z ksiag miejskich Poznania* (Burghers inventories for the years 1528 to 1635 drawn from the Court registers of the Poznan mayors), Poznan 1961, *passim*. J. PACHONSKI, *Decline of the notables...*, pp. 429 et seq., 455 et seq. *Dzieje Gniezna* (History of Gniezno), vol. I, Warsaw 1965, p. 336, etc.

[57] Cf. M. BOGUCKA, *Formy zycia « marginesu mieszczanskiego » w Gdansku polowy XVII w.* (The ways of life of the « marginal burghers », in Gdansk in the mid XVIIth century), Zapiski Historyczne, vol. XXXVIII, 1973, fasc. 4, pp. 55-79; *ibidem, Odziez mieszkancow Gdanska w XVII w.* (The dress of the inhabitants of Gdansk in the XVIIth century), Rocznik Gdanski, vol. XXXII, 1972, pp. 175-191. ANNA SUCHENI GRABOWSKA and HIERONIM WEISS, *Materialy zrodlowe do dziejow kultury materialnej chlopow w woj. sieradzkim i ziemi wielunskiej w XVI w.* (Sources for the history of the material civilization of the peasants of the voivoide of Sieradz and the Wielun lands in the XVIth century), *Studia do dziejow gospodarstwa wiejskiego* (Studies on the history of agriculture), vol. I, Wroclaw 1957, pp. 317-371.

[58] Cf. M. BOGUCKA, *« Atrakcyjnosc » kultury szlacheckiej? Sarmatyzacja mieszczanstwa polskiego w XVII w.* (The « attraction » of aristocratic culture? The *sarmatisation* of the Polish burghers in the XVIIth century), Acta Poloniae Historica in the press.

[59] *Ibidem.*

The Monetary Crisis of the XVIIth Century and its Consequences in Poland

in profiting from the general chaos, was affected by the monetary crisis. The collapse of the currency and the rise in value of the sound larger coins became the apocalyptic symbol of the misfortunes of the age, the apparent cause of all their worries and torments in the eyes of contemporaries. Neither the nobles nor the bourgeoisie was able to see these monetary difficulties as the product of the economic situation of their country and of Europe as a whole, but rather insisted on seeing the debased currency as the sole culprit. It is no surprise then that the debates on the monetary problem gave rise to impassioned controversy and polemic. The Diets and their members became involved in these debates [60] while the nobles (Gostkowski, Grodwagner, Zaremba, Starowolski),[61] and equally the burghers (Keckerbart, Boemeln, Freder,[62] Schröder, Krummhausen [63]) all wrote extensively on the subject. At the outset (1604) the burghers of the Prussian towns demanded a revaluation of the penny, a demand which was opposed by the members of the Commission of Monetary Affairs which the Diet had established.[64] After 1620, when the relation between the prices of exported and imported goods suddenly changed, it was the nobles who raised the demand for revaluation, or what was termed the « reduction of silver », in the naive belief that this would provide some miraculous cure for the rising price of imports and the falling price of exports.[65] But this was opposed by the inhabitants of Gdansk who feared that increasing the price of exports would discourage the foreign merchants who dealt in Polish goods: « high prices will drive away the foreigners who will take their trade elsewhere ».[66] Apart from these political and economic treatises and polemics, the monetary problems gave rise to a whole genre of polemical literature; tracts of every sort appeared, together with songs and verses, often satirical or mocking in tone, and which at times bordered on scarcely restrained hatred.[67]

---

[60] Cf. *Volumina Legum*, vol. III, pp. 10,135, 179-180, 206, 217, 261-262, 320-321, 379, vol. IV, pp. 131, 209, 245, 279, 447 etc.

[61] Published dissertations by Z. SADOWSKI, *Treatises on Money, passim*, and J. GORSKI and E. LIPINSKI, *Mercantile economic thought*; *passim*.

[62] *Ibidem.*

[63] Unpublished, cf. the *Library of the P.A.S. in Gdansk*, manuscript department, Ms. 1254 and 1255. (The latter Ms. in lost and its contents known only through the catalogue).

[64] They acted on behalf of the debtors: the revaluation, the increase in the standard of the penny « would bring great harm with it ... for in paying off the debts which burden a great many people in the kingdom they would pay more than they would otherwise have to ... », cf. Z. SADOWSKI, *Money and the beginning of the fall of the Republic...*, p. 172 et seq.

[65] *Ibidem.*

[66] Cf. Z. SADOWSKI, *Gdanszczanie w polskiej mysli ekonomicznej poczatkow XVII w.* (The citizens of Gdansk in Polish economic thought at the beginning of the XVIIth century), Ekonomista 1958/6, p. 1648.

[67] Cf. *Library of the P.A.S. in Gdansk*, Ms. dept., ms. 1254, p. 135. Ms. 1255, p. 384 etc.

One of the principal themes in this literature was the search for those who were responsible. *Vox populi* was unanimous in charging the «financiers» as the main culprits, together with the speculators, forgers and minters.[68] Even as early as 1601, the Diet decided « to suppress all the workshops where individuals in various towns may strike coin *in suum commodum* », at the same time giving licence to only two minting establishments (at Olkusz and Cracow) and laying down severe penalties for forgers and counterfeiters.[69] In 1611 again the Diet raised cries of indignation against the « abuses of the counterfeiters ».[70] Gostkowski and other nobles fulminated against the minters,[71] while Schröder in Gdansk called them robbers and cheats, and described in great detail how the fabulous fortunes of the detested farmers of the Royal Mint, Jacob Jacobsen,[72] Boratini and the Tymff brothers,[73] had been amassed. Amongst both the nobility and the bourgeoisie verses and couplets raging against the minters and counterfeiters were widely circulated,[74] and in practice the former was synonymous with the latter. It is interesting that there was no general feeling against the King, however, although it was he who had debased the currency. Public opinion limited itself to regretting that he had been too lenient and allowed himself to be tricked by the farmers of the Mint, who had known how to use gifts and presents to win the support of the King and the magnates.[75]

Another cause of general indignation lay in the arrival of debased foreign coin in Poland, which flooded Polish markets and aggravated the troubles still further. The nobles assembled in different Diets raised loud cries against the merchants who introduced this debased currency.[76] Gostkowski claimed that those responsible for the troubles were not only the minters, but equally « the Bohemians, our neighbours the German dukes, and the towns of Silesia ».[77] In Gdansk the Dutch merchants were blamed for the influx of

---

[68] A similar situation arose in other countries during the period of monetary crises, cf. R. DE ROOVER, *Gresham on Foreign Exchange*, Cambridge 1949, p. 200.

[69] Cf. *Vol. Legum*, vol. II, p. 426.

[70] *Vol. Legum*, vol. III, p. 10.

[71] Cf. Z. SADOWSKI, *Treatises on Money* . . ., pp. 143-145, 267-268, 291.

[72] The town-councillor of Gdansk, Schröder, called him a wretched hard-ware merchant and rogue who knew how to gain the favour of the nobles and the king, cf. *Library of the P.A.S. in Gdansk*, Ms. dept., Ms. 1254, pp.16-23.

[73] *Ibidem*, Ms. 1254, p. 135; 1256, pp. 43-52; 1255a, pp. 58-59.

[74] Most of these works were "dedicated" to the Tymff brothers and Boratini, including this prayer in verse, which freely translated reads: « But save us from Tymff and Boratini and send them to the devil, to cursed hell, for who is more to blame than they for all those *tynfs* and *orts*, not to mention *deniers* ».

[75] See note 73.

[76] In 1620 the complaint was made « that they bring foreign money into our country by all kinds of means, artifices and contrivances and buy up and export our silver of the realm, which far surpasses foreign money by virtue of its quality and weight . . . », *Vol. Legum*, vol. III, p. 180; cf. also p. 379 etc.

[77] J. GORSKI, E. LIPINSKI, *Mercantile economic thought* . . ., p. 147.

debased coin.[78] The noble memorialist Pasek thundered in 1662 against « the unworthy merchants » who had brought Wallachian *deniers* into Poland, that « cruel vengeance », the cause of « despair and horrible sufferings amongst men ».[79] There can be no doubt that monetary problems contributed to the growing xenophobia which, in the XVIIth century, became so typical of the Polish nobility.[80]

Anti-Semitism as well as xenophobia was bred by the monetary crisis. Particularly violent charges of complicity in monetary speculations were laid at the door of Jewish merchants, who were often singled out as the prime source of all these evils. In an anonymous treatise written by a noble as early as 1611 we read that « all these evils come from no other source than the trickery of the Jews ».[81] Gostkowski and Zaremba, seeking the causes of the high price of money, also blamed the Jews,[82] so giving expression to the feelings of the nobles who were becoming more and more fanatical, more and more determined to reveal — and hence explain and resolve — the source on which their economic distress might be blamed. But as the difficulties increased, so it became increasingly inadequate simply to blame the Jews and foreigners, and soon the nobility came to lay the blame for their financial problems on the entire bourgeois estate. After the 1620's the noble publicists began increasingly to accuse all the inhabitants of the towns of financial speculation and of activities which were dragging the country into ruin. The anti-bourgeois feelings, which had developed in the XVIth century, quickly spread and the nobles' writings on the subject of money are full of invective and attacks on the bourgeoisie. A treatise written as early as 1611 described the merchants as fleecers and forgers, and saw the cause of all the problems in their « tricks ».[83] Gostkowski also railed against the enrichment of « crafty men and merchants » at the expense of the honest nobles.[84] Zaremba accused the merchants not only of demoralizing society by importing luxury goods but also of « crafty expedients and intolerable profits », of forcing prices to rise, of monetary speculation and intolerable usury; « like inquisitive dogs and bloodhounds these merchants spy on our purses », he claimed.[85] The nobles were increasingly convinced that all inhabitants of towns were their enemies, money-grubbers engaged in specu-

---

78 Cf. M. Bogucka, *Zur Problematik der Münzkrise . . .*, p. 68 *et seq.*
79 J. Pasek, *Memoires*, Wroclaw 1968, p. 323.
80 Cf. J. Tazbir, *Ksenofobia w Polsce XVI i XVII w.* (Xenophobia in Poland in the XVIth and XVIIth centuries), in the volume *Arianie i katolicy* (Aryans and Catholics), Warsaw 1971.
81 Z. Sadowski, *Treatises on Money . . .*, p. 91.
82 J. Gorski, E. Lipinski, *Mercantile economic thought . . .*, pp. 148, 267 etc.
83 *Ibidem*, pp. 91, 106-107, 117.
84 *Ibidem*, pp. 160-161.
85 St. Zaremba, *Okulary na rozchody w Koronie y z Korony . . .*, 1623 (An eye-glass through which to see the expenditure of the realm and exports from the realm . . ., 1623); J. Gorski, E. Lipinski, *Mercantile economic thought . . .*, pp. 263, 267-268, 272, 291.

II

culation, parasites driving the country to ruin. « They are ruining the Realm, reducing it to poverty and stripping it of all its possessions while they are enriching foreign countries and increasing their own wealth ».[86] The old antagonism between the country (or more precisely, the castle) and the town turned into furious hatred.

One of the important consequences of the monetary problems was, then, the recrudescence of class hatred and an unprecedented increase in the antagonism between various groups, which developed into a merciless struggle among various sectors of the community. This situation is reminiscent of the psychopathic states to which a society falls victim in times of great scourges or epidemics.[87] Ignorance of the way in which such situations arise and a widespread feeling of menace lead to a feverish search for guilty parties which occasionally reaches almost the proportions of collective hysteria. Because of their widespread nature such attitudes constitute a tangible force which in turn contributes to the development of the general situation. The isolation of Polish towns and the decline of their economic fortunes owing to the increasing aggression of the nobility should be certainly connected with the effects of the monetary crisis on the psychology of the population. Thus the monetary upheavals were not only the effect of the unfavourable developments taking place in the economy at that time, but also accelerated them even further. The pressure and evolution of these attitudes in turn determined the attitudes and behaviour of specific classes and social groups, so influencing their mutual relations.

[86] *Ibidem*, p. 263.
[87] Cf. R. BACHREL, *La haine de classe en temps d'épidemie* (Class hatred in times of epidemic), *Annales, Economies, Sociétés, Civilisations*, 1953, pp. 351-360.

APPENDIX

The prices of the thaler (crown) and ducat in pennies[1]

Year	Gdansk		Lwow		Lublin		Official price (taxation by the Diet)	
	crown	ducat	crown	ducat	crown	ducat	crown	ducat
1600	36.5	59	36	60	36	60		
1604	37	60	37.33	61.5	37	63.7		
1611	41.45	70	36-42	70	42	65.7	40	70
1620	58.75	102.2	75	100-120	75	90-120	45	120
1623	76.87	129.35	75-120	120-180	75-120	120-180	70	120
1628	88.20	165	90	165	86.25	170		
1640	90	172.5	90	180	90	172.5		
1668	96.66	195	180	360	180	349.7		
1673	101.08	196	180	360	178	360		

[1] See W. ADAMCZKY, *Ceny w Lublinie XVI-XVIIIw.* (Prices in Lublin from XVIth to XVIIIth centuries), Lwow 1935. S.T. HOSZOWSKI, *Ceny we Lwowie XVI-XVIIw.* (Prices in Lwow), Lwow 1928, Y. PELE, *Ceny w Gdnasku.* (Prices in Gdansk), Lwow 1937.

III

Le commerce de Gdansk
avec la Péninsule Ibérique
à la charnière du XVI⁰ et du XVII⁰ siècle

L'établissement d'échanges directs entre Gdansk, le plus grand port de la Baltique, et la Péninsule Iberique au tournant du XVIᵉ et du XVIIᵉ siècle a attiré depuis longtemps l'attention de nombreux chercheurs [1]; c'est un élément d'une problématique plus vaste et importante de l'époque, un fragment, entre autres, de la concurrence accrue entre la Hanse, l'ancienne « souveraine des mers » au Moyen Age, et la puissance moderne, la Hollande, qui monopolisait de plus en plus hardiment le commerce de la Baltique et l'approvisionnement en denrées alimentaires et en matières premières de nombreux pays d'Europe occidentale et méridionale.

Le soulèvement déclenché en 1566, dans les Pays-Bas, contre les Espagnols, marqua un tournant car il priva les commerçants néerlandais de leur position dominante dans le commerce avec l'Espagne. Recherchant de nouveaux fournisseurs des principaux produits de la Baltique, notamment de blé et de bois, Philippe II demanda à la Hanse de rompre sa collaboration économique avec les Pays-Bas et d'organiser directement la four-

---

[1] Cf. H. KELLENBENZ, *Unternehmerkräfte im Hamburger, Portugal-und Spanienhandel*, Hamburg 1954; J. KÖSTNER, *Die Handelsverbindungen der Hansa, speciell Danzigs, mit Spanien und Portugal seit 1583*, Zeitschrift des Westpreussischen Geschichtsvereins, Heft 5, 1881; M. MAŁOWIST, *Les produits des pays de la Baltique dans le commerce international au XVIᵉ s.*, Revue du Nord, XLII, 1960; K. F. OLECHNOWITZ, *Handel und Seeschiffahrt der späten Hans*, Weimar 1964; pour des problèmes très proches — les relations commerciales entre la Baltique et la Méditerranée en même temps — on peut citer dernièrement P. JEANNIN *Entreprises hanséates et commerce méditerranéen à la fin du XVIᵉ s.*, Histoire économique du monde méditerranéen, 1450-1650, Melanges en l'honneur de Fernand Braudel, Paris 1974, et H. SAMSONOWICZ, *Relations commerciales entre la Baltique et la Méditerranée aux XVIᵉ et XVIIᵉ s.*, ibid.

niture des marchandises indispensables au fonctionnement de l'économie de ses territoires, jusqu'à la Péninsule Ibérique. Dès le commencement de 1582, des pourparlers de ce genre étaient menés avec Gdansk et d'autres villes hanséatiques; en même temps des démarches, d'ailleurs inefficaces, étaient entreprises au Danemark en vue de la fermeture du Sund aux navires néerlandais [2]. La très grande pénurie et la « cherté » du pain qui sévit, pendant l'hiver 1582-1583, dans les pays soumis à Philippe II, et surtout au Portugal uni à l'Espagne depuis 1580, créait une situation très avantageuse pour les exportateurs baltiques et encourageait les commerçants de Gdansk à tirer profit de la conjoncture favorable qui s'offrait à eux. La déchéance d'Anvers, en 1585, et la crise qui s'ensuivit pendant un certain temps dans le commerce néerlandais, devaient élargir encore les possibilités qui s'offraient aux commerçants les plus entreprenants des villes baltiques.

Cependant, des difficultés surgirent avec la guerre hispano-anglaise (1588-1604) et l'interdiction proclamée par Elisabeth d'entretenir des relations commerciales avec l'Espagne; de véritables chasses aux navires se rendant de la Baltique aux ports ibériques furent organisées par les corsaires anglais [3]. La République des Provinces Unies avait également proclamé (en 1588) le blocus de l'Espagne et enjoint aux capitaines hollandais et zélandais de capturer tous les navires soupçonnés d'entretenir des contacts avec l'ennemi [4].

Philippe II, puis son successeur Philippe III durent reboubler leurs efforts pour attirer dans les ports ibériques les commerçants des ports baltiques. L'ambassadeur du roi d'Espagne, le prince François de Mendoza, venu en Pologne à la fin de 1596, devait ainsi, entre autres missions, décider la Pologne à rompre les contacts commerciaux avec les rebelles de Hollande et de Zélande; l'Espagne était convaincue que, privés des fournitures polonaises (via Gdansk) de blé et des matériaux de construction navale, les rebelles hollandais et zélandais, sujets de Philippe II, seraient obligés de renoncer à la lutte [5]. En même

---

[2] J. H. Kernkamp, *De handel op den vijand 1572-1609*, vol. I-II, Utrecht 1931, p. 131.

[3] P. Simson, *Geschichte der Stadt Danzig*, vol. II, Danzig 1918, p. 469.

[4] J. H. Kernkamp, *op. cit.*, vol. II, pp. 229, 251, 306, 307. Plaintes de marchands dantzigois capturés par les hollandais, voir Allgemeen Ryksarchief Haag, St. Gen. 6605, lettres de 14-5-1620, 10-11-1622, 16-7-1624 etc.

[5] Cr. Archivio General de Simancas, Estado, Legajo 614, aussi 631, 2024, 2025, 2036. Déjà en 1587 un diplomate espagnol, Benito Nuñez écrivait: « es notorio que la Holanda y Zelanda comen del trigo, centeno y harina que viene de Ostelanda tanto de Dantzique como de las otras portas, todo salido de la manante fuente del Reyno de Polonia, adonde ordenando se personas que al ello hayan a comparar todo lo que habia de salir del Reyno para venir ad la Holanda y Zelanda, es cosa muy

temps, Mendoza traitait avec Gdansk d'importantes livraisons de blé à l'Espagne[6]. La question de la rupture du commerce entre la Pologne et les Provinces Unies fut encore l'objet de nouvelles démarches diplomatiques espagnoles au début du XVIIe siècle[7]. En 1598, Philippe concéda à la Hanse de larges privilèges en Espagne. Quatre ans plus tard furent ouverts des consulats hanséatiques à Lisbonne et à Séville. Les commerçants hanséatiques mettaient ainsi à profit l'excellente conjoncture politique, d'autant plus que le commerce avec l'Espagne procurait en ce temps d'importants bénéfices[8]. De même le principal port exportateur de la Baltique — Gdansk —, bien qu'il ne se soit pas décidé à rompre, comme le suggérait la couronne espagnole, les attaches, vitales pour lui, avec la Hollande et l'Angleterre, développait son commerce avec la Péninsule ibérique sur une échelle jusque-là inconnue. Vers 1560 encore étaient acheminés de Gdansk vers les ports ibériques de 2 à 4 navires par an en moyenne[9]. La situation changea après 1570: entre 1574 et 1625 partent chaque année de ce port vers l'Espagne de 10 à 40 navires, soit toute une flottille[10].

En 1606, on établit dans les ports des villes hanséatiques des droits, appelés « collecte espagnole », destinés à pourvoir aux frais d'entretien de la représentation en Espagne qui fut alors instituée[11]. Nous disposons aujourd'hui dans les Archives nationales de Gdansk, entre 1606 et 1621, d'un registre[12] contenant les données relatives aux navires partant de Gdansk pour les ports ibériques, et en revenant. Les indications, assez détaillées, précisent la date du mouillage ou de l'appareillage du navire (jour, mois, année), le nom et la ville d'origine du ca-

cierta (...) que no aviendo mantenimientos la Holanda y Zelanda seria forcada de la nombre a rendirse a merced de Su May », Archivio General de Simancas, Estado, Legajo 592.

[6] M. Bogucka, *Misja Franciszka Mendozy i jego opinie o Polce* (*Message diplomatique de Fr. Mendoza en Pologne*), Odrodzenie i Reformacja w Polsce, XIX, 1974, p. 177.

[7] Cf. « Proposiciones sobre impedir a Holandeses el Comercio en Polonia » par Felix Antonio Recirano (1622-1625), Archivio Gen. de Simancas, Estado, Legajo 2847.

[8] K. F. Olechnowitz, *Handel und Seeschiffahrt* ... pp. 27-28.

[9] N. Bang, *Tabeller over skibsfart og varetransport gennem Øresund 1497-1660*, vol. I, København 1906, pp. 415 et suiv.

[10] 1574-20, 1575-17, 1576-24, 1577-12, 1578-22, 1582-10, 1585-10, 1586-13, 1587-14, 1588-15, 1589-16, 1590-25, 1591-13, 1593-10, 1594-11, 1595-12, 1598-14, 1599-27, 1600-36, 1601-36, 1602-17, 1603-20, 1604-11, 1605-19, 1606-16, 1607-22, 1608-24, 1609-6, 1610-4, 1611-8, 1612-4, 1613-4, 1615-2, 1606-2, 1617-0, 1618-0, 1619-1, 1620-2, 1621-5, 1622-21, 1623-34, 1624-46, 1625-14, 1626-8, 1627-1, 1628/30-0, 1631-2, 1633-1, 1635-3, 1636-5, 1637-6, 1638-6, 1639-5, 1640-2, 1642-11, 1643-4, 1644-3, 1645-4, 1646-4, 1647-4, 1648-4, cf. N. Bang, *op. cit.*, pp. 415 et suiv.

[11] P. Simson, *Geschichte* ..., vol. II, pp. 485-487.

[12] Les Archives de la Vojevodie de Gdańsk, 300,19/13.

pitaine, la capacité du navire en lasts, la spécification des marchandises constituant sa cargaison avec leurs quantités et leur valeur au prix de gros à Gdansk, assez souvent aussi (surtout pour les années 1607-1609) les noms des marchands propriétaires des différents lots de marchandises. C'est une source précieuse, jusqu'à maintenant inexploitée par les chercheurs: elle nous a servi à dresser les tableaux.

Le tableau 1 illustre les échanges entre Gdansk et la Péninsule Ibérique dans les années 1607-1621. Au premier coup d'oeil, apparaît une assez grande différence entre les données du registre de la « collecte espagnole » et les registres du péage du Sund; ces derniers relèvent beaucoup moins de navires allant de

Tableau 1

Circulation entre Gdańsk et la Péninsule Ibérique (1607-1621)

Année	Voyages Gdańsk-Pén. Ib.		Voyages Pén. Ib.-Gdańsk		Total		Pourcentage 1607-100 %	
	A	B	A	B	A	B	A	B
1607	48	4044	30	2882	78	6926	100	100
1608	28	3204	16	1597	44	4801	56,4	69,2
1609	20	2279	12	1420	32	3699	41	53,4
1610	20	1832	8	817	28	2649	35,9	38,3
1611	29	2945	21	2005	50	4950	64,1	71,5
1612	13	1175	3	300	16	1475	20,5	21,3
1613	14	1389	5	425	19	1814	24,3	26,2
1614	17	1721	3	210	20	1931	25,6	27,8
1615	17	1590	1	70	18	1660	23,1	23,9
1616	22	2471	—	—	22	2471	28,2	35,7
1617	20	2071	—	—	20	2071	25,6	35,6
1618	15	1568	—	—	15	1568	19,2	22,6
1619	2	265	—	—	2	265	2,6	3,8
1620	—	—	—	—	—	—	—	—
1621	3	267	1	52	4	319	5	4,6

A = nombre des navires; B = tonnage globale en lasts.

Gdansk aux ports ibériques [13]. Il est probable qu'à l'enregistrement du Sund, on tenait souvent compte non pas du lieu de destination du navire mais du port où celui-ci devait se rendre directement après le passage du Sund. Or, nous savons par ail-

[13] Voir note 10.

leurs que les navires appareillant à Gdansk pour les ports ibériques s'arrêtaient souvent au passage dans les ports scandinaves pour y prendre une cargaison de bois, ou dans les ports anglais pour prendre du drap et d'autres marchandises semblables [14]. De ce fait, ces navires pouvaient figurer au péage du Sund comme allant en Norvège ou en Angleterre. L'enregistrement dans le cahier de la « collecte espagnole » semble ici plus digne de foi, car on peut douter que le maître de navire ait consenti à payer la collecte espagnole [15] s'il n'avait pas effectivement l'intention d'aller jusqu'en Espagne ou au Portugal. Bien sûr, certains navires ne parvenaient pas au point de destination, soit qu'ils aient eu quelque avarie, soit qu'ils aient été capturés par les corsaires: c'étaient cependant des exceptions. Les données contenues dans le registre des comptes de la « collecte » peuvent donc être considérés comme un reflet approximatif des contacts réels entre Gdansk et la Péninsule Ibérique, compte tenu évidemment des restrictions valables pour les autres registres de douane de ce temps [16].

L'analyse du tableau 1 permet de relever le dynamisme des contacts entre Gdansk et la Péninsule Ibérique. Si l'on prend pour point de référence l'année 1607, on voit que dans les années suivantes, le commerce entre Gdansk et la péninsule s'affaiblit graduellement, et qu'il s'arrête presque entièrement en 1612 environ dans la direction Péninsule-Gdansk. L'offensive des commerçants de Gdansk en direction des ports ibériques, déclenchée à la fin du XVIᵉ siècle et dans les premières années du XVIIᵉ, fut donc de courte durée ... La trêve de douze ans, signée en 1609 entre la République des Provinces Unies et l'Espagne, et permettant la reprise des échanges commerciaux légaux entre les deux pays y joue certainement un grand rôle. Mais la structure des échanges et leur rentabilité, dont il sera question ci-dessous, représentent également un facteur non négligeable. Quoi qu'il en soit, après 1612 dans le sense Péninsule-Gdansk, et Gdansk-Péninsule après 1618, le chiffre d'affaires baisse jusqu'au niveau enregistré au milieu du XVIᵉ siècle. Une certaine reprise se manifesta, on le sait, d'après les registres du Sund, dans les

---

[14] Cf. Allgemeen Ryksarchief Haag, St. Gen. 6605; Archives de la Vojevodie de Gdańsk 300,5/81 pp. 1585-6.
[15] 0,1 % *ad valorem.*
[16] Cf. A. CHRISTENSEN, *Der Handelsgeschichtliche Wert der Sundzollregister*, Hansische Geschichtsblätter, vol. LIX, 1934; A. FRIIS, *La valeur documentaire des comptes du péage du Sund, la periode 1571 à 1618*, in: Les sources de l'histoire maritime en Europe du Moyen Age au XVIIIᵉ s. Actes du IVᵉ Colloque international d'histoire maritime, Paris 1962; P. JEANNIN, *Les comptes du Sund comme source pour la construction d'indices généraux de l'activité économique en Europe (XVIᵉ-XVIIIᵉ ss.)*, Revue Historique, vol. 470, 1964.

années 1622-1625 [17], liée probablement à l'expiration en 1621 de
la trêve entre l'Espagne et les Provinces Unies. C'était toutefois
la dernière vague d'activité. Dans le second quart du XVIIe siècle,
les contacts directs entre Gdansk et la Péninsule Ibérique subis-
sent une réduction considérable: de rares navires de Gdansk
ne vont le plus souvent que dans les ports à sel du Portugal,
les contacts avec les ports espagnols étant presque complètement
rompus [18]. Il est intéressant de noter que, dans le même temps,
s'arrêtent aussi les échanges directs entre Gdansk et l'Italie [19].

Le problème de la structure du commerce entre Gdansk et
la Péninsule Ibérique présentée dans le tableau II, donne matière à réflexion. Les exportations de Gdansk vers l'Espagne et
le Portugal peuvent être réparties alors en quatre groupes:
A) les céréales (surtout le seigle et le froment) et d'autres produits agricoles (des quantités peu importantes de houblon et de
pois, un peu de lin, de chanvre et de cornichons); B) le bois
(surtout des douves et des mâts) et des produits forestiers (de
la cire, un peu de goudron, des peaux et de fourrures); C) des
métaux (plomb, cuivre, fer); D) des produits industriels et des
semi-produits (poudre, bouteilles et étuis à bouteilles, ustensiles
pour le vin, assiettes, bahuts, toutes sortes de tissus, filés, produits en cuir, articles en métal, d'assez importantes quantités
d'ambre brut et travaillé — en un mot des produits de l'artisanat de Gdansk).

Le tableau 2 montre des modifications de la structure des
exportations au cours de ces années: le centre de gravité se
déplace des céréales (1607-1608) vers le bois et les produits
forestiers. Ce n'était pas la ligne typique d'évolution des exportations de Gdansk où le blé prédominait, alors que le bois et les
produits forestiers occupaient d'année en année moins de place,
du fait notamment de la réduction des espaces forestiers. Pourquoi alors, le commerce avec l'Espagne, évoluait-il en sens
contraire? Probablement les circonstances étaient défavorables
à la vente du blé sur les marchés ibériques. Peut-être était-ce
la conséquence de la concurrence accrue des Hollandais, après
la conclusion de la trêve de 1609. Disposant d'une flotte supérieure et offrant des frêts meilleur marché, ils disposaient en
même temps de capitaux plus importants qui leur permettaient
d'acheter à bas prix de grandes quantités de céréales, et de les
entreposer dans les silos d'Amsterdam pour les placer sur le

---

[17] Voir note 10.
[18] Selon les comptes du Sund pendant des années 1626-1648 24 navires
seulement avaient quitté Gdańsk pour se rendre vers les ports espagnols.
[19] Cf. H. SAMSONOWICZ, *Relations commerciales ...*, cit., p. 543.
[20] Cf. V. BARBOUR, *Dutch and English Merchant Shipping in the Seventeenth Century*, The Economic History Review, vol. II, 1930, pp. 261-290.

Tableau 2

L'exportations de Gdańsk vers la Péninsule Ibérique
(valeur en zlotys polonais)

Groupe de marchan- dises	1607		1608		1609	
	Valeur	%	Valeur	%	Valeur	%
A	93395	80,7	47180	46,7	13587	20,3
B	18017	15,6	32279	31,9	46006	68,7
C	—	—	8632	8,5	2964	4,4
D	4228	3,7	12864	12,9	4435	6,6
Total	115640	100	100955	100	66992	100

Tableau 2 - *L'exportations de Gdańsk vers le Péninsule Ibérique*
(valeur en zlotys polonais)

Groupe de marchan- dises	1610		1611		1612	
	Valeur	%	Valeur	%	Valeur	%
A	32410	39,9	38552	51,3	8488	32,7
B	34219	42,1	31305	41,7	15813	60,9
C	4316	5,3	400	0,5	540	2,1
D	10163	12,7	4822	6,5	1095	4,3
Total	81108	100	75080	100	25936	100

Tableau 2 - *L'exportations de Gdańsk vers la Péninsule Ibérique*
(valeur en zlotys polonais)

Groupe de marchan- dises	1613		1614		1615	
	Valeur	%	Valeur	%	Valeur	%
A	13704	41,4	18529	44,1	3360	6,5
B	14867	44,9	21661	51,6	44446	86,3
C	2100	6,3	880	2,2	750	1,4
D	2464	7,4	883	2,1	2956	5,8
Total	33135	100	41953	100	51512	100

Explication due groupe de marchandises - A, B, C, D - voir page 294.

III

Tableau 2 - *L'exportations de Gdańsk vers la Péninsule Ibérique*
(valeur en zlotys polonais)

Groupe de marchan-dises	1616 Valeur	%	1617 Valeur	%	1618 Valeur	%
A	—	—	34370	50,6	45089	56,3
B	3200	99,2	23771	34,9	23678	29,3
C	—	—	6865	10,1	5702	7,3
D	26	0,8	2993	4,4	5543	7,1
Total	3226	100	67999	100	80012	100

Tableau 2 - *L'exportations de Gdańsk vers la Péninsule Ibérique*
(valeur en zlotys polonais)

Groupe de marchan-dises	1619 Valeur	%	1620 Valeur	%	1621 Valeur	%
A	—	—	—	—	18605	94,2
B	—	—	—	—	1100	5,6
C	—	—	—	—	—	—
D	63	100	—	—	48	0,2
Total	63	100	—	—	197543	100

Explication du groupe de marchandises - A, B, C, D - voir page 294.

marché au moment de la demande la plus grande[21]. Les commerçants de Gdansk n'avaient pas de telles possibilités, ce qui les excluait du marché des grains en Espagne.

Les importations en provenance de la Péninsule Ibérique (tableau 3) peuvent également se répartir en quatre groupes: A) le sel — le principal article d'importation, servant en même temps de charge du navire au lieu du ballast; B) les fruits (oranges, citrons, figues, raisins secs, etc.) ainsi que les épices (poivre, gingembre, anis, cannelle) parmi lesquelles j'inclurai aussi le sucre, le vinaigre et certaines quantités de sucreries; C) le vin (des quantités étonnamment petites, donc une impor-

[21] Cf. A. E. Sayous, *La speculation sur marchandises dans les provinces Unies au XVIIᵉ*, Bijdragen voor vaderlandsche Geschiedenis, La Haye 1902.

tation plutôt occasionnelle); D) des produits industriels (surtout les couvertures espagnoles et les bahuts) et quelques matières premières pour l'artisanat (colorants, liège, alun).

Ce qui frappe dans le tableau 3, outre la faiblesse des importations dans leur ensemble, c'est la réduction rapide des envois du produit le plus important de ces échanges, le sel, bien que dans les échanges entre Gdansk et la Péninsule Ibérique, cette denrée ait joué un rôle multiple non seulement comme marchandise, mais aussi comme ballast et comme la forme la plus sûre du transport en retour des ventes de marchandises à l'Espagne: le sel était moins convoité par les pirates que les cargaisons de métaux précieux ou de monnaies! La raison décisive en est la forte concurrence du sel français ainsi que du sel de Pologne et de Ruthénie, meilleur marché que le sel ibé-

Tableau 3

L'importation à Gdańsk provenant de la Péninsule Ibérique
(valeur en zlotys polonais)

Groupe de marchandises	1607		1608		1609	
	Valeur	%	Valeur	%	Valeur	%
A	42865	70,3	27234	78,5	22336	93
B	10311	16,9	6132	17,6	1672	7
C	3770	6,2	540	1,5	—	—
D	3998	6,6	750	2,4	—	—
Total	60944	100	34656	100	24008	100

Tableau 3 - *L'importation à Gdańsk provenant de la Péninsule Ibérique*
(valeur en zlotys polonais)

Groupe de marchandises	1610		1611		1612	
	Valeur	%	Valeur	%	Valeur	%
A	12810	79,8	30953	63,8	4595	75,2
B	2488	15,8	15365	31,6	1563	22,9
C	—	—	630	1,3	—	—
D	825	4,4	1562	3,3	750	1,9
Total	16123	100	48510	100	6908	100

Tableau 3 - *L'importation à Gdańsk provenant de la Péninsule Ibérique*
(valeur en zlotys polonais)

Groupe de marchandises	1613		1614		1615	
	Valeur	%	Valeur	%	Valeur	%
A	6189	35,1	3264	53,6	1075	64,8
B	11068	62,7	2754	45,3	584	35,2
C	—	—	—	—	—	—
D	396	2,2	63	1,1	—	—
Total	17653	100	6081	100	1659	100

Tableau 3 - *L'importation à Gdańsk provenant de la Péninsule Ibérique*
(valeur en zlotys polonais)

Groupe de marchandises	1616/20		1621	
	Valeur	%	Valeur	%
A	—	—	2192	98,6
B	—	—	30	1,4
C	—	—	—	—
D	—	—	—	—
Total	—	—	2222	100

Explication A, B, C, D - voir page 296-297.

rique: au début du XVIIe siècle, ils évincèrent efficacement le sel ibérique du marché de Gdansk [22].

En prélevant la « collecte » on notait l'assiette de l'imposition, c'est-à-dire la valeur des marchandises aux prix de gros courants à Gdansk. Il s'agit vraiment des prix à Gdansk et non des prix en Espagne ou au Portugal. On a pu le constater en vérifiant les valeur indiquées dans la source de deux articles fondamentaux des échanges — le blé et le sel — et en les confrontant avec les données d'autres sources de Gdansk — surtout les actes des litiges entre marchands, et entre marchands et nobles (qui figurent dans les registres du bourgmestre adjoint) [23].

---

[22] Cf. M. BOGUCKA, *Le sel sur le marché de Gdańsk au cours de la première moitié du XVIIe s.*, Studia Historiae Oeconomicae, vol. XI, 1976, pp. 57-69.

[23] Archives de la Vojevodie de Gdańsk, 300,5/1-93.

En se fondant sur les données relatives à la valeur des marchandises, telles qu'elles sont explicitées dans le registre de la « collecte », on peut établir la balance des échanges entre Gdansk et la Péninsule Ibérique pour les années 1607-1621 (tableau 4).

Tableau 4

Bilan commercial des échanges entre Gdańsk et la Péninsule Ibérique
(valeur en zlotys polonais)

Année	Valeur globale du commerce	Exportations de Gdańsk		Importations à Gdańsk		Solde à Gdańsk	
		Valeur	%	Valeur	%	Valeur	%
1607	176584	115640	65,4	60944	34,6	+ 54696	30,9
1608	135611	100955	74,4	34656	25,6	+ 66299	48,8
1609	91000	66992	73,6	24008	26,4	+ 42984	47,2
1610	97231	81108	83,4	16123	16,6	+ 64985	66,8
1611	123590	75080	60,7	48510	39,3	+ 26570	21,5
1612	32844	25936	78,9	6908	21,1	+ 19028	57,9
1613	50788	33135	65,2	17653	34,8	+ 15482	34,0
1614	48034	41953	87,4	6081	12,6	+ 35872	74,3
1615	53171	51512	96,8	1659	3,2	+ 49853	93,7
1616	3226	3226	100,0	—	—	+ 3226	100,0
1617	67999	67999	100,0	—	—	+ 67999	100,0
1618	80012	80012	100,0	—	—	+ 80012	100,0
1619	63	63	100,0	—	—	+ 63	100,0
1620	—	—	—	—	—	—	—
1621	21975	19753	89,8	2222	10,2	+ 17531	79,7

Comme le montre le tableau, la valeur des exportations annuelles de Gdansk était considérable: dans les années 1607-1608, elle dépasse le chiffre de 100.000 zlotys polonais, et dans les années 1609-1618, elle se maintient au niveau de plusieurs dizaines de milliers de zlotys. Les importations étaient plus modestes, et seules les années 1607, 1608, 1609 et 1611 enregistrent des valeurs de plusieurs dizaines de milliers de zlotys. Le solde annuel, en faveur de Gdansk, oscillait entre 63 et 80.000 zlotys. Il ne fait pas de doute qu'un tel solde était le résultat de la politique économique draconienne de Philippe III et Philippe IV qui prélevaient d'énormes droits sur les exportations de marchandises espagnoles. Malgré tous ses efforts, Gdansk ne réussit pas à faire exonérer ses marchands de ces droits. Dans ces conditions, il n'était pas rentable d'importer d'Espagne ni le vin, d'autant qu'on pouvait facilement s'approvisionner à Gdansk en boissons françaises et allemandes, et que la noblesse polonaise préférait les vins hongrois, ni les épices; ces dernières pouvaient être achetées moins cher chez les marchands hollandais qui entretenaient des contacts directs avec les colonies. Et comme diminuaient aussi, on l'a vu, les importations de sel, il ne restait plus à l'Espagne qu'à équilibrer la balance avec de l'argent tant qu'elle en eut la possibilité.

Le cahier de la « collecte » contient des données sur les commerçants propriétaires des marchandises expédiées de Gdansk jusqu'à la Péninsule Ibérique. 75 % des marchandises appartenaient aux bourgeois de Gdansk et environ 20 % à différents marchands néerlandais, y compris les Hollandais, qui, montant des sociétés avec ceux de Gdansk et utilisant le pavillon de cette ville, voulaient continuer leurs affaires en Espagne malgré les interdictions des autorités. Environ 5 % des marchandises appartenaient à des commerçants d'autres pays (Allemagne, Danemark et autres). Il faut rapprocher cette situation de celle de la propriété des navires. Les capitaines des navires proviennent pour la plupart de Gdansk (environ 60 %). Un assez grand nombre cependant sont originaires de Lübeck, du Danemark, etc. ..., surtout du Holland. Il serait cependant risqué d'en déduire le titre de propriété du navire [24]. Dans les premiers registres, quand les scribes étaient encore très exacts dans leurs notations, nous retrouvons des indications directes sur la propriété des navires. Plus tard, à mesure que les inscriptions deviennent moins précises, l'on se contente de mentionner le lieu — Gdansk ou un autre port hanséatique — où le navire avait payé la « collecte », ou bien son exemption comme n'appartenant pas à la Hanse. Les navires appartenant aux bourgeois d'autres villes hanséatiques, envoyés à Gdansk pour prendre une cargaison de marchandises à destination de l'Espagne, payaient en général des droits de douane calculés sur la capacité (1 shilling de Lübeck par last) dans leur port d'attache, alors qu'à Gdansk étaient imposées seulement les marchandises. Ainsi, d'après le lieu de perception des droits de douane — ou d'après leur exemption — on peut répartir les navires partant de Gdansk pour l'Espagne en trois groupes: ceux qui appartenaient à Gdansk, ceux des autres villes hanséatiques et les navires non hanséatiques. Cette division, bien qu'imparfaitement assurée, représente cependant mieux l'état de fait que le critère incertain de l'origine du capitaine.

Le tableau 5 représente sur cette base la division de la flotte circulant entre Gdansk et la Péninsule ibérique. Il en résulte

[24] Cf. M. BOGUCKA, *Anteil der Danziger Schiffer am Ostseehandel der ersten Hälfte des 17*. Jahrhunderts, Zapiski Historyczne, 1964/4, pp. 15-26; S. VON BRAKEL, *Schiffsheimat und Schifferheimat in den Sundzollregistern*, Hansische Geschichtsblätter 1916, vol. XXI, p. 211; A. CHRISTENSEN, *Dutch Trade to the Baltic about 1600*, Kopenhague 1941, pp. 60 et suiv.

Tableau 5

Provenance de navires sur la route Gdańsk-Péninsule Ibérique-Gdańsk
nombre de navires = A

	1607 A	%	1608 A	%	1609 A	%
De Gdańsk	68	87,2	36	81,8	20	62,5
D'autres ports hanséates	—	—	5 [1]	11,4	1 [2]	3,1
Non - hanséates	10 [3]	12,8	3 [4]	6,8	11 [5]	34,4
Total	78	100,0	44	100,0	32	100,0

Tableau 5 - *Provenance de navires sur la route Gdańsk-Péninsule Ibérique-Gdańsk - nombre de navires = A*

	1610 A	%	1611 A	%	1612 A	%
De Gdańsk	27	93,2	49	98	16	100
D'autres ports hanséates	1 [6]	6,8	1 [7]	2	—	—
Non - hanséates	—	—	—	—	—	—
Total	28	100,0	50	100,0	16	100,0

Tableau 5 - *Provenance de navires sur la route Gdańsk-Péninsule Ibérique-Gdańsk - nombre de navires = A*

	1613 A	%	1614 A	%	1615 A	%
De Gdańsk	19	100,0	18	90	18	100,0
D'autres ports hanséates	—	—	2 [8]	10	—	—
Non - hanséates	—	—	—	—	—	—
Total	19	100,0	20	100,0	18	100,0

302

Tableau 5 - *Provenance de navires sur la route Gdańsk-Péninsule Ibérique-Gdańsk - nombre de navires = A*

	1616 A	%	1617 A	%	1618 A	%
De Gdańsk	21	95,5	20	100,0	15	100,0
D'autres ports hanséates	1[9]	4,5	—	—	—	—
Non - hanséates	—	—	—	—	—	—
Total	22	100,0	20	100,0	15	100,0

Tableau 5 - *Provenance de navires sur la route Gdańsk-Péninsule Ibérique-Gdańsk - nombre de navires = A*

	1619 A	%	1621 A	%
De Gdańsk	2	100,0	4	100,0
D'autres ports hanséates	—	—	—	—
Non - hanséates	—	—	—	—
Total	2	100,0	4	100,0

1.3 de Wismar, 2. de Lübeck, 2. de Lübeck, 6. de Lübeck, 7. de Lübeck, 3.8 de Danemark, 1 de Angleterre, 1 inconnu, 4.2 de Holland, 1 de Danemark, 5.9 de Holland, 2 inconnus, 8. de Lübeck, 9. de Wismar.

que c'étaient pour une grosse majorité des unités de Gdansk qui transportaient souvent des marchandises appartenantés à des commerçants autres que ceux de Gdansk, entre autres à des Hollandais. En outre, l'on se servait, pour le transport, de navires hollandais, danois, lübeckois, wismariens, anglais même. Il est intéressant de remarquer qu'après 1609, les navires non hanséatiques disparaissent du tableau — fait que l'on peut sans doute attribuer à la trêve déjà mentionnée qui suspendit les hostilités entre l'Espagne et la République des Provinces Unies, et mit ainsi fin à la discrimination des marchands néerlandais;

les capitaines hollandais (et aussi danois) qu'employaient aupa-
ravant les bourgeois de Gdansk, avaient à présent trouvé de
l'emploi ailleurs.

Les données des registres de la « collecte », qui indiquent
la forte prépondérance des navires originaires de Gdansk sur
les transports peuvent-elles être considérées comme dignes de
foi? Sans aucun doute, et surtout après 1609. Avant cette date,
il pouvait arriver que l'on enregistrât tel navire comme de Gdansk
pour éviter les répressions espagnoles. Mais valait-il la peine
de le faire à Gdansk où un tel enregistrement était assorti de
l'obligation de payer la « collecte »? On pouvait en effet — et on
le faisait certainement — arborer le pavillon de Gdansk en cours
de voyage. C'était à l'époque d'autant plus facile qu il n'existait
pas de dispositions uniformes et conséquentes sur les documents
des navires. Dans la plupart des ports, on se contentait de la
déclaration du capitaine, et la production de lettres de l'arma-
teur ou d'autres certificats était rarement demandée.

Un autre aspect du problème mérite examen: le cas des
navires à double appartenance, qui étaient, le plus souvent, la
propriété de sociétés gédano-néerlandaises. De telles sociétés,
on le sait, étaient assez fréquentes et dans ce secteur de la navigation, elles pouvaient manifester une activité particulière. C'est
un problème difficile à résoudre. Il semble ici aussi que l'on
aurait pris soin d'enregistrer ces navires à Gdansk comme étrangers, et cela dans la dessein, compréhensible, d'éviter les taxes.
Comme on le voit, donc, s'il y avait à corriger les chiffres aux
tableaux 5, il faudrait le faire plutôt dans le sens de l'augmen-
tation de la part des navires de Gdansk dans les transports vers
l'Espagne.

Les registres de la « collecte » ne citent pas avec exactitude
les points d'arrivée dans la Péninsule Ibérique des navires expé-
diés à partir de Gdansk. A partir d'autres sources, et surtout
des contrats d'affrètement conservés dans les archives hollan-
daises, on peut présumer que c'étaient, en Espagne: Huelva, San
Luca de Barrameda, Cadix, Malaga, Motril, Valence, Barcelone,
Majorque. Au Portugal, les navires de Gdansk mouillaient le plus
souvent à Lisbonne et dans les ports du sel, Sétubal et S. Uvis [25].
Des données des registres de la collecte, il résulte qu'un navire
pouvait prendre une cargaison appartenant soit à un seul marchand, soit, pour plus de sécurité, à plusieurs. De toutes façons,
tout marchand ayant une part importante dans le commerce
ibérique répartissait ses exportations, pour une année donnée,
en plusieurs lots et les expédiait sur différents navires. Certains

---

[25] Cf. M. BOGUCKA, *Der Niederländisch-Danziger Handel in den Jahren
1597-1651 auf Grund der Amsterdamer Frachtverträge,* Zapiski Historyczne 1968/3 pp. 171-191.

marchands de Gdansk envoyaient en Espagne plusieurs navires, jusqu'à une quinzaine par an (Hans Schenck, Paul Dameraw). Les raisons de la courte durée des contacts directs entre Gdansk et la Péninsule Ibérique sont complexes. Au premier plan se situe ici le retour sur les marchés espagnols des marchands néerlandais; tout le développement des échanges directs entre la Baltique et les ports ibériques, organisés par les marchands de Gdansk et des autres villes hanséatiques à la fin du XVIe et au début du XVIIe siècle, reposait sur la conjoncture courte née du déclenchement de l'insurrection anti-espagnole dans les Pays Bas (1566) et de la crise subie par le commerce du sud des Pays Bas (surtout après la destruction d'Anvers en 1585), ainsi que des interdictions imposées par le gouvernement espagnol de commercer aver les marchands des Pays Bas du nord, dans l'espoir de briser la puissance des rebelles. Un certain rôle incombe ici également à tout un concours d'autres circonstances. Bien que Philippe II et ses successeurs aient à maintes reprises encouragé les marchands de Gdansk à prendre la direction de l'Espagne, ceux-ci s'y heurtaient à de graves difficultés: malveillance et chicanes des fonctionnaires de l'endroit, droits élevés, voire confiscations de marchandises et de navires entiers [26]. Un autre danger venait des corsaires espagnols stationnant à Dunkerque, ainsi que des corsaires anglais et néerlandais qui pourchassaient les navires portant des cargaisons à destination de l'Espagne [27]. Ces dangers menaçaient d'ailleurs non seulement les marchands de Gdansk, mais aussi ceux des autres villes hanséatiques désireuses d'exploiter le moment favorable pour accroître leur part dans le commerce espagnol.

Un rôle peu négligeable a aussi été joué par les modifications de la structure des échanges, et surtout par la réduction des expéditions des deux plus importants articles du commerce avec la Péninsule Ibérique: les céréales et le sel. On y rattachera d'ailleurs la question des bénéfices tirés du commerce entre la Baltique et l'Espagne, encore élevés à la fin du XVIe siècle. Au XVIIe siècle, l'exportation la plus rentable était celle du froment, et sans doute du seigle, de la région baltique vers les ports ibériques; la comparaison des prix à Gdansk et en Espagne que (après déduction des frais approximatifs du transport, des taxes douanières et d'autres charges) les bénéfices atteignaient souvent les 100 %, et parfois plus [28]. Ce commerce avait cepen-

---

[26] Cf. M. BOGUCKA, *Handel Gdańska z Półwyspem Iberyjskim w pierwszej połowie XVII w.* (*Le commerce de Gdańsk avec la Péninsule Ibérique dans la première moitié du XVIIe s.*) *Przeglad Historyczny* 1969/1 p. 3.
[27] *Ibid.*
[28] Cf. M. BOGUCKA, *Merchants' Profits in Gdańsk Foreign Trade in the First Half of the 17 th Century*, Acta Poloniae Historica, 23, 1971, p. 75.

dant son revers: l'importation du sel ibérique [29] rapportait de très faibles bénefices, et souvent même des pertes surtout que la demande du marché à Gdansk était couverte par le sel moins cher: polonais et français [30]. Le commerce du sel, abandonné peu à peu au début du XVIIe siècle, le problème se posait donc de trouver une denrée d'échange. Les très lourdes taxes douanières (30 %) imposées en 1602 par les autorités espagnoles sur toute les exportations rendirent également non rentable l'importation vers Gdansk du sucre, des épices et certainement d'autres marchandises espagnoles [31]. Ce qui explique l'insignifiance des importations au XVIIe siècle, qui figurent dans les tableaux 1 et 4. Restait l'importation des métaux précieux et des monnaies: largement pratiqueé, elle comportait un risque très grave, tant du fait du pillage possible par les pirates, qu'à cause de l'interdiction d'exporter l'argent d'Espagne, rigoureusement appliquée à l'époque par les pouvoirs locaux [32]. Nous retrouvons en effet dans les sources des informations sur les confiscations de monnaies et de métal clandestinement embarqués sur les navires, et sur les pertes importantes qui en découlent pour les bourgeois de Gdansk [33]. D'ailleurs, avec le temps, au XVIIe siècle, ce genre d'importations devenait de moins en moins rentable, le prix de l'argent augmentant considérablement en Espagne (beaucoup plus vite qu'au bord de la Baltique). Le résultat, en fut les changements défavorables dans les différences de cours des monnaies, et surtout du ducat. L'*agio* élevé du ducat à Gdansk (plus de 50 %) dans les deux premières décennies du XVIIe siècle, d'où les marchands du lieu tiraient des bénéfices supplémentaires dans leurs échanges avec la Péninsule Ibérique, baisse les années suivantes jusqu'à se muer en *disagio* [34]

Pour montrer comment cette situation influait sur les bénéfices des marchands entretenant le commerce avec l'Espagne, nous citerons un exemple. Le 9 octobre 1609, le plénipotentiaire à Amsterdam de Hans Schenck, exportateur connu de Gdansk, chargeait un certain Jean Courtoijs de retirer à Séville la somme de 33.143 réaux pour la livraison de 64 lasts et 48 boisseaux [35] de froment. Donc le prix de vente d'un last à Séville était d'environ 510 réaux, soit 19.125 maravedis (1836 g. d'argent). Comme le prix à l'exportation était à Gdansk en 1609 d'environ 1423 g.

[29] Cf. M. BOGUCKA, *Le sel* ..., voir note 22.
[30] *Ibid.*
[31] M. BOGUCKA, *Merchants' Profits* ..., p. 78-79.
[32] Voir un rapport écrit par l'ambassadeur francais 24-8-1626, concernant la pénurie d'argent en Espagne et les methodes drastiques pour l'empêcher de sortir du pays, Paris, Archives Nationales, Affaires Etrangères, Sous-Série B₇ 204, pp. 107-114.
[33] Cf. Archives Nationales de la Voivodie de Gdańsk, 300,5/87, p. 90 ab.
[34] M. BOGUCKA, *Merchants' profits* ..., p. 75.
[35] Gemeente Archief Amsterdam, Not. Arch. 118, p. 6.

d'argent pour un last, le frêt d'au moins 310,36 g., et que les autres frais (douanes, taxes portuaires, etc.) ont été calculés à 284,60 g.[36], il faudrait admettre que Schenck subit pour chaque last une perte équivalant à 181,96 g. d'argent, soit 9 % du capital dépensé. En réalité, il pouvait l'éviter grâce justement à la différence du cours des monnaies et de l'argent en Espagne et à Gdansk.

Si, en effet, Schenk reçevait son dû en ducats à raison de 10 réaux pour 1 ducat, et transportait cet argent jusqu'à Gdansk, pour chaque tranche de 51 ducats constituant le paiement d'un last de froment, il pouvait obtenir dans cette ville 2170,84 g. d'argent[37]. Ce qui signifiait en réalité un bénéfice de 152,88 g. d'argent par last, autrement dit non pas une perte mais un profit de l'ordre de 7,5 % du capital placé dans la transaction. Ce n'était pas beaucoup et c'est peut-être la raison pour laquelle, abandonnant le froment, il passa les années suivantes au commerce du bois[38]; mais ceci prouve bien que la spéculation sur l'agio du ducat était très rentable. La diminution de ces possibilités les années suivantes pesa, à n'en pas douter, défavorablement sur le commerce entre Gdansk et l'Espagne.

Les exemples trouvés dans les sources du XVIIᵉ siècle témoignent ainsi de la rentabilité décroissante du commerce espagnol, et même des pertes subies par les marchands de Gdansk. La société composée de Hans Kerschberg, Casper Klippel, Sigismund Kerschenstein, qui, dans les années 1623-1629, avait expédié à St. Lucas et à Lisbonne le navire « Die Pfarrkirche », termina son exercice, après les comptes faits au printemps 1630, par un bénéfice minime: Kerschberg toucha 12 zlotys polonais à peine de bénéfice, soit 1 % du capital placé. Les bénéfices de certaines croisières étaient, il est vrai, nettement plus élevés (19 à 34 %), mais le solde général n'encourageait pas à continuer cette branche du commerce[39]. Hans Kerschberg était membre d'une autre société qui commerçait avec l'Espagne dans les années 1624-1625 (avec le navire « Braunfisch »), dans laquelle il essuya une perte de 239 zlotys polonais, soit 49 % du capital qu'il y avait placé[40]. Les années suivantes, comme il apparaît dans son livre de comptes, Kerschberg avait abandonné le com-

[36] Cf. M. Bogucka, *Handel zagraniczny Gdańska w pierwszej połowie XVII w. (Le commerce extérieur de Gdańsk dans la première moitié du XVIIᵉ siècle)*, Wrocław 1970, p. 145.
[37] Calculé selon E. J. Hamilton, *American Treasure and the Price Revolution in Spain 1501-1650*, Cambridge 1934, pp. 358-383 et J. Pelc, *Ceny w Gdańsku w XVI i XVII w. (Les prix à Gdańsk aux XVIᵉ et XVIIᵉ ss.)*, Lwów 1937 pp. 3 et suiv.
[38] M. Bogucka, *Handel Gdańska z Półwyspem Iberyjskim ...*, p. 13.
[39] Archives Nationales de la Voievodie de Gdańsk, 300,R/F, 19 a, pp. 87 b-88 a.
[40] *Ibid.*, pp. 88 b-89 a.

merce ibérique pour développer les relations extrêmement animées avec les marchands d'Amsterdam, tant dans le domaine des échanges de marchandises que des lettres de change et du crédit [41]. Les voyages en Espagne entrepris un peu plus tard, en 1642 et 1646, par le marchand de Gdansk Dawid Mey (navire « König Dawid ») ne semblent pas non plus avoir été ni réussis ni profitables [42]. Ce genre d'expériences n'encourageaient pas les marchands de Gdansk à continuer les échanges directs avec la Péninsule Ibérique. Il y avait moins de risques à attendre dans son propre port l'arrivée de la flotte hollandaise et à vendre aux marchands hollandais les produits acheminés à Gdansk par la noblesse polonaise, en achetant en contrepartie aux mêmes Hollandais les produits d'importation. La tentative de pénétrer sans intermédiaires sur les marchés ibériques avait échoué (et pas seulement à Gdansk d'ailleurs): cet échec marque une dernière étape dans la concurrence opposant les villes hanséatiques et la puissance maritime croissante de la Hollande.

---

[41] *Ibid.*, 300,R/F, 19 b.
[42] *Ibid.*, 300,5/81, pp. 1585-86, 87, p. 90 ab.

IV

The Role of Baltic Trade in European Development from the XVIth to the XVIIIth Centuries

This is a very complex issue which despite appearances (for there is a great deal of literature on the subject of the Baltic trade), has only partly been studied. It should be examined from at least two points of views, one socio-economic and the other cultural. It is particularly the latter that has not been examined.

The XVIth and XVIIth centuries are often called the era of Baltic trade. The great geographical discoveries at the end of the XVth century changed the network of the main transport routes. The old trading centres declined and new ones rapidly developed (Antwerp, Amsterdam, Baltic ports) following the shift in world trade from the Mediterranean to the Atlantic and the Baltic sea. These changes were linked to the new forms of international commerce: the low volume and mainly luxury trade of the Middle Ages gave way in modern times to large-scale trading in basic consumer commodities, especially grain and raw materials. Hence the dependence of many countries on the products of distant regions and regular shipping and transport became an indispensable condition of existence for the peoples drawn into the orbit of international trade.

All this was mainly the consequence of the extremely rapid population growth in XVIth century Europe [1] and comparatively slow development of agriculture in the most populated countries of Western and Southern Europe.[2] The doubling of the number of inhabitants in some regions and rapid urbanisation caused a rapid increase in the demand for basic consumer goods, particularly foodstuffs. At the same time, the low level of farming techniques made it impossible to meet that demand locally. This lag in agriculture was at the root both of the XVIth century price revolution (which can only partly be attributed to the inflow of American silver to Europe) and the emergence of poverty and famine on a mass scale which, according to some scholars, had no parallel in the Middle Ages.[3] In the existing circumstances there were only two ways in which to resolve the problem of lack of food: either intensification of production (which was difficult to carry out rapidly because of slow technical progress), or the search for new sources of supply and it was that which linked the expansion of Baltic trade and the growth of its role in the life of the rapidly developing European economy.

Contemporaries were well aware of this. As early as the late XVIth century Baltic trade was described in the Netherlands

---

[1] For a review of recent studies see M. REINHARD, A. ARMENGAUD, J. DUPAQUIER, *Histoire générale de la population mondiale*, Paris 1968.

[2] Several formerly food exporting regions found themselves in a situation in which they were forced to import foodstuffs. See F. BRAUDEL, *La mediterranée et le monde mediterranéen au temps de Philippe II*, Paris 1966; G. CONIGLIO, *Il regno di Napoli al tempo di Carlo V*, Napoli 1951; J. GOY and E. LE ROY LADURIE (eds.), *Les fluctuations du produit de la dîme*, Paris, The Hague 1972; M.J. ELSAS, *Umriss einer Geschichte der Preise und Löhne in Deutschland*, Leiden 1949; M. MORINEAU, *Les faux-semblants d'un démarrage économique: agriculture et démographie*, Paris 1971; P. RAVEAUS, *L'agriculture en Haut Poitou au XVIe s.*, Paris 1926; B.H. SLICHER VAN BATH, *De agrarische geschiedenis van West-Europa, 500-1850*, Ultrecht-Antwerp 1960; H. VAN DER WEE and E. VAN CAUWENBERGHE (eds), *Productivity of Land and Agricultural Innovation in the Low Countries (1250-1800)*, Leuven 1978. Flanders and Brabant in the XVth c. already depended on the importation of Baltic grain, see M.J. TITS-DIEUAIDE, *La formation des prix céréaliers en Brabant et en Flandre au XVe s.*, Bruxelles 1975.

[3] See W. ABEL, *Massenarmut und Hungerkrisen im vorindustriellen Europa*, Hamburg 1974.

as " *moederhandel* " " mother trade." Politicians, especially in Spain, at the turn of the XVIth century, often said that it was precisely this trade that had made possible the armed rising of the Dutch provinces and the later emergence of the independent Republic of the United Provinces (Holland). Without the deliveries of Baltic grain and materials for building their fleet, the rebels would have had to capitulate quite early.[4] Contemporaries also emphasize the interdependence of England and the Baltic region through the exchange of textiles and raw materials.[5] The optimism of the Polish gentry in the XVIth and XVIIth centuries was mainly due to the firm conviction that Polish grain was and would always be indispensable for the existence of the West of Europe.[6]

Recent studies in general confirm this picture, but reduce its validity chronologically to a span of approximately one century (1550s-1660s), when every failure or delay in the arrival of a Baltic fleet caused famine in Amsterdam and other large towns in the West, and even in the South of Europe.[7] It seems that only towns with less than 20,000 inhabitants, itself a considerable size in the Middle Ages, could live on local supplies. When population exceeded 30,000-40,000, the town's neighbourhood was incapable of meeting its demand for grain in full.[8] In the XVIth century the situation became even more acute due

---

[4] Archivo General de Simancas, Estado, Legajo, 592, 614, 631, 2024, 2025, 2036, 2847. See also the opinion of an anonymous Flemish writer from the first half of the XVIIth c., " Een merkwardig aanvalsplan gericht tegen Vischerij en Handel der Vereenigde Nederlanden in de erste helft de 17de eeuw. Medegedeelt door P.I. BLOK ", *Bijdr. en Meded. Hist. Gen. Deel* XIX, 1898.

[5] *Ibidem*.

[6] See M. BOGUCKA, North European Commerce as a Solution Factor of Resource Shortage in the XVIth-XVIIIth cc., *Natural resources in European History*, ed. A. Mączak and W.N Parker, Washington D.C. 1978, pp. 9-42.

[7] H. Wätjen, *Die Niederländer in Mittelmeergebiet zur Zeit ihrer hochsten Machtstellung.* Abhandlungen zur Verkehrs- und Seegeschichte, Bd. II, Berlin 1909, p. 121.

[8] R. Mols, Population in Europe 1500-1700, in *The Fontana Economic History of Europe. The Sixteenth and Seventeenth Centuries*, ed. by C.M. Cipolla, London 1976, pp. 42-43.

to the switch in the countryside from corn growing to sheep pastures (England, Spain), to the cultivation of olive trees and vineyards (Spain, Italy), vegetables, flax and hops (Brabant, Flanders, Zeeland) and to the development of dairy farms (Holland, Friesland). Meanwhile, the number of towns with more than 40,000 inhabitants, which in the early XVIth century had been 26, nearly doubled and rose to more than 40 by the end of the century. At the end of the XVIth century, this group included some giants with more than 150,000 inhabitants (Constantinople, Naples, Paris, London, Milan, Venice) and over 100,000 (Rome, Seville, Amsterdam, Lisbon, Palermo, Antwerp). No wonder, then, that grain crises, which had been acutely felt in the first half of the XVIth century, should become extremely intense by the end of the century and were to rage mostly in the Netherlands, the Iberian Peninsula and Italy, (i.e. in the most urbanised areas of Europe). In addition, a major role must have been played by the devastation of France (which had exported grain in the XVth century), by the religious wars, as well as the crisis in the rural Netherlands caused by the anti-Spanish rising and the long drawn out war for liberation waged by the northern provinces. Throughout this most critical period for the consumer in Western and Southern Europe, which was to last until the end of the first decade of the XVIIth century, it was no longer the traditional supplies from Sicily and Africa, nor the additional transport of grain from Constantinople, but the agricultural produce from the Baltic zone that proved to be of crucial importance. Although yields there were low, the political pre´ominance of the gentry and the absence of major urbanisation allowed all the surpluses obtained (mostly at the expense of peasant consumption) to be sold abroad. We know that at the turn of the XVIth century an average of 50-70,000 lasts of grain went through the Sound annually.[10] This was a considerable amount in

9 F. BRAUDEL, La mediterranée... Polish edition Gdansk 1976, vol. II, pp. 604 ff.

10 A.J. FABER, Het probleem van de dalende graanaanvoer uit de Oostzeelanden

view of the probably somewhat modest estimate of the Amsterdam merchant Joost Nykerke, in 1630, who put the entire annual
consumption of grain in the Netherlands at the time at 40,000
last.[11] According to H. Brugmans, in the mid-XVIIth century
Amsterdam alone needed some 21,000 lasts.[12] With a population of about 140,000 [13] this would average some 0.75 kg of
grain per head per day. Calculations for other towns at the
time (Gdańsk) yield similar results (0.65-0.70 kg a day).[14] Naturally, only part of the Baltic grain remained in the Netherlands
(where, after all), domestic production was still considerable and
grain was imported from other sources as well e.g. Archangel.[15]
Considerable quantities were re-exported (or went straight from
Baltic ports) to other countries: England, France, the Iberian Peninsula, and Italy, depending on the demand in those markets. Not
only did demand fluctuate, as it depended every year on the
local harvests in various parts of Europe, but supply also fluctuated
considerably because of the irregularity of Baltic deliveries, which
in turn were tied to the varying harvests in that region and to
the political situation (war, disruption and the frequent closures
of the Sound). Consequently, there were years when more than
100,000 lasts were freighted through the Sound, but quite frequently the supplies fell to 5,000, 10,000 or 20,000 lasts or even

in do tweede helft van de zeventiende eeuw, AAG, *Bijdragen, IX Afdeling Agrarische
Geschiedenis Landsbouwhogeschool*, Wageningen 1963, p. 7 which calculates Dutch imports
alone at 50,000 lasts.

[11] See O. PRINGSHEIM, *Beiträge zur wirtschäftlichen Entwicklungsgeschichte der Vereinig-
Niederlande im 17.und 18.Jhr.*, Leipzig 1890, p. 18.

[12] H. BRUGMANS, *Opkomst en bloei van Amsterdam*, Amsterdam 1944, p. 114.

[13] P. SCHRAA, *Onderzoekingen naar de bevolkingsomvang van Amsterdam tussen 1550-
1650*, Amstelodamum, vol 46, Amsterdam 1954, p. 27.

[14] M. BOGUCKA, *Urząd zapasów a konsumpcja Gdańska w pierwszej połowie XVIIw.*
(Board of Reserves and Food Consumption in Gdańsk in the First Half of the Seventeenth
Century), *Kwartalnik Historii Kultury Materialnej*, vol. XVIII, 1970 no 2, pp. 255-260.

[15] M. BOGUCKA, *Zboże rosyjskie na rynku amsterdamskim w pierwszej połowie XVIIw.*
(Russian Grain on the Amsterdam Market in the First Half of the Seventeenth Century),
Przegląd Historyczny, 1962 no 4, pp. 611-627; Z. GULDON S. ZALEWSKI, *Eksport zbożowy
Rosji w XVI-XVIII w.* (Grain Exports from Russia in XVIth-XVIIIth cc), Zapiski
Historyczne, vol XLII, 1977, no. 1. pp. 27-45.

IV

stopped altogether for some time. The grain trade had a built-in element of risk and speculation, and the grain prices in the Netherlands and other countries of Western and Southern Europe fluctuated considerably on a monthly and yearly scale.[16] The irregularity of Baltic supplies sometimes caused quite serious, temporary, upsets in the provisioning of the largest European towns (particularly in 1557-1559, 1562-1564, 1570-1578, 1586-1587, 1590-1591, 1628-1631). In the XVIth and first half of the XVIIth century the existence of urban populations on the scale then attained made them definitely dependent on the Baltic granary in two senses of the term: both as a supplier of food and as the supplier of the materials needed for the building of ships to carry that food. The expansion of the Dutch and English merchant fleets in the XVIth and XVIIth centuries, as is well known, depended on primary materials such as timber, flax, hemp and tar, which were imported from the Baltic region.

What might be called " the grain stage " in the Baltic trade lasted up to the mid-XVIIth century. In the second half of that century and in the XVIIIth century, the food situation in Western and Southern Europe underwent a fundamental change which resulted in a diminished demand for Baltic grain.[17] The slowing down of demographiec growth, and even a decline in the number of inhabitants in certain countries due to wars and plagues, as well as the intensification of domestic agriculture (in the Netherlands, England, France) together with the introduction of new crops (rice and maize — chiefly in the Iberian Peninsula and Italy) freed some regions from their former dependence on Baltic imports.[18] D. Ormrod has emphasized recently

[16] Recently on this problem see: P. W. KLEIN, Quantitative Aspects of the Amsterdam Rye Trade During the XVIIth Century and the Economic History of Europe, Contrum voer Maatschapij geschiedenis, Rotterdam Erasmus Universiteit, Mededelingen no 2, Rotterdam 1978.
[17] A.J. FABER, Het problem van de dalende graanaanvoer... passim; M. BOGUCKA, North European Commerce... passim.
[18] Ibidem.

England's role in this process and claimed that in the second half of the XVIIth and first half of the XVIIIth century English grain replaced Baltic supplies on the international markets.[19] In the second half of the XVIIIth century the import of grain from America and increasing cultivation of potatoes, which revolutionized the structure of mass consumption, dealt the final blow to the importance of Baltic grain supplies. Other commodities then came to the fore in Baltic trade, and this could be called " the raw material stage " because at the top of the list in the exports to the West going through the Sound were timber, metals, flax, hemp and tar which were shipped to developing early capitalist factories.[20] These shifts in the content of the Baltic shipment were followed by changes in trading partners. Agricultural Poland, the West's main trading partner in the XVIth and early XVIIth century, proved unable to adapt herself to the new requirements of the international markets and was importing fewer Western products due to the impoverishment of her gentry. She was pushed aside by Sweden, Russia, Norway, Latvia, Estonia and Finland, the countries which supplied the raw materials in demand and in turn bought the goods offered by the West.[21] As a result important transformations took place in the Baltic zone. Its importance as a producer and supplier for Western Europe continued, although the nature of Baltic supplies changed and they began to play a role in sectors of the West's economy different from those at the earlier stage.

As well as, and thanks to, its role in the supply of foodstuffs

---

[19] D. ORMROD, Le déclin industriel et commercial néerlandais et la croissance britannique à la fin du XVIIe s. in: *Transition du féodalisme à la societé industrielle : L'échec de l'Italie de la Renaissance et des Pays-Bas du XVIIe siècle*, ed. by P. M. Hohenberg and F. Krantz, Montreal 1975.

[20] M. BOGUCKA, *North European Commerce...*; E. HARDER-GERSDORF, *Lübeck, Danzing und Riga. Ein Beitrag zur Frage der Handelskonjunktur im Ostseeraum am Ende des 17. Jahrhunderts*, Hansische Geschicht sblätter, 96 Jhrg. 1978, pp. 106-138.

[21] *Ibidem*. See also A. ATTMAN, *The Russian and Polish Market in International Trade 1500-1650*, Göteborg 1973.

and raw materials, Baltic trade also fulfilled extremely important functions in the sphere of capital accumulation. The studies of merchant profits in the Baltic trade show a high rate of profit — higher that in other branches of European trade, and only slightly lower than in the early colonial trade.[22] It is precisely because of the high profitability of Baltic trade that first the Hanseatic League and the Dutch, and then later the Dutch and the English fought fiercely for its mastery. The Sound was a gold mine for the Danes; the wars which dragged on for many years between Poland, Sweden, Muscovy and Denmark for the *dominium maris Baltici* were waged, to a large extent, to conquer the Baltic ports and subordinate Baltic trade. Not only did the rulers and powers of the North carry out their intrigues in this area, but also the Spanish Hapsburgs, and one of the phases of the Thirty Years' War was clearly centred on the Baltic. If we accept the records of the Sound customs books we can see that in the first half of the XVIIth century an average of some 70,000 lasts of grain went through the Sound annually to the West and that the merchant's profits amounted to 521 g of silver per last (on shipping to the Dutch ports).[23] From this we can estimate a total annual profit for the export merchants of some 36,000 kg of pure silver. In comparison, it is interesting to note that the output of the famous mines at Potosi (Peru) amounted in 1533 to 11,537 kg, in 1534 to 56,534, and in 1535 to 27,183 kg

---

[22] See M. BOGUCKA, *Zur Problematik der Profite in Handel zwischen Danzig und Westeuropa 1550-1650* (in the press).

[23] Calculated on the basis of price differences between Amsterdam and Gdańsk (with corrections suggested by P. JEANNIN, *Press-Kosten und Gewinnunterschiede im Handel mit Ostseegebiet 1550-1650*, in: *Wirtschaftliche und soziale Strukturen im säkularen Wandel. Festschrift für Wilhelm Abel zum 70 Geburtstag*, vol. II, Hannover 1974, pp. 494-517) minus transport costs, customs duties etc. See M. Bogucka, *Handel zagraniczny Gdańska w piorwszej połowie XVII w.* (Gdańsk Foreign Trade in the First Half of the Seventeenth Century), Wrocław 1970, p. 148. J. FABER estimates the average difference between the price of rye at Arnhem and the price of rye at Gdańsk in 1560-1599 at about 514 grams of silver, in the years 1600-1649 at 417 grams of silver in the second half of XVIIth c. at 446, and in the years 1700-1749 at 388 grams of pure silver, *op.cit.* p. 5, table I.

of pure silver.[24] Other branches of the Baltic trade, the export westwards of raw materials, and the imports of colonial goods and industrial products eastwards must also have been very remunerative.[25] So Baltic trade must be considered as an extremely rich source for capital accumulation, which was exploited mainly not by local Baltic merchants but by the enterprising agents of the West-European, mainly the Dutch and English, trading classes. It is difficult to assess the role of those profits in the development of the rapidly modernising societies of Western Europe (especially Holland and England) because of the lack of detailed studies. But next to the trade with colonies, it seems that it was the main source of the rapidly growing wealth of the merchants who, in the XVIth-XVIIth centuries, clearly constituted a leading social group which was slowly turning into the modern bourgeoisie.

In the early XVIth century, the Baltic markets also constituted an extremely important area for West-European industry.[26] The production of Dutch and English textiles would have been unthinkable on such scale without the export possibilities in that region. Recently scholars have pointed to the fact that the swift development of the rural Netherlands in the XVIth and early XVIIth century was also connected with the import of Baltic grain, and thus with the Baltic trade, although it may seem like a paradox.[27] It made possible specialisation of production in the Netherlands and the shift from grain to dairying, brewing, vegetable growing and the cultivation of industrial crops (flax,

---

[24] See P. VILAR, *Or et monnaie dans l'histoire, 1450-1920*, Paris 1974, p. 133.

[25] See M. BOGUCKA, *North European Commerce...* and *Zur Problematik der profite* (in print).

[26] See R.W.K. HINTON, *The Eastland Trade and the Common Weal in the Seventeenth Century*, Cambridge 1959; B.E. SUPPLE, *Commercial Crisis and Change in England, 1600-1642*, Cambridge 1959; H. ZINS, *England and the Baltic in the Elizabethan Era*, Manchester 1972.

[27] See H. VAN DER WEE, The Agricultural Development of the Low Countries as revealed by the Tithe and Rent Statistics, 1250-1800, in *Productivity...*, pp. 10 ff.

tobacco); it also facilitated the organisation of cottage industries (mainly weaving), thus stimulating the progress of early-capitalist industry in the countryside.

Baltic trade was one of the important factors in the urbanisation and industrialisation of the West of Europe, but looks somewhat different when analysed from the point of view of the other partner — North-Eastern Europe: The "colonial" thesis, put forward sometime ago by M. Małowist,[28] has been recently questioned by J. Topolski and A. Wyczański, who have tried to demonstrate from the case of Poland that the export of grain had constituted quantitatively too slight a margin of the agricultural production of the countries taking part in the Baltic trade to influence either the progress of their economic or their social development in any vital way.[29] This poses certain other problems which need to be discussed further. It also seems that other aspects of the question should be considered, particularly that of the balance of Baltic trade which in the XVIth-XVIIIth centuries was extremely positive for the entire Baltic region, as A. Attman has demonstrated.[30] One must also ask what happened to the stream of money and metals flowing through, thanks to the Baltic trade, which found its way mainly into the pockets of the Eastern magnates and the gentry. Credit operations, on one hand, and money speculation, on the other, doubtless drained that stream,[31] yet it was still powerful enough

---

[28] M. MAŁOWIST, "The Economic and Social Development of the Baltic Countries from the XVth to the XVIIth Centuries" *Economic History Review*, IIth ser. vol XII, 1959, No. 2.

[29] See J. TOPOLSKI, Commerce des denrées agricoles et croissance économique de la zone baltique aux XVIe et XVIIe s., *Annales ,Économies, Sociétés, Civilisations*, 1974 no. 2, pp. 425 ff. A. WYCZAŃSKI, La base intérieure de l'exportation polonaise des céréales dans la seconde moitié du XVIe s., in *Der Aussenhandel Ostmitteleuropas 1450-1650*, Köln-Wien 1971, pp. 260 ff.

[30] A. ATTMAN, *The Russian and Polish Markets...* pp. 10 ff.

[31] See M. BOGUCKA, Obrót wekslowo-kredytowy w Gdańsku w pierwszej połowie XVII w. (Bills of exchange and Credit Turnover in Gdańsk in the First Half of the XVIIth Century), *Roczniki Dziejów Społecznych i Gospodarczych*, vol. XXXIII, 1972, pp. 1-31;

to make a strong impact on the living standards and social relations of such countries as Poland, Lithuania, Ducal Prussia, Livonia, and somewhat later (second half of the XVIIth and XVIIIth century) Russia as well. " Here (i.e. in the Baltic trade) lies the reason why those people from the East and from Poland have become so rich, so impudent and haughty; here lies the reason that they now ride in four-in-hands though once they simply walked," wrote Joost Nykerke in 1630.[32] Baltic trade ought certainly to be examined not only from the production angle but also from the angle of national income, its division, and the nature and size of consumption within the framework of this income, and in relation to the various social groups. Baltic trade was linked with the rapid growth of the prosperity of the gentry as well as of the great nobles in the agricultural Baltic countries and the high level consumption of luxury goods which was a feature of their life-style. The same can be said of the Baltic townsfolk in the ports of Gdańsk, Elbląg, Riga, Königsberg, Klaipeda, Narva, etc. who acted as intermediaries between the feudal lords of the hinterland and West-European merchants. The trade with the Middle and Far East was an extension of Baltic trade, and the purchases of jewellery, richly ornamented arms, rugs, fabrics woven with gold and silver were possible thanks to the money produced from the sales of agricultural produce to the West.[33] The latter also contributed directly to the growth of this luxury consumption, and supplied the Baltic zone with expensive textiles, southern fruits and wine, and spices. When analysing consumption, one should remember too a characteristic phenomenon which some scholars consider as an

---

idem, Zur Problematik der Münzkrise in Danzing in der ersten Hälfte des 17.Jh., *Studia Historiae Oeconomicae*, vol. VI, 1971, pp. 65-73.

[32] Quoted after M. BOGUCKA, Zboże rosyjskie... p. 620.

[33] See M. ZAKRZEWSKA-DUBASOWA, Ormianie zamojscy i ich rola w wymianis handlowej i kulturalnej między Polską a Wschodem (*Armenians from the City of Zamość and their Role in the Trade and Cultural Exchanges between Poland and the East*), Lublin 1965.

investment, others as a form of consumption.[34] That is the expenditure connected with culture, such as the building of palaces and churches, the purchase of work of art, the pensions given to builders and artists; in brief, the whole range of cultural patronage exercised by the magnates and the gentry, as well as by the wealthiest townsmen, thanks to the profits gained in the Baltic trade.[35] On the other hand, one should not forget the phenomenon of hoarding, which in the XVIIth and XVIIIth centuries seems to have played an enormous role in the economy of the Baltic region, though the scale and consequences have not been fully studied.[36]

The impact of Baltic trade then was varied and affected different spheres of life; it was not limited solely to production and the social relations directly connected with it. Further studies in this field will doubtless elucidate the aspects which have remained controversial and studied only in part. It should also be pointed out that this survey is mainly limited to the southern part of the Baltic region. Norway and Finland which exported timber to the West,[37] and Sweden which, while exporting iron,

---

[34] See the conference in Prato, 1976: *Nona Settimana di Studio; Investimenti e civilta Urbana secoli XIII-XVIII* (in the press).

[35] M. Bogucka, Le bourgeois et les investissements culturels. L'exemple de Gdańska dans la première moitić du 17e s. *Revue Historique*, vol. CCLIX, no 2, pp. 429-440; J. Wojtowicz, Miejskie inwestycje kulturalne w Prusach Królewskich w XVI-XVIII w. (The cultural investments in the cities of Royal Prussia in the XVIth-XVIIIth cc.), *Zapiski Historyczne*, vol. XLIII, no 2, pp. 25-44.

[36] M. Bogucka, The Monetary Crisis of the XVIIth Century and Its Social and Psychological Consequences in Poland, *The Journal of European Economic History*, 1975 no 1, pp. 137-152.

[37] S.E. Åstrom, *From Cloth to Iron: the Anglo-Baltic Trade in Late Seventeenth Century*, Helsinki 1963; *Idem*, Technology and Timber Exports From the Gulf of Finland 1661-1740, *The Scandinavian Economic History Review, vol. XXIII*, no 1, 1975; *Idem*, English Timber Imports from Northern Europe in the Eighteen Century, *Scandinavian Economic History Review*, XVIII, 1970; J. Schreiner, *Nederland og Norge 1625-1650. Trelast utførsel og handelspolitik*, Oslo 1933; *Idem*, Et problem i norsk trelasthandel, *Historisk Tidskrift*, XLIII, 1964; *Idem*, Fremmede Marknader for norsk trelast, *Historisk Tijdskrift*, XLIV, 1965.

was keenly engaged in setting up her own industry,[38] were certainly drawn into the orbit of the Baltic trade just as strongly as were Poland and Lithuania, yet they reacted to it in a different way. In the XVIIth and XVIIIth centuries Russia also tried to built up her 'own industry on the basis of the Baltic trade.[39] These examples may serve as a warning not to treat that trade as a unidirectional causal factor, isolated from its context, onesidedly determining the course of economic and social development, and even the political system as the " colonial " thesis would seem to suggest. The Baltic zone, the development of which had been certainly to a large extent stimulated in the XVIth-XVIIIth centuries by the trade with the West, was not a uniform area and its various regions reacted very differently to contacts with the Western economy.

Closely associated with trade were migrations and exchanges of population. Even in the Middle Ages the Baltic was a much frequented travelling route from the East to the West and vice versa. Next to ships, masters and sailors, merchants and their agents, artisans and journeymen used it, as well as those travelling to foreign countries for business purposes, to gain education or to visit the famous towns and holy places; the scholars and artists, diplomats, rulers with their retinues, and the soldiers transported on board ships for various military operations. Between the XVIth and the XVIIIth centuries, this traffic increased massively, not only because of intensified economic and cultural contacts but also because crowds of religious and political refugees fled across the Baltic from the Netherlands, England, France and Sweden, and sought asylum in more tole-

---

[38] See E.F. HECKSCHER, *An Economic History Of Sweden*, Cambridge 1954.

[39] See E. AMBURGER, *Die Familie Marselis*, Giessen 1957; A. OHBERG, Russia and the World Market in the Seventeenth century, *Scandinavian Economic History Review*, 1955, no. 2; D.S. VAN ZUIDEN, *Bydrage tot de kennis der hollandsch-russische relaties in de 16e-18e eeuw*, Amsterdam 1911; *Idem*, Nieuwe bydrage tot de kennis wan de hollandsch-rusrische relaties in de 16e-18e eeuw, *Economisch-Historisch Jaarboek*, 1916.

rant Poland.[40] Besides the East-West exchange, migrations also followed a North-South direction; at the turn of the XVIth century in particular a considerable number of Swedes emigrated to Poland.[41] This traffic involved various different social groups which gave their movements different cousequences. The peasant immigration from the Netherlands to Poland is relatively the best known and studied; it continued the settlements which had began far back in the Middle Ages.[42] In Pomerania, Great Poland and Kujawy, experts brought from the Netherlands drained the marshes, dug canals, built windmills which later served as flour and fulling mills, and established model farms. Also the inhabitants of the Netherland towns came to Poland, especially in the XVIth and early XVIIth centuries; among them were owners of considerable financial means and various skilled specialists (architects, painters, teachers as well as weavers, haberdashers, distillers, etc.).[43] It is worth noting that the banking and credit operations in Pomerania in the XVIth-XVIIth centuries developed very much under the influence of these immigrants, both in theory and in practice.[44] In the second half of the XVIIth and in the XVIIIth century, migration across the Baltic was no longer to Poland but mainly to Sweden and Russia, whose rulers, to a large extent, with the help of Western merchants

---

[40] J. Tazbir, *A State Without Stakes. Polish Religious Toleration in the Sixteenth and Seventeenth Centuries*, New York - Warsaw 1973.

[41] St. Herbst, Swedish Emigrants in Poland at the Turn of the XVIth and the XVIIth Centuries, Poland at the *XIth International Congres of Historical Sciences in Stockhlom*, *Warszawa 1960*, 20č-216; S.M. Szacherska, Uczeni szwedzcy na emigracji w Polsce (Swedish scientists as emigrants in Poland), *Odrodzenie i Reformacja w Polsce*, vol. XVII, 1972, pp. 5-26.

[42] See R. Mauer, *Drei Jahrhunderte Bauernleben in der Weichselniederung*, Poznań 1935; R. Szpor, *Nederlandische Nederzettingen in Westpruisen gedurende den Poolschen tijd*, Enkhuisen 1913; also Polish works of B. Baranowski, St. Inglot, Z. Ludkiewicz and W. Rusiński.

[43] See M. Bogucka, *Rzeczpospolita szlacheka a Niderlandy w XVI-XVII w.* (Polish Commonwealth and Netherlands during XVIth-XVIIth centuries) (forthcoming).

[44] *Ibidem.*

and specialists, tried to develop their national industries and introduce technical innovations.[45] The exchange of people and of commodities went together with an interchange of cultural ideas and trends. The lively economic contacts with Western Europe, as well as the internal links between the Baltic countries resulted in the emergence of a specific cultural zone with distinctive common features despite the many individual ones.[46] This zone had taken shape in the Middle Ages and included, first and foremost, the Baltic ports with their characteristic architecture, their art, their specific social and political forms of life and their highly developed intellectual activity.[47] Comparative studies in this field are, unfortunately, rather modest and the problems relating to it still await thorough examination.[48] It will be important to study the impact exercised by the culture of the Baltic towns and the intellectual and artistic currents flowing through them to the more remote hinterland of the Baltic coast. This problem has received some attention in the case of Gdańsk and the impact of Dutch culture on the Polish lands between the XVIth and the XVIIIth centuries.[49] To describe the results of this research is beyond the

---

[45] See note 39 + K. KUMLIEN, Staat, Kupfererzeugung und Kupferausfuhr in Schweden 1500-1650, in: *Schwerpunkte der Kupferproduktion und des Kupferhandels in Europa 1500-1650*, ed. by H. KELLENBENZ, Köln-Wien 1977, pp. 241 ff; B. BOETHIUS, Swedish Iron and Steel, 1600-1650, *Scandinavian Economic History Review*, 1958, pp. 149 ff. Problemy razvitja feedalizna i kapitalizma w stranach Baltiki. Doklady istoriceskij konferencii 14-17 marca 1972 (On problems of the feudal and capitalistic development of Baltic countries. Rapports of a conference 14-17 March 1972), Tartu 1972.

[46] See A. MĄCZAK, H. SAMSONOWICZ, La Zone Baltique: l'un des éléments du marché européen, *Acta Poloniae Historica*, vol. XI, 1965, pp. 71-99.

[47] See K. FRIEDLAND, Träger und Gegenstände kultureller Vermittlung im spätmittelalterlichen Ostseebereich, *Studia Maritima* vol. I, 1978, pp. 29-38; H. SAMSONOWICZ, Les liens culturels entre les bourgeois du littoral baltique dans le bas moyen âge, *ibidem*, pp. 9-28.

[48] First attempt being made by J.B. NEVEUX, *Vie spirituelle et vie sociale entre Rhin et Baltique au XVIIe s.*, Paris 1967.

[49] See M. BOGUCKA,. *Rzeczpospolita szlachecka* (note 43); *idem*, Gdanski-Polski czy międzynarodowy osrodek gospodarczy (The city of Gdańsk-Polish or international economic centrum?) in: *Polska w epoce odrodzenia*, ed. A. Wyczański, Warszawa 1970,

framework of this paper, however, but they should be included as a supplement to this brief survey of the range of questions posed by the problems connected with the role of Baltic trade.

PRINCIPAL COMMODITIES PASSING VIA THE SOUND
(ANNUAL AVERAGES)
1590-1599 = 100

	First half of the XVIIth century	Index	Second half of the XVIIth century	Index	First half of the XVIIIth century	Index
Westwards:						
Grain (lasts)	68500	121,4	55800	98,9	31800	56,4
Iron (Shippound)	14713	195,6	36742	488,6	131832	1753,3
Timber-Planken						
(in sixties)	1281	193,5	12089	1826,1	53283	8048,7
Eastwards:						
Salt (lasts)	25889	106,2	21305	87,4	25821	105,9
Herrings (lasts)	7715	158,6	3077	63,3	3366	69,2
Textiles (pieces)	55646	190,9	39952	137,1	41972	144,6
Colonial-wares						
(1000 pound)	485	6956,8	2589	37118,2	7463	106614,2

* Estimated at about 40 ellen each.

Source: N. BANG, K. KORST, *Tabeller over Skibsfart og Varetransport gennem Øresund: 1497-1660,* vol. I, 2B, København 1933; *1661-1720,* vol. II, 1, København 1939; *1721-1749,* vol. II, 2, København 1945.

1970, pp. 100-125; A. BOROWKI, Polska a Niderlandy. Zwiazki i analogie kulturalne i literackie w dobie humanizmu, renesansu i baroku (Poland and the Netherlands. Connections and Analogies in Culture and Literature of the Time of Humanismus, Renaissance and Baroque), in: *Literatura staropolska w kontekście europejskim,* Wrocław 1977, pp. 233-252; K. GUTMANÓWNA, Wpły wy niderlandzkie na sredniowieczne malarstwe cechowe w srodomisku krakowskim (Influences from Netherlands on the medieval painting in Cracov), Kraków 1933; J. KIESZKOWSKI, Artysci niderlandzcy w Europie w schodniej (Artists from Netherlands in Eastern Europe), Lwów 1922; W. TOMKIEWICZ, *Z dziejów polskiego mecenatu artystycznego w XVII w.* (On polish cultural investments in the XVIIth c.), Wrocław 1952.

V

SOME ASPECTS OF COMMERCIAL RELATIONS WITHIN THE
BALTIC REGION ON THE EXAMPLE OF GDAŃSK—STOCKHOLM
TRADE IN 1643

The huge body of writings on the Baltic trade is mainly centred on
the question of the voluminous trade between East and West, less space
being devoted to the mutual ties within the Baltic region, which grew
in strength as the region itself developed [1]. For instance, in the first half
of the 17th c. Gdańsk's trade with other Baltic ports has been estimated
at some 25—30 per cent of the total volume of its trade. In order to
find out which Baltic towns took part in that trade and what was the
latter's structure one has to look through the archives of several Baltic
ports. Here the Swedish ports of Stockholm, Gotenburg and Norrköping
are among the best equipped with documentation for there whole sets
of ledgers recording the maritime customs duties levied on imported
and exported goods (tollage) have been preserved [2]. Because I was in
Sweden for a very short time, I had to limit myself to perusing only
one archive in Stockholm, concerning only one year, 1643, at that.
I selected that year because of the relatively quiet times then prevailing
in the Baltic after the Stumdorf armistice (1635) and before the hostil-

[1] These aspects are dealt with especially by: K. K u m l i e n, Sverige och han-
seaterna. Studiar i svensk politik och utrikeshandel, Lund-Stockholm 1953;
K. P. Z o e l l n e r, Vom Strelasund zum Oslofjord. Untersuchungen zur Geschichte
der Hanse und der Stadt Stralsund in der zweiten Hälfte des 16. Jahrhunderts,
Weimar 1974; H. L a n g e r, Stralsund 1600 - 1630. Eine Hansestadt in der Krise und
im europäischen Konflikt, Weimar 1970. Recently, an important article on the
subject has been published by H. L e s i ń s k i, Rozwój handlu morskiego Koło-
brzegu z krajami Skandynawii w XVII i XVIII wieku [Development of Maritime
Trade between Kołobrzeg and Scandinavian Countries in the 17th and 18th c.],
[in:] Ars historica, Poznań 1974, pp. 635 - 651. The problem has also been tackled
marginally by M. H r o c h, Obchod mezi vychodni a zapadni Evropou v obdobi
počatku kapitalizmu, "Československy Časopis Historicky", 1963, vol. 4, pp. 479 - 511.

[2] I am deeply indebted to Professor Artur Attman of Gotenburg for drawing
my attention to this important source, and to Professor Folke Lindberg of Stockholm for his help in my work at the Archive of the City of Stockholm.

V

ities at sea in the years 1644—1645 in connection with the Danish-Swedish conflict, and also because of the fact that two of the set of three books for that year, in which the levying of harbour charges was recorded in Gdańsk, have been preserved; this gives the opportunity of comparing the two sources [3]. The study attempts on this base to probe and point out some of the characteristic patterns of the trade within the Baltic region and his importance for the development of Baltic countries irrespective of their ties with Western Europe.

Even at a glance the Stockholm customs books differ from the Gdańsk ones and the difference is to the credit of the former thanks to the detailed entries. They give, besides the home port of the skipper and his name also the port of departure (when the two localities differ); next to the amount of customs duty also the value of the goods and the names of cargo owners. The specification of the goods is very accurate. Even small quantities of various articles as well as parcels carried by the passengers are entered [4]. Also the tiny quantities of goods carried by the crew are recorded in detail. But the Gdańsk customs books give only the name of the skipper and his home port and the specification of goods with the amount of duty paid; they contain no information about the route plied by the ship and about the owners of the cargo [5].

The analysis of the 1643 customs book has led to the compilation of a few tables which bring out the various sides of the trade between Gdańsk and Stockholm at the time. Table A shows the movement of ships in the harbour of Stockholm and indirectly the important size of the volume of trade with Gdańsk. The ships arriving from Gdańsk accounted for more than 20 per cent of all the ships which docked in Stockholm throughout that year; here Gdańsk heads the list followed by German ports (Stralsund, Lübeck) which traditionally played an important role in trade with Scandinavia [6], and ahead of Dutch ports. Gdańsk as the port of call for ships sailing from Stockholm occupies the second place in the table (18.3 per cent) after Dutch ports but ahead of Lübeck, Danish ports, Stralsund etc. But one must bear in mind that the ships plying between Gdańsk and Stockholm were not very big, mostly of a capacity of 20 to 60 lasts (an average of 30 lasts), rarely 50—80

---

[3] This article is based on: Stadarkiv Stockholm, Stadskakamerarensarkiv, Stadens rekenskaper verifikationer 1643 (hereinafter referred to as SS, Ver. 1643) and the Voivodship State Archives in Gdańsk, 300, 19/28, 29 (hereinafter referred to as VSA Gdańsk).

[4] Altogether, 26 passengers, including nine women, were recorded in 1643.

[5] Concerning the Gdańsk harbour dues see C. B i e r n a t, *Gdańskie księgi palowe z drugiej połowy XVIII w. oraz metoda ich opracowania statystycznego* [Gdańsk Customs Books of the Second Half of the 18th C. and the Method of Their Statistical Analysis], "Studia gdańsko-pomorskie" [Gdańsk-Pomeranian Studies"], 1964, pp. 214 - 231.

[6] Cf. K. K u m l i e n, *op. cit.*, *passim.*

Table A. Traffic in Stockholm Harbour in 1643
I. Coming in Ships

From	Number	% of Total Traffic
Gdańsk	34	20.4
Stralsund	25	15.2
Lubeck	23	13.6
Dutch Ports	21	12.6
Portugal	21	12.6
Königsberg	9	5.5
Rostock	6	3.6
Scotland	4	2.4
Szczecin	3	1.8
Kołobrzeg	1	0.6
Riga	1	0.6
Memel	1	0.6
Copenhague	1	0.6
Göteborg	1	0.6
Unknown	15	9.3
Total	166	100.0

II. Going out Ships

To	Number	% of Total Traffic
Dutch Ports	47	26.8
Gdańsk	32	18.3
Lubeck	31	17.7
Danemark	18	10.2
Stralsund	18	10.2
Riga	8	4.6
England and Scotland	7	4.0
Rostock	3	1.7
Königsberg	3	1.7
Kołobrzeg	2	1.2
Szczecin	2	1.2
Wismar	1	0.6
Memel	1	0.6
Parnau	1	0.6
Destination unknown	1	0.6
Total	175	100.0

lasts [7]. At the same time, ships plying the Portugal—Stockholm and Holland—Stockholm routes had a capacity of more than 100, usually 150 or 180 lasts [8]. So, when we examine the volume of trade in Stockholm

[7] Information about the size of ships can be obtained from the list of harbour duties of the second half of the year 1643, cf. SS, Ver. 1643, pp. 851 - 871.
[8] As above.

V

Table B. The Trade of Stockholm in 1643

I. Imports

From	Value (in Svedish dollars)	% of Total Value
Dutch Ports	522,717	33.0
Lubeck	284,519	17.9
Portugal	188,433	11.9
Gdańsk	156,721	9.9
Göteborg	107,862	6.8
Königsberg	106,707	6.7
Stralsund	55,810	3.5
Scotland	27,058	1.7
Rostock	26,817	1.7
Riga	2,288	0.4
Copenhaguen	3,522	0.3
Kołobrzeg	3,232	0.2
Szczecin	2,615	0.2
Unknown	92,089	5.8
Total	1,584,390	100.0

II. Exports

To	Value (in Swedish dollars)	% of Total Value
Dutch Ports	1,040,547	53.3
Lubeck	470,406	24.0
Gdańsk (and Elbląg)	171,984	8.8
Danemark	63,450	3.2
Stralsund	62,114	3.1
England and Scotland	61,349	3.1
Riga and Parnau	19,188	1.0
Königsberg	15,509	0.9
Kołobrzeg	6,642	0.3
Rostock and Wismar	3,175	0.2
Szczecin	2,899	0.2
Memel	1,889	0.1
Unknown	36,079	1.8
Total	1,955,231	100,0

(Table B), the share of Gdańsk appears more modest: fourth in imports (the value of imported goods amounted to 156,721 Swedish thalers i.e. 9.9 per cent) after the Dutch ports, Lübeck and Portugal; and third in exjorts (the value of exported goods amounted to 171,984 Swedish thalers or 8.8 per cent) after the Dutch ports and Lübeck [9]. Still Gdańsk

[9] Included in the study is also one ship which arrived to Elbląg from Stock-holm.

was quite an important trading partner for Stockholm. In the total turnover of Gdańsk Stockholm's share was, of course, less imposing: 3.3 per cent of the movement of ships, and 5.2 per cent of the value of the total turnover [10]. The balance of this trade was unfavourable to Gdańsk: in 1643 it amounted to 15,263 Swedish thalers i.e. 4.6 per cent on the debit side. It would be interesting to examine this phenomenon over whole decades, as well as the balance of trade of Gdańsk with other Baltic ports at the same time; only then would it be possible to determine whether and how much trade within the Baltic region differed from Gdańsk—Western Europe trade which brought a considerable surplus to that city in the 16th and 17th centuries [11].

The structure of the Gdańsk—Stockholm trade, presented in Tables C and D, shows considerable difference compared with the structure of trade between Gdańsk and the Western ports via the Sound. Agricultural and animal products and foodstuffs which in Gdańsk's overall exports accounted for more than 80 per cent [12] amounted to barely 58.3 per cent in the export to Stockholm; of that figure, rye accounted for only 24.5 per cent, flour, cereals and malt (i.e. processed products) to 12.8 per cent. The share of various industrial products in that export was quite remarkable: textiles, clothing, fancy goods, furniture, vessels, glass and articles of glass, fur and leather goods, tools (spinning wheels and other tools for the weaving industry), and, lastly, cultural goods: paintings, etchings, books, paper, chessboards etc. Children's clothing and toys were a popular item. Altogether, this branch of exports accounted for 32 per cent of Gdańsk's exports to Stockholm. It appears that Gdańsk, then a big production centre [13], manufactured goods not only for its own do-

---

[10] In 1643, 1,983 ships passed through the port of Gdańsk (M. B o g u c k a, *Handel zagraniczny Gdańska w pierwszej połowie XVII w.*, [*Gdańsk's Foreign Trade in the First Half of the 17th C.*], Wrocław 1970, p. 31); this figure includes 34+32=66 ships or 3.3 per cent plying the Stockholm route. Gdańsk's volume of trade was estimated (as above, p. 34) in 1643 at 37, 978,000 Prussian marks i.e. 4,220,000 Reichsthalers. The volume of trade between Gdańsk and Stockholm amounted to 328,705 Swedish thalers which at the rate of exchange 1 Reichsthaler=1.5 Swedish thalers (cf. E. F. H e c k s c h e r, *Sveriges Ekonomiska Historia*, Stockholm 1936, pp. 556, 613) would equal 219,136 Reichsthalers or 5.2 per cent of the overall trade.

[11] Cf. M. B o g u c k a, *Die Bedeutung des Ostseehandels für die Aussenhandelsbilanz Polens in der ersten Hälfte des 17. Jahrhunderts. Der Aussenhandel Ostmitteleuropas 1450 - 1650*, Cologne 1971, pp. 47 - 55; A. M ą c z a k, *Między Gdańskiem a Sundem. Studia nad handlem bałtyckim od połowy XVI do połowy XVII w.* [*Between Gdańsk and the Sound. Studies on Baltic Trade from Mid=16th to Mid=17th c.*], Warszawa 1972, pp. 69 - 96.

[12] In 1641 — 79.7 per cent, in 1649 — 89.7 per cent. M. B o g u c k a, *Handel zagraniczny...*, p. 36.

[13] M. B o g u c k a, *Gdańsk jako ośrodek produkcyjny od XIV do połowy XVII w.* [*Gdańsk as a Production Centre from the 14th to Mid=17th c.*], Warszawa 1964, *passim*.

V

Table C. Structure of Gdańsk Imports to Stockholm 1643

Name	Value in Svedish dollars	% of Total
I. Agricultural and breeding products, food		
Rye	38,430	24.5
Flour, grit, malt	20,185	12.8
Hop	12,431	8.0
Salt	6,216	4.0
Cucumber, peas, vegetables	3,875	2.5
Liquors	2,879	1.9
Fruit (aples, prunes)	1,870	1.2
Meat and fat	1,447	0.9
Bred, gingerbred, biscuits	1,120	0.7
Flax and hem	822	0.5
Colonial goods	702	0.4
Wool, hair, yarn	574	0.4
Feathers, down	475	0.3
Fish	348	0.2
Total	91,375	58.3

II. Manufactured goods		
Textiles, knittedware, haberdashery	38,234	24.4
Fur — and leather goods	5,702	3.6
Furniture, utensils	2,089	1.3
Glassware	2,012	1.3
Cultural goods*	1,887	1.2
Tools**	236	0.2
Total	50,160	32.0

III. Metals, minerals, chemicals, forests products*	15,186	9.7

* Paintings, books, chessboards, toys for children.
** Mostly spinning wheels.
*** Lead, sulfur, salpeter, powder.

mestic market and for the Polish gentry but also for the highly absorptive Scandinavian market. This type of expansion is very symptomatic and interesting for it is without precedent in the economic history of the Polish Commonwealth. Besides the Gdańsk-made products, the ships carried from Gdańsk to Stockholm goods manufactured in Pomerania (cloth, linen, glass) and Silesia (textiles, clothing, fancy goods). The structure of the exports from Stockholm to Gdańsk shows an overwhelming majority of raw materials: more than 85 per cent is accounted for by metals (chiefly iron bars) probably for use by the Gdańsk and neighbouring metallurgical factories; also small quantities of forest

Table D. Structure of Stockholm Exports to Gdańsk 1643

Name	Value in Swedish dollars	% of Total
I. Metals		
Iron (mostly in bars)	142,414	82.8
Copper and brass	2,994	1.7
Armor plates	1,460	0.8
Total	146,868	85.3
II. Other goods		
Fish oil	7,740	4.5
Other fats	455	0.3
Pitch	4,395	2.6
Wood	4,310	2.5
Fish	4,293	2.5
Leather and furs	2,568	1.5
Other	1,355	0.8
Total	25,116	14.7

products, fish and fish oil. In consequence, in 1643, trade between Gdańsk and Stockholm exhibited features reversing the pattern of Gdańsk's trade as a whole in that period: the big role of industrial goods in exports, and of industrial raw materials in imports. It would be extremely interesting to investigate whether those features also dominated the trade between Gdańsk and other Baltic ports, particularly the Swedish ones, and when they appeared first: at the close of the 16th or only in the first half of the 17th century. But there is no doubt as to the short time they lasted, the chief reason for this being the Polish-Swedish war of 1655—1660 which constituted a turning point for the entire Polish economy.

The analysis of the Stockholm customs books provides interesting insight into the organisation of commerce within the Baltic region at the time. Each ship's cargo was usually divided between four, six or even more merchants, in two cases only did it belong to one person. The skipper and the crew carried, as a rule, certain quantities of goods on their own account. The skipper's share amounted usually to from 5 to 10 per cent of the value of the entire cargo; members of the crew such as cooks, bosuns, helmsmen and even seamen traded in more modest quantities. But there were cases when the greater part of the cargo belonged to the crew, e.g. in September 1643, the ship which arrived in Stockholm from Gdańsk, captained by Jorgen Holst, declared goods to the value of 2,670 Swedish thalers including 2,188 thalers worth of goods belonging to the skipper, and 4 thalers worth of goods to the bosuns, which means that 82.1 per cent of the cargo was owned by the crew [14]. As a matter of fact, Holst appears among the leading group of merchants who organised shipping on that route (Table G). Another ship which arrived also in September, its skipper being Hindrich Hinderson, declared 756 Swedish thalers worth of goods including the skipper's 432 thalers, the helmsman's 7, three bosuns' 27, 9 and 6, totalling 492 thalers worth of crew's goods i.e. 65 per cent of the value of the whole cargo [15]. All in all, the goods imported from Gdańsk to Stockholm by skippers amounted to 10,171 thalers or 6.5 per cent of the overall value of imports; the goods belonging to other members of the crew accounted for 3,152 thalers or 2 per cent, the total being 13,323 thalers or 8.5 per cent. The crew's share of exports from Stockholm to Gdańsk seems to have been smaller: the skipper goods account for 3,898 Swedish thalers or 2.2 per cent, other crew members' for 119 thalers or 0.07 per cent, the total being some 2.3 per cent. Perhaps this total would be somewhat higher if we tried to interpret and to widen the definition in the source of "skipper's goods". In two cases, no names of the owners of the cargo are entered so it is logical to assume that it belonged entirely to the skippers, in this case Peter Bertils and Jorgen Holst. In May 1643, Peter Bertils brought to Stockholm from Gdańsk goods to the value of 622 Swedish thalers [16]. We know from other sources that Bertils was a merchant because he is mentioned in the books four times as the owner of cargoes shipped from Gdańsk: in June aboard his own ship goods worth 596 thalers, in July on board Claes Boetke the Elder's ship goods worth 447 thalers, in August 220 thalers worth of cargo on board Jochim Kramer's ship, and in September 101 thalers worth of goods aboard Zacharias Droghe's ship [17]. In the records of exports from Stockholm he is quoted as the owner of two shipments valued jointly at 751 thalers [18]. He was certainly one of the smaller (low total value of cargo) but busier merchants on this route. Similarly, there are no names of owners as concerns the cargo worth 2,849 Swedish thalers shipped in June from Stockholm to Gdańsk aboard skipper Jorgen Holst's ship [19]. He was also the owner of three other cargoes carried by other skippers, their total value being 6,532 Swedish thalers [20]. On the Gdańsk—Stockholm route his name is quoted in connection with as many as seven cargoes totalling 4,633 thalers (on board ships commanded by Claes Boetke and Zacharias

[14] SS, Ver. 1643, pp. 333 - 334.
[15] As above, pp. 392 - 393.
[16] As above, p. 34.
[17] As above, pp. 116, 318, 301, 330.
[18] As above, pp. 34, 319.
[19] As above, p. 179.
[20] As above, pp. 37, 176, 408.

Droghe) [21]. Both these skippers and traders at the same time can be found in the records of the ship's duties levied in Stockholm [22]; Peter Bertils (Bartels) was entered on August 8 as a native of Gdańsk commanding a 30-last ship, Jorgen Holst on September 1, as a Stockholm skipper of a 20-last ship. Also in several other cases the names of skippers coincide with those of the merchants, so it seems right to assume that they were the same persons each performing two functions [23]. So in reality the share of skipper's cargo may have been much bigger than the above figures would suggest; it amounted probably to 10—15 per cent of the total turnover between Gdańsk and Stockholm. But it shows up the backward, medieval nature of that trade featuring a very weak division of labour and far for complete separation of the functions of skipper, merchant and, perhaps, shipowner. The skippers, beside having some cargo of their own on board small ships commanded (perhaps also owned) by them, were also often the owners of cargoes carried by other ships in order to lessen the risks. Another characteristic feature was the participation of members of the same family in a trading operation; it certainly increased the feeling of security, but also added to the backward nature of the trade [24].

The analysis of the structure of the cargoes belonging to various merchants brings out their low degree of specialisation: the majority traded in mixed goods shipping textiles, grain, salt, wood and glass products etc. from Gdańsk to Stockholm. On the Stockholm—Gdańsk route specialisation was also practically non-existent although, because of the smaller variety of goods carried, the cargoes belonging to particular merchants were of a more uniform nature. Trade, as we may assume from the names, was mainly in the hands of Swedish merchants. Some Gdańsk and Dutch merchants, including the famous Ludwig de Geer, also had some business interests in that trade. But most of them were small merchants, their trading operations being on a small scale. The great number of persons (in 1643, on the Gdańsk—Stockholm route

[21] As above, pp. 216, 330, 341, 369, 588, 595, 628.

[22] As above, pp. 851 - 871.

[23] For instance, Zacharias Droghe of Kalmar, commanding a 50-last ship, entered in the list of harbour duties on September 1, 1643, is quoted as the owner of goods worth 26 thalers, freighted from Gdańsk on board his own ship in September. Skipper Claes Boetke the Younger of Stockholm, commanding a 80-last ship entered in the list of harbour duties on October 3, 1643, figures as the owner of two shipments of goods carried from Stockholm to Gdańsk: in June, 365.5 thalers worth of goods aboard Claes Boetke the Elder's ship, and in August, 674.5 thalers worth on Sigfryd Erichson's ship. In August he also figures as the owner of a shipment of goods worth 447 thalers freighted to Stockholm aboard Claes Boetke the Elder's ship. There are many similar examples.

[24] Very often the skipper is a member of the family carrying goods belonging to his son or father, the terms "Younger" and "Elder" are quite frequent.

V

Table E. Frequency of the Participation in the Turnover
Gdańsk – Stockholm

Number of Merchants	Number of Cargoes in 1643	Total Number of Cargoes
129	1	129
28	2	56
22	3	66
2	4	8
7	5	35
4	6	24
2	7	14
2	8	16
1	9	9
1	10	10
Total 198		367

Table F. Frequency of the Participation in the Turnover
Stockholm – Gdańsk

Number of merchants	Number of Cargoes in 1643	Total Number of Cargoes
36	1	36
14	2	28
5	3	15
7	4	28
6	5	30
1	6	6
1	9	9
Total 70		152

198 merchants and 70 on the Stockholm—Gdańsk route) is evidence of considerable disintegration of this trade. Tables E and F show the frequency of shipping organised by particular merchants, Table G contains the list of the more important merchants taking part in the trade: it gives the names of 33 persons who exceeded the figure of 1,700 Swedish thalers worth of goods over the year; in their hands was concentrated 73.1 per cent of the overall trade. This was certainly small-scale trading with small capital but quite intensive if one takes into account the number of cargoes shipped by some of the merchants during a single sailing season. In order to form a general idea of the total volume of trade between Gdańsk and Stockholm at the time it is necessary to note that, with a still very medieval traditional organisation (weak division of functions, disintegration, strong family ties), its structure showed, at least from Gdańsk's point of view, an interesting novel feature: breaking away from the traditional model of export of agricultural produce and import of industrial goods, and a 180° turn in the exchange which meant

V

Table G. Most Important Merchants and Their Turnovers in 1643

Name	Number of Cargoes			Value of Cargoes*			% of Global Turnover
	Gd.–St.	St.–Gd.	Total	Gd.–St.	St.–Gd.	Total	
Rÿnn Robert	6	4	10	6,602	15,306	21,908	6.7
Delfendal Gabriel	7	6	13	12,522	8,981	21,503	6.5
Hindrichson Joens	10	5	15	7,918	12,488	20,406	6.2
De Keyser Didrich	5	1	6	4,980	7,839	12,819	3.9
Hanson Peter	3	4	7	5,343	6,856	12,199	3.7
Jonson Johan	9	5	14	6,234	5,319	11,553	3.5
Holst Joran	7	4	11	4,633	6,532	11,165	3.4
Martemar Hans	3	2	5	3,232	7,051	10,283	3.1
Behm Peter	2	4	6	2,440	7,665	10,105	3.1
Dawidson Arfwed	5	9	14	2,692	7,174	9,866	3.0
Peterson Johan	10	4	14	1,172	6,005	7,777	2.4
Göw Hindrich	1	2	3	3,500	3,983	7,483	2.2
Nyman Christopher	5	2	7	3,173	4,203	7,376	2.2
Güttery Walter	6	3	9	1,915	5,365	7,280	2.2
De Geer Lois	–	2	2	–	5,818	5,818	1.7
Olofson Johan	8	4	12	1,509	4,154	5,663	1.7
Fintzke Christian	1	1	2	4,254	1,354	5,608	1.7
Boÿ Oliver	1	2	3	959	4,582	5,541	1.6
Hartman Claes	2	5	7	184	5,271	5,455	1.6
Berendt Frantz	5	1	6	4,204	475	4,679	1.4
Brünn Anthony	3	2	5	2,242	1,699	3,941	1.2
Smit Claes	2	3	5	917	2,851	3,768	1.1
Foss Carl	3	4	7	984	2,637	3,621	1.1
Smit Jochim	5	5	10	1,472	2,097	3,569	1.1
Sÿlfaet Simon	–	5	5	–	3,499	3,499	1.1
Dürkeyster Dirck	1	–	1	3,382	–	3,382	1.0
Mandt Hans	6	3	9	1,369	1,779	3,148	0.9
Behm Hans	8	1	9	2,269	181	2,450	0.7
Silfert Joran	–	3	3	–	2,187	2,187	0.7
Israelson Hans	1	–	1	1,927	–	1,927	0.6
Debett Dirck	6	1	7	350	1,735	2,085	0.6
StrewingAlbrecht	–	1	1	–	1,909	1,909	0.6
Anderson Hans	5	1	6	1,459	256	1,715	0.5
						Total	73.1

* In Swedish dollars.

export of craftsmen's articles from Gdańsk in exchange for raw materials necessary for their production. This was, naturally, a consequence of the economic changes which had occurred in Gdańsk in the first half of the 17th century and turned this city into the first big Baltic manufacturing centre looking to Scandinavia both for convenient selling markets and for sources of supply. A chronological and geographical enlargement (other Baltic ports besides Stockholm) of this probe would make it possible to check this assertion and perhaps support it more fully.

The examination of a bigger number of Swedish customs books will

V

also allow for a critical check up of the Gdańsk customs books. For a comparison of materials concerning the year 1643 suggests that not only were the Swedish customs declarations more carefully drawn up and more accurate, containing more items (ports of origin and call, names of cargo owners and of passengers, etc.) but also that the Gdańsk books may have been deliberately and perhaps to a large extent rigged. The declarations made by the same skippers commanding the same ships differ fundamentally as concerns the quantity of goods in Gdańsk and in Stockholm. Two examples will suffice. The customs declaration made by Claes Boetke the Younger, who sailed from Gdańsk in July 1643, as entered in the customs book, shows: 55 lasts of rye, 20 lasts of rough flour, 6 lasts of medium flour, 60 stones of down, 12 bolts of Silesian cloth, 1 bolt of white Gdańsk cloth, felt articles worth 130 zlotys, linen worth 200 zlotys, 300 black rabbit skins, 12 bales of forty ermine skins each and one table worth 15 zlotys [25]. His declaration in Stockholm lists 49 lasts of rye, 6 lasts and 226 barrels (1 last=12 barrels?) of flour, 6 barrels of beer, 120 barrels of malt, some amounts of butter, beer, vodka and fish, 1 last+2 pounds of down (1 last=some 60 stones), 12 bolts of Silesian cloth, 1 bolt of heavy cloth (probably of Gdańsk manufacture), large quantities of various kinds of linen probably much more than 200 zlotys worth, large quantities of felt articles, a casket and 16 chairs besides the one table and, finally, besides the rabbit and ermine skins also chamois leather worth 30 thalers [26]. Peter Bertils' declaration of May 1643 in Gdańsk lists 18 lasts of rye, 400 quintals of calamine and 4 quintals of lead [27]. The same skipper, having docked in Stockholm in the same month of May declared: 17 lasts of rye, 60 barrels of flour, 133 1/3 shippound of calamine, 2.5 shippounds of lead, 38 bolts of linen, 10 dozen gloves and 40 bundles of leather thongs as well as goods carried by the crew: 3 barrels of bucklings, 400 bundles of marline, 5 spinning wheels, 12 sets of chessmen, 18 caskets, 6 chests, 144 chairs, a certain quantity of gingerbreads [28]. The short time that elapsed between departure from Gdańsk and arrival in Stockholm excludes any possibility of docking somewhere en route and taking on board some more cargo. The comparison suggests that the Gdańsk customs books did not enter all the goods taken out, and the differences are so big that they hardly seem to be due solely to smuggling or swindling on the part of the skippers. More probably, the city authorities, bound to pay half the port dues to the king, lowered their amount in the relevant documents and so appropriated more than a half of the sums levied. I have elsewhere drawn

---

[25] VSA Gdańsk, 300, 19/28 p. 20a.
[26] SS, Ver. 1643, p. 216. The small difference in the number of lasts of rye may be due to the difference between the Stockholm and the Gdańsk last.
[27] VSA Gdańsk, 300, 19/28 p. 7a.
[28] SS. Ver. 1643, p. 28.

attention to the practices of the customs authorities in Gdańsk in connection with their gambling on the differences between the rates of exchange of coins levied as customs duties and paid to the King, which made it possible for the city to gain a considerable "surplus" every year [29]. The comparison of Gdańsk and Stockholm customs books seems to indicate that Gdańsk was not satisfied with indulging in such dealings. In order to confirm or reject such a supposition it would, of course, be necessary to consult a whole set of records and compare them. Without concluding the matter this or that way it seems, however, that the suspicion that the customs books regularly lowered the figures concerning Gdańsk's volume of trade may, unfortunately, affect all the studies conducted on the basis of those books.

To sum up, it is possible to assume on the example of the trade between Gdańsk and Stockholm in 1643 that there was a considerable difference in the structure of trade within the Baltic region and that of the whole Baltic zone with Western Europe. The incentives were different and the nature of ties depended on the local conditions of the Baltic partners. But despite the considerably backward, medieval trading methods and techniques prevailing within the Baltic region there were emerging at the opening of the 17th century the first signs (perhaps stimulating the economic development?) of certain towns (Gdańsk) expanding towards economically less developed areas (Scandinavia). Further comparative studies covering longer periods and larger areas (other Baltic ports and their mutual contacts) may complete and enrich the picture presented here in outline only. They will also make possible a more effective critique of customs sources originating in various places, which may substantially alter the views entertained hitherto and the studies carried out so far illustrating the size of the Baltic trade.

Translated by Krystyna Kęplicz

[29] Cf. M. B o g u c k a, *Spór nie tylko wokół apogeum gdańskiego handlu [Dispute not only about the Apogee of Gdańsk's Trade]*, "Zapiski Historyczne" ["Historical Notes"], 1972, vol. 1, p. 122.

DUTCH MERCHANTS' ACTIVITIES IN GDANSK IN THE FIRST HALF OF THE 17th CENTURY

I. GENERAL REMARKS

This article should be seen as a complementary one to the study "Amsterdam and the Baltic in the First Half of the 17th Century" published more than 15 years ago[1]. Towards the end of the 16th century the Baltic region became the most important trade area for the Netherlands. In the 17th century Baltic trade was often described as *moederhandel*[2]. In those years more than 50 per cent of the Baltic trade was concentrated in Gdansk, where Dutch sailors and merchants acquired the dominant role in the overseas commerce: 60-90 per cent of the total number of ships plying Gdansk were Dutch ships[3]. Because of the high technical qualities of the Dutch fleet Dutch freights were low: 1.5-3 times cheaper than the freights in Gdansk's own fleet[4]. It resulted in the Dutch control over the Gdansk shipping in the first half of the 17th century.

The Dutch merchants were not only the biggest exporters of the Polish agricultural and forestry products to the West, but they were also the main importers of luxurious goods to Gdansk: fine textiles, wines, fruits, spices. The expansion and elaboration of Dutch activities took place already in the 16th century[5], but its peak was formed in the first decades of the 17th century.

---

[1] M. Bogucka, "Amsterdam and the Baltic in the First Half of the 17th Century", in: *The Economic History Review* (Second Series) XXVI (1973) 3, 433-447.

[2] D.W. Davies, *A Primer of Dutch Seventeenth Century Overseas Trade* (The Hague, 1961) 10.

[3] St. Hoszowski, "The Polish Baltic Trade in the 15th-18th Centuries", in: *Poland at the XIth International Congress of Historical Sciences in Stockholm* (Warszawa, 1960) 143; M. Bogucka, *Handel zagraniczny Gdanska w pierwszej polowie XVII w. (Gdansk's Overseas Trade in the First Half of the 17th Century)* (Wroclaw, 1970) 68-69.

[4] Bogucka, *Handel zagraniczny*, 116.

[5] A.E. Christensen, *Dutch Trade to the Baltic about 1600* (The Hague, 1941) 380 ff.

II. FAMILY STRUCTURE OF BUSINESS

The structure of the Dutch connections with Gdansk was built mostly on the base of family relations. Family ties helped to avoid the difficulties met in Gdansk by foreign tradesmen because of the monopoly granted to Gdansk's citizens in their own harbour. The family structure of business also gave the enterprise a feeling of security: the partner who belonged to the family was expected to be loyal and trustworthy[6]. Usually a son or younger brother was sent from Amsterdam to Gdansk to establish his residence there and to manage the family business as a resident or a citizen of Gdansk[7]. The arrangement of Pels' firm could be regarded as an example of such an enterprise. The head of the firm was Pieter Pels, living in Amsterdam, its representatives in Gdansk were three brothers: Marcus, Pieter and Abraham Pels[8]. The firm was exporting goods from Gdansk and supplying other merchants with credit, in 1617 e.g. they financed a big operation, the export of grains, conducted by Wessel Schenk, merchant in Amsterdam, with the help of his brother Hans residing in Gdansk[9]. On European scale big businesses were conducted by the Dutch family of Pilgrom. One of the Pilgroms, Arndt, had not only settled in Gdansk in the beginning of the 17th century, but had become a citizen of this city[10]. To Pilgrom's trading company in Amsterdam belonged Paul, Stephen and Herman Pilgrom as well as the husband of Arndt's sister, Claes Outgertsen[11]. The Pilgroms were trading along two routes:

1. Gdansk-Hamburg-Amsterdam
2. Wroclaw in Silesia-Hamburg-Amsterdam

They were exporting grains, potash, powder, saltpetre and copper from Poland; Arndt Pilgrom was also a partner from 1636-1641 in a company formed in Gdansk for refinement of saltpetre[12].

Very lively activities were conducted by merchants of the Dutch family Van Tweenhuysen: one of two brothers took up his residence in Gdansk, the second, Lambrecht, in Amsterdam. They were trading not only with Gdansk, but also

---

[6] There are some examples of it; e.g. A(rchives of) G(dansk) 300, 5/47, 96ab.

[7] G(emeente) A(rchief in) A(msterdam), N(otarieel) A(rchief) 134, 65; 151, 128-131, 140-142, 174-175; 879, 67. Also letters written by Gdansk city council, GAA, A(rchief) B(urgermeestern), M(issiven van) D(anzig), p(ortefeuille) 2.

[8] GAA, NA 116, 358-359; 150, 73.

[9] Bogucka, *Handel zagraniczny*, 11, 106; M. Bogucka, "Handel Gdanska z polwyspem Iberyjskim w pierwszej polowie XVII w." ("Gdansk Trade with the Iberian Peninsula in the First Half of the 17th Century"), in: *Przeglad Historyczny* LX (1969) 1, 11.

[10] Bogucka, *Handel zagraniczny*, 95.

[11] GAA, NA 103, 171; 132, 156; 201, 460-461.

[12] M. Bogucka, "Saltpeter Production and Saltpeter Trade between Gdansk and Amsterdam in the First Half of the 17th Century", in: W.G. Heeres (ea) (eds), *From Dunkirk to Danzig, Shipping and Trade in the North Sea and the Baltic, 1350-1850. Essays in honour of J.A. Faber* (Hilversum, 1988) 167-170.

with Szczecin and Frankfurt, dealing with goods as well as conducting large financial operations[13]. The well-known family Le Maire, originally from the Southern Netherlands, but already established in Amsterdam[14], had also a factor in Gdansk: Daniel Le Maire, Isaac's brother or son; he was also related to the big merchant of Gdansk Hans Schenck, his sister's husband. Daniel traded mostly in pepper and powder and acted as a banker in commission of several merchants of Amsterdam[15]. The factor of the family Thibaut, originally French but settled in Amsterdam, in Gdansk was Gilles Thibaut, trading in grains, lumber, wax, hem, tallow and seeds[16]. A large trade in grains and spices between Gdansk and Iberian peninsula or Italy was carried on by the Dutch family Voyrknecht; one of them, Salomon, was living in Amsterdam, the other, his brother or son Jan, became a resident in Gdansk; Jan was acting as an agent not only for his family but also for other Dutch merchants[17]. Similar activities were conducted in Gdansk by several other Dutch tradesmen who became residents in this city: Dirck Brasser, brother of merchant Joost Brasser living in Amsterdam, Hans Ghysbrechtsen de Veer, who was sent to Gdansk by his father, merchant of Amsterdam, Ghysbrecht Jansen de Veer, Willem Sitterich de Jonge, son of Willem van Sitterich merchant of Amsterdam, François Clenterinck, son of Pieter Clenterinck, merchant of Amsterdam, Jacob Jacobsen, brother of Isaac Jacobsen, merchant of Amsterdam, David Rothe, brother of Hans Rothe, merchant of Amsterdam. Floris Haskelaer de Jonge became a citizen of Gdansk and acted there for the husband of his sister, Hans Hongers, merchant of Amsterdam. It is worth noting that Cornelis Vlaminck, a very busy merchant and citizen of Gdansk, was also of Dutch descent: his brother Pieter Dircksen Vlaminck with the help of Cornelis imported grain into the Netherlands and was a member of the Amsterdam city council[18].

Companies not based on family ties were less frequent. On 26th May 1625 such a *contracte van compagnie* was established by Jan Pieterssen Van Nes, father, and Pieter Jansen van Nes, son, both merchants of Amsterdam, with Jan Jourenssen van Lier, actually settled in Gdansk. Jan Jourenssen promised to manage Van Nes' business in Poland. From a settlement made after Jan's death in 1635 it shows however that he was acting as a factor rather than as an associate of his patrons in Amsterdam[19].

---

[13] Bogucka, *Handel zagraniczny*, 107.
[14] J.G. van Dillen, "Isaac Le Maire en de handel in actiën der Oost-Indische Compagnie", in: *Economisch-Historisch Jaarboek* XVI (1930) 1 ff.
[15] Bogucka, *Handel zagraniczny*, 107.
[16] *Ibidem*.
[17] Bogucka, *Handel zagraniczny*, 107-108.
[18] *Ibidem*.
[19] Bogucka, *Handel zagraniczny*, 108.

Besides the above mentioned merchants several other Dutch tradesmen were interested in an exchange with Gdansk. In the thirties of the 17th century a great grain trade was conducted in Gdansk by the brothers Gabriel and Selio Marselis; they were also trading with other Baltic ports and even with Russia[20]. Lively contacts with Gdansk were kept by such Dutch merchants as Adriaen van de Graef, Jacob and Jost Fransensoons de Vryes, Cornelis Pietersen Jongkees van Lantsmeer, David van de Kercke, Adriaen Wereringh, Casper van Hoogenraet, Paul de Hoog, Gysbert and Claes van Broeck, Arndt Dircksen, Dirck Bell, Anthony Moens[21].

III. DUTCH FACTORS IN GDANSK

Many Dutch merchants were doing their business in Gdansk with the help of Dutch factors, residents of Gdansk, who were not members of the family of the patron. The factors' salaries were usually established at 1-2 per cent of the global transaction; sometimes he could also participate in his patron's commerce[22]. A contract between factor and patron was running for several months or years, but it could also be made for one individual transaction only. The factor was usually under the obligation to draw the bills of exchange for his patron and also was he responsible for the best placement of his patron's capital.

Most of the Dutch factors in Gdansk did not act for just one but for several merchants living in Amsterdam or in other towns in the Netherlands. They were also doing some transactions on their own account. Some factors resided in Gdansk permanently, other were coming here only for the shipping season, spring, summer and early autumn. In the year 1618 the number of Dutch calvinists in Gdansk exceeded 300 persons[23]. Living in Gdansk as permanent resident were the brothers Nicolaes and Jeronimus Ginsons, Loef Pietersson van Goir, Hans op ten Hoof, Cornelis van Foorest, Pieter Hans, Jan de Hahn, Willem Hendricsen Verbruggen, Leon Cambier, Gerrit Adriaensen, Cornelis Grauwaert, Simon Claese van Oossanen, Anthony Cuiper, Jan Passavandt, Nicolas Press, Dirck Brasser, David Hesters[24]. In the forties of the 17th century the number of Dutch permanent residents in Gdansk rose to 40-50 and soon to 75 persons[25]. The majority were tradesmen and bankers or moneydealers; there was also a group of craftsmen and

---

[20] M. Bogucka, "Zboze rosyjskie na rynku amsterdamskim w pierwszej polowie XVII w." ("Russian Grains on the Amsterdam Markets in the First Half of the 17th Century"), in: *Przeglad Historyczny* LIII (1962) 4, 622.

[21] Bogucka, *Handel zagraniczny*, 109.

[22] AG 300, 5/90, 76a-77a; Bogucka, *Handel zagraniczny*, 117.

[23] L(ibrary of the Polish Academy of Sciences in) G(dansk) D(epartment of) M(anuscripts) Ms. 865.

[24] Bogucka, *Handel zagraniczny*, 119-120.

[25] Roll of foreigners from May 1650, in: AG 300, 10/27, 186-192.

A MOTLOU B: GRINE BRUCK C DIE WAGE D KHU THOR

Fig. 1. View on Danzig. Copperplate by Johann Dickman (1617)
Bibliothek Gdansk (Gdansk)

organisers of production, propagating the putting-out system[26]. Some of the Dutch newcomers to Gdansk were successful enough to obtain the citizenship of this city.

Also Gdansk's merchants, such as Christoffel Pruyn, Willem and Cornelis Simonsens -obviously of Dutch descent- Abraham van Ackersdyck, Thomas Uphagen, Reyer Claesen, Georg Hewel, Jean Devaud, Dirck van Bancken, Tobias Everdtsen, Hans Lutke, Nicolas von Duren, Hans von Hamel, Frantz Ross, Friedrich Donawerts, Hans and Heinrich Dorbecks served as factors to Dutch merchants[27]. It means that every year hundreds of persons -Dutchmen or others-working for Dutchmen, were acting in Gdansk on behalf of Dutch trading companies.

In spite of Gdansk's official monopoly of exchange with the Polish hinterland, Dutch businessmen tried to penetrate deep into the country, where the prices of agricultural products were lower; the city's authorities often made complaints against such proceedings[28]. In 1625 the council of Gdansk decided, that all foreigners coming to the city should swear the oath to trade only with local burghers and to postpone trips into the Polish hinterland[29]. This demand, however, met the refusal of Dutch residents in Gdansk, who declared that such an oath would not be accepted by their patrons in the Netherlands[30]. The controversy resulted in more serious control over the foreigners in Gdansk. They were watched very closely indeed and forbidden even to speak with Polish noblemen, lest they should do some business with them. On September 12th 1638, the Dutch consul in Gdansk, Niclaes de By, wrote to the States-General:

"Mitsdien and eene sijde de vrembde natien strictelijck verboden
wert, niet alleen mette Polsche natie niet te sprecken, ja indien
bewonden wert een nederlandsch coopman met een polsch edelman
gesprocken te hebben, allwaert oick twintich mijlen buijten de Stadt
Dantsig denselven doen citeeren end dringen sijn selven met Eede te
purgeeren, eghene negotie mete inwoonders der Crone Polen gedreven
te hebben behalven dat deselffde dickwils in een groote boete
gecondemneert werden"[31].

---

[26] M. Bogucka, "Les relations entre la Pologne et les Pays-Bas, XVIe siècle - première moitié du XVIIe siècle", in: *Cahiers de Clio* (1984) 78-79, 5-18.
[27] Bogucka, *Handel zagraniczny*, 119-120.
[28] AG 300, 10/21, 324a; 22, 27b, 38b, 102 ff, 113b, 328ab; 23, 172a, 179; 24, 415a.
[29] AG 300, 10/22, 206a, 304b-305a.
[30] LG DM Ms 540, 52 ff.
[31] Algemeen Rijksarchief (The Hague), Staten-Generaal 6578.

Dutch merchants in Gdansk

But Dutch merchants were so much needed in Gdansk, that it was impossible to keep those restrictions too long. To Gdansk's merchants, who had rather modest means to conduct their own trade -the rich patrician in the first half of the 17th century was already less and less interested in urban activities- because they were representatives of the middle groups of the city, the partnership with Dutch tradesmen came to be of vital importance. They used to lend their own names to the Dutch companies just to allow them to operate freely under such cover, not only in Gdansk but also in the Polish lands. In the forties of the 17th century about 80 per cent of the Gdansk's overseas trade was already in the hands of Dutch merchants[32], both in the form of Dutch enterprises and of mixed Dutch-Gdansk companies.

IV. THE PROBLEM OF PROFITS

The exchange with Gdansk was a great source of profit for the Dutch tradesmen. According to Maczak and my own studies the average profit in the grain trade on the route Gdansk-Amsterdam in the years 1597-1647 should be estimated at 30-40 per cent of the invested capital. Similar profits were achieved in the trade in forestry products on the same route[33]. If one accepts the Sound records as the base of one's calculation, one can assume that, as in the first half of the 17th century an average of 70,000 lasts of Baltic grain -mostly from Gdansk- annually went to the West, and profit per last amounted to 521 grams of silver[34], the merchant's profit could be estimated globally at 36,000 kg of pure silver yearly. This was more than the output of the famous mines at Potosi in Peru[35].

No wonder, that Dutch residents in Gdansk are described in the roll of foreigners of 1649 as very rich: four of them owned a house in Gdansk, two were owners of parts of a house; others were living in apartments let to them by Gdansk's citizens for high prices -between 300 and 1,000 guldens per year- which testifies both to the luxurious standard of the housing and to the wealth of the tenant[36]. It is worth noting that Dutchmen mostly lived in the best quarters of the city, in

---

[32] Bogucka, *Handel zagraniczny*, 123.
[33] A. Maczak, *Miedzy Gdanskiem a Sundem. Studia nad handlem baltyckim od polowy 16 do 17 w. (Between Gdansk and Sound. Studies on the Baltic Trade in the 16th-17th Centuries)* (Warszawa, 1972) 82; M. Bogucka, "Zur Problematik der Profite im Handel zwischen Danzig und Westeuropa, 1550-1650", in: *Hansische Studien* V (1984) 42.
[34] M. Bogucka, "The Role of the Baltic Trade in European Development from the 16th to the 18th Centuries", in: *(The) J(ournal of) E(uropean) E(conomic) H(istory)* IX (1980) 1, 12.
[35] Ibidem. During the years of 1534 and 1535.
[36] M. Bogucka, "Obcy kupcy osiadli w Gdansku w pierwszej polowie XVII w." ("Foreign Merchants Residing in Gdansk in the First Half of the 17th Century"), in: *Zapiski Historyczne* XXXVII (1972) 2, 68.

the streets occupied by members of the upper strata of the urban society; some groups however, mostly craftsmen who came to Gdansk from the Southern Netherlands as well as from Holland, were situated in the suburbs[37].

V. CREDIT AND BANKING

The activities of the Dutch merchants were not limited to trade. Another big field of operation was credit-giving and banking. The great accumulation of capital in the Netherlands and the need of capital in Gdansk resulted in a constant flow of capital, mainly in the form of cash and bullion, form the West to the East; large traffic in bills of exchange was going on in the opposite direction[38]. The interest rate in Gdansk was high enough, 6-12 per cent, when in Amsterdam it was only 3.5-4 per cent[39]. Some information on the credit functioning is given to us by the declaration of Barent Sweerts, merchant of Amsterdam, who testified before a notary that in the beginning of May 1618 Hans Clase, another merchant of Amsterdam, notified him that his -Clase's cousin- Abraham Keuben "gaerne op Dantsick wilde trecken ende door sijn factor, Hans Ghijsberts van de Veer aldaer laten befallen die somme 4,000 guld. corent geld". Hans Clase proposed to Barent Sweert to join him in this enterprise and to put half of the capital destined for loans in Gdansk[40]. With this capital the Dutch factor in Gdansk could lend money to merchants in this city, who were in need of cash. Such operations were often very big: in the years 1608/9 a merchant of Gdansk, Bartel Schultze, obtained from Amsterdam a loan credit for his grain trade 300,000 carolus guldens[41]. In 1612 a merchant of Gdansk, Heinrich Dreier went broke; his debt to Amsterdam amounted to 71,253 Polish zlotys, which were borrowed from the Dutchman Asaris Cornelisen[42]. In 1617 Wessel Schenck, a merchant from Amsterdam, used a credit of 10,800 carolus guldens (6,750 Polish zlotys) in Gdansk to buy

---

[37] Ibidem.

[38] A. Attman, *The Bullion Flow between Europe and the East, 1000-1750* (Gothenburg, 1981); idem, *Dutch Enterprise in the World Bullion Trade, 1550-1800* (Gothenburg, 1983); M. Bogucka, "La lettre de change et le credit dans les échanges entre Gdansk et Amsterdam dans la première moitié du XVIIIe siècle", in: *Actes du Cinquième Congres International d'Histoire Economique* (Leningrad, 1970; Moscou, 1975) IV, 31-41.

[39] AG 300, 5/24, 66b; 70, 37a-38b; 71, 150b; 73, 74a, 413ab; 75, 13b; 82, 803; 83, 540ab; 87, 66b; 300, 10/23, 199a, 216b; 300, R/F 16; for the Netherlands: H. Richardot, B. Snapper, *Histoire des faits économiques* (Paris, 1963) 308. The importance of the traffic with the bills of exchange was underlined already by A.E. Christensen, *o.c.*, 388 ff.

[40] GAA, NA 196, 529-530.

[41] Bogucka, *Handel zagraniczny*, 11.

[42] AG 300, 5/47, 73b-74a, 94b-95a, 134b-136a.

grain[43]. It seems that most of the operations of buying grain in big quantities were paid in Gdansk with money provided by the Netherlands[44].

The credit operations were linked to the speculation called gambling on arbitrage, *le jeu de l'arbitrage* or *cambio arbitrio*, based on the difference in prices of bills of exchange in Gdansk and in Amsterdam. That difference was caused by the great need of capital in Baltic ports, where large quantities of agricultural products had to be bought and where the Polish gentry seeked loans to buy luxurious goods or to travel abroad. With the use of the *cambio arbitrio* the Dutch owners of capital were able to cash significant profits, as is shown in Table I.

The *cambio arbitrio* was given profits from 3.7 to 26.6 per cent, which is rather high compared to the rate of interest in the Netherlands, which was 3-4 per cent[45]. The beginning of the 17th century was most profitable, especially the years 1617-1618, when the very large extent of the purchase and export of grain resulted in an extremely big demand for ready capitals[46]. In the thirties and forties the profits from *cambio arbitrio* became more stable on the lower level, but still they were good ones: twice as high as the interest rate in the Netherlands.

VI. MARITIME LOANS

A specific form of credit linked closely to shipping and trade constituted the maritime loans, called *bodmery -Bodmerei-*. They are represented in Table II.

The scale of an individual loan was not very large, some hundreds of carolus guldens; usually it was enough to prepare a ship for the trip. As it was a short-termed credit, the loan had to be returned in 10-14 days after the arrival of the ship in the harbour mentioned in the contract. The capital almost completely belonged to merchants of Amsterdam, as they were especially interested in the trade with Gdansk. The interest rate was not very high, on the route Amsterdam-Gdansk it was about 6 per cent, in the opposite direction it was a little more, 8-13 per cent; this resulted from the difference in prices of cash and silver in Gdansk in comparison with Amsterdam[47]. The fact that in those days the usual

---

[43] GAA, NA 140, 73, 74.

[44] M. Bogucka, "Obrot wekslowo-kredytowy w Gdansku w pierwszej polowie XVII w." ("The Traffic with the Bills of Exchange in Gdansk in the First Half of the 17th Century"), in: *Roczniki Dziejow Spolecznych i Gospodarczych* XXXIII (1972) 1-31.

[45] See note 39.

[46] Bogucka, *Handel zagraniczny*, 15, 37.

[47] Jan and Isaac Passavandt lent 300 dollars to the skipper of the ship *De Nachtegaell* going from Gdansk to Amsterdam in 1645 on the condition that he should pay to the Amsterdam merchant Reyner de Haes not only the usual 8 per cent but an additional 5 per cent "voor de differentie vant gout en silver", in: GAA, NA 1573, 184.

Table I

The price of bills of exchange from Gdansk in Amsterdam, yearly average*.

Year	In Polish grosz for one pound flamish	In grams of silver for one pound flamish	In %
1609	105.50	64.99	8.2
1610	104.50	61.97	7.1
1613	107.50	62.35	10.2
1614	107.00	62.27	9.7
1617	114.00	63.50	16.9
1618	112.50	61.20	15.3
1619	123.50	61.13	26.6
1630	221.50	59.80	5.4
1631	221.20	59.72	5.3
1632	224.10	60.50	6.7
1633	222.10	59.97	5.7
1634	217.75	58.79	3.7
1635	219.75	59.33	4.6
1636	218.60	59.02	4.1
1637	220.10	59.43	4.8
1638	223.80	60.43	6.5
1640	221.50	59.81	5.4
1641	221.80	59.89	5.6
1642/43	220.00	59.94	5.7
1645	226.10	61.05	7.6
1646	227.60	61.45	8.3
1648	222.80	60.16	6.1
1649	221.80	59.87	5.6
1650	219.70	59.32	4.6

*Calculated by:
M. Bogucka, "Obrót wekslowo-kredytowy w Gdansku w pierwszej polo Traffic in the Bills of Exchange and Credit Operations in Gdansk in the First Half of the 17th century"), in: Roczniki Dziejów Spolecznych i Gospodarczych XXXIII (1972) 15.

Table II

Bodmery letters issued for Gdansk in the years 1626-1649*.

Date	Route	Ship's loading capacity in lasts	Loan in carolus guldens	%
Nov. 1626	Amsterdam-Gdansk	?	600	3.5
Nov. 1626	Amsterdam-Gdansk	?	1,200	3.5
Apr. 1633	Amsterdam-Gdansk-Amsterdam	130	300	9
Apr. 1633	Amsterdam-Gdansk	?	200	5
June 1633	Amsterdam-Gdansk	?**	?	5
June 1633	Amsterdam-Gdansk	?***	2,000	4
Oct. 1633	Amsterdam-Gdansk	140	150	9
Mar. 1635	Amsterdam-Gdansk	130	500	10
Apr. 1635	Amsterdam-Gdansk	?	700	?
Nov. 1635	Amsterdam-Gdansk-Amsterdam	?	50	12
Mar. 1641	Amsterdam-Gdansk	60	250	6
June 1642	Amsterdam-Gdansk-Amsterdam	100	550	10
July 1643	Rotterdam-Gdansk-Emden	100	1,125	15
July 1643	Amsterdam-Gdansk-Amsterdam	100	1,000	11.5
May 1644	Amsterdam-Gdansk-Amsterdam	130	300	12
Aug. 1644	Amsterdam-Gdansk-Amsterdam	150	400	5
Sept. 1644	Amsterdam-Gdansk	?	600	11
Nov. 1644	Gdansk-Amsterdam	?	3,500	8
Apr. 1645	Gdansk-Amsterdam	?	765	13
Apr. 1645	Amsterdam-St. Ubes-Gdansk	?	590.5	28
June 1645	Amsterdam-Gdansk-Amsterdam	160	500	12
Aug. 1645	Amsterdam-Gdansk-Amsterdam	?	700	10
Sept. 1645	Amsterdam-Gdansk-Amsterdam	150	200	12
Apr. 1646	Amsterdam-Gdansk-Norway	140	2,000	10
June 1648	Amsterdam-Gdansk-Amsterdam	?	550	10

* Based on the sources: GAA, NA, 763; 1568,69; 1589, 238; 1570, 179, 186; 1572, 274, 446, 476; 1573, 184, 209, 285, 393, 477; 1574, 265; 1575; Rechtelijk Archief, 2064.

** The loan was secured not on the ship but on the cargo (2 barrels of sugar).

*** The loan was secured on 3 barrels of sugar.

rate of interest on bodmery was only a little higher than the usual interest rate in Holland testifies to that:

1. The shipping on the route Amsterdam-Gdansk-Amsterdam was regarded as a rather safe business; on the route Amsterdam-St. Ubes-Gdansk the higher rate -28 per cent- shows that it was not only a much longer trip but also a risky one.

2. The abundance of capital in Amsterdam pushed the Dutch owners of capital to seek several possibilities to invest their money.

VII. MONETARY SPECULATION

The great importance of the credit operations in the Gdansk-Amsterdam trade was also caused by the monetary perturbations of the 17th century, which were felt very strongly in Poland[48]. When most of the merchants tried to avoid cash operations with the help of the bills of exchange, there were some who used the monetary crisis as the opportunity to speculate with money. Gdansk became a place where good coins were sought and bought in large quantities in order to export them to other countries, e.g. Silesia, Turkey or the Netherlands. In the beginning of the 17th century special companies composed of local and foreign money dealers were operating in Gdansk. At the head of one of those were two Dutchmen, Isaac van Eicken and Jacob Jacobson van Embden, associated with the local banker and merchant Herman Wolf. The company exported good coins -old Rixdollars- to the Low Countries, where they were turned into coins of lower silver-content and them reimported to Gdansk as *liondollars -Löwenthalers-* or *dollars with the cross, Kreuzthalers*[49]. The inhabitants of Gdansk complained bitterly against this speculation[50]. Isaac van Eicken was even imprisoned for his activities, but it did not prevent the scarcity of *good* money on Gdansk's monetary market ant its leakage abroad[51]. The authorities of the city were openly afraid to take stronger measures against bad Dutch coins circulating in the city[52]. When in the forties an order of the Polish King forbade inhabitants of Gdansk to accept *liondollars*, the city council hastily informed Amsterdam and other Dutch towns lest their merchants should suffer any losses[53]. The interdiction was issued at the end

---

[48] M. Bogucka, "The Monetary Crisis of the 17th Century and its Social and Psychological Consequences in Poland", in: *JEEH* IV (1975) 1, 137-152.

[49] AG 300, 5/73, 115ab. Cf. M. Bogucka, "Zur Problematik der Münzkrize in Danzig in der ersten Hälfte des 17. Jhs", in: *Studia Historiae Oeconomicae* VI (1971) 66-73.

[50] AG 300, 10/21, 154a, 293a; 22, 31b, 106b-107a; LG MS 54, 60b, 61a; 403, 34.

[51] AG 300, 10/153, 167a, 175b ff.

[52] AG 300, 10/26, 144, 148, 149, 177, 190, 240, 241, 244, 251, 285, 286, 314, 385, 461.

[53] AG 300, 10/26, 244, 286; also GAA, AB MD, p 2, letters from 7 February and 18 December, 1642.

Dutch merchants in Gdansk

of 1642, but until the end of March 1643 the Gdansk authorities allowed the prohibited coins to circulate in the city -every transaction, it was said, could in 10 per cent be realised by using them- in order to protect the Dutch merchants from heavier damages[54]. The enforcement of the King's order met big difficulties; in the years 1644 and 1645 Gdansk's merchants were still complaining, that they were forced to accept *liondollars* as well as other bad Dutch coins in the trade with Dutch traders[55]. The confiscation of bad coins happened only incidentally, just to show the submission of the authorities of Gdansk to the King's will[56]. As a result bad money was circulating quite openly; the proposition issued in 1647 by the Third Order of Gdansk to establish a law that in all transactions over 100 Polish zlotys only 1/3 could be paid with bad money and 2/3 should be realised with good, could be seen as evidence to prove this[57].

In the thirties of the 17th century a project to establish a bank in Gdansk was prepared in order to avoid the consequences of the monetary crisis and monetary speculation. The project was elaborated by a Dutch banker and factor settled in Gdansk, Anthony Kuiper[58]. His paper entitled "Gutachten über Anlegung einer Wechselbank. Bedenken Antoine de Cuypers über die Frage, ob man dieses Ortes könne Wechselbanken aufrichten"[59] contemplated the foundation of a bank under the direction of two members of the city council, experienced in trade and two merchants from the middle class, which in this time was the main active group of the urban society. The bank was to employ two bookkeepers as clerks and several cashiers; the opening hours were to be from 9 till 11 in the morning every day. Gdansk's citizens as well as foreign merchants as shareholders would be accepted. The smallest share was to be 200 Prussian marcks = 133 Polish zlotys. The activities of the bank were to be larger than those of the bank of Amsterdam, established in 1609. The bank in Gdansk was to be the place to exchange money, to accept gold and silver bullion deposits, to issue loans. The project never came to execution, probably because of the resistance of the private bankers.

---

[54] AG 300, 10/26, 286, 306 ff., 314.
[55] AG 300, 10/26, 385, 461.
[56] In 1645 the Dutch consul in Gdansk, Paulus Pels, was complaining that many Dutch merchants suffered heavy losses because of the confiscations of the *liondollars*, GAA, AB DM 106.
[57] AG 300, 10/26, 634-636.
[58] His name was written on many bills of exchange; he was acting in Gdansk in the name of some merchants of Amsterdam, transferring their capitals and advising in financial matters, e.g. AG 5/75, 398.
[59] LG DM Ms 540, 17a-18b.

VIII. CONCLUSIONS

The part played in Gdansk's economy and trade by the Dutch merchants was of an extremely big importance in the first half of the 17th century. The Dutch were attracted to Gdansk by great profits which could be derived from commerce with agricultural goods bought in Gdansk cheaply enough and sold for high prices in Amsterdam. Baltic trade should be regarded as a rich source for capital accumulation which was exploited mainly not by local, Gdansk's inhabitants, but by the enterprising agents of Dutch merchants. The trading business was organised mostly by means of family ties. Relatives of Dutch merchants settled in Gdansk to conduct commercial activities there for their cousins and patrons from Amsterdam as well as from other cities in the Low Countries. Closely associated with trade were credit operations and monetary speculation. The Netherlands and Gdansk were linked by complex financial relations involving the settling of accounts and bills of exchange as well as trading in money. The Dutch had a great deal of capital at their disposal which enabled them to supply Gdansk with silver in bars as well as with loans in cash. The profits derived from those operations combined with commercial gains brought to the Dutch merchants great possibilities of quick enrichment. It resulted in the growing Dutch control over the Gdansk's overseas trade and shipping till the middle of the 17th century.

VII

TOWNS IN POLAND AND THE REFORMATION.
ANALOGIES AND DIFFERENCES WITH OTHER COUNTRIES

The Reformation was undoubtedly one of the greatest events
in the evolution of Early Modern Europe and the attitude taken
by particular societies towards it determined their development
for centuries to come. A. Peyrefitte, the author of a recent
French bestseller,[1] using a metaphor taken from the New Testament, contrasts the "countries of Martha" developing favour-
ably until today, i.e. those countries in which the Reformation
was victorious, with the "countries of Mary", i.e. those in which
adherence to Catholicism determined, according to him, the
backwardness of the social and economic structure up to and
including the 20th century. This reasoning can be considered
as referring, to a certain degree, to that found in the already
classic works of Max Weber and R. H. Tawney;[2] the problem
of a correlation between social and economic progress and the
Reformation occurs in numerous other historical works (in
England : H. R. Trevor-Roper, C. Hill, D. Little). However, we
are not at this time interested in the consequences of the
Reformation but in the causes which resulted in its specific
course in particular countries and especially in Poland.

Scholars who have conducted research on the history of the
Polish Reformation (H. Barycz, O. Bartel, J. Tazbir) in ascertain-
ing its predominantly gentry character, perceive in this trait
a national specificity of a movement which practically in all of
Europe (England, Switzerland, the Netherlands and partially
also France and Germany) overwhelmingly embraced the masses

---

[1] A. Peyrefitte, *Le mal français*, Paris 1976.
[2] M. Weber, *Die protestantische Ethik und der Geist des Kapita-
lismus*, Berlin 1964 - 65 ; R. H. Tawney, *Religion and the Rise of Capitalism*, 1 ed., London 1926.

of the urban population.[3] Yet we know that the Reformation trends reached Polish towns rather quickly; it is with them that, to a great extent, one should connect the wave of social disturbances which took place in the years 1517 - 1526. The course of the upheavals in Gdańsk, Toruń, Elbląg, Braniewo, Warsaw and Lublin are best known;[4] these centres do not, however, end the list in which unrest of the town poor and the middle class burghers occurred: altogether 27 towns of the Polish Crown, including Royal Prussia and Warmia, excluding Silesia and Lithuania.[5] All of these movements, however, ended relatively quickly; they did not change the social and political urban structure to any great extent. It is true that in many towns they resulted in the introduction of institutions of the so-called third order (a representation of the middle class burghers, artisans and small merchants in the city authorities) but as a rule they were soon taken over by the richer representatives of the middle class and made dependent upon the patriciate; nowhere did the revolts bring about even a temporary victory of the Protestant faith.

---

[3] Works directly related to this problem are: G. M o e l l e r, *Reichstadt und Reformation*, Gütersloh 1962 and B. H a l l, *The Reformation City*, "Bulletin of the John Rylands Library," vol. LIV. 1971 - 72, p. 103 sqq.; recently: S. E. O z m e n t, *The Reformation in the Cities. The Appeal of Protestantism to Sixteenth Century Germany and Switzerland*, New Haven 1975.

[4] For Gdańsk cf. S. G l u e c k s m a n n, *Ruchy społeczne w Gdańsku w początkach reformacji 1522 - 1526* [*Social Movements in Gdańsk at the Beginning of the Reformation*], Warszawa 1937, and among recent works: M. B o g u c k a, *Walki społeczne w Gdańsku w XVI w.* [*Social Struggles in Gdańsk in the 16th century*] in: *Pomorze średniowieczne*, ed. by G. Labuda, Warszawa 1958; G. S c h r a m m, *Danzig, Elbing und Thorn als Beispiele städtischen Reformation (1517 - 1558)*, in: *Historia Integra. Festschrift für E. Hasinger zum 70. Geburtstag*, Berlin 1977. For other towns cf. among the recent and most important works: J. B u ł a w a, *Walki społeczno-ustrojowe w Toruniu w pierwszej połowie XVI w.* [*Social and Political Struggles in Toruń in the First Half of the 16th century*], Toruń 1971; H. Z i n s, *Rewolta w Elblągu w r 1525* [*The 1525 Revolt in Elbląg*], "Zapiski Historyczne," vol. XXII, 1958, No. 1; i d e m, *Początki reformacji na Warmii* [*The Beginnings of the Reformation in the Region of Warmia*], "Odrodzenie i Reformacja w Polsce", vol. II, 1957; T. S t r z e m b o s z, *Tumult Warszawski 1525 r.* [*The Warsaw Disturbance of 1525*], Warszawa 1959; R. S z c z y g i e ł, *Konflikty społeczne w Lublinie w pierwszej połowie XVI w.* [*Social Conflicts in Lublin in the First Half of the 16th Century*], Warszawa 1977.

[5] Cf. R. S z c z y g i e ł, *op. cit.*, pp. 98 - 99.

The end of the revolts did not mean, however, an end to the infiltration of the Reformation into the towns. In this second phase of penetration, however, which occurred in the second half of the 16th century, it was adopted not only by the middle class burghers and the poor, but also by the upper strata of urban society. Only in the towns of Royal Prussia did the Reformation gain a definitive victory which was also recognized by the state authorities. In 1557, using a favourable political and economic situation, and after paying an enormous sum of 100,000 Polish złotys. (30,000 as a gift and 70,000 as a loan) into the royal treasury, did Gdańsk, Toruń and Elbląg receive privileges from the King guaranteein religious freedom for their inhabitants; on this basis a Lutheran Church strongly connected with the city authorities was organized. The situation of the followers of the Protestant faith in the towns of Warmia, an episcopal domain, was much more difficult.[6] The fate of the Reformation was also not very fortunate in the towns of Central Poland. The greatest successes of the Reformation took place in the medium-sized towns of Greater Poland (Wschowa, Brojce, Międzyrzecz, Skierzyna, Czaplinek, Wałcz as well as partially in Kościan, Konin and Kalisz);[7] Protestant communities also existed under the patronage of the magnate Górka and Ostroróg families in Poznań up to the beginning of the 17th century. In 1619, however, it was prohibited to grant non-Catholics town rights in Poznań.[8] Limited successes were won by the Reformation in the towns of Little Poland; but during the second half of the 16th century one finds here a rather numerous group of adherents in Cracow itself[9] and also in such smaller towns as Biecz, Jasło,

---

[6] H. Zins, *Początki reformacji na Warmii* [*The Beginnings of the Reformation in Warmia*], p. 53 sqq.
[7] J. Dworczakowa, *Wprowadzenie reformacji do miast królewskich Wielkopolski* [*The Introduction of the Reformation to the Royal Towns of Greater Poland*], "Odrodzenie i Reformacja w Polsce," vol. X, 1965, p. 53 sqq.
[8] *Ibidem*, p. 76 sqq.
[9] R. Zalewski, *Zaburzenia wyznaniowe w Krakowie. Okres przewagi różnowierców 1551 - 1573* [*Religious Upheavals in Cracow. The Period of the Predominance of the Dissidents 1551 - 1573*], "Odrodzenie i Reformacja w Polsce," vol. VI, 1961, p. 91 sqq.; cf. also G. Schramm, *Reformation und Gegenreformation in Krakau. Die Zuspitzung des konfessionellen Kampfes in der polnischen Haupstadt*, "Zeitschrift fur Ostforschung," vol. XIX, 1970, pp. 1 - 41.

58

Ciężkowice, Gorlice, Osiek and Dębowiec.[10] It is worthwhile to remember that one of the outstanding representatives of the Reformation movement in Little Poland was Jakub from Iłża, a burgher.[11] In the socond half of the 16th century one can also speak about a dissemination of the seeds of the Reformation in the cities of Lublin,[12] Lwów,[13] and Wilno (in Lithuania).[14] On the other hand the Reformation was completely unaccepted in the towns of Mazovia including Warsaw.[15]

This second stage of the spreading of the Reformation in Polish towns did not last long since it waned already at the end of the 16th and at the beginning of the 17th centuries. In addition, this was not a mass movement since it embraced relatively small groups of burghers with but a few exceptions. As a rule the Polish urban population remained faithful to Catholicism.

In order to explain such a course of events it is necessary to analyze briefly the situation of the Polish towns in the period under discussion, especially considering that many historians (in Poland—J. Dworzaczkowa and of the German scholars F. Arnold and A. Rhode) perceived the solution to the puzzle precisely in a general "weakeness of their position".

As far as the degree of urbanization was concerned, the Polish state presented itself not unfavourably even against the European background of the 16th century. Practically 20 per cent of the inhabitants lived in towns. Of course, the degree of

---

[10] W. U r b a n, *Reformacja mieszczańska w dawnym powiecie bieckim* [*Burgher's Reformation in the Former District of Biecz*], "Odrodzenie i Reformacja w Polsce," vol. VI, 1961, p. 130 sqq.

[11] H. B a r y c z, *Z epoki renesansu i baroku* [*From the Renaissance and Baroque Epoch*], Warszawa 1971, p. 222 sqq.

[12] G. S c h r a m m, *Lublin und das Scheitern der stadtischen Reformation*, "Kirche im Osten," vol. XII, 1969, pp. 33 - 57; S. T w o r e k, *Zbór lubelski i jego rola w ruchu ariańskim w Polsce w XVI i XVII w.*, [*Community of Antitrinitarians in Lublin and Its Role in the Polish Reformation in the 16th and 17th Centuries*], Lublin 1966.

[13] G. S c h r a m m, *Lemberg und die Reformation*, "Jahrbücher für Geschichte Osteuropas," vol. XI, 1963, pp. 343 - 350.

[14] I d e m, *Protestantismus und stadtische gesellschaft in Wilna (16 - 17 Jahrhundert)*, "Jahrbücher für Geschichte Osteuropas," vol. XVII, 1969, pp. 187 - 214.

[15] G. S c h r a m m, *Problem reformacji w Warszawie w XVI w.* [*The Reformation in Warsaw in the 16th Century*], "Przegląd Historyczny," vol. LIV, 1963, No. 4, pp. 557 - 571.

VII

urbanization of particular regions was unequal ; alongside highly urbanized areas where the inhabitants of the towns constituted over 30 per cent of the entire population (Greater Poland, Little Poland, Pomerania) in certain regions the town population reached only up to 15 per cent (Mazovia) or a few per cent in the Eastern parts of the country. Historians agree that in the second half of the 16th century there existed about 700 towns and small townships in the socalled Polish Crown (Central Poland), including Royal Prussia. However, only 8 of them had more than 10,000 inhabitants : these were Gdańsk (over 50,000 at the close of the 16th century), Cracow (ca. 28,000), Poznań (ca. 20,000) as well as Toruń, Elbląg, Lublin, Warsaw and Lwów. At the close of the 16th century Wilno (ca. 15,000) was a significant town in the Grand Duchy of Lithuania. Towns with from 4,000 to 5,000 inhabitants were considered medium-sized (Sandomierz, Kazimierz Dolny, Gniezno, etc.). Dominant were those urban centres with inhabitants numbering from 500 to 2,000.[16] The problems of urban demography are, however, still rather controversial.

The 16th century is considered as a period of a favourable development and enrichment of the Polish towns which at that time grew significantly and gained magnificent Renaissance architectural and decorative forms. Those towns which participated in the export of grain and agricultural products to the West (mainly Gdańsk, but also numerous others along the Vistula, e.g. Cracow, Sandomierz, Kazimierz Dolny, Warsaw and other Mazovian towns, Włocławek and Toruń) seemed to develop and thrive economically particularly rapidly. The same applies to the great markets and centres of big international trade (Lwów, Lublin, Poznań) which lay along the routes running from Lithuania, Russia and the Black Sea to Greater Poland or Silesia and further to Western Europe. Of lesser importance for the wealth of the towns was their artisan production although the artisans constituted the majority of the population of many towns (from 50 to 75 per cent). Already at that time Polish artisans began to feel the impact of the competition of industrial

---

[16] S. H e r b s t, *Miasta i mieszczaństwo renesansu polskiego* [*Polish Towns and Their Inhabitants during the Renaissance*], Warszawa 1954, p. 7.

articles imported from Western Europe and preferred by the Polish gentry. Production was conducted in the Polish towns in the outdated but still strong guild system and based on small establishments where, just as in the Middle Ages, a master employed two or three helpers. The elements of early capitalism appeared rarely and most frequently in the form of a domestic system and the dependence of direct producers upon the richer master or merchants. One can speak about the occurrence of these elements on a larger scale only, however, in the rich and well developed towns of Pomerania.[17] Larger establishments which came close to early manufacture, were to be found sporadically and mainly in such branches of production as the iron and ship industry, paper and glass works as well as in mining—salt in Wieliczka and Bochnia, silver and lead in Olkusz; the latter was a leading terrain for the development of the elements of early capitalism.[18] In general, however, the beginnings of the new system of production were weak and this made the economic level of the Polish Commonwealth unfavourable in comparison to the level achieved in the 16th century by the rapidly developing economy of many of the West European countries, especially of England. Particularly unfavourable was the fact that only a very small part of commercial capital accumulated in Polish towns was destined for productive investments. The largest part of it was absorbed by consumption expenses, connected with an extravagant style of life in the towns (construction of magnificent houses and their opulent furnishings, luxury in clothing, jewelry, etc.) or spent, despite legal prohibition, on purchasing property in the countryside. Both these trends in expenditures resulted from a fascination, common among the burghers, with the gentry way of life, from a yearning to

---

[17] Cf. M. B o g u c k a, *Gdańsk jako ośrodek produkcyjny w XIV - XVII w.* [*The City of Gdańsk as a Centre of Production in the 14th - 17th Centuries*], Warszawa 1962, *passim*.

[18] Cf. D. M o l e n d a, *Kopalnie rud ołowiu na terenie złóż śląsko-krakowskich w XVI - XVII w.* [*Lead Ore Mines of the Silesia-Cracow Region in the 16th - 18th Centuries*], Wrocław 1972; A. W y r o b i s z, *Szkło w Polsce od XIV do XVII w.* [*Glass in Poland in the 14th - 17th Centuries*], Wrocław 1968; B. Z i e n t a r a, *Dzieje Małopolskiego hutnictwa żelaznego XIV - XVII w.* [*The History of Ironworks in Little Poland in the 14th - 17th Centuries*], Warszawa 1954, *passim*.

equal it and even to penetrate into the ranks of the nobility either through official ennoblement or at least illegally. This was linked with a specific pattern of social and political relations which emerged in the Commonwealth during the 16th century.

The second half of the 15th and the first half of the 16th century constituted a period in which the form of the so-called Commonwealth of the gentry was taking shape in Poland ; at the same time it was a turning point in the history of Polish towns. Both of these phenomena were closely connected with each other. By the middle of the 15th century the future was still unsolved, it remained an open question whether in the consolidation of the country and remodeling of the Polish State, the Monarch would lean on the gentry or use the burghers, for purposes of strengthening his own power as was the case in numerous European countries at that time. The specificity of the development of Poland consisted of, among other things, the fact that for different reasons the gentry became the main ally of the King in his undertakings and, subsequently, a force which he was dependent upon ; already in the second half of the 15th century the gentry constituted the head of Polish society as its most active leading group. The winning of social and political predominance by the gentry was accompanied by limiting of the role played by the towns. Anti-urban laws, initiated already in the 15th century, with a prohibition of purchasing landed property by the burghers (1496) were continued throughout the entire 16th century (a 1538 repetition of the prohibition of land purchasing with the exception only of the inhabitants of a few of the largest towns, attempts at abolishing guilds in 1538 and 1552, introduction of price lists for urban products and prohibition of conducting an active foreign trade by the Polish merchants in 1565).[19] There was no room for representatives of the towns in the emerging Polish Parliament at the end of the 15th and the beginning of the 16th centuries. Only a few of the most important towns such as Cracow, Poznań,

---

[19] A. Popiół-Szymańska, *Problematyka handlowa w polityce "miejskiej" szlachty w Polsce centralnej w XV i XVI w.* [*The Problems of Trade in the "Anti-Urban" Policy of the Polish Gentry in the 15th and 16th Centuries*], "Roczniki Dziejów Społecznych i Gospodarczych," vol. XXI, 1970, pp. 45 - 83.

Lublin and, after the Lublin Union of 1569—the city of Wilno, as well as the towns of Pomerania were allowed to send to the Polish Diet [the Seym] their representatives who had, however, only the right to take the floor as advisers in connection with urban problems (1565). Gradually burghers also lost their right to hold state offices while special prohibitions limited their access to higher Church positions.

The majority of towns at the beginning of the 16th century had complete or almost complete self-government won in the course of the preceding centuries. In the 16th century this self-government was subject to a gradual limitation in favour of the interests of the gentry (e.g. the constitutions of 1538 and 1567). In the royal towns the influence of the King's officials-the *starostas*, grew (limitation of the authority of the municipal council and the influence of the *starosta* upon its choice, control over finances and urban administration, etc.). In private towns, the number of which grew rapidly, self-government was even more limited and its scope was dependent upon the will of the owner of the town.[20] Competition between particular towns (conflicts concerning storage privileges, the rights of merchants to trade in those urban areas where they did not have city rights, trials concerning the competence of guild authorities, etc.) resulted in the fact that each of them jealously guarded its mediaeval laws and privileges against the burghers of other centres. An inter-urban solidarity and a developed social consciousness could not arise in such conditions and was unable to play a defensive and unifying role in the face of the aggressive policy of the gentry.

The only exception within a weak and internally divided Polish bourgeoisie were the three great Pomeranian towns headed by Gdańsk. They owed their position to an exceptionally favourable economic situation. During the 16th century Gdańsk had practically acquired a complete monopoly on Polish foreign trade (ca. 80 per cent of the export of manor farm products and a large part in import); Toruń and Elbląg played a supplementary

---

[20] A. Wyrobisz, *Rola miast prywatnych w Polsce w XVI i XVII w.* [*The Role of Private Towns in Poland in the 16th and 17th Centuries*], "Przegląd Historyczny," vol. LXV, 1974, No. 1, p. 19 sqq.

role.[21] The legal basis for the exceptional position of Gdańsk in the Polish state was ensured by a number of privileges granted in 1455 - 1477 by King Casimir the Jagiellonian as a reward for the intensive participation in the Thirteen-Year War against the Teutonic Knights (among others, Gdańsk was granted enormous rural properties and a broad autonomy, certain customs were abolished, privileges concerning the administration of the seacoast and regulation of marine traffic were bestowed, etc.).[22] The economic strength and the convenient legal and political status of the towns in Royal Prussia was expressed in the fact that they participated in the sessions of the regional diet known as the Prussian Little Seym. This consisted of two houses : the Land House of the gentry and the Town House with representatives of the towns. The burghers of Royal Prussia also had the right to purchase and own landed property, (confirmed in' the constitution of 1538). The three great cities of Gdańsk, Toruń and Elbląg sat alongside the highest Pomeranian dignitaries in the autonomous government of Royal Prussia, the so-called Prussian Council. When after 1569 the government of Royal Prussia was transformed according to the Polish structure, the situation of the local towns was influenced by it only to a slight degree. The Prussian Council, however, was liquidated. Its gentry members obtained place in the Polish Diet, but the towns of Gdańsk, Toruń and Elbląg were from that time on to send their observers only ; however, such an arrangement suited them since they were separatistically indifferent towards the majority of the common problems of the State and mindful solely of the interests of the local patrician groups. The authorities of the Pomeranian towns, and especially of Gdańsk, knew that they could anyhow effectively defend themselves against any aggression of the gentry. The representatives of the towns remained members of the Prussian regional diet until the end of the

[21] S. H o s z o w s k i, The Polish Baltic Trade in the 15th - 18th Centuries, in : Poland at the XIth International Congress of Historical Sciences in Stockholm, Warsaw 1960, p. 119 sqq.
[22] E. C i e ś l a k, Przywileje Gdańska z okresu wojny 13-letniej na tle przywilejów niektórych miast bałtyckich [The Privileges of the City of Gdańsk from the Time of the Thirteen-Year War Against a Background of the Hanseatic Privileges], "Czasopismo Prawno-Historyczne," vol. VI, 1954, No. 1, p. 61 sqq.

existence of the Commonwealth of the gentry (only the representatives of small towns lost their places in 1662),[23] always playing a dominating role in its sessions.

Thus, the situation of the towns in Poland, with the exception of Royal Prussia, differed substantially from the situation in Western Europe and even more so since in the 16th century the burghers of many countries expanded their political privileges and entered into a victorious competition with the gentry in numerous spheres of life. This state of affairs also influenced the development of the Polish Reformation although undoubtedly we have here an opportunity to deal not with one causal factor but with a whole sequence of them.

Some scholars consider that the reason for a weak reception of the Reformation in the Polish towns lay in the fact that in the 16th century these towns were already fully Polonized (contrary to the 14th and 15th centuries when patricians of German or Italian origin retained their national and cultural distinctiness). This would explain the victory of the Reformation in the towns of Royal Prussia and also its relatively strong development in some of the towns in Greater Poland where, as late as the 16th century, there existed a strong and un-Polonized German population. However, one should remember that in spite of the "German character" of Protestantism it was possible for a significant part of the Polish gentry and magnates to accept it. Undoubtedly one of the stimulating factors could be the linguistic and national closeness, stressed by G. Schramm while examining the course of the Reformation in Gdańsk, Elbląg and Toruń. But Schramm, at the same time, points to the fact that one should not identify this closeness with a feeling of state allegiance.[24] A certain role was played by the geographic factor—wherever the important centres of the Reformation were not too distant and lively contacts were maintained (e.g. Gdańsk and Wittenberg) the progress of the Reformation could be facilitated and the reception of the new ideas accelerated. One should, however,

---

[23] *Historia państwa i prawa Polski* [*The History of the Polish State and Law*], vol. II, ed. by J. Bardach, Warszawa 1966, p. 161 sqq., 435 sqq.
[24] G. S c h r a m m, *Danzig, Elbing und Thorn als Beispiele...*, p. 131 sqq.

remember that even such a fully Polonized and far away town as Lwów maintained contacts with the centres of the Reformation (merchants' and students' journeys and migrations) and this created a basis for the passage of new ideas despite the great distance. There must also have occurred other factors, resulting in the failure of the Reformation in Polish towns.

Among these factors one must place the problem of the attitude, of the King towards the Reformation as recently correctly emphasized by J. Dworzaczkowa.[25] The victory of the Reformation in many of the German towns was certainly connected either with an open support or at least with the vacillating attitude of the local dukes towards the new creed. In England the entire process was initiated by a break with Rome by Henry VIII. In Poland, however, the situation was quite different. Both Sigismund I and Sigismund Augustus remained faithful to Catholicism and this made an eventual adopting of the new confession by the Royal towns, (a group of the largest towns in Poland) very difficult. The peak of the Reformation movement in the Commonwealth occurred at the Piotrków Diet in 1555, when it seemed that a Polish National Church, independent of Rome, would emerge. Sigismund Augustus agreed, at the time, under the pressure of the gentry, to suspend Church jurisdiction and to send an envoy to the Pope in order to gain permission to call a national synod. The gentry was granted the right to keep Protestant ministers in their estates and to receive communion in both kinds. However, the King simultaneously took care that none of these resolutions should pertain to the towns where he even intensified his action against the Protestants. Only a week after the close of the debates conducted by the Diet, on June 27, 1555, there appeared another mandate against the Protestants in Poznań. On January 20, 1556, a similar mandate was directed to Konin in Greater Poland. On March 1, 1556 the King proclaimed the next three edicts, two of which once again pertained to Greater Poland, the region most threatened by the progress of the Reformation. The first addressed the *starostas* and ordained them to suppress religious innovations and not to permit the dissenters to congregate, preach or worship in villages

---

[25] J. D w o r z a c z k o w a, *Wprowadzenie reformacji...*, p. 67 sqq.

and royal towns, even in homes owned by the gentry and thus exempt from city jurisdiction. The second edict, addressed to the Starosta General added that he should arrest all the Bohemian Brethern living in Poznań.[26] During the Warsaw Diet in 1556 - 1557 the King agreed to prolong the Piotrków interim but already very clearly excluded all towns from its resolutions. "*Item* the royal towns and others since they cannot equal the gentry either in freedom or in dignity, should not be included into this permission [...] this is why His Royal Majesty does not wish to make them equal by this freedom with you [i.e. the gentry— *M.B.*] but leaves them all *sui ipsius dispositioni*". This formulation which flattered the gentry was not questioned by the deputies— noble adherents of the Reformation. What is even more, they did not support attempts for revoking this decision undertaken at the Diet by representatives of Cracow, who, as a result, were unsuccessful.[27]

Of course, royal power in Poland was not very strong or efficient. This was the reason why the development of the situation in private towns depended exclusively on the attitude of the owner. As a result in certain private towns Protestant communities developed and survived even when the Counter-Reformation was winning victories in the whole country; a good example of this phenomenon was the town of Węgrów in Podlasie, the property of the powerful magnate Radziwiłł and Kiszka families.[28] In royal towns it was most important who was holding office of the *starosta*. In Greater Poland, for example, a significant role was played by the fact that in the decisive years of 1552 - 1564 Janusz Kościelecki, a fervent Catholic held the office of Starosta General.[29] In the town of Wschowa the Reformation was introduced with the support and the co-participation of the Lutheran starosta Maciej Górski from Miłosław.[30] In Między-

---

[26] *Ibidem*, p. 68.

[27] *Diariusz sejmu walnego warszawskiego z r. 1556 - 7* [*Warsaw Diet's Diary 1556 - 57*], ed. S. B o d n i a k, Kórnik 1939, p. 50.

[28] T. W y s z o m i r s k i, *Z przeszłości zboru protestanckiego w Węgrowie w XVII i XVIII w.* [*From the Past of the Protestant Community in the City of Węgrów in the 17th and 18th Centuries*], "Odrodzenie i Reformacja w Polsce," vol. IV, 1959, p. 137 sqq.

[29] J. D w o r z a c z k o w a, *Wprowadzenie ...*, p. 69.

[30] *Ibidem*, pp. 70 - 71.

rzecze the Protestants were also upheld by the local starosta, Mikołaj Myszkowski[81] while in Warsaw a group of protestants acted under the patronage of the Warsaw starosta, Zygmunt Wolski and the Rawa Voievode, Anzelm Gostomski;[82] these examples can be multiplied. Thus, the success or failure of the Reformation in towns depended upon the *starosta* who influenced the course of town matters; it was also important whether the nearby region was inhabited by Protestant magnates who were willing to support their urban co-religionists.[83] This personal factor which was of an entirely accidental character, decided frequently the fate of the entire movement. In addition, support given to Protestant burghers by the gentry was not only often insufficiently strong and consistent but also, as J. Dworzaczkowa correctly pointed out, frequently harmed the interests of the towns as a whole (among others by excluding the gentry homes from urban jurisdiction) and thus could not have been very popular. It was obvious that the Reformation opened up for the gentry an additional path for intervention into urban questions; in this situation the burghers received not so much advantages from a change of religion, it rather brought further limitation of their rights. In the royal towns a certain role was also played by a fear of the King's disfavour and eventual repressions. All this limited the mass character of the movement, especially where neither linguistic ties nor national factors appear in its favour. Thus in Polish towns one sees a lack of the most important factor which elsewhere was the basis for the victory of the Reformation, i.e. the support of numerous groups of people who were not so much engaged because of the ideological values of the new faith, but because of their definite economic or social interests. This was linked with a rather weak connection between the Reformation movements and social movements in Polish towns during the second half of the 16th century. After the disturbances in the 1520s, struggles between the guilds and the middle merchants and the town councils ceased in many town centres for a long time to come. In the

---

[81] *Ibidem.*
[82] G. Schramm, *Problem reformacji w Warszawie...*, p. 562.
[83] J. Tazbir, *Społeczeństwo wobec reformacji* [*Polish Society and the Reformation*], in: *Polska w epoce odrodzenia*, Warszawa 1970 p. 215.

second half of the 16th century more serious disturbances among the urban poor also did not occur. This was the result of various factors such as a relative prosperity of many Polish towns connected with an economic boom and favourable for Poland's terms of trade which was felt to a certain extent by all groups of the towns' inhabitants, and of a weak development of the elements of early capitalism which elsewhere at that time sharpened the class struggle and antagonisms within the town population. The intensification of social conflicts and a new wave of movements both of the urban poor and the middle class was to occur in Polish towns in the following "crisis" century, when the unfavourable fate of the Reformation was already decided not only in the towns.

In order to obtain a full picture of the situation it would seem, however, that one cannot omit a group of psychological factors. Until now scholares did not often take these factors into consideration since the studies on "states of mind" and so-called history of social mentality in general are rather a novelty and have been developing, especially in Poland, only recently. Here the question of the education of the town population would be a fundamental one; already L. Febvre stressed that the Reformation could not develop in a milieu deprived of "a high intellectual civilization".[34] Literacy must have been particularly important since individual study of the Bible played a basic role in the Protestant Church. According to Peter Clark and Peter Slack literacy in England during the 17th century amounted to more than 60 per cent in provincial towns and about 75 per cent in London.[35] French scholar E. Le Roy Ladurie estimates the literacy among the French burghers at the end of the 16th century at about 90 per cent[36] which seems to be far too optimistic. The Italian (or rather American) scholar C. M. Cipolla

---

[34] *A New Kind of History. From the Writings of Lucien Febvre*, edited by Peter B u r k e, London 1973, p. 115.

[35] P. C l a r k, P. S l a c k, *English Towns in Transition 1500 - 1700*, London 1976, pp. 73, 153. See also L. S t o n e, *Literacy and Education in England 1640 - 1900*, "Past and Present," vol. XLII, 1969 and R. S c h o - f i e l d, *The Measurement of Literacy in Pre-Industrial England*, in: *Literacy in Traditional Societies*, ed. J. G o o d y, Cambridge 1968.

[36] E. L e R o y L a d u r i e, *Les paysans de Languedoc*, Paris 1966, p. 321.

believes that the average literacy for the 16th century in Western countries should be estimated at more than 50 per cent of the towns' population.[37] It means better conditions and a more developed culture than we perceive in the Polish towns in this time.

Latest research shows enormous disproportions in this sphere among the Polish urban population. For example, in the towns of Little Poland, at the close of the 16th century, the ability to both read and write characterized around 70 per cent of the patriciate while among the middle burghers about 40 per cent, and the poor—only 8 per cent.[38] This means that only the more prosperous burghers participated in an animated intellectual life of Poland's "Golden Age" as a result of attending outstanding academic secondary schools of the period (the schools in the cities of Gdańsk, Toruń and Elbląg which won the well-deserved titles of "Academies" achieved a particularly high level), of studying in Polish and foreign universities and travelling abroad extensively. Thus, only the "upper" strata of the town population was intellectually fully prepared to receive the Reformation and it was they who introduced it in the Polish towns during the second half of the 16th century. This coincided with the fact that anti-clericalism, the feeling which could bring the illiterate burgher to the new creed—was in Poland most strongly developed among the gentry but in towns various positive results of the activity of the clergy prevailed (the organization of hospitals, schools, charity work, etc.). Anti-clerical propaganda and literature was not as developed in Poland during the 14th and 15th centuries as it was in England ; a trend of anti-clericalism did exist but we had neither Langland nor Chaucer although the life of the Polish clergy furnished many causes for

---

[37] C. M. C i p o l l a, *Literacy and Development in the West*, London 1969, 50 pp. See also R. E n g e l s i n g, *Analphabetentum und Lektüre. Zur Sozial Geschichte des Lesens in Deutschland zwischen feudaler und industrieller Gesellschaft*, Stuttgart 1973.

[38] W. U r b a n, *Umiejętność pisania w Małopolsce w drugiej połowie XVI wieku* [*Knowledge of Writing in Little Poland in the Second Half of the 16th Century*], "Przegląd Historyczny," vol. LXVIII, 1977, No. 2, p. 251.

reproach.[39] It also seems that in Polish towns, beginning with the 15th century, conflicts with the gentry played a much more important role than the collisions with the clergy ; the struggle between the gentry and the burghers thus overshadowed the conflict with the Catholic clergy which played such an important role in the development of the Reformation in Germany and in England. The strongest anti-clerical feelings appeared in the towns of Royal Prussia which, due to their strong economic and legal position, did not feel the aggressiveness of the gentry. Anticlericalism in Poland was mainly of a peasant and gentry character (controversies over tithes) while in the towns it lacked a sufficient basis, if only because the urban clergy and monks had to observe appearances more. It seems that the country parsons could permit themselves more easily to keep young and pretty housekeepers while in the towns a great discipline was observed as the sad events from the life of old Copernicus had proved.[40] The excesses committed by the church dignitaries (for example the legendary conduct of Bishop Gamrat) were well-known rather in the court and gentry circles and, at any rate, they gave rise more to antimagnate than to anti-clerical feelings ; but the burghers were not interested in a struggle with the magnates. One also should not forget that in conditions when for the burgher any secular career was difficult to attain, a church career appeared frequently to be the only path towards desired social advancement.

Reformation in Western Europe was closely connected with a nobilitation of town professions which in Poland were still treated with disdain ; this attitude was reflected in the works of the most outstanding gentry writers of the 16th century (Rej, Orzechowski). The burghers themselves did not take pride in their professions, they demanded to be portrayed on family gravestones in armour (Seweryn Boner and his famous sepulchre in the Church of Our Lady in Cracow) and manufactured for

---

[39] Cf. J. T a z b i r, *Znaczenie obyczajów kleru dla rozwoju i upadku polskiej reformacji* [The Role of the Moral Conduct of the Clergy for the Development and Decline of the Polish Reformation], "Odrodzenie i Reformacja w Polsce," vol. VIII, 1963, p. 91 sqq.
[40] J. S i k o r s k i, *Mikołaj Kopernik na Warmii* [Nicolaus Copernicus in the Region of Warmia], Olsztyn 1968, pp. 109 - 112.

themselves knightly genealogies. To praise work, thriftiness or a productive and not consumptive way of life was alien to the ideology not only of the gentry but also of the majority of the burghers. Isolated voices of progressive authors (Frycz-Modrzewski, Rozdzieński) could not change this image. Already in the 16th century the Polish burghers, with but a few exceptions, found themselves under the influence of models and ideals spread among those "of gentle birth"; by the use of all means they strove to enter into that group. The hierarchy of values valid in the Polish towns referred either to the Middle Ages (egalitarian tendencies, the treatment, at least in theory, of the entire life on earth as a preparation for a better existence after death through ascetism and contempt for material prosperity) or it was an adaptation of values promoted by the gentry (disdain for commerce and artisanship, an idealization of the style of life typical for the gentry). This was linked with a recognition of land as the highest value, a characteristic trait of the mentality of an agrarian society with a predominance of landowning gentry. "The land will remain but we shall die" said the Warsaw patrician Michael Fukier in the autumn of 1618, to his colleague Alexander Giza, who later complained in court : "And he plowed up some fields of my land and added it to his own".[41] This anecdotic fragment from Warsaw court acts illustrates the principal trait of the mentality of the Polish burghers of that period. The new social group—the modern bourgeoisie in Western Europe—emerged already in the 15th century, participated in large trade, navigation and geographical discoveries, invested large capital in the development of manufactures and gained profits from all these undertakings which demanded a willingness to take risks. This modern Western bourgeoisie needed a new and bold religion to supply it in its risky undertakings with an ideological support.[42] The Polish burghers, on the other hand,

---

[41] Archiwum Główne Akt Dawnych w Warszawie, Stara Warszawa [The Central Archives of Old Acts in Warsaw, The Old Warsaw Section], 545, p. 117.
[42] Cf. M. N e r l i c h, *Kritik der Abenteuer-Ideologie. Beitrag zur Erforschung der bürgerlichen Bewusstseinsbildung 1100 - 1750*, Bd. I - II, Berlin 1977.

did not seek or need such a religion; they were apathetic, conservative and showed little initiative; they gazed upon their own fading greatness and did not even attempt to struggle for a better place in society. They were unable to create a social solidarity which would counterbalance the local interests of the individual towns. Such a solidarity was achieved only from time to time by the towns of Royal Prussia despite the fact that they also conducted among themselves sharp competition, especially Gdańsk with Elbląg and Toruń. Perhaps the lack of larger and united economic actions which in England or in the Netherlands took the form of colonization enterprises, overseas expeditions and the activity of great trading companies, was of decisive significance. In Poland trading companies, as a rule, did not extend beyond one town; perhaps only Gdańsk was an exception with its numerous Gdańsk-Dutch companies, but they also generally were based on agency rights and not equal partnership. Foreign trade and navigation were dominated by Gdańsk and foreign merchants who did not permit the inhabitants of the majority of Polish towns to be active in this field; this policy enjoyed the support of the gentry. The Seym constitutions of 1565 forbade Polish merchants to engage in foreign trade or to travel abroad. Thus the political and social passivity of the Polish burghers in the 16th century was matched by deepening economic stagnation in the towns. This was however a broader phenomenon which certainly expanded beyond the towns although it was there that it occurred especially sharply. Particularly from the end of the 16th century the entire Polish economy, enclosed within the narrow borders of the manor farm, became ever more passive and strongly characterized by a conservative quietism, which expressed itself, among other things, in a general conviction that it was the "foreigners" who needed greatly Polish grain and should come for it.[43] Only an extreme danger (the Turks, Cossacks and Swedes in the 17th century) could awaken such a society to some military

---

[43] C. C z u b e k, *Pisma polityczne z czasów pierwszego bezkrólewia* [*Political Writings from the Times of the First Interregnum*], Kraków 1906, p. 422.

effort; while, on the other hand, all social and political or economic activities for any improvement or simply for a change cannot but fail. This was probably the reason why a struggle for the "Reform of the Commonwealth" and even the gentry Reformation died down so quickly; quietism, typical of agrarian societies was here of great significance, it enabled the victory of the Counter-Reformation which meant a return to the old, facile forms of worship which appealed more to the imagination and emotions than to the intellect and eliminated the risk connected with the search for new expressions of piety. Thus an unwillingness to undertake an economic risk, to introduce more progressive, modern methods in production and commerce had to be linked with a reluctance towards changes in the sphere of religion, i.e. with religious conservatism.

To sum up: the Reformation had various aspects and was linked with equally various political, social, economic and psychological needs which appeared in the 16th century. The situation and characteristic traits of the Polish bourgeoisie in this period made it impossible, however, for this movement to become more deeply enrooted in the urban milieu. In Poland the Reformation, as a form of political struggle and an instrument of competition for power, became the monopoly of the gentry. Polish towns relegated to the sidelines of political life, did not participate in the struggle for the "Reform of the Commonwealth", which flared up in the 16th century. Even the gentry, once the struggle for "Reform" died down, put aside arms supplied by the Reformation and returned *en masse* to the fold of Catholicism and, as if with certain relief, to the old, comprehensible, well-known and facile forms of piety offered by the Catholic Church. The Reformation could have been, as was the case in many Wester European countries (the Netherlands, partly England), a form of a social, political, economic and even mental overturn, but the Polish towns were not mature enough for it. As a result and at the same time as a catalysis of new mental attitudes connected with transformations in the sphere of political, social and economic relations, the Reformation proved to be alien to the Polish burghers. The victory of the Re-

74

formation in the towns of Royal Prussia, at a different level of development and in a legal and social situation which differed from other towns of the Polish Commonwealth, only confirms the remarks presented above.

VIII

Les villes et le développement de la culture sur l'exemple de la Pologne aux XVIe-XVIIIe siècles

Le rôle des villes et de la bourgeoisie en tant que facteur puissant de création de la culture est de plus en plus souligné par les chercheurs. Les études intensives sur les progrès de l'urbanisation au seuil de l'ère moderne mettent dernièrement l'accent non seulement sur les aspects économico-sociaux de ces processus, mais aussi sur leur immense signification pour la civilisation et la culture[1]. Le caractère bourgeois du siècle d'or de la culture hollandaise en est un exemple, extrême sans doute, mais pas entièrement isolé. Au cours des XVIe—XVIIIe siècles, la bourgeoisie en voie d'enrichissement dans plusieurs pays européens apportait une contribution de plus en plus grande au développement des cultures nationales, entrant avec succès sous ce rapport en compétition avec les féodaux et conférant à la culture de l'époque des marques par lesquelles elle différait considérablement de la culture créée par le Moyen Age. Du fait de leur spécificité, les processus intervenant en ce temps en territoire polonais méritent une attention particulière.

Dès les débuts de son existence, la ville offrait au développement de la culture des conditions particulièrement favorables, et cela du fait d'une forte concentration dans son enceinte du potentiel créateur, humain et économique. En tant que centre compact de production de biens matériels et spirituels, elle offrait également à ses habitants des possibilités de large accès aux biens culturels. La saturation de la ville, dès le haut Moyen Age, d'une grande quantité d'oeuvres d'art (architecture, arts plastiques) faisait que le bourgeois frayait quotidiennement avec elles, ce qui ne pouvait pas rester sans influence sur sa sensibilité esthétique et son niveau intellectuel. Plus facile y était aussi l'accès à l'instruction, y compris les écoles supérieures, aux bibliothèques publiques et privées; les occupations de ville réclamant un certain minimum d'ins-

---

[1] Sans entrer dans une discussion démesurée sur la définition de la culture et de la civilisation, nous entendrons par culture dans le présent article aussi bien l'ensemble des produits (matériels et non matériels) de l'homme, que les modes d'existence et les systèmes de valeurs socialement reconnus.

154

truction, ainsi que le rythme rapide, vivant, de la vie urbaine, détermi-
naient une sphère d'expériences psychiques autre qu'à la campagne et
formaient des structures mentales spécifiques. Dès le Moyen Age donc
se concentrait dans les villes la vie intellectuelle la plus intense du pays,
naissaient et se développaient les groupes de la pré-intelligentsia
(fonctionnaires municipaux, clergé, enseignants, etc.); en même temps,
vu l'accès large et relativement facile aux biens culturels, naissaient,
à côté de la culture des élites, des embryons de culture de masse englobant les bas-fonds de la population urbaine [2]. Les recherches sur la
culture urbaine en Pologne médiévale relèvent son rapide développement et son haut niveau, surtout au déclin du Moyen Age, à quoi cor-
respondait en même temps l'épanouissement rapide des villes polonaises [3].

Les siècles, faisant l'objet de notre propos, apportent de profonds
changements dans les structures socio-économiques et juridico-politiques
de la Pologne. La conquête de la suprématie dans l'Etat par la noblesse
(à peine env. 10% de la population), à l'époque certainement le groupe
le plus actif, le plus conscient et intérieurement solidaire de la société,
équivalait au refoulement de la bourgeoisie, d'ailleurs assez nombreuse
déjà (dans la deuxième moitié du XVIe siècle près de 20%, au XVIIIe s.
sans doute environ 16% de la population du pays [4]) en marge de la vie
non seulement politique. Le refoulement de la bourgeoisie de la vie
économique active et le sapement de son bien-être du fait de la mono-
polisation par la noblesse d'une grande part de l'exportation des produits agricoles vers les ports (Gdańsk) où celle-ci s'approvisionnait directement en produits de l'industrie étrangère importés, allaient de pair
avec la discrimination juridique de la bourgeoisie (interdiction de posséder des biens fonciers, 1496, 1538, élimination des bourgeois des hautes
dignités de l'Eglise, 1496, perte du titre de noblesse pour la pratique
des professions bourgeoises, 1633, 1677). Ces mesures se doublaient dans
la République nobiliaire de l'atmosphère spécifique, étrangère aux
autres pays, de mésestime, voire même de mépris pour les habitants
des villes. Leurs représentants étaient absents du parlement polonais
définitivement constitué à la charnière des XVe et XVIe siècles [5]. Le

---

[2] Sur les notions de culture élitaire — culture de masse, cf. l'introduction
de l'ouvrage collectif sous la direction de B. Geremek, *Kultura elitarna a kultura
masowa w Polsce późnego średniowiecza* [*La culture des élites et la culture de*
masse dans la Pologne du bas Moyen Age], Warszawa 1978, p. 5 et suiv.

[3] Cf. H. S a m s o n o w i c z, *Złota jesień polskiego średniowiecza* [*L'automne*
d'or du Moyen Age polonais], Warszawa 1971, p. 156 et suiv.; d u m ê m e, *Nowe*
wartości w kulturze średniowiecznych miast polskich [*Nouvelles valeurs dans*
la culture des villes médiévales polonaises], „Zapiski Historyczne", 1974, fasc. 2.

[4] Ce sont des chiffres prêtant à discussion; certains chercheurs considèrent
que la proportion de la bourgeoisie était quelue peu plus élevée. Cf. H. S a m-
s o n o w i c z, *Das polnische Bürgertum in der Renaissancezeit*, „Studia Historica",
53, Budapest 1963, p. 93.

[5] *Historia państwa i prawa Polski*, t. I [*Histoire de l'Etat et du droit de*
Pologne], I, ss la dir. de J. Bardach, 3e éd. Warszawa 1968, p. 442.

meurtre d'un noble entraînait une amende beaucoup plus élevée que celui d'un bourgeois[6]. L'autonomie urbaine, conquise au Moyen Age, avait subi d'importantes limitations[7]. Tous ces phénomènes devaient se répercuter, et assez rapidement, dans la sphère du développement de la culture. Il est remarquable que la bourgeoisie, soumise aux restrictions dans d'autres domaines d'activité et humiliée, se lance tout d'abord d'autant plus intensivement dans le tourbillon de l'activité culturelle pour, de cette façon, défouler au moins partiellement ses frustrations sociales[8]. Le XVIe s. apporte un magnifique, mais dernier accord dans le développement de la culture bourgeoise en Pologne. Elle se manifesta sans conteste le plus magnifiquement et le plus pleinement dans l'architecture et les arts plastiques connexes. On peut même risquer l'affirmation que tout le resplendissant départ de l'architecture Renaissance polonaise s'était accompli, pour une grande part, justement sous les auspices du mécénat bourgeois[9]. Parmi les mécènes extrêmement actifs de la Renaissance polonaise, on doit ranger aussi bien les autorités municipales (surtout des centres urbains riches, tels que Gdańsk, Toruń, Elbląg, Cracovie, Poznań et autres), que les confréries et les corporations (nous en connaissons des exemples remarquables, mais pas uniques, à Gdańsk et à Cracovie), et enfin les familles particulières de patriciens où l'on peut relever des exemples de geste large et ambitieux (les Ferber de Gdańsk, les Boner de Cracovie, les Baryczka de Varsovie, les Boim de Lwów, etc.). Le XVIe siècle, et surtout sa seconde moitié, se situe sous le signe d'une reconstruction et d'un agrandissement intense dans le style Renaissance des villes polonaises, résultat d'une activité décuplée de la bourgeoisie[10]. Les motivations sociales de cette activité n'étaient pas inconnues même des contemporains[11]. En même temps d'ailleurs fonctionnaient certaines motivations économiques: parmi les plus importantes pouvait se trouver, dès le XVIe siècle, la recherche d'un placement sûr et avantageux des capitaux. Dans la conjoncture défavorable aux investissements dans le commerce ou la production[12], et vu les obstacles créés à l'achat des

---

[6] *Ibidem*, p. 342, II, p. 121 et suiv.

[7] *Ibidem*, p. 58 et suiv.

[8] M. B o g u c k a, *Les bourgeois et les investissements culturels. L'exemple de Gdańsk aux XVIe et XVIIe siècles*, „Revue Historique", CCLIX, 1978, 2, pp. 429—440.

[9] Cf. A. M i ł o b ę d z k i, *Zarys dziejów architektury w Polsce [Précis d'architecture en Pologne]*, Warszawa 1968, p. 96.

[10] *Ibidem*. Cf. aussi S. H e r b s t, *Miasta i mieszczaństwo renesansu polskiego [Les villes et la bourgeoisie de la Renaissance polonaise]*, Warszawa 1954, et d u m ê m e, *Polska kultura mieszczańska XVI/XVII w. [La culture bourgeoise polonaise des XVIe/XVIIe s.]*, „Studia Renesansowe", Wrocław 1956.

[11] Cf. *Pisarze polskiego Odrodzenia o sztuce [Les écrivains de la Renaissance polonaise sur l'art]*, éd. par Wł. Tomkiewicz, Wrocław 1955, surtout pp. 200—207.

[12] W. K r a s s o w s k i, *Przesłanki gospodarcze programów architektonicznych w Polsce około r. 1600 [Les prémisses économiques des programmes architecturaux en Pologne vers 1600]*, in: *Sztuka około roku 1600*, Warszawa 1974, p. 130 et suiv.

terres par les bourgeois, du fait aussi des possibilités limitées d'acheter un nombre important de parcelles en ville (vu le territoire limité des villes [13]), le capital était investi dans les parcelles déjà acquises et dans les immeubles, de façon à en rehausser au maximum la valeur, donc par voie de remaniement et d'agrandissement des maisons (principalement en hauteur) et d'embellissement de leurs façades [14]. L'évaluation globale, même approchée, de la grandeur des capitaux bourgeois placés dans les grandes réalisations du bâtiment et d'architecture et dans les travaux plastiques décoratifs au XVIe et même au début du XVIIe siècle, est impossible du fait de la carence des sources et de la littérature. C'était cependant, à n'en pas douter, la principale orientation des investissements culturels de la bourgeoisie en ce temps [15], bourgeoisie que l'on peut sans crainte d'exagérer appeler créatrice de l'architecture et des arts plastiques Renaissance polonais.

Le début du XVIIe siècle s'est exprimé par les dernières réalisations de l'architecture bourgeoise, tant privée que municipale [16]. La cause en est, sans nul doute, dans la crise monétaire des années 1618—1621 et la forte détérioration en ce temps des „terms of trade" de la Pologne; à côté cependant des facteurs purement économiques jouaient également les facteurs socio-politiques et la pression de plus en plus forte exercée sur les villes par la noblesse. Celle-ci adoptait même la forme de restrictions imposées aux activités du bâtiment de la bourgeoisie par voie de pression administrative [17]; une autre cause résidait dans l'invasion des nobles et magnats dans les villes les plus importantes de la Couronne (Varsovie, Cracovie, Lublin, Lwów, Poznań), aboutissant au rachat des parcelles à bâtir et à la construction de gentilhommières nobles et de palais aristocratiques sur le territoire des villes [18]. Ce phénomène était déjà intervenu plus tôt, aux XVe et XVIe s., mais il n'adopta des dimensions massives qu'au XVIIe siècle. De même, le développement rapide des complexes plus étendus de propriétés féodales, dits juridictions (iurisdictiones), qui segmentaient le territoire de la ville, correspond aux mêmes années [19]. Le développement rapide de l'architecture sacrale dans les villes, lié à la Contre-réforme et alimenté par les nombreuses fondations pieuses, était pour une grande part sti-

---

[13] M. B o g u c k a, Quelques problèmes de la sociotopographie des villes les plus grandes de Pologne aux XVIe—XVIIe s., „Acta Poloniae Historica", XXXIV, 1976, p. 131 et suiv.

[14] D'après les évaluations de Krassowski, les Przybyła avaient accru leurs dépenses pour la construction de leurs maisons de Kazimierz-sur-la-Vistule, donc également leur valeur, par la richesse des façades, d'environ un quart, ibidem, p. 135.

[15] M. B o g u c k a, Les bourgeois et les investissements culturels, p. 433.

[16] M. B o g u c k a, Kultura miejska w Polsce XVI—XVIII w. [La culture urbaine en Pologne aux XVIe—XVIIIe s.], (ss presse).

[17] Ibidem.

[18] M. B o g u c k a, Quelques problèmes, p. 136 et suiv.

[19] Ibidem.

mulé par des facteurs non-urbains (le roi, les magnats, les nobles riches). Ainsi, si l'architecture Renaissance polonaise était pour une grande part une architecture bourgeoise (hôtels de ville et autres édifices municipaux d'utilité publique, maisons de patriciens, greniers à blé etc.), le Baroque polonais en revanche, puis le Classicisme, est représenté pour une immense part par des églises et des palais nobles [20]. Le dernier coup fatal à la magnificence de l'architecture urbaine a été porté par la période du „Déluge" suédois qui a entraîné la ruine des bâtiments de nombreux centres urbains à 60—80%/o [21]. Seule Varsovie s'est très rapidement relevée des ruines, mais en tant que centre résidentiel de la noblesse, ville de palais féodaux et de gentilhommières, avec par endroits seulement des maisons bourgeoises modestes [22]. L'échec du mécénat bourgeois et le passage des initiatives dans l'architecture aux mains de la riche noblesse et des magnats, est en outre attesté par le développement caractéristique, surtout des XVIIe et XVIIIe siècles, des villes privées de différents types: résidentielles (Zamość, Żółkiew, Nieśwież, Białystok, Rydzyna, Siedlce, Biała Podlaska), „artisanales" (Grande-Pologne: Bojanowo, Rawicz, Szlichtyngowo, Rakoniewice), „agricoles" centres de latifundia (Ulanów, Janów etc.). Leur plan et leur construction se caractérisent par la subordination des demeures bourgeoises à la résidence du magnat, éventuellement à l'église, fait que l'on peut considérer comme un reflet symbolique des rapports sociaux de l'époque dans les conceptions d'urbanisme et d'architecture.

Une évolution semblablement peu favorable, quoique certainement moins violente, s'est produite dans le rôle de la bourgeoisie au plan de la stimulation de la création artistique au sens large L'exemple le plus manifeste peut en être fourni par le peinture, au XVIe siècle encore, réalisant pour une grande part les commandes des milieux bourgeois et portant un fort caractère bourgeois. Le portrait polonais du XVIIe siècle, en revanche, est surtout un portrait du style dit „sarmate", représentant des magnats, ou peint d'une manière réaliste sur les cercueils des magnats et des nobles, répond aux goûts et aux besoins spécifiques du client féodal. En Poméranie uniquement s'est perpétuée la riche tradition du portrait bourgeois (B. Strobel, D. Schultz, A. Boy, A. Stech) et de la peinture représentant, à la manière dont le faisait au début

---

[20] Wł. T a t a r k i e w i c z, *O sztuce polskiej XVII i XVIII w.* [*De l'art polonais aux XVIIe et XVIIIe s.*], Warszawa 1966; cf. aussi M. K a r p o w i c z, *Sztuka oświeconego sarmatyzmu* [*L'art du sarmatisme éclairé*], Warszawa 1970.

[21] Z *Zniszczenia gospodarcze w połowie XVII w.* [*Les destructions économiques au milieu du XVIIe s.*], in: *Polska w okresie drugiej wojny północnej 1655—1660*, Warszawa 1957. Des exemples caractéristiques sont cités par D. T o l l e t, *Skutki wojen drugiej połowy XVII w. dla miast polskich wedle relacji podróżnych i komentatorów francuskich* [*Les effets des guerres de la deuxième moitié du XVIIe s. pour les villes polonaises d'après les relations des voyageurs et commentateurs français*], „Rocznik Gdański", XXXVII, 1977, pp. 11—12.

[22] W. K a l i n o w s k i, *The city development in Poland up to the mid-19th century*, Warszawa 1966, p. 50 et suiv.

du XVIᵉ siècle le célèbre *Codex* cracovien de Behem, la vie quotidienne de la ville et de ses habitants (particulièrement la peinture de l'école de Gdańsk fondée par A. Moeller). Il est symptomatique cependant que les artistes poméraniens ci-dessus cités n'aient que partiellement travaillé pour le client bourgeois, réalisant surtout les commandes du mécène féodal: la cour royale, les magnats, la noblesse cossue. En même temps, les contacts avec les créateurs étrangers et l'achat des oeuvres d'art à l'étranger, largement pratiqués par la riche bourgeoisie des grandes villes encore à la charnière des XVIᵉ et XVIIᵉ siècles, deviennent, dans la seconde moitié du XVIIᵉ siècle et au XVIIIᵉ, le domaine presque exclusif des agents de la cour royale et des magnats [23].

Le XVIᵉ siècle peut également être reconnu comme l'apogée du mécénat bourgeois dans le domaine de l'éducation et de la science. L'excellent développement de l'enseignement Renaissance était en Pologne surtout l'oeuvre de la bourgeoisie. Les cadres enseignants des écoles de tous types, y compris les supérieures, étaient principalement d'origine bourgeoise, et la nouvelle pensée pédagogique humaniste était surtout développée par les bourgeois [24]. Les excellents Gymnases Académiques de Gdańsk, Toruń et Elbląg, mis en place du fait du mécénat bourgeois, rivalisaient efficacement avec les écoles existant grâce au mécénat du roi, des nobles et des magnats (Académies de Cracovie, de Wilno et de Zamość, gymnases de Raków, Pińczów, Leszno, Sieraków). La jeunesse bourgeoise ne le cédait en rien à la noblesse dans la course à l'instruction, généralisée au XVIᵉ siècle, d'autant plus que les fils plus ambitieux de bourgeois voyaient dans l'instruction la chance souhaitée de promotion sociale sur la voie de la carrière ecclésiastique ou universitaire. Selon les récentes recherches, vers la fin du XVIᵉ siècle, dans les villes de Petite-Pologne savaient écrire 70% des patriciens, 40% de la couche moyenne et 8% des pauvres [25]; dans le même temps, chez les nobles de la voïvodie de Cracovie il y avait environ 69% d'analphabètes [26]. Ceci indiquerait une supériorité considérable de la bourgeoisie dans le domaine de l'éducation fondamentale. Dans l'instruction moyenne et supérieure, les proportions étaient analogues, et en tout cas elles n'étaient pas défavorables aux habitants des villes [27]. A partir seule-

---

[23] M. B o g u c k a, *Kultura miejska* (ss presse).

[24] *Historia wychowania* [*Histoire de l'éducation*], ss la dir. de Ł. Kurdybacha, Warszawa 1967, I, p. 371 et suiv.

[25] W. U r b a n, *Umiejętność pisania w Małopolsce w drugiej połowie XVI w.* [*La capacité d'écrire en Petite-Pologne dans la deuxième moitié du XVIᵉ s.*], „Przegląd Historyczny", 1977, n° 2, p. 251.

[26] A. W y c z a ń s k i, *Oświata a pozycja społeczna w Polsce XVI stulecia* [*L'éducation et la position sociale en Pologne du XVIᵉ s.*], in: *Społeczeństwo staropolskie*, I, Warszawa 1976, pp. 27—55.

[27] Les bourgeois constituaient plus de 90% des élèves des Gymnases Académiques de Gdańsk, Toruń et Elbląg, plus de 40% des étudiants de l'Université de Cracovie, cf. B. K ü r b i s, *Mieszczanie na Uniwersytecie Jagiellońskim i ich udział w kształtowaniu świadomości narodowej w XV w.* [*Les bourgeois à l'Université*

ment du deuxième quart du XVIIe siècle probablement a commencé à baisser le niveau des écoles urbaines, ce qui, dans le contexte de l'épanouissement de l'enseignement jésuite, destiné principalement à former les fils de nobles, et de la diminution du nombre de départs des jeunes bourgeois pour les études à l'étranger, devait aboutir dans la seconde moitié du XVIIe et au XVIIIe siècle à un renversement des proportions défavorable pour les villes [28].

Immense était la contribution de la bourgeoisie au développement de la science dans toute la période considérée. La science était pratiquée en Pologne principalement par des hommes d'origine bourgeoise, les nobles se trouvant plus rarement au nombre des intellectuels [29]. Le mécénat bourgeois, dans le domaine de la science, rivalisait aux XVIe et XVIIe siècles avec le mécénat royal et des magnats, et il devait rester vivant également au XVIIIe siècle; plusieurs villes étaient devenues des centres importants de la pensée scientifique, fondés exclusivement sur le mécénat local des bourgeois (Gdańsk, Toruń, Elbląg). Les fondations scientifiques bourgeoises se retrouvaient d'ailleurs également dans d'autres centres, surtout dans les villes universitaires (Cracovie, Zamość, Wilno) ou d'une manière générale là, où se trouvait un patriciat riche, culturellement développé (Varsovie, Poznań, Lwów). La bourgeoisie a particulièrement mérité de l'organisation de la vie scientifique, surtout par la création de collections de livres et l'organisation (aux XVIIe — XVIIIe s.) de „cabinets de curiosités", de laboratoires physiques et chimiques, d'observatoires astronomiques, de collections d'histoire naturelle, etc. [30] Certaines familles patriciennes, parmi les plus importantes, sont passées dans l'histoire comme protecteurs particuliers de la littérature et des sciences: ils subventionnaient les recherches, versaient des pensions et des allocations aux écrivains et chercheurs (les Boner de Cracovie, les Strobandt de Toruń, les Ferber de Gdańsk, les Boim de Lwów, les Baryczka de Varsovie). Dans les cercles bourgeois étaient aussi créées les premières sociétés savantes [31]. Il semble cependant que les sommes, affectées par les bourgeois aux fins du mécénat scientifique, étaient incomparablement inférieures aux capitaux placés dans les realisations

---

Jagellonne et leur participation à la formation de la conscience nationale au XVe s.], in: Studia nad literaturą staropolską, Wrocław 1957, pp. 40—41 et 78.

[28] *Historia wychowania,* pp. 437—438.

[29] Une statistique de sondage dressée à partir des biogrammes contenus dans le vol. VI de *Historia Nauki Polskiej [Histoire de la science polonaise]* ss la dir. de B. Suchodolski, Wrocław 1974, permet de constater que plus de 80% des hommes de science qui y sont cités sont des bourgeois.

[30] M. B o g u c k a, *Kultura miejska* (ss presse).

[31] A Gdańsk, elles bourgeonnaient déjà dans les années 70 du XVIIe s. Définitivement la Societas Litteraria y a été créée en 1720. En 1767 fut fondée la Warszawskie Towarzystwo Fizyczno-Chemiczne [Société varsovienne physico-chimique] qui fonctionnait pour une grande part en se fondant sur la bourgeoisie. Nous ne citons pas ici le précurseur de ces organisations, la Societas Vistulana de Kallimach, étant donné qu'elle possédait un caractère plutôt littéraire.

architecturales et l'achat des oeuvres d'art, ce qui devait devenir d'ailleurs la cause de sérieuses lacunes dans les investissements au profit de la science en Pologne. Les causes en étaient diverses. Il ne fait pas de doute que le mécénat scientifique produisait moins d'effet visible que le mécénat au plan de l'architecture et des arts et jouait beaucoup moins dans l'affermissement de la position sociale du mécène. Non sans importance aussi était le fait qu'on ne pouvait traiter les dépenses pour la science comme un placement sûr et apportant des bénéfices considérables, des capitaux, comme c'était le cas de la construction d'une maison ou de l'achat d'oeuvres d'art [32]. Ainsi, dans les conditions où le prestige social et la concurrence entre les états et groupes sociaux étaient le principal mobile du mécénat, la science devait souffrir du manque d'investissements. Plus „avantageuses", du point de vue de l'investisseur, étaient les dépenses pour la littérature, d'où le soutien zélé accordé par la riche bourgeoisie au XVIe et dans la première moitié du XVIIe siècle aux poètes et aux artisans de la plume, et, avec cela, le développement, surtout à l'époque du Baroque, de la littérature occasionnelle et panégyrique. Dans ce secteur cependant, dès le XVIe siècle, se manifestait la supériorité du mécénat de la cour, des magnats et des nobles. Considérable à l'échelle du pays tout entier était en revanche la contribution de la bourgeoisie au développement des spectacles, qui constituaient l'embryon de la vie théâtrale. Ceux-ci étaient organisés par les autorités municipales et diverses institutions de la ville (confréries, corporations, écoles), et cela à diverses occasions: fêtes publiques (visite des souverains, couronnements des rois, anniversaires, fêtes familiales de la dynastie régnante), festivités locales (tournois, compétitions de tir, etc.), fêtes religieuses (carême-prenant, spectacles du carnaval, festivités de Noël, de Pâques, de la Fête-Dieu, etc.) et autres. L'apogée de ces spectacles correspond à la première moitié du XVIIe siècle: l'appauvrissement progressif de la bourgeoisie après le „Déluge" réduisit considérablement les initiatives dans ce domaine.

Les exemples présentés ci-dessus, dans un grand raccourci évidemment, témoignent de l'activité culturelle intense et diversifiée de la bourgeoisie dans la République au XVIe et encore dans la première moitié du XVIIe siècle, et de l'extinction progressive de cette activité à la période de dépression économique et sociale, notamment la deuxième moitié du XVIIe et le début du XVIIIe siècle. Ayant perdu dans la concurrence avec la noblesse sur le champ économico-politique, les bourgeois perdent dans la deuxième manche de la compétition, celle touchant au domaine de la culture. Ce processus trouve sa meilleure illustration dans l'analyse du domaine spécifique et extrêmement important qu'est l'idéologie.

---

[32] M. B o g u c k a, *Les bourgeois et les investissements culturels,* passim.

La mesure du dynamisme au plan de la création culturelle de tel groupe défini et l'exposant de sa contribution à la culture nationale, est justement le degré de développement de sa propre idéologie, entendue comme un ensemble d'idées et d'opinions sur le monde et la vie, propre au groupe donné, formé en tant que reflet de son existence sociale, servant à la défense et à l'expression de ses intérêts [33]. H. Samsonowicz situe la naissance de l'idéologie bourgeoise en Pologne aux XIIIe—XIVe siècles, et en souligne le caractère novateur et le rôle important joué dans les transformations générales de l'époque [34]. Les XVe et XVIe siècles se sont soldés par un nouveau développement en la matière, comme que — il faut le soulinger — notre bourgeoisie n'ait pas formé, comme cela avait lieu en Europe Occidentale, une auto-conscience développée, dépassant le cadre d'une seule ville. Au sein de l'état bourgeois polonais naissaient uniquement des solidarités très étroites et bornées. Chaque ville polonaise constituait aux XVe et XVIe siècles, comme dans le haut Moyen Age, une communauté close, englobant uniquement les citoyens locaux (*cives*), luttant jalousement pour ses privilèges locaux (nombreux encore étaient au XVIe s. les litiges portant sur le droit d'entrepôt, l'obligation de la route, etc.). On ne relève pas en Pologne de traces de constitution d'unions de villes ou de conclusion d'arrangements (à l'exclusion des arrangements entre corporations artisanales de signification limitée) pour engager des actions socio-politiques solidaires et d'envergure [35]. La transformation du bourgeois médiéval, citoyen d'une seule ville, en „bourgeois" moderne, aux vastes horizons, raisonnant non plus à l'échelle d'une ville mais de l'état tout entier, n'a commencé chez nous ni au XVIe, ni au XVIIe siècle: il faut en chercher les embryons au déclin du XVIIIe siècle seulement [36]. Cette désintégration de la bourgeoisie polonaise la plaçait justement dans une position très désavantageuse par rapport à la noblesse, au sein de laquelle l'auto-conscience et la solidarité d'état s'étaient développées tôt et très fort [37].

On peut, en revanche, parler de l'accroissement de l'autoconnaissance bourgeoise au XVIe siècle à l'échelle d'une ville; cette croissance était sans doute d'autant plus importante que la bourgeoisie ressentait plus fortement la menace pesant sur sa position du fait de l'agressivité croissante de la noblesse. Ce sont des questions assez mal étudiées, néanmoins des sondages sporadiques mènent à des conclusions très inté-

---

[33] J. W i a t r, *Socjologia a ideologia* [*Sociologie et idéologie*], Studia Filozoficzne, t. IV, 1958.
[34] H. S a m s o n o w i c z, *Ideologia mieszczaństwa w Polsce XIII w.* [*L'idéologie bourgeoise en Pologne du XIIIe s.*], in: *Sztuka i ideologia XIII w.*, Wrocław 1975.
[35] M. B o g u c k a, *Miasta w Polsce a reformacja* [*Les villes en Pologne et la Réforme*], „Odrodzenie i Reformacja w Polsce", XXIV, 1970, pp. 17—18.
[36] M. B o g u c k a, *Kultura miejska* (ss presse).
[37] J. M a c i s z e w s k i, *Szlachta polska i jej państwo* [*La noblesse polonaise et son Etat*], Warszawa 1969, p. 38 et suiv.

162

ressantes [38]. L'auto-conscience croissante des bourgeois à l'échelle d'une ville est attestée, entre autres, par les programmes idéo-politiques mis au point dans la deuxième moitié du XVIe et au début du XVIIe siècle par certaines villes riches (Gdańsk, Poznań) et par la représentation de ces programmes dans le décor des façades et les intérieurs des hôtels de ville [39]. Des études plus larges sur l'architecture et l'art en villes polonaises de la Renaissance et du Baroque précoce comme l'expression d'une idéologie municipale, malheureusement non entreprises jusqu'à ce jour, permettraient très certainement de mettre au jour le fonctionnement de nombreux éléments de ce domaine dans différents centres urbains, là particulièrement où s'était formé un patriciat riche et ambitieux. On pourrait également risquer l'affirmation que, dans l'abondante production artistique des épitaphes et monuments funéraires du XVIe et du début du XVIIe siècle, attachée au mécénat bourgeois, interviennent certains éléments de l'auto-conscience bourgeoise et des embryons de l'idéologie d'état, quoique dès le XVIe s. on voit s'y manifester aussi la fascination par les modèles de vie nobles et chevaleresques [40]. Il faut en effet constater que les villes polonaises n'avaient pas su créer (même à l'époque de leur plus grand épanouissement) ni propager un système cohérent d'idéaux de la vie, typiques du milieu bourgeois. Dans la littérature polonaise, extrêmement peu nombreuses sont les traces d'éloge du travail du non-agriculteur. Là se situe la proposition des „inspecteurs" royaux de la terre de Cracovie, de 1564, dans le sens de la reconnaissance de l'immense utilité pour le pays de l'activité minière, et leur constatation que „ceux qui font d'habitude ce métier sont comme des chasseurs par nature et comme des chevaliers vertueux" [41]. Le travail du fondeur devait être vanté plusieurs dizaines d'années plus tard par Walenty Rozdzieński, dans le poème maintes fois cité „*Officina ferraria abo huta i warstat z kuźniami szlachetnego dzieła żelaznego*" [*Officina*

---

[38] Cf. p.ex. S. M. S z a c h e r s k a, *Próba walki o główszczyznę szlachecką w XV w.*, in: *Cultus et cognitio. Studia z dziejów średniowiecznej kultury. Księga ku czci Al. Gieysztora w 40-lecie pracy naukowej* [Tentative de lutte pour l'amende en cas de meurtre d'un noble au XVe s., in: *Cultus et cognitio. Etudes sur l'histoire de la culture médiévale. Livre en hommage à A. Gieysztor pour ses 40 ans d'activité scientifique*], Warszawa 1976, p. 551 et suiv.

[39] Cf. E. I w a n o y k o, *Apoteoza Gdańska. Program ideowy malowideł stropu wielkiej sali rady w Gdańskim ratuszu Głównego Miasta* [Apothéose de Gdańsk. Le programme idéel des peintures du plafond de la grande salle du conseil de l'hôtel de ville de la Ville Principale], Gdańsk 1976; T. J a k i m o w i c z, *Architektura świecka w Wielkopolsce w latach około 1540 do około 1630* [L'architecture profane en Grande-Pologne dans les années v. 1540—v. 1630], in: *Studia nad renesansem w Wielkopolsce*, Poznań 1970, p. 19 et suiv.

[40] Un exemple typique de cette fascination peut être fourni par le monument funéraire du banquier du roi Sigismond le Vieux, Seweryn Boner, en l'église Notre-Dame à Cracovie, représentant le patricien cracovien, mort en 1549, anobli de fraîche date, en tant que chevalier en armure.

[41] *Lustracja dóbr królewskich woj. krakowskiego 1564* [Inventaire des domaines royaux de la voïv. de Cracovie 1564], éd. J. Małecki, IIe partie, Warszawa 1964, pp. 50—51, 53, 56.

*ferraria ou four de fer et ateliers de forge du noble ouvrage de fer,
1612]* [42]. Une tentative assez timide d'excuser des opérations de crédit
et de l'usure, entreprise par l'imprimeur Jakub Siebeneicher dans son
avant-propos du livre *Gospodarstwo [Economie]* écrit par le voïvode de
Rawa Anzelm Gostomski (1588) [43] ou encore la défense des plébéiens de
Krzysztof Warszewicki (1598) ont, dans ce contexte, une éloquence
extrêmement courageuse. En revanche Sebastian Fabian Klonowic, très
souvent présenté comme un idéologue bourgeois, ne s'écarte pas dans
son *Flis [Le Flotteur,* 1595] de la mentalité du noble satisfait de son
existence rurale, pour qui le comble de l'activité économique était la
transportation du blé jusqu'à Gdańsk, et qui considère les occupations
des gens de ville avec les yeux nettement méprisants et hostiles des
„bien nés" [44].

Le rapide développement de l'idéologie nobiliaire, imposée comme
l'idéologie pilote du pays tout entier, n'a pas permis, semble-t-il, de
venir à maturité l'ensemble d'idées et d'opinions d'orientation bourgeoise. Dès le XVIe siècle, à l'époque donc où le mécénat intense des bourgeois constituait une large base du développement de la culture urbaine,
naissaient déjà dans la mentalité sociale des embryons de dédain pour
les habitants des villes. Avec le temps, ce dédain a égalé en profondeur
celui manifesté aux paysans, devenant même peut-être plus violent, les
occupations urbaines étant mises en question du point de vue éthique.
Selon les écrivains nobles qui se faisaient en l'occurence les porte-paro-
les de l'ensemble de la noblesse, la ville est „un nid de vices et de men-
songe" et la pratique des occupations des villes est un procédé infa-
mant et, de par sa nature, même malhonnête. On doit se maculer
dans un milieu aussi criminel: „le marchand, vivant de perte du temps,
doit nécessairement oublier et la vérité et la foi et c'est pourquoi le
droit polonais interdit au noble les occupations urbaines", écrivait
St. Orzechowski, démontrant en même temps que „la nature de tous les
métiers est telle qu'ils sont licencieux et puants" [45]. Le créateur de la
littérature nationale polonaise, M. Rej, démontrait que l'apprentissage
de la profession marchande consistait en l'acquisition du savoir sur la
manière d'induire en erreur et de tromper le client [46]. Même A. Frycz-
Modrzewski, qui combattait la discrimination juridique des bourgeois
et soutenait que „tout homme doit manger son pain dans la peine [...]

---

[42] W. R o z d ż e ń s k i, *Officina Ferraria. A Polish Poem of 1612 Describing
the Noble Craft of Iron work,* Cambridge, Mass. 1976.
[43] Cf. *700 lat myśli polskiej. Filozofia i myśl społeczna XVI wieku* [700 ans
de pensée polonaise. La philosophie et la pensée sociale du XVIe s.]. Choix ét. et
réd. par. L. Szczucki, Warszawa 1978, p. 609 et suiv.
[44] M. B o g u c k a, *Kultura miejska* (ss presse).
[45] Cité d'après J. P t a ś n i k, *Miasta i mieszczaństwo w dawnej Polsce* [Les
villes et la bourgeoisie dans l'ancienne Pologne], Kraków 1934, pp. 368—369.
[46] *Ibidem,* p. 130.

et qui ne travaille pas qu'il ne mange pas", prisait plus haut le travail des champs que les occupations urbaines et louait la noblesse de ce qu'elle „ne s'occupe pas de métiers sales ni ne tire pas de bénéfices qui éveilleraient l'envie des hommes" [47]. Au XVIIᵉ siècle, à mesure que s'amplifiait la crise économique, que s'envenimaient les troubles monétaires et que baissait (du fait de la montée des prix des marchandises industrielles étrangères alors que les revenus des domaines restaient stagnants ou même se rétrécissaient) le niveau de vie de la noblesse, les attaques des publicistes nobles contre la bourgeoisie connurent une recrudescence. Déjà, le traité anonyme de 1611 caractérisait les marchands comme des usuriers et des faussaires et justifiait les difficultés par leurs „ruses" [48]. W. Gostkowski lance, en 1622, des imprécations contre l'enrichissement „des hommes avides et des marchands" aux dépens de la noblesse honnête [49], St. Zaremba accuse, en 1623, les marchands de démoraliser la société par l'importation d'articles de luxe, de pratiquer une „usure insupportable, de faire de la spéculation monétaire, de pousser artificiellement les prix et de toutes sortes d'autres „ruses" [50]. De là un pas seulement séparait de l'attaque violente d'Al. Olizarowski qui, au milieu du XVIIᵉ siècle, devait accuser les marchands de trahison, d'espionnage et d'actions pour le compte des ennemis du pays [51].

Même les „mercantilistes nobles" — W. Gostkowski, K. Opaliński, A. M. Fredro, qui voyaient pourtant la nécessité de développer les villes et les avantages découlant d'un commerce et d'une industrie développés, ne surent pas se défaire des accents de mépris pour les occupations des bourgeois. „Il ne sied pas au noble de s'amuser au métier marchand", constatait sans ambages Starowolski [52].

Les Lumières n'ont changé que partiellement cette situation. Les propagateurs de l'émancipation des villes étaient principalement des représentants de nobles et des magnats éclairés qui considéraient la chose, au fond, du point de vue des intérêts de la noblesse elle-même [53]. L'éveil de la bourgeoisie se faisait très lentement et surtout à Varsovie; aussi à propos de ce milieu varsovien seulement peut-on parler de

---

[47] A. F r y c z M o d r z e w s k i, *Dzieła Wszystkie* [*Oeuvres complètes*], Warszawa 1953, I, pp. 175 et 261.

[48] Cf. *Rozprawy o pieniądzu w Polsce pierwszej połowy XVII w.* [*Traités sur l'argent en Pologne dans la première moitié du XVIIᵉ s.*], éd. Z. Sadowski, Warszawa 1959, p. 85 et suiv.

[49] J. G ó r s k i, E. L i p i ń s k i, *Merkantylistyczna myśl ekonomiczna w Polsce XVI i XVII w.* [*La pensée économique mercantiliste en Pologne aux XVIᵉ et XVIIᵉ s.*], Warszawa 1958, p. 129 et suiv.

[50] *Ibidem*, p. 257.

[51] E. L i p i ń s k i, *Historia polskiej myśli ekonomicznej do końca XVIII w.* [*Histoire de la pensée économique polonaise jusqu'à la fin du XVIIIᵉ s.*], Wrocław 1975, p. 259.

[52] Sz. S t a r o w o l s k i, *Reformacja obyczajów polskich* [*Réforme des moeurs polonaises*], Kraków 1859, p. 168.

[53] M. B o g u c k a, *Kultura miejska* (ss presse).

la naissance au déclin du XVIIIe siècle d'éléments d'auto-conscience bourgeoise et de la formation d'un programme d'idées bourgeois indépendant, se trouvant dans l'opposition par rapport aux conceptions sarmates [54]. Le désastre du partage de la Pologne étouffa cependant dans l'oeuf ces phénomènes, consacrant la subordination idéologique de la bourgeoisie polonaise à la noblesse pour plusieurs décennies encore. Dans les conditions de la perte de l'indépendance politique, la noblesse — ce pilote des luttes armées pour la liberté — se plaça une fois de plus à la tête de la société polonaise et garda cette position tout au long du XIXe siècle.

Cet état de choses avait des répercussions très sensibles dans la sphère de la culture, et surtout dans celle de la mentalité sociale. A mesure que le sarmatisme habillait de couleurs de plus en plus chatoyantes la généalogie de la noblesse, célébrait ses vertus, son style de vie, son rôle politique et sa mission historique, le personnage du bourgeois devenait de plus en plus équivoque. La faible bourgeoisie polonaise n'était pas en mesure de s'opposer efficacement aux idées qui la désavouaient ni de créer son propre éthos qui célébrerait les vertus bourgeoises. Un rôle peu banal y est sans aucun doute incombé à la faiblesse de la Réforme dans le milieu bourgeois qui, en Europe Occidentale, avait nanti les habitants des villes d'une arme idéologique importante et accéléré leur émancipation [55]. Au profit du sarmatisme jouaient aussi l'horreur croissante de la menace turque et le développement de l'idéologie du „rempart" grâce à laquelle le modèle du chevalier-défenseur de la foi et de la patrie tout à la fois avait obtenu au XVIIe siècle une position particulière, se hissant au rang de modèle national [56]. Non sans importance aussi était la polonisation de la plupart des villes de la Couronne, accélérée à partir du XVIe siècle. Les groupes de nationalités allemandes, arméniennes, italiennes, à mesure qu'ils perdaient leur caractère distinct et se fondaient en une même entité, s'assimilaient ce qui, en ce temps, était la plus complète expression de la polonité — donc la culture créée par la noblesse, culture spécifique, teintée de fortes influences orientales, tranchant nettement sur les modèles culturels généralisés dans l'Occident plus „bourgeois" de l'Europe.

La noblesse des XVIe—XVIIIe s. en effet non seulement s'identifiait avec la nation; elle en était de fait la partie la plus avancée, la

---

[54] *Ibidem*. Cf. aussi K. Z i e n k o w s k a, *Sławetni i urodzeni. Ruch polityczny mieszczaństwa w dobie sejmu czteroletniego* [*Bourgeois et nobles. Le mouvement politique de la bourgeoisie pendant la Diète de Quatre Ans*], Warszawa 1976.

[55] M. B o g u c k a, *Towns in Poland and the Reformation. Analogies and Differences with Other Countries*, „Acta Poloniae Historica", XL, 1979.

[56] J. T a z b i r, *Les modèles personnels de la noblesse polonaise au XVIIe s.*, „Acta Poloniae Historica", XXXVI, 1977, p. 137 et suiv., souligne cependant le caractère défensif de ce modèle.

plus éveillée pour une vie nationale consciente mûre. Dans ces conditions, la polonisation devait nécessairement s'exprimer par la subordination à la noblesse et l'acceptation de son programme et de son idéologie — le sarmatisme. Ceci allait habituellement de pair avec la consolidation des influences de la Contre-réforme et l'épanouissement du catholicisme. Il est à remarquer que seuls les milieux qui avaient gardé une certaine spécificité ethnique et confessionnelle restaient récalcitrants au sarmatisme et à ses modèles idéologiques et éthiques. Un exemple caractéristique en la matière est fourni par les Juifs qui formaient d'importants groupes, hermétiquement fermés sous le rapport religieux et culturel et celui des moeurs, dans de nombreuses villes et bourgades. Plus caractéristique encore est l'exemple du milieu bourgeois poméranien. Du fait tant de leur force et de leur richesse que de leur faible polonisation (conditionnée entre autres par leur confession luthérienne et calvinienne, les contacts serrés avec la bourgeoisie hollandaise, allemande et scandinave, le sentiment de leur spécificité institutionnelle et juridique), les villes de la Prusse Royale constituaient des centres créateurs de culture comportant des traits originaux, spécifiques. La bourgeoisie poméranienne se caractérisait aussi aux XVIIe et XVIIIe s. par une indépendance de la pensée considérable, s'exprimant entre autres dans un criticisme marqué, et même agressif, à l'encontre de la noblesse et de son programme socio-politique. Ceci s'est exprimé notamment par la composition dans ces milieux justement du drame connu: *Tragedia o bogaczu i Łazarzu* [*Tragédie du riche et de Lazare*], avec ses accents antinobiliaires et antiaristocratiques osés [57], et par le développement d'une littérature historico-politique et juridico-économique d'orientation bourgeoise, souvent polémique contre les conceptions avancées par les écrivains nobles. Dans cette littérature apparaît visiblement la conscience de la force des grandes villes, le sentiment du caractère distinct de leurs intérêts, la fierté de l'appartenance à la communauté urbaine de Gdańsk, Toruń ou Elbląg, constituant comme une „petite patrie". Il faut cependant se souvenir que ce même milieu, fort et éveillé, ne se préoccupait pas de solidarité avec les intérêts des villes à l'échelle du pays tout entier, exploitant même, an alliance avec la noblesse, les rapports juridico-économique généraux en Pologne, défavorables pour la bourgeoisie [58]. Ce milieu a également créé, surtout au XVIIe siècle, des dizaines de poèmes historiques et politiques, de panégyriques, de vers, etc., toutes oeuvres teintées nettement de la mytho-

---

[57] Attribué autrefois (Al. Brückner) à Jan Guliński, lecteur de polonais au Gymnase de Gdańsk, il est considéré d'après les recherches récentes comme ayant été écrit par Marcin Gremboszewski, un musicien et poète au service du conseil municipal de la ville de Gdańsk, cf. T. W i t c z a k, *Teatr i dramat staropolski w Gdańsku* [*Le théâtre et le drame de l'ancienne Pologne à Gdańsk*], Gdańsk 1959, p. 30 et suiv.
[58] M. B o g u c k a, *Kultura miejska* (ss presse).

logie et des notes émotionnelles du sarmatisme, souvent dédiées directement aux souverains et aux magnats. Ainsi, même la culture de la Prusse Royale, ce territoire fortement urbanisé au regard des conditions polonaises et même européennes [59] et disposant d'une considérable spécificité sociale, nationale, morale et confessionnelle (victoire de la Réforme), se caractérisait par un mariage des éléments bourgeois et nobles, au point qu'il est difficile de parler ici de l'existence de deux modèles culturels égaux en droits: on a plutôt affaire à un modèle formé de la symbiose de courants diversifiés [60].

Vu son incapacité à développer un modèle propre de culture, la bourgeoisie, surtout ses couches supérieures, commence, dès le XVIe siècle, à subir l'influence de la culture nobiliaire, s'assimilant son idéologie, sa vision du monde, et même les mœurs nobles-sarmates avec, en tête, le penchant pour la consommation fastueuse. C'était un style bien éloigné du modèle de vie de la bourgeoisie occidentale où se développaient les idéaux de l'épargne, de la limitation de la consommation au profit des investissements productifs et de la multiplication du capital [61]. La fascination par l'éclat du blason se manifestait dans la tendance très forte non pas tant à abolir les barrières d'état qu'à se trouver de l'autre côté, „le meilleur", de ces barrières. L'idéal de la vie, surtout de la bourgeoisie cossue, est dès le XVIe siècle l'anoblissement, éventuellement l'entrée furtive dans les rangs de la noblesse par l'un des portillons illégaux [62]; aux XVIIe—XVIIIe siècles ces tendances connurent encore une recrudescence. Toute la bourgeoisie plus ambitieuse, désireuse de porter plus haut son statut social, fait siens les attributs considérés comme les symboles de la noblesse: l'opulent costume, multicolore, modelé sur la mode orientale avec le sabre indispensable au côté, la tenue orgueilleuse, la pratique d'un hobby noble (p.ex. la chasse), l'aménagement de gentilhommières à proximité des villes. Les protestations irritées de l'opinion nobiliaire, revendiquant des châtiments pour ce genre d'imitation, restaient en principe impuissantes [63]. De même l'intérieur du logis du bourgeois cossu différait peu aux XVIe—XVIIIe siècles de l'aménagement de la gentilhommière noble. Les plus récents dépouillements des inventaires bourgeois de ce temps mettent en lumiè-

---

[59] Les bourgeois y constituaient plus de 30%/o des habitants, cf. M. B o g u c k a, *Les villes en Pologne du XVe jusqu'à la fin du XVIIIe s.; structures sociales, morphologies urbaines, place dans la société*, „Studia Historiae Oeconomicae" (ss presse).
[60] M. B o g u c k a, *Kultura miejska* (ss presse).
[61] Cf. M. H o r w i t z ó w n a, *Reformacja polska a zagadnienie zbytku* [La Réforme polonaise et le problème du luxe], Reformacja w Polsce, vol. IV, 1926, et, dernièrement, St. S a l m o n o w i c z, *De la réglementation des coutumes et des mœurs bourgeoises à Toruń aux XVIe—XVIIIe siècles (aperçu de la problématique)*, in: *Studia Maritima*, vol. III (ss presse).
[62] M. B o g u c k a, *L'attrait de la culture nobiliaire? Sarmatisation de la bourgeoisie polonaise au XVIIe siècle*, „Acta Poloniae Historica", XXXIII, 1976, p. 30 et suiv.
[63] *Ibidem.*

re le faste des meubles, des tentures, des kilims, des armes, des collections de toiles, de l'argenterie, ainsi que la présence d'éléments caractéristiques des influences orientales, constituant la dominante des intérieurs nobles de ce temps. Le slogan sarmate „donne en gage mais montre-toi" était également suivi par la bourgeoisie dans les plaisirs de la table ou les fêtes de famille telles que baptêmes, fiançailles, mariages, enterrements, dont le cérémonial se modelait jusque dans les détails sur celui des „bien nés"[64]. Ainsi, les moeurs, les goûts et les prédilections des deux milieux sociaux, la noblesse et la bourgeoisie, se rapprochaient, surtout aux XVIIe—XVIIIe s., très considérablement. Un rôle peu négligeable y a sans doute été joué par la Contre-réforme et par les moyens baroques d'action de l'Eglise sur les fidèles, mis en oeuvre surtout par les jésuites, grâce à quoi s'uniformisaient les formes de dévotion et les rites qui s'y rattachaient, déterminant en même temps le rythme de la vie de famille et de société. Les fêtes et les célébrations y attachées, telles que la vigile de Noël, l'usage „chanter Noël", la sainte crèche, les festins du carnaval et du Carême-prenant, les célébrations du Carême et de Pâques, de la Pentecôte et de la Fête-Dieu, se ressemblaient assez sensiblement à la campagne et dans les villes. De même les jeux et divertissements de société dans les demeures bourgeoises et nobles ne différaient pas considérablement: on se passionnait pour les contes et les devinettes aux arguments identiques parce qu'itinérants, on jouait aux gages, à colin-maillard, au „mondain" et autres jeux d'ensemble peu compliqués; étaient aussi généralisés les osselets, les échecs, les cartes, la danse et la pratique de la musique. Dans les deux milieux régnaient des idées semblables sur la vie familiale et érotique, les canons de beauté et d'élégance différaient peu[65]. Sous ce rapport aussi la bourgeoisie s'efforçait de faire siennes les manières de la classe possédante, ses goûts et ses inclinations.

L'appréciation du rôle des villes et de la bourgeoisie dans le développement de la culture polonaise des XVIe—XVIIIe siècles est une chose compliquée. L'infériorité juridique et le refoulement de la bourgeoisie en marge de la vie politique et économique de la République, entraînèrent à n'en pas douter — dans une certaine mesure en tant que réaction à ces phénomènes — une activité culturelle décuplée de cette même bourgeoisie au XVIe et au début du XVIIe siècle. Cette activité était particulièrement intense dans le domaine de l'architecture, des arts, de l'enseignement et de la science, apportant à n'en pas douter des fruits abondants et diversifés. Dans la seconde moitié du XVIIe siècle et au XVIIIe, l'appauvrissement drastique arrêta cette activité de

---

[64] *Ibidem*. Cf. aussi J. A. C h r ó ś c i c k i, *Pompa funebris. Z dziejów kultury staropolskiej* [*Pompa funebris. Pages d'histoire de la culture de l'ancienne Pologne*], Warszawa 1974.
[65] M. B o g u c k a, *L'attrait*, p. 30 et suiv.

la bourgeoisie et l'accula à la défaite, dans la concurrence avec la noblesse, dans d'autres domaines encore. C'était un échec d'autant plus significatif que, dans le domaine de l'idéologie et de la mentalité sociale au sens large et des moeurs, la bourgeoisie subissait visiblement dès le XVIe s. les influences de la noblesse pour s'assimiler sous peu en entier la vision du monde et les usages sarmates. La ,,sarmatisation" de la bourgeoisie polonaise avait des conséquences immenses pour l'orientation générale du développement de la culture polonaise. A partir du XVIIe siècle, on peut pour une grande part l'identifier avec la culture nobiliaire, et cela du fait de l'absence de modèles culturels concurrentiels et de la subordination de toute la société en fait au modèle lancé par les ,,bien nés". La conséquence, ce devait être l'uniformité de la vision du monde, construite exclusivement à partir des modèles et des valeurs propagés par la noblesse [66]. Dans cette conjoncture devient compréhensible le culte des occupations argicoles et des vertus militaires, et le mépris pour les professions marchandes et artisanales, l'absence des impératifs d'épargne et d'assiduité au travail, la course après le luxe et l'envie de briller se substituant à la modestie, le manque du talent d'organisation au travail qui n'a pu se former — mais en revanche l'esprit de sacrifice, la faiblesse de vues mesquines et d'hypocrisie, traits véhiculés par le modèle mental bourgeois et petit-bourgeois [67]. Dans l'affrontement bourgeoisie-noblesse, la victoire incomba dans la République polonaise à cette dernière également sur le champ de la culture; la prise par la noblesse du ,,gouvernement des âmes" perpétué longtemps pendant l'époque des partages, devait être déterminante pour la spécificité de la culture nationale polonaise et la mentalité nationale jusqu'au XXe siècle.

(Traduit par Lucjan Grobelak)

---

[66] Cf. J. T a z b i r, *Modèles personnels*, p. 135 et suiv.; d u m ê m e, *La culture nobiliaire polonaise au XVIIe s.*, ,,Acta Poloniae Historica" XL, 1979; d u m ê m e, *Kultura szlachecka w Polsce. Rozkwit—upadek—relikty* [*La culture nobiliaire en Pologne. Epanouissement—décadence—vestiges*], Warszawa 1978.
[67] *Ibidem.*

IX

The towns of East-Central Europe from the fourteenth to the seventeenth century

Historians who study the specific features of the development of East-Central Europe in the late Middle Ages and in modern times usually concentrate on the transformations which took place in the countryside. For it is easy to assume that these are precisely the kind of studies that are of fundamental value to largely agrarian countries where the gentry were predominant in social, political and even cultural life. Only the past thirty years have brought increased interest in the history of towns in those areas, and this trend is particularly clear in Polish and Hungarian historiography. Since the special role of towns in the development of civilisation in the broadest meaning of the term has been acknowledged,[1] it follows that the analysis of their functioning is an important, even indispensable element in the attempts at elucidating the historical processes occurring in East-Central Europe. Here I shall discuss the fourteenth to the seventeenth centuries and, more particularly, the late fifteenth to early seventeenth century as a time of rapid changes in Europe. I shall concentrate mainly on Poland, with Bohemia and Hungary as a comparison, for their development shows considerable analogies alongside certain characteristic differences.

The urbanisation processes which in East-Central Europe began as early as the ninth to tenth centuries, proceeded at an increased pace during the fourteenth to fifteenth centuries. It is assumed that, as a result, by the end of the fifteenth century there were more than 600 towns in Poland (without Lithuania). Only five or six of them approached the figure of 10,000 inhabitants or exceeded it, this figure being considered, in accordance with medieval European standards, the threshold between a medium and large town. They were Gdańsk (30 thousand), Cracow (nearly 18 thousand), Lvov, Toruń, Elbląg (some 8 thousand each), Poznań and Lublin (some 6–7 thousand) and Warsaw (some 5–6 thousand). Nearly 80 towns numbered 2–3 thousand inhabitants, the rest were boroughs with 500 to 1,500 inhabitants. Thus, even if the density of the urban network on the Polish lands was considerable (one town for some 210 sq km), they were mostly small centres and placed much lower on the scale than the small towns of the West European type. The share of townsfolk in the population structure was also modest, amounting probably to some 15 per cent.[2] Urbanisation in Bohemia was similar at the time, with Prague (30 thousand inhabitants) occupying the first place; the other centres were much smaller (Brno some 8 thousand, Cheb and Kutná Hora some 5 thousand, České Budějovice, Hradec Kralové, Chrudim 3–4 thousand each).[3] Hungary's urban network was made up of even smaller centres. Only Buda's population amounted in the fifteenth century to 8 thousand; the rest had 4–5 thousand each (Bratislava, Sopron, Košice and Cluj; of mining towns, Banská Bystřica and Banská Štiavnica), or some 3 thousand (Pest, Szeged, Székesfehérvár, Trnava, Prešov, Bardějov, Levoča, Brașov and Sibiu; of mining towns Gelnica and Kremnica). Altogether it is assumed that in the late Middle Ages there were in Hungary some 30–35 towns, all small by European standards, whose population was estimated at around 3 per cent of the country's total population.[4] But next to them there existed some 800 boroughs (*oppida*) without full legal and political municipal status, subordinated to feudal jurisdiction, the economy of which rested on farming and breeding, but which functioned in part as towns in the field of trade and production and even social life (parishes, schools, hospitals).[5] Their rapid development was one of the characteristic features of urbanisation in Hungary at the time. These boroughs numbered 500–1,000 inhabitants on average.[6]

The process of urbanisation in East-Central Europe in the sixteenth to seventeenth century is a controversial subject. The slowing down of that process and the crisis of towns in that area have been variously dated, which is partly due to the specific features of particular regions. It seems that the earliest urban crisis occurred in Hungary, namely as early as the mid-fifteenth century (according to L. Mákkai and J. Szücs), perhaps in the early sixteenth (A. Kubinyi). In Bohemia, the first symptoms of a crisis appeared in the sixteenth century, and mostly in its later half (J. Janáček). Polish historians have shifted the beginning of the urban crisis to the late sixteenth century, some even to the later half of the seventeenth. Indeed, there is no doubt that throughout the sixteenth century, and partly also in the seventeenth, a colonisation was carried out on the Polish lands (according to A. Wyrobisz's calculations, 25 per cent of Polish towns were then established); in many existing towns the population increased considerably up to the mid-seventeenth century. At the end of the sixteenth century, the urban population amounted probably to some 20 per cent of Poland's inhabitants (Lithuania not included).[7] Some historians have raised this estimate to 22.5 per cent. Naturally, the degree of urbanisation in different parts of the country was not the same. Next to highly urbanised regions where the townspeople amounted to more than 30 per cent (Royal Prussia), or over 20 per cent of the total population (Great Poland, Little Poland, Silesia which in the fourteenth century belonged to the Kingdom of Bohemia), there were areas where the urban population constituted only upwards of 10 (Mazovia) or just a few per cent (the eastern borderlands).[8] Worth recalling, by way of comparison, is the fact that according to K. J. Beloch's calculations the inhabitants of towns at that time in some parts of northern Italy constituted over 50 per cent of the total population.[9] During the sixteenth century, the urban population in Holland increased from 46 per cent (1514) to 54 per cent (1622). The level of Poland's economic development, measured in terms of urbanisation, was thus much lower than in Western Europe, particularly in its leading regions. Although the urban network became denser in the Polish lands during the sixteenth century and by its end numbered more than 700 centres (without Lithuania and Silesia), yet only eight of them exceeded 10,000 inhabitants: Gdańsk (50 thousand by the end of the sixteenth century and probably some 70 thousand in the first half of the seventeenth), Warsaw (probably around 30 thousand in the early seventeenth century), Cracow (28 thousand), Poznań (some 20 thousand), Toruń, Elbląg, Lublin and Lvov (some 10 thousand). In the Grand Duchy of Lithuania, Vilna was quite an important town (15 thousand inhabitants by the end of the sixteenth century, 20 thousand in the mid-seventeenth). Towns with 4–5 thousand were considered medium size (Sandomierz, Kazimierz Dolny, Gniezno, etc.), but the majority consisted of townships with a population of 500–2,000[10] with farming as the predominant occupation, which invested them with a half-rural character.

At the time, Silesia, which as mentioned earlier did not then form part of the Polish state but was closely connected with it economically, had attained a high degree of urbanisation. Wrocław, which by the end of the fourteenth century numbered 20 thousand inhabitants, exceeded 30 thousand in the early seventeenth century. In the sixteenth century, Świdnica had over 11 thousand, Głogów some 10 thousand, Nysa 7–8 thousand; of the other Silesian towns, Lwówek had around 4 thousand, Bolesławiec, Jawor, Jelenia Góra and Strzegom 3 thousand each, while the rest (38 centres) had from a few hundred to 2 thousand inhabitants. Strangely enough, in the second half of the sixteenth century a certain decline in the proportion of townspeople in the population of Silesia as compared with the fourteenth century has been noted.

Wars drastically influenced the development of the urbanisation processes. In Silesia, the Thirty Years' War and the accompanying epidemics caused the Wrocław population to fall in 1640 to under 20 thousand; these losses were made good in the seventies of that century, but only in the eighteenth century did the population increase significantly. Other Silesian towns also suffered painful losses in population which were only very slowly made good. Apart from sporadic exceptions, no new towns were being chartered. Consequently, at the end of the seventeenth century, the percentage of the urban population in the demographic make-up of Silesia fell to 17; at the same time, the importance of agricultural occupations in towns increased. In Poland, similar results followed the devastation caused by the Swedish invasion in the mid-seventeenth century. Sixty per cent of the architectural substance in many towns was destroyed (the figure for Great Poland was 62.5 per cent); the losses in the demographic substance have been estimated on a similar scale, especially as they occurred as a consequence both of the hostilities and of plagues. The revival was very slow and so the share of the townsfolk in Poland's population in the eighteenth century has been estimated at barely 16 per cent. Thus the end of the seventeenth century was something of a return to the situation obtaining in the late Middle Ages. Another factor in the decline of Poland's urbanisation, a factor difficult to measure, was the extremely rapid growth of rural occupations in towns, where an estimated two-thirds of the population were employed in this way.

In Bohemia, as in Poland, the urban network became denser in the sixteenth century, but there, too, small and very small centres predominated. The only big town on the European scale was the capital city of Prague which had 50 thousand inhabitants in the second half of the sixteenth century, and even 60–70 thousand at the beginning of the seventeenth century, according to some scholars. The other Bohemian towns did not exceed 10 thousand (Cheb 7–8 thousand, Olomouc 5–7 thousand, Brno 4–5 thousand, České Budějovice, Hradec Kralové, Kutná Hora, Plzeň 3.5–4 thousand each) most of them numbering less than three thousand. There were cases of rapid growth in towns connected with a temporary development of, for example, mining: here a classic example is that of Jáchymov, whose inhabitants grew from one thousand in 1516 to 14 thousand by 1526. But these were short-lived growths. Altogether, the inhabitants of Czech towns at the end of the sixteenth century probably constituted over 20 per cent of the country's population.[11] The Thirty Years' War was responsible there, too, for considerable population losses; Prague fell to 30 thousand, and it was only in the early eighteenth century that it reached the figure of 40 thousand. In the sixteenth to seventeenth century the number of townsfolk engaged in farming also rose, although it seems that there this phenomenon did not reach the proportions noted in Poland and Hungary.

In Hungary, noticeable disturbances in her urban development appeared as early as the beginning of the sixteenth century, especially after the defeat at Mohács in 1526 and the division of the country into three parts, of which one remained under Turkish rule for 150 years; the rapidly depopulating towns of that zone (e.g. Buda and Pest) declined to the level of garrison towns. The situation was worsened by the military operations of 1591–1604 and conflicts with the Habsburgs in the seventeenth century. In the sixteenth to seventeenth century the population of the majority of Hungarian towns did not exceed the fifteenth-century level.[12] Some development was noticeable in a few trading centres (due, amongst other things, to the influx of fugitives from Buda and Pest), such as Pozsony and Trnava and in mining centres such as Banská Štiavnica. But in most towns the population declined so that they numbered barely 2–3 thousand inhabitants.[13] At the same time, the rank of agricultural occupations rose in towns.[14] The development of half-urban boroughs (*oppida*) was also characteristic of the time; besides cattle-breeding, vineyard cultivation and corn growing, trade and crafts were concentrated there; the urban functions of such boroughs expanded and their size grew, e.g., Debrecen numbered 7–8 thousand inhabitants in the mid-sixteenth century.[15] The urbanisation of Hungary in the sixteenth to seventeenth century rested mainly on the network of such boroughs.

This very brief survey suggests that a characteristic feature of East-Central Europe in the fourteenth to seventeenth century was its fairly dense urban network, made up of very small centres, often half-rural. As a matter of fact, only five towns in this region can be reckoned well-developed medium, perhaps even large, centres: Gdańsk, Prague, Warsaw, Wrocław and Cracow. The rise of the so-called second serfdom hindered the influx of peasants as early as the late fifteenth century in Poland, and later on in Bohemia and Hungary, and this in turn had an extremely adverse impact on the growth of towns in that zone. If the fourteenth to fifteenth century was a period of rapid urban development, the next period, sixteenth to seventeenth century, brought a reverse trend. At that time, urbanisation in East-Central Europe consisted mainly of the multiplication and development of small, half-rural centres, whereas in Western Europe this period saw the growth of big towns, numbering over 100,000 inhabitants (there were only five in the early sixteenth century, but twelve in the late seventeenth).[16] Consequently, both as regards quantity (the proportion of town-dwellers in the total population) and quality (the prevailing demographic type, the role of farming occupations) the urban backwardness of East-Central Europe as compared with the West was increasing.

In the opinion of the majority of historians, this backwardness should not be linked with the military events mentioned earlier. They played a significant but not decisive role in the history of the towns of Poland, Bohemia and Hungary. According to the latest studies, a much more important factor was the specific nature of the trade linking East-Central with Western Europe which emerged in the fifteenth century and continued to grow in the sixteenth to seventeenth century. It consisted of a broad range of imports of industrial and luxury goods and exports of raw materials, agricultural and forest produce (Poland exported grain and forest produce; Bohemia grain, wine, cattle and metals; Hungary wine, cattle and metals).[17] Such a structure of trade slowed down the development of these countries' own industrial production which was deprived of opportunities to sell its goods not only to the great nobles and the gentry but also to the townsfolk and the better-off among the peasants who, according to many studies of Poland and Hungary, would buy foreign commodities to the detriment of the local producer.[18] Hungarian (E. Fügedi, A. Kubinyi, L. Mákkai, J. Szücs), Polish (M. Małowist, A. Mączak, H. Samsonowicz, B. Zientara) and Czech historians (J. Janáček, A. Míka, J. Petráň,

J. Zemlička) have emphasised the weakness of urban artisans, caused by such a situation, and their petrification in guilds in the sixteenth and seventeenth centuries. Characteristically, the number of guilds rose in that period, sometimes reaching the figure of 50–60, and there developed fierce demarcation disputes among them, their backwardness in techniques and organisation increasing all the time. It is interesting to note that the idea of suppressing guilds, entertained by the gentry in Poland, and by the gentry and the rulers (Charles IV in Bohemia and later also the Habsburgs) in Bohemia and Hungary, was not carried out in practice, so that the guild system survived in East-Central Europe at a time when in the West it was gradually disintegrating. The guild system was too weak here to offer effective opposition to the competition of foreign goods; yet it was strong enough to monopolise production in the hands of a small number of privileged masters, limit the possibilities of enlarging particular workshops and oppose technical innovations.

The urban artisans were also adversely affected by the competition from craftsmen often supported by the gentry or even organised by them not only in the countryside but also in the property owned by the gentry in towns; the question of the so-called *a parte* or non-guild craftsmen became acute in the sixteenth to seventeenth century, because, among other things, of the restrictive policy of the guilds. In Poland such crafts were centred in an increasing number of houses and even whole town quarters belonging to the gentry (called *iurisdictiones*) and remaining outside the municipal law.[19] The situation was similar in Silesia and some Czech towns. In Hungary there was a rapid development of an artisan class in the half-agrarian *oppida*.[20] Yet production remained essentially small-scale, all the more so as at the turn of the sixteenth century the worsening economic conditions in the countryside and the shrinking purchasing power of the peasantry restricted demand. Consequently, in East-Central Europe very few big manufacturing centres emerged which would supply both the immediate neighbourhood and also the more outlying areas. The few exceptions only confirmed the rule. Among them was Gdańsk, which at the turn of the sixteenth century expanded into a large manufacturing centre with 3 thousand workshops supplying various commodities (textiles, furniture, arms, metal products, glassware, pottery, tools, toys, etc.) to customers throughout Poland and exporting to Scandinavia. Next came Wrocław (with 1,200–1,400 workshops at the turn of the sixteenth century). But in general East-Central European towns did not develop their own crafts (except, perhaps, the food industry) to a degree sufficient even to meet the local demand. Characteristic examples are those of the big residential centres at the end of the sixteenth century such as Warsaw and Prague, where the number of local workshops was very small and the demand for industrial products was met by foreign imports. Particularly 'stunted' was the development of crafts in Hungary where the share of artisans in the professional make-up of the towns was strikingly low (20–30 per cent).[21] The situation in Bohemia was different, with craftsmen making up 40–50 per cent of the population in many towns; it is there that in the late Middle Ages several regions emerged making textiles for large-scale export abroad (to Austria, Poland and Hungary). This flourishing of Bohemian and Moravian cloth-making did not last long; it declined in the last quarter of the sixteenth century. Also short-lived was the development of textile-manufacturing regions of some strength in Poland (Sieradz and Łęczyca voivodships in the sixteenth century, Great Poland and Royal Prussia in the seventeenth).

The organisation of production in the areas of interest to us did not undergo any large-scale transformations so characteristic of Western Europe, particularly towards the end of the Middle Ages. Even in the sixteenth to seventeenth century the small workshop with a slight output capacity, the master working personally with the help of 2–3 journeymen and apprentices, was typical of Poland, Bohemia and Hungary. The guilds fiercely resisted all attempts at increasing the size of workshops and all technical innovations. The example of Gdańsk, where in the sixteenth to seventeenth century a crisis of the guild organisation occurred and biggish manufacturing units developed fairly strongly, is an exception. Bohemian, Moravian and Polish textile-exporting townships worked on the basis of a putting-out system: attempts at organising centralised manufactories did not really appear in East-Central Europe until the second half of the seventeenth century (Bohemia), and still more in the eighteenth century (Poland).[22] This was related to the weakness of early capitalism. Indeed, the development of such manufactories can only be linked with some branches of production: mining, especially Bohemian and Hungarian,[23] production of iron and glass, and shipbuilding (Gdańsk, Elbląg). The development of various forms of the putting-out system, mostly organised by merchants, only increased the backwardness of East-Central European crafts. Numerous Polish, Czech and Hungarian scholars have emphasised that the craftsmen in those regions were poor and that they achieved prosperity by engaging in other occupations rather than plying their crafts. In the market conditions prevailing in these parts, productive activity did not allow of any accumulation of capital on a larger scale. Doubtless, a significant role was played by the prices policy extorted by the gentry. In Poland, after attempts made in the fifteenth century (1423, 1454, 1465, 1496), the regulation of prices for industrial products was entrusted to the palatines in 1565. Somewhat later, at the turn of the sixteenth century, such price lists were issued by the gentry in Bohemia and Hungary.[24] The crafts, poor and weak, became a prey to large-scale expansion of usurers and merchants, often foreigners; good examples of this can be seen in the activity of south-German merchants, as well as of the English and Dutch in Bohemia and Silesia.[25] Foreign capital also exploited Hungarian and Bohemian mining.[26] Another characteristic feature was the increased involvement of the gentry and magnates in the sphere of mining as is evident in Poland (Olkusz and the salt mines of Wieliczka and Bochnia) and

Bohemia (Jáchymov). Capital expenditure in mining was limited and it exhibited a tendency towards a wasteful exploitation which resulted in declining production.

The movement of foreign capital to the territories of East-Central Europe was particularly forceful in the field of credit and big trade. Gdańsk's overseas trade, which developed in the fourteenth to fifteenth century, turned in the next two centuries into a passive intermediary in its own port between the gentry and foreign skippers. It is assumed that at the end of the sixteenth century some 80 per cent of the Baltic trade was in the hands of the Dutch, who earned enormous profits from it.[27] Dutch merchants tried also to control the trade between Gdańsk and its hinterland by way of credits and the dependence of Gdańsk firms on their capital. A similar activity was carried out by south-German merchants in Hungary and Bohemia (direct organisation of imports and exports or the control of local merchants through credits).[28] It can safely be asserted that the development of trade in East-Central Europe was considerably weaker than in the West. Capital accumulation proceeded on a much more modest scale; truly big banker and merchant fortunes were rare and emerged only in the more developed centres of the region. The banking house of the Loitz family in Pomerania in the sixteenth century dealt in hundreds of thousands of thalers; its activity (loans to rulers, mining projects, big commerce) brings to mind the dealings of the famous Fuggers: even the bankruptcy of both the Loitz family and the Fuggers was to a large extent caused by the same factors.[29] But there are not many such analogies. At the close of the fifteenth century, the fortunes of the big merchants in Gdańsk amounted to from 14 to 30 thousand marks, that is, from 230 to 280 kg of pure silver. In the first half of the seventeenth century, there were in Gdańsk some merchants whose property amounted to 300–600 thousand Polish florins, that is the equivalent of some 2,500–4,500 kg of pure silver.[30] Yet in Warsaw the fortune of the biggest merchant in the late sixteenth century, Sigismund Erkemberger, amounted to barely 50–60 thousand Polish florins (i.e., the equivalent of only 1,000–1,200 kg of pure silver). On the Gdańsk level were the fortunes of the wealthiest Prague merchants in the first half of the seventeenth century: Eustachius Betengel's estimated at some 312,500 Rhine guldens, and Lorenz Stark's estimated at some 212,500 Rhine guldens; the Jewish banker of Prague, Markus Maisel, left half-a-million Rhine guldens in ready money. But the rest of the Prague merchants ranked far below those three, only a dozen or so having reached the figure of 37,500 Rhine guldens. In Hungary a few thousand guldens were thought to be quite a fortune for a merchant.[31] For the sake of comparison it is worth recalling that the Fuggers' legendary riches ran into millions of guldens (in 1527 their firm's assets totalled three million guldens, in 1557 two million guldens).[32] In the first half of the seventeenth century, the accumulated capital of the Netherlands firm of De Groote-Hureau-van Colen amounted to 500,000 Flemish pounds or more than

30,000 kg of pure silver.[33] Moreover, such a fortune was nothing extraordinary in Western Europe.

Besides the competition on the part of strong foreign merchants, the East-Central European middle class also felt keenly the competition of the gentry which, particularly in the sixteenth and seventeenth centuries, organised its own sales of agricultural crops and the purchase of foreign goods, by-passing the local burghers. This happened particularly in Poland where the gentry, having obtained exemption from customs duties in 1496, almost monopolised the transport of grain down the Vistula to Gdańsk where, in turn, they bought various industrial products. In the early seventeenth century, the share of the gentry in the trade with Gdańsk amounted to some 70 per cent, that of the townsfolk only 20 per cent. Similar trends developed in Bohemia, where throughout the sixteenth century the gentry vied with the towns for economic rights.[34] In Hungary not only the gentry but also the wealthy peasants competed with the burghers by attempting to monopolise the cattle, wine and corn trade.[35] During the sixteenth century, both the Bohemian and Hungarian gentry obtained exemption from paying customs duties and tolls which the townspeople were obliged to pay.[36]

A feature characteristic of the development of East-Central Europe, and one with far-reaching consequences, was the rapid outflow of merchant capital from the towns. The purchase of landed estates occurred as early as the fourteenth to fifteenth century, but in the following centuries it became the chief means of spending money earned from commerce (besides hoarding, luxury consumption and artistic and building patronage). Both entire towns (among particularly big landowners were Gdańsk and Prague)[37] and single merchants owned villages and landed estates. In Poland this was a procedure formally legalised in the sixteenth to seventeenth century only in respect of the inhabitants of towns granted 'noble rights' (Cracow, Vilna, Lvov), and to towns in Royal Prussia (Gdańsk, Elbląg, Toruń), but in practice it was quite common and was followed by inhabitants of all the major urban centres.[38] The situation in Silesia was similar,[39] as well as in many Bohemian and Hungarian towns.[40] Of course, investing capital in land was not exclusive to those areas. In the sixteenth and seventeenth centuries, the wealthy English, French, German and Dutch townspeople also invested considerable sums in landed estates; R. Mandrou has even considered this tendency a permanent feature, a mental structure characteristic of the early modern era, and emerging almost all over Europe.[41] But the point is that, in the territories covered by this survey, the outflow of capital from the towns caused by this tendency was not, as in the West, made good by increased economic activity in other fields, primarily in production and trade; it created gaps which weakened the economic potential of towns in a permanent way. This led to a so-called 'feudalisation' of the East-Central European burghers and their merging into the gentry. A complete break with urban occupations and a move to the countryside would often occur as early as the second generation.[42] Even those people who stayed in towns tried to imitate the gentry's life-style and took over its cultural patterns and ideals.[43] This subordination of the urban culture to the nobles was particularly strong in the seventeenth century in Poland and Hungary; after the wiping out of the Bohemian gentry in the battle of the White Mountain (1620) and the emigration which followed, the development of culture in Bohemian towns proceeded along different paths.

The outward movement of the rich townspeople and their capital went parallel to an opposite movement, that of the influx of the gentry into towns. In the fourteenth and fifteenth centuries, the right to own property in town was enjoyed in principle exclusively by its burghers, although there were exceptions to this rule.[44] It was the constitution of 1550 which opened the doors wide to the development of gentry property in Polish towns; it allowed the gentry to own property in towns provided the municipal taxes were paid.[45] This condition was not fulfilled and the urban real estate belonging to the clergy, gentry and magnates increased at a quick pace, in some centres such as Warsaw and Cracow reaching over 50 per cent of all property.[46] Similar processes took place in Bohemian towns, the most glaring instance being Prague which, like Warsaw, became in the seventeenth century a large agglomeration of mansions of the gentry and palaces belonging to magnates. In Hungary the influx of the gentry into towns in the sixteenth and seventeenth centuries was magnified by the fear of the Turks.[47] The Diets of 1553 and 1563 ordered the towns to accept the gentry provided they did not free themselves from municipal taxes; ultimately in 1647, the Hungarian gentry was definitively allowed to settle in towns and exempted, their servants included, from all municipal burdens and jurisdictions.[48]

The dwindling of burghers' property in towns meant the defeat of that estate, all the more painful as it was suffered on their own territory, in that stronghold which (both in reality and in the social feeling) was constituted in the Middle Ages by an area encircled with walls and reserved for the burghers alone, to whom had been granted numerous monopolistic rights and privileges relating to its surroundings. Strongly connected with this is the problem of the development of the estate consciousness of the burghers in East-Central Europe as well as of the political role played by towns in the fourteenth to fifteenth century, and which was later, in the sixteenth to seventeenth century, linked with the question of the towns' autonomy and rights.

Not all the towns in East-Central Europe had the autonomy and legal freedom characteristic of West European cities as early as the twelfth to thirteenth century; they were enjoyed only by the free royal towns. In central Poland (not including the Ruthenian lands) there were 264 of them by the close of the seventeenth century out of the total of 741 urban centres. In Bohemia, the proportions were very similar, whereas in Hungary the number of royal towns did not exceed 30 to 35. The other towns were the private property of feudal lords: their burdens were very much like those of the rural villein services (including rent in kind and sometimes even labour services); they were subjected to feudal jurisdiction and had a more-or-less restricted self-government. The number of private towns increased rapidly in the sixteenth to seventeenth century in Poland, Bohemia and Hungary, and they became typical of that part of Europe. Their development strengthened neither the burghers nor the ruler but the rich noblemen, that is, the feudal elements in the socio-political structure. Moreover, during the sixteenth to seventeenth century, the royal towns became enfeebled and the range of their self-government and legal freedoms shrank visibly. In Poland, the royal towns came under the burdensome control of royal officials. A similar subordination developed in Bohemia, where the years between the Hussite revolution and the late fifteenth century are considered the peak of the self-government and judicial autonomy of the royal towns. The famous Diet of 1547 put the Bohemian royal towns under the control of special royal officials, as had been the case in Poland. The Hungarian royal towns also went through a flourishing period of self-government and legal freedom in the later half of the fifteenth century.[49]

As regards the political rights of towns, there was greater differentiation. The situation was worst in the Polish towns. Only in the fourteenth and fifteenth centuries did they take part in important political events, such as elections of kings, approval of international treaties, etc. The second half of the fifteenth century brought a considerable weakening of such activity and, consequently, the exclusion of the towns from the just emerging Polish Diet. The Bohemian and Hungarian towns were politically extremely active throughout the fifteenth century. In the early sixteenth century (1517) the representatives of Bohemian towns obtained, despite the gentry's opposition, the confirmation of their right to what was called the third voice in the national Diet. In 1547 this right was taken away, yet a limited representation of the towns in the Diet was maintained. The Hungarian towns also retained – albeit with difficulty – their participation in the Diet up to the late seventeenth century.[50]

The politically inferior situation of the Polish townsfolk was certainly bound up with their less-developed estate awareness. One of the criteria of such awareness is the ability to cooperate with other towns and to set up unions for the promotion of interests covering more than a single town. According to the scheme proposed by E. Lousse, three levels should be distinguished: (1) the capacity to establish *ad hoc* defensive coalitions; (2) the capacity to establish permanent unions in the defence of common interests; (3) the capacity to force the granting of estate privileges.[51] The Polish townsfolk attained the first level in the fourteenth and first half of the fifteenth century (urban confederations in 1349, 1350, accession to the gentry confederations in 1464 for the last time). From the second half of the fifteenth century, the Polish towns did not have it in them to undertake any broader solidary action even of an occasional defensive type. The Bohemian and Hungarian towns, on the other hand, exhibited a strong activity in forming unions (according to the second level of Lousse's scheme) not only in the fifteenth century but throughout the sixteenth and well into the seventeenth century. It was due to their active role in the great social and national movements such as the Hussite revolution and later the Reformation as well as to their participation (in alliance with the gentry) in the opposition against the Habsburgs in the sixteenth and seventeenth century. Although the townspeople suffered repression after the defeats inflicted on this opposition, their participation alongside the gentry awakened their estate consciousness. In this regard, they were nearer to the conscious and politically active Dutch and English town dwellers – who in the sixteenth to seventeenth century were slowly getting ready for a bourgeois revolution – than were the inhabitants of the Polish towns, politically immature and incapable of forming any ideology of their own.[52] These are matters very little studied so far and they certainly require broad comparative studies, particularly from the national and ethnic aspect. The undertaking of such studies would also mean examining, in a broader way than heretofore, the specific features of the development of burgher culture in East-Central Europe and its obvious slowing down precisely at a time when it reached its peak in the West (the Netherlands and Italy).

The considerations here have, of necessity, been stated with extreme brevity, and only the most important questions relating to the development of East-Central European towns have been touched upon. But even such a summary review reveals the specificity of the urban processes in the areas of interest to us. This specificity was doubtless one of the important elements in the different paths of the general development followed by East-Central Europe in the fourteenth to seventeenth century.

NOTES

7. The towns of East-Central Europe

1 Mumford (1961), chap. 1; Sjöberg (1960), pp. 5f; Rausch (1963), pp. 9, 13f; Abrams and Wrigley (1978), pp. 215f.
2 According to H. Samsonowicz, 'Liczba i wielkość miast późnego średniowiecza Polski', *Kwartalnik Historyczny*, 86, 1979, part 4, p. 16.
3 Zemlička (1978).
4 Bonis (1974); Fügedi (1956); Granasztoi (1956); Györffy (1960); *History of Hungary* (1973), pp. 87, 103; Kubinyi (1977); Mályusz (1927); Szücs (1955, 1963).
5 *History of Hungary* (1973), p. 87; Mályusz (1953); Szabó (1960); Székely (1960, 1963).
6 *History of Hungary* (1973), p. 105.
7 Samsonowicz (1963), p. 92.
8 *ibid.*, p. 93.
9 Beloch (1961), pp. 339–85.
10 Bogucka (1976b), p. 131.
11 It is estimated that at this time the royal towns in Bohemia had about 200,000 inhabitants.
12 Szücs (1963), pp. 149–50.
13 There was decline in Košice, Bardějov, Prešov, and Levoča; Szücs (1963), pp. 149–51. Higher figures have recently been given for Košice.
14 In sixteenth-century Hungary, the proportion of the urban population involved in vine growing rose from 63 per cent to 80 per cent: Szücs (1963), p. 125.
15 Székely (1963), p. 83.
16 Cipolla (1976), p. 42; Mauersberger (1960); Mols (1954–6).
17 Bog (1971). Cf. Amber (1960); Hoszowski (1960); Mákkai (1963); Małowist (1959); Rusiński (1959).
18 Mákkai (1976); Mákkai and Zimányi (1978); Samsonowicz (1976).
19 Bogucka (1976b), pp. 140–1.
20 Szücs (1963), pp. 118f, 141f.
21 *ibid.*, pp. 100, 103.
22 It is worth emphasising the fact that in many of these industries, organised by the rich gentry, serf-labour was used. The establishments did not have a capitalist character.
23 Molenda (1976); Paulinyi (1971); Probst (1966); Vozar (1971).
24 Szücs (1963), pp. 148, 160.
25 Aubin (1942); Zimmermann (1885); Zimmerman (1956–8).
26 Ehrenberg (1896); Pölnitz (1960); Strieder (1935).
27 In a forthcoming study, the author estimates the annual profit from the exports of Baltic grain to Western Europe in the first half of the seventeenth century as the equivalent of 26–36,000 kg of pure silver.
28 Szücs (1963), pp. 111f.
29 Papritz (1957).
30 See the author's forthcoming history of Gdańsk, vol. 2.
31 Szücs (1963), pp. 110, 135.

32 Ehrenberg (1896).
33 Baetens (1976), vol. 2, pp. 82–3.
34 These rights included the organisation of fairs and the production and sale of beer as well as the cattle and grain trade.
35 Pach (1968b); *History of Hungary* (1973), p. 137.
36 Szücs (1963), pp. 128, 136, 137.
37 In the middle of the fifteenth century, Gdańsk became the owner of more than 70 villages, thanks to the privileges of King Casimir, and the figure was to be increased later by purchase. At the end of the fifteenth century the city of Prague owned about 100 villages, and more still at the beginning of the sixteenth century; all this property was confiscated in 1547. The property of Hungarian towns was more modest; at the end of the fifteenth century, for example, the city of Košice owned 24 villages (Szücs, 1963, p. 101). After attempts to take their rural property away from the towns, in 1608 the Hungarian Diet declared that only communities owning land and serfs should be regarded as towns. The point was to reduce the number of places with the rights of towns (Szücs, 1963, p. 154).
38 The Polish Diets of 1496 and 1536 forbade burghers to own land, but this rule was broken all the time: Bogucka (1976a).
39 Petry (1935), pp. 147f.
40 Szücs (1963), pp. 114–15, 118, 125, 135–7.
41 Mandrou (1969), pp. 12f.
42 In Warsaw, for example, all the old families disappear from the city in the second half of the seventeenth century.
43 Bogucka (1976a); Szücs (1963), pp. 158f; see also McCagg (1972).
44 Bogucka (1976b), p. 135.
45 *ibid.*, pp. 135–6.
46 *ibid.*, pp. 136–8.
47 Szücs (1963), p. 156.
48 *ibid.*, pp. 157–8.
49 Bonis (1974), pp. 79–92.
50 Szücs (1963), p. 158.
51 Lousse (1937).
52 Bogucka (1976a, 1980).

Bibliography

This bibliography contains all the works cited in the references to chapters 1–12, whether directly concerned with East-Central Europe or not.

APH   Acta Poloniae Historiae
AÉSC   Annales: Économies, Sociétés, Civilisations
EcHR   Economic History Review
JEEH   Journal of European Economic History
P&P   Past and Present
SHASH   Studia Historica Academiae Scientiarum Hungariae
SHO   Studia Historiae Oeconomicae
VSWG   Vierteljahrschift des Sozial- und Wirtschaftsgeschichte

Abel, W. (1935) Agrarkrisen und Agrarkonjunktur, Berlin. Trans. Agricultural Fluctuations in Europe, London 1980.
    (1973) 'Hausse und Krisis der europäischen Getreidemärkte', in Mélanges F. Braudel, Toulouse.
Abrams, P. and Wrigley, E. A. (eds., 1978) Towns in Societies, Cambridge.
Amber, G. (1960) 'Zur Geschichte der Aussenhandels Ungarns im 16.Jh.', SHASH 44.
Ammann, H. (1970) Die wirtschaftliche Stellung der Reichstadt Nürnberg, Nuremberg.
Anderson, P. (1974) Lineages of the Absolutist State, London.
Angyal, E. (1961) Die slawische Barockwelt, Leipzig.
Arnoldsson, S. (1960) La leyenda negra, Gothenburg.
Attman, A. (1973) The Russian and Polish Markets in International Trade, Gothenburg.
Aubin, G. and Kunze, A. (1940) Leinenerzeugung im östliche Mitteldeutschland, Stuttgart.
Aubin, H. (1942) 'Die Anfänge der grossen schlesischen Leinweberei und Handlung', VSWG 35.
Backvis, C. (1957) 'Les thèmes majeurs de la pensée politique polonaise au 16e siècle', Annuaire Institut Philologie Histoire Orientale Slave 14.
Baetens, R. (1976) De nazomer van Antwerpen welvaart, 2 vols., Brussels.
Balogh, J. (1975) Die Anfänge der Renaissance in Ungarn, Graz.
Barkan, C. (1957) 'Les données des registres de recensement dans l'empire ottoman', Journal of Economic and Social History of the Orient 1.
Bastian, F. (1944) Das Runtingerbuch, Regensburg.
Belényesi, M. (1957) 'Der Ackerbau und seine Produkte in Ungarn in 14.Jh.', Acta Ethnographica 6.
Bellettini, A. (1973) 'La popolazione italiana', Storia d'Italia 5, ed. R. Romano and C. Vivanti, Turin.

191   Bibliography

Beloch, G. (1900) 'Die Bevölkerung Europas im Mittelalter', *Zeitschrift für Sozial-wissenschaft* 16.
Beloch, K. J. (1961) *Bevölkerungsgeschichte Italiens*, 3, Berlin.
Benda, G. (1973) 'Production et exportation des céréales en Hongrie, 1770–1870', in Köpeczi and Balázs.
Berend, I. and Ránki, G. (1974) *Economic Development in East Central Europe in the Nineteenth and Twentieth Centuries*, New York and London.
Bergier, J. F. (1963) *Genève et l'économie européenne* , Paris.
Białostocki, J. (1976) *The Art of the Renaissance in Eastern Europe*, Oxford.
Biraben, J. N. (1975) *Les hommes et la peste*, Paris and The Hague.
Blaschke, K. H. (1967) *Bevölkerungsgeschichte von Sachsen*, Weimar.
Bog, I. (ed., 1971) *Der Aussenhandel Ostmitteleuropas 1450–1650*, Cologne and Vienna.
Bogucka, M. (1976a) 'L'attrait de la culture nobiliaire', *APH* 33.
      (1976b) 'Quelques problèmes de la socio-topographie des villes de Pologne', *APH* 34.
      (1977a) 'Le sel sur le marché de Gdańsk', *SHO* 11.
      (1977b) 'The Vasa Dynasty in Poland', *Kungliga Akademiens Årsbok*.
      (1980) 'Towns in Poland and the Reformation', *APH* 40.
Bökönyi, S. (1961) 'Die Haustiere in Ungarn im Mittelalter', in *Viehzucht und Hirtenleben in Ostmitteleuropa*, Budapest.
Bonis, G. (1974) 'Die ungarischen Städte am Ausgang des Mittelalters', in Rausch.
Braudel, F. (1949) *La Méditerranée et le monde méditerranéen à l'époque de Philippe II* . Second ed. 1966. English trans. 2 vols., London 1972–3.
Browne, E. (1673) *A Brief Account of Some Travels*, London.
Bruce, W. (1598: ed. C. H. Talbot, 1965) *Relation of the State of Polonia*, Rome.
Burke, P. (ed., 1972) *Economy and Society in Early Modern Europe*, London.
Cipolla, C. (ed., 1976) *Fontana Economic History of Europe* 2, London.
Cipolla, C. (*et al.*, 1963–4) 'Economic Depression of the Renaissance', *EcHR* 16.
Cynarski, S. (1968) 'The Shape of Sarmatian Ideology in Poland', *APH* 12.
Dávid, G. (1977) 'The Age of Unmarried Children in the Tahrir Defters', *Acta Orientalia* 31.
Długosz, J. (1863) *Liber Beneficiorum Diocesis Cracoviensis*, Cracow. *Domande e consumi*, Florence 1978.
Ehrenberg, R. (1896) *Das Zeitalter der Fugger*, Leipzig. Abridged English trans. by H. M. Lucas, *Capital and Finance in the Age of the Renaissance*, London 1928.
Ember, G. (1971) 'Ungarns Ausserhandel mit dem Westen um die Mitte des 16.Jhs.', in Bog.
Evans, R. J. W. (1973) *Rudolf II and his World*, Oxford.
Faber, J. A. (1966) 'The Decline of the Baltic Grain-Trade in the Second Half of the 17th Century', *Acta Historiae Neerlandicae* 1.
Faber, J. A. (*et al.*, 1965) 'Population Changes and Economic Development in the Netherlands', *Afdeling Agrarische Gschiedenis Bijdragen* 9.
Filipowicz, T. (1932) 'The Accomplished Senator', *Proceedings of the American Society for International Law*.
Fügedi, E. (1956) 'Kaschau, eine osteuropäische Handelstadt am Ende des 15.Jh.', *Studia Slavica* 2.
      (1969) 'Pour une analyse démographique de la Hongrie médiévale', *AÉSC* 24.
Gieysztorowa, I. (1958) 'Guerre et régression en Masovie aux 16e et 17e siècles', *AÉSC* 13.
      (1968) 'Research into the Demographic History of Poland', *APH* 18.
Glamann, K. (1976) 'European Trade 1500–1750', in Cipolla.
Goldenberg, S. (1976) 'Les échanges économiques entre les pays roumains et l'occident', *Fifth International Congress of Economic History*, vol. 6, Moscow.

X

The Typology of Polish Towns during the XVI th - XVIII th Centuries

They are hundreds of definitions of a town resulting from a large variety of urban situations occurring in different regions and in different periods. Polish scholars regard the special juridical situation as the main feature of a town; the settlements endowed with city rights (among others — personal freedom of the inhabitants according to the saying 'Stadtluft macht frei') are acknowledged as towns — even if their size, inner structure of functions sometimes differ substantially from the Western type of town.

The diversity of urban centres leads inevitably to attempts at their classification. Polish towns, as everywhere else, can be classified though with considerable simplification, according to some basic criteria, such as their legal position, their size, their functions. In this article we will try to establish the typology of Polish towns in early modern times according to those three basic criteria.

1. A crucial element defining the status and character of a town in Poland was its legal position, which resulted mostly from the circumstances of its origin and its foundation. Polish towns in the early modern period should be thus divided into royal, referred to the sources also as 'free cities' and private ones. Of the 1,336 towns existing in Polish territory at the beginning of the seventeenth century 368, that is only 27.5%, were royal towns; 964, that is 72.2%, others owed their existence to the organising efforts of private landowners: magnates, clergy, rich gentry.[1] The

---

[1] See M. Bogucka - H. Samsonowicz, *Dzieje miast i mieszczaństwa w Polsce przedrozbiorowej* (The History of Towns and Towndwellers in Pre-partitioned Poland), (Wrocław 1986), p. 400.

urbanisation process, which in Poland began as early as the nineth century, accelerated during the sixteenth century and following centuries. According to A. Wyrobisz's recent estimates, 25% of Polish towns were established in the sixteenth century and 8% in the first half of the seventeenth century; this means that overall in this period one third of Polish towns were created.[2] Their foundation resulted mostly from the urbanising activity of the nobility. In Little Poland in the sixteenth and seventeenth centuring only 19 out of 186 towns were royal ones - that is, 10,2%. In Great Poland only 5 out of 50 towns which were founded in the sixteenth to eighteenth centuries were royal ones - that is about 10%. In Mazovia in the sixteenth century they were 40 towns - of which 4 were royal ones - again 10%.[3]

The growth in number of private towns had a big impact on Polish urbanisation. Historians rightly stress the fact that this phenomenon resulted in cutting off the majority of town-dwellers process in Poland from the direct protection both of the Polish state as well as of Polish Kings. It is true that private town-owners very often asked the King to confirm the foundation and endorse the privileges given to the new town; nevertheless they controlled every aspect of town life, even though its inhabitants enjoyed - at least to some extent - personal freedom and were given many privileges and rights comparable to those possessed by the inhabitants of the royal towns. The right to take legal action against the owner was limited to a very small group of private towns.[4] Private towns were also usually smaller than royal towns, they belonged mostly to groups III and IV shown below in our tables. The modest demographic size of the private towns contributed to their general weakness and increased their subordination to the

---

[2] A. Wyrobisz, "Rola miast prywatnych w Polsce XVI i XVII w." (The Role of Private Towns in Poland during the XVIth and XVIIth centuries), *Przeglad Historyczny*, 1974, no. 1, passim.
[3] M. Bogucka, H. Samsonowicz, *Dzieje miast*, p. 399.
[4] *Ibid.*, pp. 395-96.

owners. The existence of private cities on such a large scale - a phenomenon well known also in Bohemia and Hungary - greatly influenced the whole structure of urban society in Central Europe and gave the urbanisation process in those parts of the European continent quite distinct features.

2. The size of Polish towns constitutes another important factor of their typology. Some elements of the demographic classification can be found directly in documents of the sixteenth to eighteenth centuries. Besides the main division into two groups, *civitates and oppida,* more diversified and specific qualifications were in usage. The tax register of 1520 distinguishes, for example, 4 groups of towns: 1. *civitates maiores* (Cracow, Poznań, Lwow); 2. *civitates et oppida secundi ordinis* (Kazimierz, Wieliczka, Bochnia, Sącz, Biecz, Pilzno, Tarnów, Proszowice, Miechów, Lelów, Sandomierz, Lublin, Radom, Opoczno, Wiślica, Szydłów, Opatów, Iłża, Bodzęcin, Kalisz, Kościan, Wschowa, Bydgoszcz, Brześć, Płock, Wieluń, Łęczyca, Gniezno, Łowicz, Wolborz, Uniejów, Koźmin, Żnin, Buk, Słupca, Rawa, Sochaczew, Brzeziny, Piątek, Szamotuły, Grodzisko, Koło, Przemyśl, Krosno, Sanok, Jarosław, Przeworsk, Łańcut, Rzeszów, Brzozów); 3. *oppida habentia fora annua et septimanalia; 4. oppida non habentes fora.*[5] In 1590 towns were also divided into 4 groups: 1. *civitates primi ordinis;* 2. *civitates secundi ordinis;* 3. *civitates tertii ordinis;* 4. *oppida non habentes fora.*[6] In 1673 the Seym Constitution divided all towns into two classes. The first one included a) extra big towns (according to Polish standards) such as Cracow, Poznań, Lublin, Warsaw, Zamość; b) *civitates primi ordinis;* c) *civitates secundi ordinis;* d) *civitates tertii ordinis.* The second class included small towns and townships subdivided again into three sub-classes: *prima, secunda,* and *tertia.*[7]

5   *Corpus iuris Polonici,* ed. O. Balzer, (Kraków 1906), vol. III, p. 597.
6   *Volumina legum,* ed. J. Chryzko, (Petersburg 1859), vol. III, p. 597.
7   Ibid., vol VIII, p. 88.

In 1775 Polish towns were divided according to their size, importance and occupation structure into 4 groups.[8] Only Warsaw was included in the first group. The second group included larger towns such as Cracow, Poznań, Wschowa; and the third, smaller townships, which were endowed, however, with urban rights and had more than 300 households. The 4th group was composed of small rural townships with fewer than 300 households. In 1793 a new classification was drawn up for the first time with the use of administrative and not only demographic criteria.[9] The towns were grouped into three categories: 1. 'main centres', such as Warsaw, Cracow, Lublin, Sandomierz, Łuck, Wilno, Grodno, Brześć Litewski, Kowno, Nowogródek; 2. towns with over 400 households in which the meetings of the gentry from *voivodships* and the provinces were held; 3. townships endowed with city rights and where at least one parish was established, even if they had actually fewer than 400 households.

The classification used in the sources from early modern times - however instructive - lacks precision; the dividing lines between groups are rather fluid and many towns appear at one time in one group and another time in another group. Greater accuracy was possible only after more sophisticated methods of analysis were used. The global results of recent demographic research on Polish towns are given in the two tables set out below.

As we can see, at the end of the sixteenth century (Table 1) group I (towns with more than 10 thousand inhabitants) comprised only 7 centres: Poznań (18-20 thousand), Warsaw (10-12 thousand), Cracow (22-25 thousand), Gdańsk (40 thousand), Toruń (12 thousand), Elbląg (15 thousand), Lwów (20 thousand), that is 0.5% of the total. Likewise, there were only a few towns with between 2 and 10 thousand inhabitants (a little more than 15% of the total). In Great Poland in this group there were: Gniezno

[8]   *Ibid.*
[9]   *Ibid.* vol. VIII, p. 398.

1. Polish towns according to their size at the end of the sixteenth century.[10]

Province	I		II		III		IV	
	Number	%	Number	%	Number	%	Number	%
Great Poland	1	0.5	27	10.5	200	78.5	27	10.5
Mazovia	1	0.9	27	25.2	35	32.7	44	41.2
Royal Prussia	3	8.3	4	11.1	25	69.5	4	11.1
Warmia	-	-	1	8.3	7	58.3	4	33.4
Podlachia	-	-	2	8.0	21	84.0	2	8.0
Little Poland	1	0.5	32	15.2	98	46.2	80	38.1
Red Ruthenia	1	0.4	10	4.7	119	55.4	85	39.5
Wolhynia, Podolia, Ukraine	-	-	45	10.6	62	14.6	319	74.8
Total	**7**	**0.5**	**148**	**11.5**	**567**	**44.1**	**565**	**43.9**

I - more than 10 thousand inhabitants
II - between 2 and 10 thousand inhabitants
III - 600-2000 inhabitants
IV - less than 600 inhabitants

2. Polish towns according to their size in the second half of the eighteenth century.[11]

Province	I		II		III		IV	
	Number	%	Number	%	Number	%	Number	%
Great Poland	1	0.5	29	13.9	103	49.5	75	36.1
Mazovia	1	0.8	3	2.9	46	44.3	54	52.0
Royal Prussia	3	7.0	2	4.7	38	88.3	-	-
Warmia	-	-	1	8.3	11	91.7	-	-
Podlachia	-	-	2	5.4	21	40.5	20	54.1
Little Poland	1	0.6	8	4.7	104	61.2	57	33.5
Total	**6**	**1.0**	**45**	**7.8**	**317**	**55.3**	**206**	**35.9**

[10] The table does not cover the Grand Duchy of Lithuania. See M. Bogucka - H. Samsonowicz, *Dzieje miast*, p. 371.
[11] *Ibid.*, p. 379

(4-5 thousand), Kalisz (3-4 thousand), as well as Sieradz, Szadek, Łęczyca, Wschowa, Kościan, Konin, Koło, Piotrków, Leszno, Warta, Żnin, Międzyrzecz, Szamotuły, Śrem, Pyzdry.[12] In Mazovia in group II we find Plock, Lomz´a, Przasnysz, Ciechanów, each with more than 4 thousand inhabitants, then Łowicz, Pułtusk, Rawa, Sochaczew, Brok, Ostrw, each with more than 3 thousand inhabitants.[13] Even in Royal Prussia small towns were the most numerous (the III group accounting for 88.3%) and the high urbanisation of this province (the share of burghers in the total population of this province was 36.5%[14]) was based on the existence of three big centres (Gdańsk, Elbląg, Toruń), where 61.8% of Prussian burghers lived[15]. In Warmia the biggest town - Braniewo - had between 5 and 6 thousand inhabitants; other towns (91,7% in group III) had from 1,500 to 2,500 inhabitants. In Little Poland group II was comparatively large (15.2%), with mining centres such as Wieliczka (4-5 thousand), Olkusz (5-6 thousand), Bochnia (3 thousand) as well as lively trade centres such as Sandomierz, Kazimierz, Biecz and Nowy Sącz (each between 4 and 5 thousand inhabitants). But the most numerous group here was also group III (46.2%). In Red Ruthenia the biggest towns were - beside Lwów - Przemyśl (5-6 thousand) and Zamość (4-5 thousand). But again the most numerous was group III (55.4%). In Ukraine, group II included Kijów, Bracław, Winnica, Kaniów which together made up only 10.6% of the total. The most numerous group in this region were the smallest towns found in group IV, counting less than 600 hundred inhabitants. Almost 75% of Ukrainian towns belonged to this group.[16]

To sum up: at the end of the sixteenth century the large and

---

[12] *Dzieje Wielkopolski* (The History of Great Poland), ed. J Topolski, (Poznan 1969), p. 461 nn.
[13] *Atlas historyczny Polski: Mazowsze w drugiej polowie XVI w.* (Historical Atlas of Poland: Mazovia in the Second Half of the XVIth century), (Warszawa 1973), p. 83.
[14] M. Bogucka - H. Samsonowicz, *Dzieje miast*, p. 364.
[15] *Ibid.*
[16] *Ibid.*, p. 375.

medium-sized towns of group I and II made up only about 12% of the total while 88% were small or very small towns. Another characteristic was the ratio between group III and IV in different parts of the country. In the so-called eastern borderlands group IV totalled 43.9% and group III - 44.1%, that is, they were almost equal. In central Poland, however, the largest was group III (58.7%); group IV, composed of the smallest towns, made up only 28.6% of the total. In general at the end of the sixteenth century the burger's share could be estimated at around 20-25% of the total population.[17] Both the size of Polish towns as well as the share of town-dwellers in the population structure of the country were rather insignificant, at least according to West-European standards. It was, however, a situation rather similar to the situation in all Central European countries, e.g. Bohemia and Hungary.

After many devastating wars and rapid agrarianisation of the country since the middle of the seventeenth century, the urban underdevelopment of Poland grew worse in the second half of the eighteenth century. Table 2 (restricted to central Poland and Royal Prussia, not including the south-eastern regions lost to Poland in the first partition of 1772), shows only 6 towns in group I: Poznań (11-12 thousand inhabitants), Cracow (21 thousand), Gdańsk (50 thousand), Toruń (10 thousand), Elbląg (11-12 thousand), Warsaw (90-100 thousand).[18] At the end of the sixteenth century the number of urban centres in group II fell from 11.5% to 7.8%. Small centres in groups III and IV, which in table 1 made up 88%, in table 2 rose

---

[17] *Ibid.*, p. 360 nn. In my article "The Grain Fields, Lords and Serfs" in: *Rural Landscapes*, ed. Wim Blockmans and Juan Gelabert (series Making of Europe), Connecticut 1994, Educational Corporation, p. 58, the editors included (neglecting my protests!) an evidently erroneous statement: "around 80% of Poland's population in the late Middle Ages were free peasants", which underrates Polish urbanisation. Because of this error and others I warn the readers against this publication. At the end of the Middle Ages the urban population in Poland should be estimated at about 15-20%, nobility at about 8-10%, which means that peasants made up at most 70% only of the total population, A law in 1496 decided that only one peasant could leave the village yearly - how could we truthfully speak about a free peasantry in those times?
[18] M. Bogucka - H. Samsonowicz, *Dzieje miast*, p. 381.

to 91% of the total. In some regions the number of very small towns in group IV rose very quickly - for instance in Great Poland from 10.5% to 36.1%, in Mazovia from 41.2% to 52.0%, in Podlachia from 8% to 54.1%. Unfortunately the situation in Little Poland in tables 1 and 2 could be not compared because table 2 does not cover the eastern regions of this province, lost in 1772, in which the small towns were the most numerous.

In general it could be said that the share of very small towns in Poland's urban structure grew rapidly during the early modern period. At the same time the share of burghers in the total structure of the country's population shrank - at the end of the eighteenth century it should be estimated at about 16% only.[19]

3. If we now move to the classification category which emphasizes towns' functions we first should point out that about 90% of all Polish towns were of the mixed kind, with both commercial and manufacturing activities geared mostly to the needs of a local market. Only a few large towns were involved in long- distance trade, which included international commerce. In this group we find sea-ports (Gdańsk, Elbląg), big river-ports (Cracow, Warsaw, Toruń) and the centres situated at major crossroads of overland routes (Poznań, Lwów, Zamość, Lublin - but also Cracow and Warsaw). As a special group of commercial towns, the medium-sized centres along the river should be mentioned, where grain, and forest products were bought and where ships and rafts for their further transportation were built, repaired, sold or rented (such as Sandomierz, Kazimierz, Włocławek). Some medium-sized towns situated on land routes were also involved in long-distance, overseas trade (Biecz, Stary and Nowy Sącz, Gniezno and others). In fact, every Polish town in the sixteenth-eighteenth centuries fulfilled some commercial function. Medium-sized and even small centres collected the agricultural products of their regions, selling at the same time imported luxury goods to the

---

[19] *Ibid.*, p. 366 nn.

gentry. Small towns were engaged in busy local trade with petty nobles and peasants, buying and selling agricultural products as well as all basic commodities. Some of those small townships also acted as intermediaries between their rural hinterland and large cities. In many towns services for the transit trade flourished: they offered merchants in transit accomodation, meals, waggon transport, repairs, etc. These towns could also be included in the commercial category.

There were few centres of specialized production in Poland - such as the mining towns of Wieliczka, Bochnia and Olkusz in Little Poland, or the textile-producing towns of Great Poland (Brzeziny, Wschowa, Bojanowo, Rawicz, Szadek). The towns of Iłża, Łagów and Potylicz in Little Poland were famous for their pottery, which was sold in the whole country and even as far as the Duchy of Lithuania.[20] In general, however, production was rather dispersed with a variety of crafts and other semi-specialist occupations in every town. The biggest centre of production (textiles, ship-building, ironware production, glass production etc.) was Gdańsk with its more than 3 thousand legal craftshops and an equal number of illegal craftshops in the first half of the seventeenth century.[21] But even in the small towns more than 20 different occupations were recorded.[22] Crafts were particularly numerous in private towns, whose owners wanted to have many different specialists at their disposal and service. As a result the emergence of some really big production centres, which manufactured goods on a large scale, cannot be regarded as typical in Poland in early modern times.

No banking centres emerged in Poland in the same period, at least not centres which are comparable to Italian, German or French ones. The biggest financial operations were concentrated in

---

[20] Cf. A. Wawrzyńczyk, *Studia z dziejów handlu Polski z Wielkim Księstwem Litewskim i Rosją w XVI w.* (Studies in the History of Trade between Poland and the Grand Duchy of Lithuania and Russia in the XVIth C.), (Warszawa 1956), p. 67-68.
[21] M. Bogucka, *Gdansk jako ośrodek produkcyjny w XIV-XVII w.* (Gdańsk as a Production Centre in the XIVth-XVIIth Centuries), (Warszawa 1962), pp. 163-165.
[22] M. Bogucka, H. Samsonowicza, *Dzieje miast*, p. 436 nn.

Gdansk and in other big towns, such as Cracow, Lwów, Lublin, where rich merchants encountered the gentry. In the second half of the eighteenth century Warsaw did become a large modern banking centre. Credit operations were also conducted during the so-called 'contract gatherings' held in different cities such as Poznań, Lwów, Przemyśl, Łuck, Bełz and others. Contract gatherings had developed from fairs where transactions for the sale and purchase of landed property, leasings and rentings were carried out; they were attended by magnates and the gentry as well as by rich burghers who offered loans and other financial services to the gentry.

Many towns, such as Głogów, Cegłów, or Szczuczyn, were founded in the sixteenth to eighteenth centuries as markets for the big landed estates owned by magnates and rich nobles. This category of town had a characteristic layout with a very big central square, rural architecture and large plots used often as gardens and fields. The inhabitants of these townships combined urban activities - trade and crafts - with rural or semi-rural occupations: brewing beer, rearing cattle and pigs, cultivating gardens and fields. Some scholars maintain that in the middle of the seventeenth century every second Polish burgher earned more than a half of his livelihood from agriculture and gardening. The agrarian functions of Polish towns - production of foodstuffs and of alcohol - greatly affected the economy of the country, especially from the middle of the seventeenth century.

A very important group of new towns founded in this period mostly in the eastern borderlands, were residential cities. They served as a context to the magnate's residence, built in Italian style (we could cite here the example of Zamość, Żółkiew and later Rydzyna). Often at the same time they served as a fortress against the permanent threat of Turkish and Tartar invasions (the most famous examples of this category were Żółkiew and Brody). Many of these cities, however, quickly gained considerable importance in trade, too, keeping up extensive commercial relations between East and West. They fulfilled the complicated residential and military as well as economic functions, at the same time serving as fortresses and markets, or transit places. Therefore they hardly fit into one typology.

Foundations which grew out of religious feeling should be regarded as a distinct group of towns. These consisted of so-called "Calvaries": chapels and routes conceived as a reproduction of the Stages of the Cross along with monasteries. The surrounding small towns based their existence upon catering for clergy and pilgrims. The most famous examples are Kalwaria Zebrzydowska in Little Poland, Pakość in Kujavien, Wejherowo in Royal Prussia. As a typical pilgrimage centre we should mention Częstochowa with its famous monastery and church as well as others centres for religious worship of the Mother of God such as Święta Lipka, Gidle, Borki, Piekary Śląskie, Berdyczów etc., where church and monastery were the centre of the city and where the urban social structure was dominated by butchers, bakers, shoemakers, that is, by crafts which were certainly most necessary in a place playing host to a large number of pilgrims every year.

Many Polish towns fulfilled administrative and socio-political functions. There were two capitals in Poland in this period: the old one, Cracow, where coronations and burials of the kings were celebrated and - since 1596 - the new capital, Warsaw, where the residences of kings and dignitaries of the state were established. Here general diets as well as royal elections were also held.

Several medium and small-sized towns also fulfilled socio-political functions. They served as meeting places for the gentry's conventions (so-called *sejmiki*) and law tribunals (Koło, Kalisz, Środa, Wieluń, Wschowa, Łęczyca, Sieradz, Dobrzyń in Great Poland; Piotrków, Korczyn, Proszowice, Opatów, in Little Poland; Czersk, Ciechanów, Liw, Łomża, Różan, Raciąż, Zakroczym in Mazovia; Malbork and Grudziądz in Royal Prussia; Chełm, Bełz, Wisznia, Halicz in Red Ruthenia). They housed offices of jurisdiction and were seats of royal officials, the so called *starostas*. Because of these functions some of the medium-sized towns, such as Piotrków or Radom, retained many characteristic features of a capital town. The Polish gentry preferred to choose a small town rather then a larger one for their conventions. It is difficult to establish the exact reason for such behaviour: was it to reduce the high costs of a stay in a large city or rather a wish to avoid, if possible, contact with urban life, regarded by the Polish gentry as inferior in comparison to rural living? Another factor was possibly the long distance to the large towns - hence the natural wish to make a shorter trip and be home earlier, which meant assembling in the nearest urban centre. This is why the category of administrative towns and those where the nobility's conventions were held were especially numerous.

An important group of towns were centres especially connected with science and education. During the period there were only two university towns in Poland: Cracow in Little Poland and (since 1579) Wilna, in the Great Duchy of Lithuania. But in the sixteenth century, the Academy of Lubrański in Poznań and, from the middle of the sixteenth century, the famous high schools in Gdańsk and Toruń, virtually operated as universities, drawing young people from the whole country as well as from abroad. In Zamość an academy was founded in 1594, which was intended to become a rival to the University of Cracow. In many medium-sized towns there was a mushrooming of secondary schools with an extremely high level of teaching and with a wide range of research activities, such as the Protestant schools in Raków, Pińczów, Leszno, Sieraków and Jesuits colleges in Pułtusk and Braniewo. The number of scholars and students in some medium-sized and small towns sometimes exceeded the number of burgers. The existence of an academy or of a high school always had a strong impact on the town's life and often superseded its original functions. In Wilna, however, and in Cracow and Zamość, which were large towns with diverse economic and social functions, the professional bodies of teachers and students numbered a few hundred persons and represented only a small sector of a much bigger and diversified urban community.

To sum up: the number of funtional categories of Polish towns was rather large. It would, however, be hard to find many "pure" examples of towns of a certain type: nearly every Polish town in the period under study could fit into several of the above mentioned functional categories.[23] The classification according to legal status (royal-private) and size appears clearer, though we should remember that demographic factors were also changing constantly. Nevertheless attempts at classifying towns are very important for building a general picture of the urbanisation process of Polish lands in early modern times.

---

[23] A. Wyrobisz came to similar conclusions in 'Functional Types of Polish Towns in the XVIth-XVIIIth Centuries', *The Journal of European Economic History*, vol. 12, no 1, 1983, pp 69-103.

XI

Krakau - Warschau - Danzig.
Funktionen und Wandel von Metropolen 1450-1650

Zur Erforschung der Stadttypologie haben mehrere Historiker beigetragen[1]. Trotz vieler Arbeiten sind jedoch die Begriffe Hauptstadt, Residenzstadt, Metropole, auch der Begriff Zentralort, nicht klar definiert und werden sehr oft als Synonyme benutzt. Darum wollen wir zu Beginn nach einer Definition suchen.

Das Wort "Zentralort" paßt zu allen Stadttypen. Jede Stadt ist für ihre Umgebung, ihre Region, ihr Land ein "Zentralort"; in dieser Bedeutung eines Zentralpunktes bündelt sich die tiefste, doch sehr allgemeine Stadtnatur. Das heißt aber zugleich, daß diese Bezeichnung für die Unterscheidung der verschiedenen Stadttypen nicht brauchbar ist.

Die Begriffe Hauptstadt und Residenzstadt hat am besten Edith Ennen definiert. Sie schreibt: "Die Besonderheit dieses Stadttyps ergibt sich primär aus der politischen Funktion der Hauptstadt ... Eine Hauptstadt ist Sitz der zentralen Organe und Behörden eines Staates, zum mindesten der wichtigsten, also 1. des Staatsoberhauptes, wenn es nicht als Fürst eine Residenzstadt neben der Hauptstadt besitzt oder durch seine Anwesenheit in der Hauptstadt diese zur Residenz- und Hauptstadt macht; 2. des Parlamentes bzw. der Ständeversammlungen; 3. der klassischen Ministerien bzw. vor 1800 der diesen entsprechenden obersten Kollegialbehörden ...; 4. der diplomatischen Vertretungen; 5. meistens, aber nicht unabdingbar, des obersten Gerichtshofes und des zentralen Archivs. Die Hauptstadt beherbergt also die Spitze der Staatsapparatur ..., von der Hauptstadt gehen die entscheidenden

---

1 Vgl. Hauptstadt, Zentren, Residenzen, Metropolen in der deutschen Geschichte. Hg. v. Bodo-Michael Baumunk/Gerhard Brunn. Köln 1989; Hauptstädte. Entstehung, Struktur und Funktion. Hg. v. Alfred Wendehorst/Jürgen Schneider. Neustadt an der Aisch 1979; Hauptstädte in europäischen Nationalstaaten. Hg. v. Theodor Schieder/Gerhard Brunn. München/Wien 1983; Residenzen. Aspekte hauptstädtischer Zentralität von der frühen Neuzeit bis zum Ende der Monarchie. Hg. v. Kurt Anderman. Sigmaringen 1992; Kersten Krüger: Die deutsche Stadt im 16. Jahrhundert. Eine Skizze ihrer Entwicklung. In: Zeitschrift für Stadtgeschichte, Stadtsoziologie und Denkmalpflege 2 (1975) Heft 1, S. 31-47; Heinz Stoob: Über frühneuzeitliche Städtetypen. In: Dauer und Wandel der Geschichte. Festgabe für Kurt von Raumer. Münster 1965, S. 163-212; Andrzej Wyrobisz: Functional Types of Polish Towns in the 16th-18th Centuries. In: The Journal of European Economic History 12 (1983), S. 69-103.

politischen Impulse aus; die dort verabschiedeten Gesetze und gefaßten Beschlüsse werden über die der zentralen Exekutive unterstehenden Behörden im ganzen Land durchgeführt"[2].

Im Unterschied zu mehreren anderen Forschern sieht Ennen die Verknüpfung einer Hauptstadt mit dem Nationalstaat nur als eine Möglichkeit, nicht als Conditio sine qua non[3]. Eine Residenzstadt dagegen ist eine Stadt, in der sich die Residenz eines Königs, Fürsten oder Magnaten befindet[4]. Hauptstadt und Residenzstadt sind oft, wenngleich nicht immer, ein und dieselbe Stadt, haben aber viele Berührungspunkte[5]. Es ist zu unterstreichen, daß nur wenige Forscher eine Metropole zu definieren versucht haben. In der Literatur kann man aber eine allgemeine, fast instinktive Überzeugung verspüren, daß die Metropole eine sehr große Stadt sein müsse; man knüpft den Begriff der Metropole an deren demographische Dimensionen[6]. Philip S. Florence definiert eine Metropole als die größte Stadt in einem Land, zumindest zweimal so groß wie die nächst große Stadt[7]. Roger Finlay führt in seinem Buch über London aus, daß in der zweiten Hälfte des 16. Jahrhunderts London schon als eine Metropole bezeichnet werden könne. Um 1600 zählte die Stadt ca. 200 000 Einwohner, das waren etwa 5% der gesamten Landesbevölkerung. Londons demographische Größe war in dieser Zeit in England ohne Beispiel: die Metropole überragte die größte Provinzstadt um das Zwanzigfache[8].

Auf die Übergröße der Stadt wie auch auf die Übergröße ihres Hinterlandes - erstes Kennzeichen einer Metropole - stützen sich die verschiedenen Funktionen, die eine Metropole ausübt. Eine ausgebaute Multifunktionalität soll also als ein zweites wichtiges Merkmal einer Metropole genannt werden.

Das Wort Metropole stammt vom altgriechischen Wort *metropolis*, d. h. Mutterstadt[9]. Und unabhängig davon, ob wir die Metropole vom Stadtstaat streng abgrenzen, kann man doch behaupten, daß quasi "mütterliche" Funktionen für eine Metropole typisch sind. Die Übergröße bildet nämlich einen Grund für die außergewöhnliche Anziehungs- und Ausstrahlungskraft, durch die eine Metropole mit ihrem Hinterland verbunden ist. Die Größe dieses Hinterlandes entspricht der Größe der Metropole und deckt sich meist mit einer ganzen Region oder mit einem ganzen Land; das Hinterland einer Metropole kann auch

2 Edith Ennen: Funktions- und Bedeutungswandel der "Hauptstadt" vom Mittelalter zur Moderne. In: Hauptstädte in europäischen Nationalstaaten (wie Anm. 1), S. 154f.

3 Ebd., S. 155f.

4 Vgl. Edith Ennen: Residenzen. Gegenstand und Aufgabe neuzeitlicher Städteforschung. In: Residenzen (wie Anm. 2), S. 189-198.

5 Dies. (wie Anm. 2), S. 154.

6 Vgl. Roger Finlay, Population and Metropolis. The Demography of London 1580-1650. Cambridge 1981; Patterns of European Urbanisation since 1500. Hg. v. H. Schmal. London 1981.

7 Philip S. Florence: Economic Efficiency in the Metropolis. In: The Metropolis in Modern Life. Hg. v. Robert M. Fisher. New York 1955, S. 85.

8 Finlay (wie Anm. 6), S. XI.

9 Vor kurzem behandelte das Problem Basilica Papoulia: Megalopolis in the Greek World. In: Chronia 50 (1992), S. 141-148.

weltweite Dimensionen haben. Wir werden also eine Regionalmetropole von einer Natio-nalmetropole oder einer Weltmetropole unterscheiden.

Um diese außergewöhnliche Anziehungs- und Ausstrahlungskraft ausüben zu können, muß eine Metropole ein leicht zugänglicher Ort sein[10]. In älteren Zeiten bedeutete das die Lage an einer Kreuzung wichtiger Landstraßen oder am Wasser, in der Neuzeit am Kno-tenpunkt von Zug- und Flugverkehr. Leichte Zugänglichkeit wird man also als das dritte wichtige Kennzeichen einer Metropole nennen. Selbstverständlich steht das auch mit der Entwicklung der Transporttechnik in Verbindung. Ein bestimmtes Entwicklungsniveau des Transports ist also eine Conditio sine qua non für die Entstehung und Entwicklung einer Metropole.

Die Anziehungskraft der Metropole bedeutet, daß der Zustrom von Neuankömmlingen sehr groß ist; neue Einwohner kommen nicht nur aus der Umgebung der Stadt, sondern auch aus entfernten Regionen, sogar aus dem Ausland. Diese Zuwanderung bildet die Grundlage eines außergewöhnlich raschen demographischen - auch wirtschaftlichen und kulturellen - Wachstums der Metropole. Für das Hinterland ist die Auswirkung dieser Er-scheinung jedoch zweischneidig: Sie kann die Probleme der Überbevölkerung im Lande lösen oder das Land demographisch, wirtschaftlich und kulturell veröden lassen. Hier be-rühren wir das oft umstrittene Problem des angeblichen Parasitentums der Metropole. Wir kommen später darauf zurück.

Die Ausstrahlungskraft einer Metropole, die die Ausstrahlungskraft benachbarter Städte um ein Vielfaches übertrifft und oft zu ihrer Dominanz führt, wirkt in verschiedene Rich-tungen, die mit der Multifunktionalität der Metropole verknüpft sind und Wirtschaft und Politik, Kultur und Religion betreffen. Die Ausstrahlungskraft einer Metropole bildet also die Grundlage für die Herausarbeitung einer Typologie von Metropolen, zu der vier Haupttypen gerechnet werden sollen: die wirtschaftliche Metropole, die kulturelle Metro-pole, die religiöse und sakrale Metropole, die politische Metropole, letztere auch Haupt-stadt genannt. Das bedeutet, daß eine Hauptstadt zur gleichen Zeit eine Metropole sein kann, wie z.B. Paris oder London. Es kann aber auch sein, daß Hauptstadt und Metropole als verschiedene Zentralorte eines Landes existieren, wie z.B. Den Haag und Amsterdam, Washington DC und New York, Ankara und Istanbul, im 16. Jahrhundert Brüssel und Antwerpen. Selbstverständlich können auch gemischte Typen von Metropolen existieren, und diese sind in der Realität am häufigsten anzutreffen.

Mit der Multifunktionalität, die besser ausgebaut ist als in anderen Städten, verknüpfen sich Intensität des Lebens und struktureller Reichtum der Metropole. In der Metropole konzentrieren sich vielfältig entwickelte Bereiche von Handel, Gewerbe, Kreditwesen, kul-turelle Einrichtungen (Schulen, Universitäten, Gesellschaften, Bibliotheken, Museen, Druk-kereien, Buchverlage, später auch Zeitungsredaktionen), religiöse Einrichtungen (Kirchen

---

10 Florence (wie Anm. 7), S. 149.

und Klöster, religiöse Bruderschaften, kirchliche Ämter). Hier entstehen neue Formen des Denkens, neue künstlerische Strömungen, von hier aus gehen Impulse technischer, kultureller und wissenschaftlicher Innovationen auf das ganze Hinterland aus. Das soll nicht heißen, daß Fortschritt nur in einer Metropole entstehen kann, sondern daß die Intensität des technischen, wissenschaftlichen und kulturellen Lebens in einer Metropole einen besonders günstigen Boden für einen solchen Fortschritt schafft. Auch diese Erscheinung hat jedoch - wie im Fall der Demographie - eine zweischneidige Wirkung. Eine Metropole kann als ein Faktor der Entwicklung für ihr ganzes Hinterland wirken, sie kann aber auch wie ein Parasit alles in sich einsaugen. Die Diskussion über einzelne Beispiele ist in dieser Hinsicht sehr lebhaft[11].

Mehrere Forscher unterstreichen nicht nur die äußere zweischneidige Wirkung einer Metropole, sondern betonen auch ihre inneren Widersprüche und Kontraste. Robert M. Fisher schreibt: "The metropolis displays many of the most advanced and most retarded aspects of national life. It ist a breeder of slums and palace; an incubator of artistic and scientific progress and of disease, crime and delinquency"[12]. Der "metropolitan way of life"[13] - eine besondere Art zu leben im guten und schlechten Sinne dieses Wortes - soll also auch als ein wichtiges Kennzeichen der Metropole erwähnt werden.

Zum Schluß dieser - notwendigerweise kurzen - Betrachtungen schlagen wir sieben Kennzeichen einer Metropole vor:

1. Übergröße der Stadt selbst
2. Übergröße des Hinterlandes
3. leichte Zugänglichkeit
4. außergewöhnlich starke Anziehungskraft im Bereich der Demographie, Wirtschaft, Kultur und Politik
5. außergewöhnlich starke Ausstrahlungskraft (Dominanz) in allen diesen Bereichen
6. außerordentlich ausgebaute Multifunktionalität
7. eine besondere Lebensweise, die von tiefen Widersprüchen und Kontrasten geprägt ist.

Man kann sagen, daß alle diese Kennzeichen - in begrenztem Umfang - auch für andere Stadttypen gelten. Das wichtigste Merkmal einer Metropole, ihr Wesen, liegt in den Dimensionen. Eine Metropole ist eine Stadt, die in allen Aspekten und Bereichen an Elephantiasis leidet.

Die wichtigste Funktion jeder Metropole ist ihre Integrationsfähigkeit. Dank ihrer Ausstrahlungs- und Anziehungskraft integriert sie ein Land oder eine Region im kulturellen

---

11 Auf eine solche Diskussion zu Danzig werden wir später zurückkommen.
12 Preface to: The Metropolis in Modern Life (wie Anm. 7), S. VII.
13 Ebd.

oder im wirtschaftlichen Sinne. Die politische Integration ist als wichtige Funktion und Aufgabe einer politischen Metropole, also einer Hauptstadt, zu betrachten[14].

Es unterliegt keinem Zweifel, daß die Metropole eine historisch und geographisch bestimmte Erscheinung ist. Unsere Betrachtungen sollen sich chronologisch auf die Zeit zwischen 1450 und 1650 und geographisch auf Ostmitteleuropa konzentrieren. Es sollen hier nicht die klassischen oder außereuropäischen Metropolen oder die Metropolen des 20. Jahrhunderts analysiert werden. Es ist jedoch festzustellen, daß Metropolen von mehreren Forschern als eine moderne Erscheinung, als ein Phänomen gesehen werden, das typisch für die Zeit nach den großen Industrialisierungs- und Verstädterungsprozessen des 19./20. Jahrhunderts ist. Kann man also überhaupt von Metropolen im Mittelalter oder in der frühen Neuzeit sprechen?

Die Entstehung und Entwicklung von Metropolen war ohne Zweifel mit dem allgemeinen Prozeß der Urbanisierung Europas verbunden. Man kann drei Etappen dieser Urbanisierung unterscheiden:

1. Mittelalter: kleine (10 000-20 000 Einwohner) Städte, bewegliche Zentren von Macht und Kultur ("ambulante" oder Reiseherrscher), schwachentwickelter Verkehr und niedriger Stand der Technik. Es existiert - mit wenigen Ausnahmen (etwa Paris) - kein günstiger Boden für die Entstehung von Metropolen.

2. Frühe Neuzeit: schnelle demographische Entwicklung Europas, Fortschritt von Technik und Verkehr, Wachstum der Städte (mehrere schon mit 50 000-100 000 Einwohnern), Entwicklung neuer Typen von Städten (Haupt- und Residenzstädte). Es gibt schon mehrere Zentren, die als Metropolen bezeichnet werden können: London, Antwerpen, Amsterdam.

3. 19./20. Jahrhundert: auf Grund der Industrialisierung, der Entwicklung neuer Technik und einer Welle demographischer und gesellschaftlicher Umbrüche entsteht eine dichte Verstädterung, die mehrere Metropolen umfaßt[15].

Dieses Modell entspricht den Verhältnissen in Westeuropa. Für Mittel- und Ostmitteleuropa, wo die Urbanisierungsprozesse schwächer waren und sich später entfalteten, sollte man an ihm einige Korrekturen anbringen. Vor allem ist zu unterstreichen, daß es im allgemeinen zwei Verstädterungstypen gab: die monozentrische Verstädterung (Frankreich, England) und die polyzentrische Verstädterung (Deutschland, Polen), was auf die Entstehung und Ausbildung von Metropolen einen großen Einfluß ausübte. Leider sind wir hier nicht imstande, auf die Ursachen dieser Erscheinung einzugehen. Man muß jedoch hervorheben, was die Bezeichnung polyzentrische Urbanisierung überhaupt beinhaltete. Sie bedeutete nämlich, daß im Lande keine Stadt zur wichtigsten heranwuchs, sondern im Gegenteil, daß mehrere Zentralorte existierten, die sich nebeneinander entwickelten und je-

---

14 Vgl. Hauptstädte in europäischen Nationalstaaten (wie Anm. 1).
15 G. Hurd: Human Societies. An Introduction to Sociology. London 1973, S. 45f. beschreibt drei Etappen der Verstädterung: 1. bis zum Ende des 18. Jahrhunderts, 2. Frühindustrialisierung, 3. die Zeit der "metropolisation".

weils nur durch einige Merkmale metropolitanen Charakters gekennzeichnet waren. In Polen gab es zumindest drei Städte, die in den Jahren 1450-1650 bestimmte Kennzeichen von Metropolen ausbildeten - es waren Krakau, Warschau und Danzig.

Die Karriere von Krakau begann in der zweiten Hälfte des 11. Jahrhunderts, als nach der Zerstörung der ersten polnischen Hauptstadt, Gnesen, durch den böhmischen Fürsten Břetislav (1039) der Sitz der staatlichen Zentralinstitutionen hier eingerichtet wurde. Die Stadt spielte auch die Rolle eines religiösen Zentrums, weil hier schon im Jahre 1000 ein Bistum gegründet wurde. Während der feudalen Zersplitterung Polens war Krakau als Sitz des Seniorfürsten (*princeps*) im ganzen Lande anerkannt. Seit 1320 (der Krönung von Wladislaw Ellenlang und dem symbolischen Ende der Zersplitterung) war Krakau für über 200 Jahre unumstrittene Hauptstadt Polens: das Wawelschloß wurde zum Sitz des Königs und der höchsten Regierungsinstitutionen und Ämter. Hier fanden die großen politischen Ereignisse statt, z.B. der berühmte Monarchenkongreß im Jahre 1364, die Säkularisierung des Deutschen Ordens (1525), die Huldigungen für polnische Könige (die letzte im Jahre 1550). Die Stadt spielte in diesen Jahren auch eine führende kulturelle Rolle (seit 1364 Sitz einer Universität, seit Ende des 15. Jahrhunderts größtes polnisches Zentrum der Druckkunst) und war wirtschaftlicher Zentralort (umfangreicher Handel mit Deutschland, Italien, Böhmen, Ungarn; ausgedehntes Kreditwesen)[16]. Krakaus demographisches Wachstum war ebenfalls bedeutend: hatte die Stadt im 14. Jahrhundert ca. 10 000 Einwohner, so waren es Ende des 15. Jahrhunderts 15 000, im 16. Jahrhundert mehr als 20 000[17]. Im Durchschnitt war also Krakau zweimal so groß wie andere große Städte Polens in dieser Zeit. Es ist aber bemerkenswert, daß Krakau kein ständiger Versammlungsort des polnischen Adels geworden ist. Von den 67 Zusammenkünften des Sejm in den Jahren 1493-1569 fanden nur 19, das sind ca. 30%, in Krakau statt; 34 tagten dagegen in Petrikau, vier in Lublin, vier in Warschau, zwei in Sandomir, eine in Radom, eine in Thorn, eine in Bromberg, eine in Parczów[18]. Das kann als Beweis dafür dienen, daß der polnische Adel das polyzentrische Modell der Urbanisierung unterstützte und die Entstehung eines einzigen mächtigen Zentrums des Staates fürchtete.

Nicht die eigene innere Entwicklung, sondern drei wichtige politische Ereignisse haben im Laufe des 16. Jahrhunderts das weitere Schicksal von Krakau bestimmt: die Umwandlung Polens aus einer Ständemonarchie in eine Adelsrepublik, die Inkorporation des Fürstentums Masowien in die polnische Krone im Jahre 1526 und die polnisch-litauische Union von Lublin im Jahre 1569. In der Folge dieser Ereignisse befand sich Krakau plötzlich nicht mehr im Zentrum, sondern am Rande des Staates: die westliche Staatsgrenze

---

16 Vgl. Andrzej Żaki: Początki Krakowa [Die Anfänge von Krakau]. Kraków 1965.
17 Vgl. Dzieje Krakowa [Geschichte von Krakau] Bd. 1: Jerzy Wyrozumski: Kraków do schyłku wieków średnich [Krakau bis zum Ende des Mittelalters]. Kraków 1992, S. 314; Bd. 2: Janina Bieniarzówna/Jan M. Małecki: Kraków w wiekach XVI-XVIII [Krakau im 16.-18. Jahrhundert]. Kraków 1984, S. 13.
18 Bronisław Włodarski: Chronologia polska [Polnische Chronologie]. Warszawa 1957, S. 481-483.

war jetzt 55 km von der Stadt entfernt, während die Ostgrenze 1200 km und die Nord-grenze 1100 km von Krakau entfernt verliefen. Zum Mittelpunkt dieses riesigen neuen Staates wurde nun Warschau: als Versammlungsort des polnisch-litauischen Parlaments proklamiert (1569) und bald (1572) auch als Ort der Königswahlen bestimmt, wurde Warschau schließlich auch zur königlichen Residenz.

Kann man diese Umwandlungen als einen totalen Übergang der Hauptstadtfunktionen von Krakau an Warschau interpretieren? Die Tradition spielte in der frühen Neuzeit - wie im Mittelalter - eine sehr große Rolle im gesellschaftlichen Leben wie in der gesellschaft-lichen Mentalität. Krakau blieb offiziell eine Hauptstadt des Landes und wurde in den Quellen immer als *caput Regni Poloniae, civitas metropolitana, totius Poloniae urbs cele-berrima* bezeichnet[19]. In Krakau wurden die sogenannten *regalia* - Krone, Apfel und Szep-ter - bis zum Ende des 18. Jahrhunderts aufbewahrt sowie das königliche Archiv (bis 1765) belassen[20]. Hier wurden die Könige gesalbt und gekrönt - eine Zeremonie, die we-gen ihres sakralen Gehalts als höchste Staatsangelegenheit zu gelten hatte. Als im Jahre 1637 Königin Cecilia Renathe in Warschau gesalbt wurde, geriet das ganze Land in Auf-regung, und der nächste Sejm beschloß, daß die Salbung - nach alter Tradition - immer in Krakau durchgeführt werden solle[21]. Hier in Krakau wurden auch die polnischen Könige beigesetzt[22].

Warschaus Sieg über Krakau war also nicht vollständig. Man muß auch betonen, daß die Verlegung des Zentralortes des Staates nach Warschau keineswegs das Resultat eines Kon-kurrenzkampfes zwischen beiden Städten war. Die entscheidende Rolle hatten hier die all-gemeinen politischen Ereignisse und die Politik des Adels gespielt, also außerstädtische Faktoren.

Krakaus demographische Stagnation seit dem Ende des 16. Jahrhunderts wie auch sein ökonomischer und kultureller Niedergang (Verfall des Handels und des Gewerbes, Redu-zierung des städtischen Marktes zum Lokalmarkt mit einem Radius von 25-30 km, der Verfall der Universität)[23] sind im Zusammenhang mit der allgemeinen wirtschaftlichen und kulturellen Konjunktur in Polen zu sehen[24]. Auch hier sind also außerstädtische Faktoren zu beachten.

---

19 Jan M. Małecki: La dégradation de la capitale. Cracovie aux XVIe, XVIIe et XVIIIe siècles. In: Studia Historiae Oeconomicae 19 (1988), S. 90.
20 Ebd.
21 Maria Bogucka: Między stolicą, miastem rezydencjonalnym i metropolią. Rozwój Warszawy w XVI-XVIII w. [Zwischen Hauptstadt, Residenzstadt und Metropole. Warschaus Entwicklung im 16.-18. Jahrhundert]. In: Rocznik Warszawski 18 (1993), S. 173.
22 Małecki (wie Anm. 19), S. 89.
23 Ebd., S. 92ff.
24 Vgl. Maria Bogucka/Henryk Samsonowicz: Miasta i mieszczaństwo w Polsce przedrozbiorowej [Städte und Bürgerschaft in Polen vor den Teilungen]. Wrocław 1986, S. 321ff.

Gleichwohl kann man Krakau in diesen Jahren als ein mächtiges religiöses Zentrum Polens bezeichnen. Hier konzentrierten sich - wie ausgeführt - die wichtigsten staatlich-sakralen Funktionen (Salbung und Beisetzung der Könige), hier entstand die größte Konzentration kirchlicher Institutionen in Polen und entwickelten sich intensiv verschiedene Formen des religiösen Lebens. Im Jahre 1580 besaß die katholische Kirche in Krakau 35% der Parzellen, im Jahre 1667 schon 55%[25]. In der ersten Hälfte des 17. Jahrhunderts gab es in Krakau 65 Kirchen und Klöster, unter denen 17 Klöster seit dem Ende des 16. Jahrhunderts entstanden waren[26]. Die Stadt wurde zum Sitz fast aller in Polen damals existierenden männlichen (17 von 20) und weiblichen (9 von 13) Konvente[27]. Der Klerus machte schon mehr als 40% der städtischen Bevölkerung aus. Die Forschung unterstreicht, daß Krakaus Stadtraum in dieser Zeit durch die Existenz religiöser Gebäude geprägt war, und nennt diese Erscheinung "kirchliche Agglomeration Krakaus"[28]. Trotz des politischen und ökonomischen Niedergangs entwickelte sich also Krakau im Laufe des 17. Jahrhunderts als ein mächtiges religiöses Zentrum, dessen Ausstrahlungs- und Anziehungskraft ganz Polen erfaßte. Krakau ist ein sehr interessantes Beispiel für die Umwandlung von einer politischen zu einer sakralen Hauptstadt, zu einer sakralen Metropole, die trotz politischer und wirtschaftlicher Stagnation ein religiöser Zentralort des Staates blieb.

Die rasche Karriere von Warschau war mit Krakaus Niedergang verknüpft; auch sie wurde nicht durch die eigene innere Entwicklung der Stadt, sondern durch äußere politische Ereignisse bestimmt. Warschau lag sehr vorteilhaft an der Kreuzung wichtiger Landwege von Osten nach Westen und von Süden nach Norden, zudem an der Weichsel, dem größten schiffbaren Fluß Polens, hatte also eine gute Verbindung nach Danzig. Von allen Teilen des polnisch-litauischen Staates konnte man Warschau schnell und bequem erreichen. Diese günstige Situation machte die Stadt zu einem gefragten Versammlungsort für den König, für die Magnaten sowie auch für den Adel. Eine Rolle spielte zusätzlich der Umstand, daß das noch kurz zuvor selbständige Masowien, das keine bedeutendere Anzahl großer Landbesitzer aufwies und zumeist vom Kleinadel bewohnt war, sich hinsichtlich der komplizierten politischen Verhältnisse zwischen Polen und Litauen sozusagen neutral verhielt. So war das in dieser Region gelegene Warschau sowohl für die litauischen als auch für die polnischen Magnaten und den polnischen Adel als Versammlungsort und Zentrum des Staates durchaus annehmbar.

Mit der neuen Würde als königliche Residenz und Versammlungsort des Sejm gewann Warschau - ein kleine Stadt, die noch am Anfang des 16. Jahrhunderts nur 3 000 bis

---

25 Mieczysław Niwiński: Stanowy podział własności nieruchomej w Krakowie w XVI i XVII w. [Stände und Immobilienbesitz in Krakau im 16. und 17. Jahrhundert]. In: Studia historyczne ku czci Stanisława Kutrzeby. Bd. 2. Kraków 1938, S. 549-585.
26 Henryk Gapski: Klasztory krakowskie w końcu XVI i w pierwszej połowie XVII w. [Krakauer Klöster am Ende des 16. und in der ersten Hälfte des 17. Jahrhunderts]. Lublin 1993, S. 291.
27 Ebd.
28 Ebd.

4 000 Einwohner zählte[29] - eine neue Dimension echter "metropolitaner" Großzügigkeit. Ein erstes Zeichen für die Wandlung war die enorme Bautätigkeit, die die Stadt schon seit Ende des 16. Jahrhunderts zum größten und lebendigsten Bauplatz im Lande machte[30]. An diesen Bauinitiativen hatte jedoch das Warschauer Bürgertum nur einen bescheidenen Anteil, obwohl eben in jener Zeit die Anzahl der Bürgerhäuser in Alt- und Neu-Warschau von 706 (1564) auf 861 (1655) stieg[31]. Die wichtigsten Bauten wurden vom König (Umbau des Warschauer Schlosses, des Schlosses von Ujazdów, Bau der Villa Regia) und von Magnaten ausgeführt[32]. Charakteristisch für das Warschau jener Zeit war die sprunghafte Entwicklung der sogenannten *iurisdictiones*, der Besitztümer der Geistlichen und des Adels. Die Residenzstadt und der Versammlungsort des Sejm zogen Magnaten und Adel aus dem ganzen Lande magnetisch an, und am leichtesten konnte man sich hier einrichten, indem man ein eigenes Haus baute.

Der Adel und die Magnaten siedelten sich nicht im Stadtzentrum, sondern vor allem in den ausgedehnten Vorstädten an. In der ersten Hälfte des 17. Jahrhunderts war aus der Krakauer Vorstadt ein Stadtteil geworden, in dem schon 75% der Parzellen Adligen gehörten[33]. Neben den früheren bescheidenen Bürgerhäusern wurden hier prachtvolle Barockpaläste der Magnaten (der Kazanowski, Koniecpolski, Ossoliński usw.) erbaut, die den königlichen Residenzen in nichts nachstanden. Herrliche Paläste entstanden auch an anderen Stellen der Stadt, z.B. das Ossoliński-Palais an der Wierzbowa-Straße und der Palast der Krakauer Bischöfe an der Ecke der Miodowa- und Senatorska-Straße. Auch zahlreiche Sakralbauten wurden in Warschau errichtet, und die alten gotischen Kirchen im neuen Renaissance- und später im Barockstil umgebaut[34].

In der ersten Hälfte des 17. Jahrhunderts war Warschau also ein bedeutsamer Residenzort des Königs und der Magnaten, in dem aber kein Zentrum bestand, das die ganze Stadt zu dominieren vermochte; viele Magnatensitze kann man hier dank ihrer Prachtentfaltung und Herrlichkeit dem Wohnsitz des Königs vergleichen. Waren der königliche Hof in Warschau und die Stadt selbst Ende des 16. und im 17. Jahrhundert Mittelpunkt des kulturellen Lebens für das ganze Land - ein Zentrum, das Vorbilder für das Land schuf, wie das in der ersten Hälfte des 16. Jahrhunderts der Krakauer Hof in der Regierungszeit Sigis-

---

29 Wanda Szaniawska: Mieszkańcy Warszawy w latach 1525-1655 [Die Bewohner von Warschau in den Jahren 1525-1655]. In: Rocznik Warszawski 7 (1966), S. 135.
30 Maria Bogucka: Warschau als königliche Residenzstadt und Staatszentrum zur Zeit der Renaissance und des Barock. In: Zeitschrift für Ostforschung 33 (1984), S. 180-195.
31 Szaniawska (wie Anm. 29), S. 128.
32 Bogucka (wie Anm. 30), S. 181-183.
33 Wanda Szaniawska: Zmiany w rozplanowaniu i zabudowie Krakowskiego Przedmieścia do 1733 [Die Änderungen in der Planung und Bebauung der Straße "Krakauer Vorstadt" bis 1733]. In: Biuletyn Historii Sztuki i Kultury 29 (1967), S. 285-316.
34 Bogucka (wie Anm. 30), S. 183.

munds des Alten und noch Sigismund Augusts vermochte[35]? Sowohl Sigismund III. als auch sein Sohn Wladislaw IV. waren ausgesprochene Kunstliebhaber, sie kauften Bücher, Bilder, Skulpturen, sammelten Kunsthandwerkserzeugnisse und Kuriosa jeglicher Art[36]. Dank des Mäzenatentums der Wasa entwickelten sich in Warschau das Theater sowie Musik und Oper[37]. Das literarische und wissenschaftliche Mäzenatentum war dagegen schwächer ausgebildet, obwohl es besonders im Bereich der Historiographie nicht gering war[38]. Die aus Frankreich stammende Gemahlin von Wladislaw IV., später auch von Johann Kasimir - Louise Marie Gonzague - eröffnete in Warschau einen "wissenschaftlichen Salon", wo man nicht nur diskutierte, sondern auch physikalische und astronomische Experimente durchführte[39]. Obwohl am Königshof berühmte Gelehrte wirkten, fehlte es Warschau doch an einem günstigen Boden, auf dem ein bedeutenderes intellektuelles Zentrum entstehen konnte, weil hier keine höhere Schule existierte[40].

Im großen und ganzen war der Königshof in Warschau zweifelsohne ein intensives Kulturzentrum, doch wirkte dieses nur auf einen begrenzten gesellschaftlichen Bereich. Die Forscher sind der Meinung, daß der königliche Hof in Polen als das alleinige Vorbild hinsichtlich der Kultur und Lebensweise von der zweiten Hälfte des 16. Jahrhunderts an seine Bedeutung zu verlieren begann. Im Gegenteil - jetzt bemühten sich die Magnaten und der Adel, dem König ihren Lebensstil und ihre Gewohnheiten aufzuzwingen. Eine scharfe Konkurrenz für die von Warschau ausgehenden kulturellen Strömungen bildeten in jener Zeit die Magnatenhöfe im Lande, die oft dem königlichen Hof in nichts nachstanden und überdies dem Adel näher waren, da sie nicht unter jenen fremden Einflüssen standen, die am Hofe der Wasa vorherrschten und die den Unwillen der "sarmatischen", immer stärker fremdenfeindlichen Gesellschaft hervorriefen. Im Endergebnis befand sich der polnische Adel unter dem Einfluß der Magnaten, und zwar nicht nur kulturell, sondern auch in politischer Hinsicht. Er hegte Mißtrauen gegen alle fremden Neigungen der Wasa, gegen deren Hof mit seinen absolutistischen Ambitionen und ebenso gegen ganz Warschau, das als Groß- und Residenzstadt für den einfachen adligen Landbewohner ein "Sitz des Lasters

35 Vgl. dies.: Bona a rola dworu monarszego jako centrum kulturalno-obyczajowego 1518-1548 [Bona Sforza und die Rolle des königlichen Hofes als Kultur- und Sittenzentrum 1518-1548]. In: Tryumfy i porażki. Studia z dziejów kultury polskiej XVI-XVIII w. [Triumphe und Niederlagen. Studien zur Geschichte der polnischen Kultur vom 16. bis 18. Jahrhundert]. Red. Maria Bogucka. Warszawa 1989, S. 97-120.
36 Władysław Tomkiewicz: Z dziejów polskiego mecenatu artystycznego w XVII w. [Aus der Geschichte des polnischen Kunstmäzenatentums im 17. Jahrhundert]. Wrocław 1952.
37 Bogucka (wie Anm. 30), S. 186.
38 Ebd.
39 Karolina Targosz: Uczony dwór Ludwiki Marii Gonzagi 1646-1667 [Der gelehrte Hof von Louise Marie Gonzague 1646-1667]. Wrocław 1975.
40 Bogucka (wie Anm. 30), S. 186.

und der Lüge"[41] war. Er verwarf also die meisten von hier ausgehenden Impulse und Vorbilder[42], was die Einflußmöglichkeiten Warschaus auf das ganze Land im Bereich von Kultur, Sitten und Lebensweise sehr begrenzte. Das war von großem Nachteil für Warschaus Werdegang zu einer Metropole.

Es erhebt sich auch die Frage, in welchem Maße man Warschau im hier behandelten Zeitabschnitt als politisches Zentrum des Landes, also als eine wirkliche Hauptstadt betrachten kann. Gewiß, die Stadt war nicht nur der Sitz des Königs und der Reichstage - die Königswahlen inbegriffen -, sondern auch der zentralen Ämter der Adelsrepublik: des Marschalls, des Schatzmeisters und des Kanzlers, die im Königsschloß wirkten. Von nicht geringer Bedeutung war ferner die Tatsache, daß einflußreiche Magnaten wenigstens einige Wochen oder Monate im Jahr in Warschau verbrachten. Hierher pflegten auch die ausländischen Gesandten zu kommen, hier wurden wichtige Verhandlungen geführt, hier konzentrierten sich die politischen Kämpfe zur Zeit der Königswahlen ebenso wie die feierlichen politischen Akte (Triumphzüge, Huldigungen usw.). Doch der Kronschatz wurde nicht in Warschau, sondern in einem kleinen masowischen Städtchen - Rawa Mazowiecka - verwahrt (1563); die höchsten Appellationsgerichte wurden im Jahre 1578 für Polen in Petrikau, für Litauen in Lublin eingerichtet. Hier wirkte ganz offensichtlich die mißtrauische Politik des Adels gegenüber großen Städten. An der Wende vom 16. zum 17. Jahrhundert war also Warschau sicher ein Staatszentrum, doch seinen kulturellen und politischen Rang kann man nicht mit der Bedeutung der absolutistischen Zentren jener Zeit, wie z. B. Paris oder London oder einiger Hauptstädte deutscher Fürstentümer, vergleichen.

Die Tatsache, daß Warschau zur Residenzstadt des Königs gewählt wurde, brachte eine schnelle Zunahme der Einwohnerzahl mit sich. In der ersten Hälfte des 17. Jahrhunderts zählte die Stadt schon ca. 25 000-30 000 Einwohner (die Vorstädte inbegriffen) und während der Königswahlen bis zu 100 000[43]. Damit war Warschau zu einem der größten Zentren des Landes geworden und stand neben Danzig mit 100 000 sowie vor Lemberg und Krakau mit je 20 000-25 000 Einwohnern in der Reihe der mittelgroßen europäischen Städte jener Zeit[44]. Es ist bemerkenswert, daß diese demographische Entwicklung auf einem Zustrom der Bevölkerung nicht nur - wie im Mittelalter - aus dem dicht besiedelten Masowien, sondern auch aus weiter entfernten Gegenden der Adelsrepublik beruhte. Es gab auch einen Zuzug aus dem Ausland, der von 3,7 bis 9,7% im 16. Jahrhundert auf 17 bis 18% im 17. Jahrhundert wuchs[45]. Die demographische Entwicklung Warschaus zeigt also einige Merkmale eines "Metropolentums".

41 Dies.: L'attrait de la culture nobiliaire? Sarmatisation de la bourgeoisie polonaise au 17e siècle. In: Acta Poloniae Historica 33 (1976), S. 25.
42 Dies. (wie Anm. 30), S. 186.
43 Ebd., S. 188.
44 Ebd.
45 Szaniawska (wie Anm. 29), S. 123; Stanisław Gierszewski: Obywatele miast Polski przedrozbiorowej [Die Stadtbürger Polens in der Zeit vor den Teilungen]. Warszawa 1974, S. 131-132.

Die gesteigerten Bedürfnisse in bezug auf die Versorgung des königlichen Hofes und der Magnatenhöfe führten in Warschau bald zu einer Wirtschaftskonjunktur. Es blühte vor allem der Großhandel, der die Einfuhr von Luxuswaren umfaßte, die aus dem Westen wie aus dem Osten, aus Danzig, Thorn, Posen, Krakau, Lublin, Lemberg oder direkt aus Nürnberg und Augsburg, aus italienischen und französischen Städten kamen[46]. Was den Export von Agrarerzeugnissen betrifft, so waren die Warschauer Kaufleute weniger daran beteiligt, da die Konkurrenz des Adels und der Danziger in diesem Bereich sehr stark war[47]. Warschau entwickelte sich dagegen schnell zu einem Zentrum für das Kredit- und Bankwesen, wo der Geldverkehr mit dem Ausland vermittelt wurde und wo der König, die Magnaten, der Adel und sogar die Bauern mit Anleihen bedient wurden[48]. Doch Großhandel und Kredit wurden zum großen Teil mit Hilfe von Kapital aus Danzig betrieben[49].

Die Konjunktur für das Warschauer Gewerbe entwickelte sich dagegen nicht so gut, wofür der sehr starke Import ausländischer Erzeugnisse verantwortlich war. So verfielen die im Mittelalter für die Stadt und ihre Umgebung arbeitenden Gewerbe der Weberei, Töpferei und Zinngießerei. Das Handwerk stellte sich vor allem auf die Befriedigung des Bedarfs des königlichen Hofes sowie des die Stadt besuchenden Adels ein. Es entfalteten sich die Produktion von Lebensmitteln und verschiedene Dienstleistungen (Schneiderei, Kürschnerei, Bortenmacherei, Schuhmacherei, Wagenbauerei usw.). Im Zusammenhang mit den Bedürfnissen des Hofes, der Magnaten, der Edelleute und auch der reich werdenden Bürger entwickelten sich die Goldschmiedekunst und verschiedene mit dem Bauwesen zusammenhängende Gewerbe[50]. Im großen und ganzen war jedoch Warschau zu jener Zeit nicht ein Produktions-, sondern ein Handels-, vor allem aber ein Importzentrum[51].

Die neue Situation hatte zu einer Umschichtung innerhalb der Warschauer Bevölkerung geführt. Die ansehnliche Zahl der hier ansässigen Magnaten mit ihrem Gefolge und der Edelleute gemeinsam mit vielen Geistlichen machte schon am Anfang des 17. Jahrhunderts gegen 25% der Gesamtbevölkerung aus, also mehr als in anderen Städten der Adelsrepublik (mit Ausnahme Krakaus)[52]. Als Resultat der Wirtschaftskonjunktur bildete sich in Warschau eine verhältnismäßig reiche Führungsschicht aus[53]. Sie war durch viele verwandtschaftliche Beziehungen miteinander verbunden und im Großhandel und Kreditwesen tätig, oft zusammen mit Kaufleuten aus Danzig[54]. In ihren Händen konzentrierte sich

46 Warszawa w latach 1526-1795 [Warschau in den Jahren 1526-1795]. Hg. v. Andrzej Zahorski. Warszawa 1984, S. 52ff.
47 Ebd. S. 46 ff.
48 Ebd. S. 74.
49 Ebd.
50 Ebd. S. 60, 194, 339.
51 Bogucka (wie Anm. 30), S. 190.
52 Ebd. S. 189.
53 Warszawa w latach 1526-1795 (wie Anm. 46), S. 85ff.
54 Ebd.

ein bedeutender Immobilienbesitz in der Stadt und auch außerhalb derselben. Die War-schauer Patrizier wollten als Mäzene von Kultur und Kunst auftreten; die ehrgeizigsten unter ihnen strebten nach Adelstiteln, was zur Folge hatte, daß die hervorragendsten Ver-treter der Bürgerschaft schon in der zweiten oder dritten Generation die Stadt verließen[55]. Bereits am Ende des 16. Jahrhunderts wurde Warschau - wie jede Metropole - zum Ort großer Gegensätze. Vor allem muß die Diskrepanz zwischen der Pracht und dem Luxus des königlichen Hofes und der Magnatenhöfe sowie der Bescheidenheit der Bürgerhäuser erwähnt werden. Die Gegensätze innerhalb der Bürgerschaft selbst nahmen zu. Der Ab-stand zwischen den reichen Kaufleuten und den Handwerkern vertiefte sich[56]. Dazu kam ein schnelles Anwachsen der Unterschichten; in immer größerer Zahl wurden Gesellen, Knechte und Mägde in den Palästen und reicheren Häusern als Hausgesinde benötigt. Dienstleute beiderlei Geschlechts machten schon im 17. Jahrhundert in einigen Stadtvier-teln etwa 40% der Bewohner aus[57]. Die Vermögens- und Sozialunterschiede brachten be-merkenswerte Kontraste im Lebensstandard und in der Lebensweise mit sich. In der un-mittelbaren Nachbarschaft eines Adelshofes, eines prächtigen Kaufmannshauses, einer ge-werblichen Werkstatt, wo reges Leben herrschte, befanden sich kleine Holzhütten der Ar-men sowie landwirtschaftliche Parzellen, wo Geflügel, Schweine und anderes Vieh gemä-stet wurden[58].

In jenen Jahren, in denen Warschaus Wachstum es nahelegt, diese Stadt als politisches und kulturelles Zentrum Polens - vielleicht als Metropole? - zu bezeichnen, war Danzig zweifellos eine wirtschaftliche Metropole nicht nur für ganz Polen, sondern auch für den gesamten Ostseeraum. Die Stadt paßt genau zu dem Modell, das der englische Wirt-schaftshistoriker Norman Gras vor fast 80 Jahren so beschrieben hat: "The metropolitan market may be described as a large district having one center in which is focused a consi-derable trade. Trade between outlying ports of course may take place, but it is that bet-ween the metropolitan town and the rest of the area that dominates all. This is chiefly the exchange of the raw products of the country for the manufactured or imported goods of the town. The prices of all goods sent to the metropolitan center are 'made' there, or, in other words, prices diminish as the distance from the center is increased"[59]. Es finden sich in dieser Definition alle charakteristischen Merkmale des Danziger Handels im 16./17.

---

55 Ebd., S. 332ff.
56 Maria Bogucka: Mieszczaństwo Warszawy w XVI i w pierwszej połowie XVII w. [Die Bürgerschaft von Warschau im 16. und in der ersten Hälfte des 17. Jahrhunderts]. In: Społeczeństwo Warszawy w rozwoju historycznym [Die Warschauer Gesellschaft in der geschichtlichen Entwicklung]. Warszawa 1977, S. 465-406. Zu Beginn des 17. Jahrhunderts verhielt sich das kleinste zum größten Vermögen Warschauer Bürger wie etwa 1:150, wie auf Grund von Steuerlisten geschätzt werden kann.
57 Ebd., S. 405.
58 Etwa 70 Prozent der Bevölkerung, insbesondere in Neu-Warschau und in den Vorstädten, befaßten sich mit Viehzucht und Ackerbau; vgl. ebd.
59 Norman S. B. Gras: The Evolution of the English Corn Market. Cambridge 1915, S. 95.

Jahrhundert: 1. ein übergroßes Hinterland, das nach den neuesten Forschungsergebnissen nicht nur Masowien, Groß- und Kleinpolen, sondern auch Podolien und die Ukraine zusammen mit großen Teilen Litauens umfaßte; 2. eine Dominanz des sich in Danzig konzentrierenden Großhandels über den zwischen anderen Städten des polnisch-litauischen Staates betriebenen Kleinhandel; 3. eine Struktur des Handels, die im Austausch von Rohstoffen und Lebensmitteln gegen Industriewaren bestand, die teilweise importiert, teilweise direkt in Danzig hergestellt wurden; 4. die bestimmende Rolle Danzigs bei der Preisgestaltung, was zur Folge hatte, daß mit zunehmender Entfernung von Danzig die Preise für polnische Exportwaren fielen, während die Preise für importierte Waren anstiegen[60].

Die Voraussetzungen für die Karriere Danzigs als Metropole waren durch die Entwicklung des gemeinsamen europäischen Marktes um die Wende zur Neuzeit entstanden[61]. Mit dem schnell wachsenden Bedarf an Lebensmitteln in Westeuropa, der sich in jener Zeit bemerkbar machte, nahm die Bedeutung des Danziger Hafens rasch zu. Die Ausfuhr von Getreide stieg besonders schnell an: im Jahre 1557 waren es 40 000 Last, 1583 schon 62 000, 1618 und 1619 bereits mehr als 100 000 Last pro Jahr. Der Wert der Umsätze schwankte in der ersten Hälfte des 17. Jahrhunderts zwischen 25 000 und 45 000 Preußischer Mark, dreimal so viel wie in den Hafenstädten Rostock, Königsberg oder Riga[62]. Obwohl Danzig offiziell nie das Stapelrecht besaß, war es seit dem 16. Jahrhundert das wichtigste Emporium des polnischen Gebietes, da hier ca. 80% des polnischen Überseehandels abgewickelt wurden. Auch für den Ostseeraum insgesamt kam dem Danziger Hafen eine besondere Bedeutung zu; seit Ende des 16. Jahrhunderts waren hier ca. 50% des Handels von Amsterdam - dem größten Handelspartner der Ostsee - konzentriert[63].

Mit der Steigerung des Umfangs des Danziger Handels ging eine Vermehrung der städtischen Produktion einher, was zur Folge hatte, daß Danzig schon in der zweiten Hälfte des 16. Jahrhunderts zum größten Produktionszentrum an der Ostsee und in Polen wurde. Die Bewohner von Danzig nutzten hier die ausgezeichnete Konjunktur für handwerkliche Erzeugnisse aus, die sich alljährlich einstellte, wenn die Edelleute zum Verkauf ihrer Agrarerzeugnisse aus ganz Polen anreisten und auf diese Weise ihren Bedarf an verschiedenen anderen Gütern decken konnten. Auch auf dem städtischen Markt wuchs der Bedarf an Handwerksartikeln, da sich der Wohlstand der Bewohner Danzigs steigerte und ihre An-

---

60 Maria Bogucka: Handel zagraniczny Gdańska w pierwszej połowie XVII wieku [Der Außenhandel Danzigs in der ersten Hälfte des 17. Jahrhunderts]. Wrocław 1970, S. 124ff.
61 Vgl. dies.: Danzig an der Wende zur Neuzeit: Von der aktiven Handelsstadt zum Stapel- und Produktionszentrum. In: Hansische Geschichtsblätter 102 (1984), S. 91-103.
62 Dies. (wie Anm. 60), S. 30ff.
63 Dies.: Amsterdam and the Baltic in the First Half of the 17th Century. In: The Economic History Review, Second Series 26 (1973), S. 433-447; dies.: Dutch Merchants' Activities in Gdańsk in the First Half of the 17th Century. In: Baltic Affairs. Relations between the Netherlands and North-Eastern Europe 1500-1800. Hg. v. Jacques Ph. S. Lemmink/John S. A. M. van Koningsbrugge. Nijmegen 1990, S. 19-32.

zahl zunahm[64]. So kam es zu einer raschen Entwicklung der holzverarbeitenden Gewerbe (darunter der sich eines ausgezeichneten Rufes erfreuenden Möbelherstellung), der Textilien und Leder verarbeitenden Gewerbe, der Metall- und Rüstungsindustrie, der Herstellung von Glas und Präzisionsgeräten (u.a. der berühmten Danziger Uhren), der Erzeugung von Papier und Büchern, der dem Luxus dienenden Gold- und Silberschmiedekunst, der Verarbeitung von Bernstein usw.[65]. An der Wende vom 16. zum 17. Jahrhundert arbeiteten in Danzig schon über 3150 Zunftmeister, wobei solche Handwerker, die keiner Innung angehörten, die sogenannten freien Künstler, nicht mitgezählt sind, z.b. die Bortenmacher und die Färber. Auch die sogenannten Bönhasen, also die unzünftigen Handwerker, die ihre Arbeit illegal betrieben, sind in dieser Zählung nicht berücksichtigt. Im ganzen bestanden in der ersten Hälfte des 17. Jahrhunderts in Danzig und in seinen Vororten etwa 7000 Handwerksstätten verschiedener Größe, in denen zuweilen ein Dutzend oder noch mehr Menschen arbeiteten[66]. In einigen Produktionszweigen bildete sich das Verlagssystem heraus, z.b. bei der Textilherstellung[67]. Fast die Hälfte der Gesamtbevölkerung lebte in jener Zeit in Danzig von gewerblicher Produktion[68]. Zum Vergleich sei erwähnt, daß Krakau in denselben Jahren nur etwa 700 - dazu noch recht kleine - Werkstätten zählte. In den Ostseestädten Königsberg und Riga gab es deren auch nur einige hundert[69].

Die Herstellungsweise hatte in Danzig einen hohen Grad technischer Vollkommenheit erreicht. Erzeugnisse aus Danzig - Möbel, Keramik, Borten und Posamenten, Uhren, Schmuck - waren im ganzen Land begehrt und wurden massenweise gekauft[70]. Wie im Handel, so auch in der Nachfrage nach Handwerkserzeugnissen deckte sich das Hinterland von Danzig mit dem gesamten Territorium des damaligen polnisch-litauischen Staates: es reichte von der Ostsee bis zu den Karpaten und zum Schwarzen Meer. Danzig exportierte in der ersten Hälfte des 17. Jahrhunderts einige Gewerbeerzeugnisse wie Textilien, Möbel, Glas, Papier, Spinnräder usw. sogar ins Ausland (Schweden, Finnland)[71].

Danzig wurde in dieser Zeit auch zum größten Kredit- und Finanzzentrum des polnischen Staates und des Ostseeraumes, wahrscheinlich dank seiner lebhaften Beziehungen

---

64 Vgl. dies.: Gdańsk jako ośrodek produkcyjny w XIV-XVII w. [Danzig als Produktionszentrum im 14.-17. Jahrhundert]. Warszawa 1962, S. 7ff., 207ff.
65 Ebd., S. 7ff.; vgl. auch dies.: Gdańskie rzemiosło tekstylne od XVI do połowy XVII w. [Danziger Textilgewerbe vom 16. Jahrhundert bis zur ersten Hälfte des 17. Jahrhunderts]. Wrocław 1956.
66 Dies. (wie Anm. 64), S. 281ff.
67 Ebd., S. 272ff.; vgl. auch dies. (wie Anm. 65), S. 133ff.
68 Dies. (wie Anm. 64), S. 392ff.
69 Vgl. dies. (wie Anm. 61), S. 93.
70 Dies. (wie Anm. 64), S. 207ff.
71 Dies.: Handelsbeziehungen im Ostseeraum: Der Handel zwischen Danzig/Gdańsk und Stockholm in der ersten Hälfte des 17. Jahrhunders. In: Seehandel und Wirtschaftswege Nordeuropas im 17. und 18. Jahrhundert. Hg. v. Klaus Friedland/Franz Irsigler. Ostfildern 1981, S. 38-47; dies.: Trade between Gdańsk and Turku (Åbo) in the 16th and the First Half of the 17th Century. In: Acta Poloniae Historica 67 (1993), S. 141-148.

zu den Hauptzentren des damaligen Bankwesens, zu Antwerpen und Amsterdam[72]. Mit Bank- und Kreditoperationen beschäftigte sich in Danzig eine große Anzahl von Institutionen und Personen: der Stadtrat, die Patrizier, wohlhabende Kaufleute, auch Handwerker und ganze Zünfte. Es gab in der Stadt zahlreiche größere und kleinere Pfandhäuser, die die ärmere Bevölkerung aus der Stadt und ihrer Umgebung bedienten. In den dreißiger Jahren des 17. Jahrhunderts wurde in Danzig die Gründung einer öffentlichen Bank geplant[73]. Das Projekt, von einem holländischen Kaufmann, Anthony Kuiper, entworfen, wurde jedoch nicht verwirklicht, wahrscheinlich infolge einer kräftigen Opposition der Privatbankiers, die die Konkurrenz fürchteten[74].

Die Entwicklung des Danziger Kreditwesens stützte sich teilweise auf eigene, in der Stadt angesammelte Geldmittel, teilweise aber auch auf nach Danzig kommendes niederländisches, vor allem holländisches Kapital. Diese Tatsache verweist auf die weiten internationalen Beziehungen der Metropole Danzig. Interessante Ergebnisse bietet auch eine Analyse der Herkunft der Danziger Kreditnehmer. Zu ihnen gehörten in jener Zeit zahlreiche Herrscher, sowohl polnische - Sigismund August, Wladislaw Wasa - als auch schwedische und dänische Könige, polnische Magnaten und polnischer Adel sowie Bürger und sogar Bauern[75]. Die von Danzigern gewährten Kredite hingen oft mit Handelsoperationen zusammen, u.a. mit dem System der Kontraktierung von Getreide auf dem Halm und von Waldprodukten am Stamm (Vorkauf). Dieses System, das schon im 16. Jahrhundert Anwendung fand, entwickelte sich im 17. Jahrhundert zur Hauptform der Versorgung des Danziger Marktes. Vorauszahlungen, die den polnischen Magnaten und dem Adel bei dieser Gelegenheit gewährt wurden, bildeten in der Regel eine versteckte Form verzinster Anleihen. Das ganze Ausmaß dieser Anleihen wird in den vierziger Jahren des 17. Jahrhunderts auf 1 bis 2 Millionen polnischer Złoty pro Jahr geschätzt[76].

Danzig zeigt sich also an der Schwelle zur Neuzeit nicht nur als der größte Hafen der Ostsee, sondern gleichzeitig auch als mächtiges Produktions- und Finanzzentrum, das sich auf die Befriedigung der verschiedenen Bedürfnisse des Adels aus dem riesigen Hinterland

---

72 Vgl. dies.: The Baltic and Amsterdam in the First Half of the 17th Century. In: The Interactions of Amsterdam and Antwerp with the Baltic Region 1400-1800. Leiden 1983, S. 51-70; dies.: Les relations entre la Pologne et les Pays-Bas; XVIe siècle - première moitié du XVIIe siècle. In: Cahier de Clio 78-79 (1984), S. 5-18; dies.: La lettre du change et le credit dans les échanges entre Gdańsk et Amsterdam dans la première moitié du XVIIe siècle. In: Actes du Cinquième Congres International d'Histoire Economique. Bd. 4, Moskau 1975, S. 31-41.
73 Ebd.
74 Ebd.
75 Ebd.; vgl. auch dies.: Obrót wekslowo-kredytowy w Gdańsku w pierwszej połowie XVII w. [Das Kreditwesen in Danzig in der ersten Hälfte des 17. Jahrhunderts]. In: Roczniki Dziejów Społecznych i Gospodarczych 33 (1972), S. 1-31.
76 Vgl. dies.: Gdańskie kontrakty zbożowe w pierwszej połowie XVII wieku [Danzigs Getreidehandelsverträge in der ersten Hälfte des 17. Jahrhunderts] In: Kwartalnik Historii Kultury Materialnej 17 (1969), S. 711-719.

spezialisierte und als Vermittler zwischen Ost- und Westeuropa fungierte. Die Ausstrahlungskraft dieser Metropole hat die staatlichen Grenzen weit überschritten.

Dasselbe kann man über Danzigs Anziehungskraft sagen. Infolge der Handelskonjunktur und der bedeutenden Nachfrage nach Spezialisten wie nach einfachen Arbeitskräften kamen jährlich zahlreiche Immigranten nach Danzig. Ihr Zustrom wurde durch die damaligen internationalen Ereignisse beschleunigt. In der zweiten Hälfte des 16. und zu Beginn des 17. Jahrhunderts emigrierten der religiösen Verfolgung wegen Tausende von Menschen aus den Niederlanden, aus Deutschland, Frankreich, Böhmen, Schlesien und Schweden nach Polen - und vor allem nach Danzig. Da im polnisch-litauischen Staat und auch in Danzig selbst in dieser Zeit religiöse Toleranz herrschte, konnten sich hier Angehörige von Sekten ansiedeln, die besonders heftigen Verfolgungen ausgesetzt waren, wie Wiedertäufer, Böhmische Brüder und Mennoniten. Eine besondere Rolle für die Entwicklung Danzigs spielte die Immigration aus den Niederlanden, denn mit ihr kamen hervorragende Architekten, Maler und Bildhauer, die einen starken kulturellen Einfluß auf die städtische und polnische Kultur ausübten[77]. Weniger bekannt ist die wirtschaftliche Bedeutung der niederländischen Immigration von Kaufleuten und Handwerkern nach Danzig und in dessen Umgebung. Die Ankömmlinge brachten nicht nur bedeutende Geldmengen mit, sondern auch breite Bekanntschaft mit der Welt und gute Beziehungen zu westeuropäischen Handelsfirmen. Unter ihnen waren Fachleute verschiedener Spezialisierung, wie z.B. Weber, Bortenmacher und Färber, die bessere, neue Produktionsmethoden einführten, das Kreditwesen entwickelten und mit neuen Formen der Produktion, des Handels und des Kredits bekannt machten[78].

Es ist nicht möglich, die genaue Zahl der an der Wende vom 16. zum 17. Jahrhundert aus verschiedenen Ländern nach Danzig Eingewanderten zu bestimmen. Meist erwarben die Neuankömmlinge kein Bürgerrecht und sind dann in Bürgerbüchern nicht nachweisbar. Doch ohne Zweifel ging die Zahl der Immigranten in die Tausende. Sie ist spürbar in der sprunghaften Entwicklung der Bevölkerungszahl Danzigs: sie wuchs von 30 000 zu Beginn des 16. Jahrhunderts auf 40 000 in den achtziger Jahren, um am Anfang des 17. Jahrhunderts um die 70 000 bis 100 000 zu erreichen[79]. Danzig hatte sich also zu einem städtischen Mittelpunkt neuzeitlichen Gepräges entwickelt, der demographisch und strukturell den mächtigen Metropolen Westeuropas ähnelte - vergleichbar schon mit Antwerpen und Amsterdam - und im Rahmen des Ostseeraumes und des polnisch-litauischen Staates eine ungewöhnliche Erscheinung darstellte: es war mindestens dreimal so groß wie die nächstfolgenden Städte Krakau, Warschau und Königsberg.

---

77 Dies. (wie Anm. 72, Les relations).
78 Ebd.; vgl. auch dies. (wie Anm. 65), S. 66f.
79 Dies. (wie Anm. 61), S. 95.

88

Leider ist hier nicht der Raum, auf die Folgen des Metropolewerdens für die innere gesellschaftliche Struktur Danzigs gründlicher einzugehen. Ich möchte nur einige wichtige Erscheinungen erwähnen, u.a. die Entstehung der ersten Elemente des Frühkapitalismus im Handel und Gewerbe und die Zersetzung des klassischen mittelalterlichen Zunftsystems. Das entspricht meiner Sicht auf die Rolle einer Metropole beim Hervorbringen von Innovationen[80]. Sie hatten eine gewaltige Umwandlung in den Lebensverhältnissen der Danziger Einwohner zur Folge: das Aufkommen der Gruppe vermögender Unternehmer und Verleger auf der einen Seite, auf der anderen die Proletarisierung der armen Meister und die Umwandlung zahlreicher Handwerksgesellen in ewige Lohnarbeiter[81]. Dieser Prozeß hat zur Entstehung tiefer Gegensätze - wichtiges Kennzeichen einer Metropole - beigetragen[82].

Die Widersprüche wurden auch dadurch verschärft, daß sich im 17. Jahrhundert das Interesse der Oberschichten in Danzig von Handel und städtischen Geschäften auf den Ankauf von ländlichen Gütern verschob[83]. Das bedeutete eine Entfremdung der Führungsschichten, die durch die luxuriöse, immer deutlicher auf Konsum eingestellte Lebensweise in prächtigen Residenzen noch gefördert wurde[84]. Solch ein Lebensstandard wurde durch die tüchtige Handelstätigkeit der Generationen ermöglicht, die enorme Profite im Danziger Hafen zu schaffen wußten. Die Analyse des Gewinns, den die Danziger Kaufleute durch Ankauf von Getreide und Verkauf desselben an fremde Schiffer oder auch durch den Verkauf von importierten Waren (Tuch, Wein, Spezereien) erzielten, ergibt eine durchschnittliche Rate von 30-40, zuweilen sogar über 100%[85]. Es war ein "Metropolengewinn", der aus der Differenz in der Preisgestaltung zwischen der Metropole einerseits und ihrem Hinterland andererseits gezogen wurde[86].

Da die Führungsschicht sich immer weniger für die spezifisch bürgerlichen Tätigkeiten interessierte, übernahmen die Mittelschichten deren bisherige Obliegenheiten in den Bereichen Handel, Reederei und Finanzen. In dieser Zeit wuchsen die Mittelschichten nach Schätzungen bis auf 40% der Bevölkerung, und sie vermehrten ihren Reichtum sehr schnell. Weil gleichzeitig die Unterschichten sich relativ schnell proletarisierten, kam es zur Entstehung großer Unterschiede im Lebensstandard und in der Lebensweise, die für eine Metropole typisch sind[87].

---

80 Dies. (wie Anm. 64), S. 264ff.
81 Ebd., S. 307ff.
82 Dies.: Zur Lebensweise des Danziger Bürgertums im 16. Jahrhundert. In: Hansische Studien 7 (1984), S. 81-90.
83 Dies. (wie Anm. 61), S. 96f.
84 Ebd.
85 Dies.: Zur Problematik der Profite im Handel zwischen Danzig und Westeuropa 1550-1650. In: Hansische Studien 5 (1981), S. 41-50.
86 Ebd.; vgl. auch dies. (wie Anm. 60), S. 124ff.
87 Vgl. dies. (wie Anm. 82).

Mehrere Forscher unterstreichen parasitäre Züge aller Metropolen, die scheinbar ihr Hinterland ausbeuten und sich auf Kosten von dessen Bevölkerung enorm bereichern. Man behauptet, daß die Ungleichheit im Verhältnis Metropole - Hinterland, die einseitige Dominanz, die in dieser Beziehung herrscht, Voraussetzungen für die unvermeidliche Ausbeutung des Hinterlandes bilden müßten. Es gibt aber auch Historiker, die eine positive Rolle der Metropolen betonen, indem sie ihre Wirkungen als stimulierendes und innovatives Phänomen betrachten.

Angesichts des soeben Gesagten ist die Beurteilung des Einflusses des Danziger Handels auf die Entwicklung des Ostseeraumes und des polnisch-litauischen Staates an der Schwelle zur Neuzeit nicht eindeutig. Einerseits, hauptsächlich dank des Danziger Hafens, erlangten Polen sowie in bedeutendem Ausmaße auch Litauen und Livland enge Wirtschaftskontakte mit den internationalen Märkten. Die Folge war eine Umstellung der gesamten Wirtschaft dieser Länder in Richtung eines maximal hohen Exportes landwirtschaftlicher Produkte und Rohstoffe. Dieser Export, der vom Adel mit großer Energie betrieben wurde, bedeutete Reichtum und Macht für die adlige Gesellschaft, ermöglichte u.a. die rasche Entwicklung der altpolnischen Kultur, die in der Renaissance und im Barock ihren Höhepunkt erreichte. Die andere Seite dieses Aufschwungs bildeten jedoch die Unterdrückung und Ausbeutung der Bauernschaft und die Verarmung des Bürgertums, das von den Exportgeschäften fast ausgeschlossen war und dessen gewerbliche Produktion infolge der Konkurrenz zwischen ausländischen und in Danzig hergestellten Industriewaren seit dem Ende des 16. Jahrhunderts immer deutlicher abzunehmen begann. Auch Danzigs Rolle als Finanzzentrum war eine zwiespältige. In erster Linie drängt sich hier die finanzielle Abhängigkeit der Magnaten und des Adels von den Danziger Kaufleuten auf. Das System der Kontraktierung von Getreide auf dem Halm begünstigte zweifellos ein Leben ohne jede Fessel, was - um die Kreditgeber zu befriedigen - oft zu einer Raubwirtschaft auf den Landgütern führte. Anderseits jedoch bewirkten diese Kreditformen, daß wenigstens ein Teil des Geldes für Land- und Waldprodukte nicht in Danzig als Äquivalent für die hier eingekauften Waren zurückblieb, sondern ins Landesinnere gelangte. Dies hatte eine große ökonomische Bedeutung, was übrigens schon von den Zeitgenossen bemerkt und betont wurde[88]. Dieser Geldstrom wirkte ohne Zweifel stimulierend auf die Entwicklung des Hinterlandes, das ohne diesen Silberzufluß noch rascher in die Stagnation hineingeglitten wäre.

Unter den polnischen Forschern formulierte vor fast 40 Jahren Marian Małowist die These vom entscheidenden Einfluß der "kolonialen" Abhängigkeit der an der Ostsee gelegenen Länder von den wirtschaftlich und sozial höher entwickelten Ländern Westeuropas durch

---

88 Dies. (wie Anm. 76), S. 711ff.

Rohstoffexport und Einfuhr von Gewerbeerzeugnissen[89]. Diese Ansicht wurde von anderen Historikern, wie z.B. Antoni Mączak, Henryk Samsonowicz, Jerzy Topolski, weiterentwikkelt[90]. Man unterbreitete sogar eine Definition des Ostseeraumes, als deren Hauptgrundlage weniger geographische Kriterien, als vielmehr die Tatsache dieser Kolonialabhängigkeit angenommen wurde[91]. Die Kolonialthese fand in Kreisen der Historiker einen breiten Widerhall, da sie tatsächlich recht überzeugend die sozialen, verfassungsmäßigen und politischen Besonderheiten der im Ostseeraum gelegenen und sich in der Neuzeit anders als Westeuropa entwickelnden Länder berücksichtigte, wobei insbesondere auf das Problem der sogenannten zweiten Leibeigenschaft zu verweisen wäre[92].

Danzigs Rolle in der Wirtschaft des damaligen Polen wurde schon im 16. und 17. Jahrhundert diskutiert. Der bekannte polnische Dichter des 16. Jahrhunderts, Sebastian Fabian Klonowic, zeigte in seinem berühmten Poem "Der Flößer" eine farbenreiche Vision Danzigs, des großen Ausbeuters, der sich auf Kosten seines Hinterlandes mästet[93]. Ähnlich wird dieses Problem in zahlreichen danzigfeindlichen Anfragen während der polnischen Reichstage des 16. und 17. Jahrhunderts dargestellt[94].

Wie oben ausgeführt, wurde allen Metropolen häufig die Rolle eines Ausbeuters zugeschrieben. Auf Kosten des Hinterlandes und auf Kosten anderer holländischer Städte sei z.B. im 17. Jahrhundert Amsterdam zu seiner kolossalen Macht herangewachsen. Wir wollen hier wenigstens in aller Kürze auf die Ähnlichkeit der Tätigkeit der Kaufleute dieser beiden Städte - Danzig und Amsterdam - hinweisen: breites Wuchertreiben auf dem Lande, Landaufkauf, räuberische Preispolitik. Die gleiche Handlungsweise hatte jedoch in beiden Fällen ganz verschiedene soziale und verfassungsmäßige Folgen. Auf diese Unterschiede in den Folgen sollte sich also das Hauptaugenmerk richten, nicht auf das Problem der Ausbeutung, da der ganze Komplex der Wirkungen einer Metropole auf ihr Hinterland nicht in moralischen, sondern ökonomischen, politischen und sozialen Kategorien betrachtet werden sollte. Das Beispiel Danzig scheint nur die These zu bestätigen, daß die Wirkung einer Metropole auf ihr Hinterland oft vielschichtig ist.

---

89 Marian Małowist: The Economic and Social Development of the Baltic Countries from th 15the to the 17th Centuries. In: Economic History Review, Sec. Series 17 (1959), S. 155-189.
90 Vgl. Henryk Samsonowicz/Antoni Mączak: Feudalism and Capitalism: a Balance of Changes in East-Central Europe. In: East-Central Europe in Transition. From 14th to 17th Century. Hg. v. Antoni Mączak/Henryk Samsonowicz/Peter Burke. Cambridge 1985, S. 6-23; Jerzy Topolski: Sixteenth-Century Poland and the Turning Point in European Economic Development. In: A Republic of Nobles. Studies in Polish History to 1864. Hg. v. Jan K. Fedorowicz. Cambridge 1982, S. 70-90.
91 Vgl. Antoni Mączak/Henryk Samsonowicz: Z zagadnień genezy rynku europejskiego: strefa bałtycka [Zur Entstehung eines europäischen Marktes: die Ostseezone]. In: Przegląd Historyczny 55 (1964), S. 198-225.
92 Vgl. Jerzy Topolski: Economic Decline in Poland from the 16th to the 18th Centuries. In: Essays in European Economic History 1500-1800. Hg. von Peter Earle. Oxford 1974, S. 127-142.
93 Sebastian Fabian Klonowic: Flis [Der Flößer]. Hg. v. Stefan Hrabec. Wrocław 1951.
94 Historia Gdańska [Geschichte Danzigs]. Hg. v. Edmund Cieślak. Bd. 2. Gdańsk 1982, S. 579ff.

Zugleich bestätigt der Fall Danzig auch die These, daß die Hauptstadt und kulturelle Metropole mit der grundlegenden nationalen Idee verknüpft sein muß. Danzigs ethnische und konfessionelle Struktur, die vor allem deutsche und niederländische Herkunft seiner Einwohner und deren protestantische Konfession erlaubten es dieser Stadt nicht, eine überragende politische und kulturelle Rolle im Polen der Neuzeit zu spielen.

Im Laufe des 16. und 17. Jahrhunderts wurde Danzig, wie bekannt, zum mächtigen Kulturzentrum - Blütezeit des Danziger Gymnasiums, der Architektur, Malerei, Skulptur, Buchdruckerei usw. -, welches auf ganz Polen ausstrahlte[95]. Auf der anderen Seite besaß die polnische Adelskultur für Danzigs Bürger beachtenswerte Attraktivität. Man kann also bei der Charakterisierung der Metropole in diesem Falle eher von Symbiose als von Dominanz sprechen[96]. Politisch wurde Danzig in der Adelsrepublik oft als ein schwieriges Problem angesehen, und der stadtfeindliche Adel wählte das schwache, dafür aber polnische und katholische Warschau zum Staatszentrum. Diese Entscheidung gefiel auch den Danziger führenden Schichten, die immer dem König und nicht dem Sejm ihre Untertänigkeit bekundeten[97].

So läßt sich abschließend sagen, daß die polyzentrische Urbanisierung zwischen 1450 und 1650 in Polen zumindest für drei Städte Grundlagen für die Metropolenentwicklung bildete: Krakau durchlief den Weg von einer Hauptstadt, einer politischen Metropole, zur sakralen Metropole. Warschau als Residenzstadt der Könige und Versammlungsort des Sejm entfaltete sich teilweise auch als Metropole im Bereich von Demographie, Politik und Kultur. Danzig wurde eine wirtschaftliche Metropole. Man muß unterstreichen, daß diese Situation - mit Ausnahme von Danzig - nicht durch die eigene innere Entwicklung dieser Städte, sondern durch außerstädtische Ereignisse verursacht wurde. Das ist ein Zeugnis dafür, daß in Polen Städte und Bürgerschaft in der Neuzeit nur eine passive Rolle zu spielen vermochten.

---

95 Ebd., S. 352ff., 686ff.
96 Vgl. Bogucka/Samsonowicz (wie Anm. 24), S. 574ff.
97 Władysław Czapliński: Problem Gdańska w czasach Rzeczypospolitej szlacheckiej [Das Danziger Problem in der Zeit der Adelsrepublik]. In: Przegląd Historyczny 43 (1952), S. 273-286.

XII

ECONOMIC PROSPERITY OR RECESSION AND CULTURAL PATRONAGE: THE CASE OF GDANSK IN THE 16TH-18TH CENTURIES

The relations between economy and culture are multiform and complicated and the *communis opinio* that cultural investments are the first to be reduced drastically during an economic crisis should be reexamined. First steps in this direction were already made during the Prato Conference on *Investments and Urban Culture*[1] held in 1977, but it seems that there are still some more points to be analysed.

Let me first state that cultural patronage in the Early Modern period was not only a simple expression of the patron's wealth – it was also an important social obligation serving to maintain the prestige and social status of an individual as well as of the whole group. Cultural patronage thus played an extremely important role in the shaping of the structures of social differentiation especially on the higher levels of the social hierarchy. It seems that the psychological and political factors greatly influenced the behaviour of the Early Modern patrons, often counterbalancing their economic intentions and conditions. The case of Gdańsk gives a very convincing proof for this hypothesis.

The history of Early Modern Gdańsk can be divided into two parts:

1. The 16th and the first half of the 17th century – a period of economic prosperity and rapid general development of the city;

2. The second part of the 17th century and the 18th century – a period of economic decline due to wars, depopulation and changes in the international trade in the Baltic region.

The number of inhabitants rose from 30,000 to 100,000 during the first period and dropped to 50,000 in the second. Grain exports which rose from 10,000 to more than 100,000 lasts at the beginning of the 17th century, fell to 20-30,000 lasts. The decline encompassed the industrial production of the

---

[1] *Investimenti e civilta urbana seccoli XIII-XVIII. Nona settimana di Studio "Istituto Francesco Datini", Prato 1977.

city.[2] A comparison of cultural patronage in these two periods shows a rather balanced picture, and it seems that it could serve well as the basis of some more general reflections on the relationship between economy and culture.

There are two kinds of cultural patronage: individual and collective. Because of the lack of sources it is difficult to compare systematically individual patronage activities in Gdańsk in those two periods. It seems, however, that the "great", conspicious forms of patronage prevailing in times of prosperity (like large building activities) were replaced by smaller, more modest forms (like investments in collections of books, paintings, sculptures etc.) in times of crisis. I have already written about this.[3] In this paper I therefore would like to concentrate on collective patronage, that is the patronage displayed by the urban authorities of Gdańsk.

We have at our disposal data on Gdańsk's communal expenses on culture, that is on building activities, reconstruction and maintenance work on the Town Hall, the acquisition of paintings and sculptures, the salaries of artists and school masters, the scholarships for students, gratifications for scholars and writers etc. This information is contained in the following table.[4]

	Times of Prosperity			Times of Recession	
Year	florins	global expenses (%)	Years	florins	global expenses (%)
1540	11,576	34.4	1770-78	1,232,390	25.48
1551	14,045	34.9	1778-87	400,471	8.95
1593	13,046	7.5	1787-93	448,227	14.69
1602	25,060	12.3			
1616	35,994	17.4			

[2] E. Cieślak (ed.), Historia Gdańska (The History of Gdańsk), II, Gdańsk 1983, passim, III, Gdańsk 1993, passim.

[3] M. Bogucka, Les bourgeois et les investissements culturels: L'exemple de Gdańsk aux XVIe et XVIIe siècles, Revue historique 259 (1978), pp. 429-440; eadem, Mecenat w czasie kryzysu gospodarczego: Wydatki władz miejskich Gdańska na kulturę w XVIII w. (The patronage during an Economic Crisis: the Municipal Expenses in Gdańsk on Culture in the 18th Century), M. Bogucka, J. Kowecki (eds.), Kultura polska a kultura europejska, Warszawa 1987, pp. 80-88; eadem, Die Kultur und Mentalität der Danziger Bürgerschaft in der zweiten Hälfte des 17. Jahrhunderts, S.O. Lindquist (ed.), Economy and Culture in the Baltic 1650-1700, Visby 1989, pp. 129-140; eadem, Testament burmistrza Hansa Speymanna z 1625 r. (The Last Will of the Gdańsk's Mayor Hans Speyman in 1625), Kultura staropolska i średniowieczna: Studia ofiarowana A. Gieysztorowi, Warszawa 1991, pp. 587-597.

[4] Source: M. Foltz, Geschichte des Danziger Stadthaushalts, Danzig 1912, pp. 463, 474-476, 486, 489.

This table shows more than a tenfold rise of nominal (expressed in florins) expenses on culture in the Gdańsk's municipal budget between 1540 and 1793. However, the deterioration of money and inflation should be taken into consideration. From 1540-1593 one florin was the equivalent of 2.28-1.875 grams of pure silver, from 1602-1616 it was 1.997-1.692 grams, while from 1770-1793 it was only 0.189 grams.[5] This means that real expenditure on culture remained almost the same in times of prosperity or recession.

The examination of the place of culture within the city's budget shows similar results. The share of expenses on culture in times of prosperity oscillated between 7.5% and 34.9% of the total expenses, while in times of economic decline they were between 8.95% and 25.48%. Thus there was no drastic decrease and the inferior limit had even slightly risen. The analysis of the structure of expenditure shows similar tendencies. In times of prosperity, expenditure on building activities oscillated between 7.1% and 34.4% of the city's budget.[6] During recessions they fluctuated between 4.7% and 19.35% — this was a serious but not drastic decline.[7] At the same time the share of expenditure on schools, salaries of scientists and artists, scholarships, writers' gratifications etc. rose — in periods of prosperity they amounted to less than 1%, while in periods of recession they reached about 4.25%-8.97% of the whole budget. The rise is obvious,[8] and supports our thesis that in times of economic decline cultural patronage concentrated mostly on small activities while abandoning great building enterprises.

The comparison of municipal budget structures in times of prosperity with those in times of recession shows some stability of the expenditure on culture in the Early Modern era. It seems that in spite of a crisis, town authorities tried to keep up the old level of the city's cultural patronage. With the decline in trade and in crafts, with depopulation as well as with the rise in political unrest, the town's council attempted to support the cultural role of the city. In the Early Modern era prestige was so closely linked to cultural patronage that Gdańsk's authorities believed it would be possible to save the social and political image of the town if cultural accomplishments were maintained despite the economic decline.

However, in order to display such policy some financial means were needed. Gdańsk did have enough resources because of the accumulation of wealth and capital during the first period. Other towns were less well off. Let me recall the case of Toruń — the second great city of Royal Prussia after Gdańsk. According to Jerzy Wojtowicz' estimates, 5% of Toruń's budget in the 16th century was used to support culture and at the end of the 16th and

---

[5] J. Pelc, Ceny w Gdańsku (Prices in Gdańsk), Lwów 1937, pp. 2ff.
[6] Bogucka, Mecenat, p. 86.
[7] Ibidem.
[8] Ibidem.

the beginning of the 17th century it was even 15%.[9] After the Polish-Swedish wars in a crisis situation expenses on culture decreased to 3%-4% in Toruń; in the second half of the 18th century they oscillated around 8%.[10] The comparison between Gdańsk and Toruń leads to the observation that the stability of expenses on culture depends to some extent on the dimensions of the wealth of the patron: the richer a patron, the more stable the share of cultural expenditure in his budget. Changes in the economic situation certainly result into changes in expenditure on culture, but in wealthy urban centres (or in rich individual households) the expenses were usually not drastically cut down. In the Early Modern world, when culture was regarded not only as a pleasure or entertainment but also as a social obligation, as legitimation of one's social position, it was not easy to decide to spare expenditure in this direction, because such savings could upset the delicate balance of respect and social approval. Social and political as well as personal desire to maintain prestige and the superior place achieved in the social hierarchy advised the Early Modern patron to avoid reducing the expenses on culture as long as possible. Significant economies in this field would occur only in a situation of major economic troubles, for instance when all the patron's resources were already spent and his choice in financial matters was exhausted. Thus the phenomenon of the belated reflection of an economic crisis in the sphere of culture, the shift between economy and cultural decline, was especially typical for the Early Modern era, an epoch when psychological and social factors in cultural patronage were almost as important as economic ones.

---

[9] J. Wojtowicz, Miejskie inwestycje kulturalne w Prusach Królewskich w XVI-XVIII w. (Municipial Cultural Investments in Royal Prussia in the 16th-18th century), Zapiski Historyczne 1978, No 2, pp. 42-43.

[10] Ibidem. See also L. Koczy, Dzieje wewnętrzne Torunia do r.1793 (The History of the City of Toruń until 1793), Toruń 1933, Table XXIV.

XIII

Health care and poor relief in Danzig (Gdansk)
The sixteenth- and first half of the seventeenth century

GENERAL REMARKS

Danzig in the early modern era was a prosperous Baltic port of 30–40,000 inhabitants in the sixteenth century and about 100,000 in the first half of the seventeenth century.[1] In the social structures of Danzig the proportion of poor people – that is of those who were not paying any urban taxes – could be estimated at the beginning of the sixteenth century at between 20 and 25 per cent of the total population and was rising constantly.[2]

The town had a diversified commercial and industrial economy and was built around the greatest port of the Baltic region.[3] Since Danzig was bursting with trade and offered excellent opportunities for different jobs it was a focus of a constant stream of immigrants – permanent as well as temporary. Seamen, foreign merchants, craftsmen, wandering journeymen, Polish noblemen and their servants, poor people of both sexes seeking support through begging or temporary work – all these people were daily coming to the city. Some of them had no money to pay for their food and shelter, others who came for a short stay had to prolong their sojourn because of sudden illness. Such transients who lacked family or friends to look after them were a serious problem in most port cities. Thus illness and poverty were important social phenomena that met with a social response from municipal authorities as well as from individual town dwellers.

POOR RELIEF

The victory of the Reformation and the new approach to the problem of poverty resulted in Danzig in changes to poor relief organisation.[4] An urban law passed in 1525 stated that beggars should be mustered. All people able to work must leave the town; those coming back would be punished by marking one ear; if caught a second time they were to be imprisoned and sentenced to work in jail for life. Only the very ill and the weak were to be offered lodging in the town's hospitals, but even in these institutions they were to perform some work according to their abilities.[5] The innkeepers were warned not to shelter any beggars or 'idle people' and all parents were admonished not to allow their children to speak to or even approach a beggar.[6]

A second poverty law was passed in 1551. The city was divided into districts headed by special beggars' officers. They had to muster all beggars periodically; foreign ones were to be expelled from the city; local beggars genuinely in need of help were to be registered and given tokens allowing them to beg alms in strictly determined places.[7] In spite of these laws, similar to those issued across the whole of Europe in this period,[8] the city was full of beggars of both sexes, and rich burghers complained that they were constantly molested by poor people, often sick or invalid, both men and women, old people as well as children, who begged for money or bread.[9] Some of these poor were even dying on the streets.[10] The problem was very acute because of the association of beggars with criminality; indeed, many thefts were committed by beggars. They also acted as snoopers and feelers, gathering information for robbers and organised gangs; female beggars were often suspected of prostitution or even of witchcraft, and were feared because of their 'evil eye'.

To control this poverty the town authorities tried to develop and improve the network of urban hospitals. Since the Middle Ages there had been several hospitals in Danzig:

- In the city centre: the Hospital of the Holy Spirit (established 1253, extended in the sixteenth century by developing the so-called Back Hospital), as well as the Hospital of St Elisabeth (established before 1308) and the Hospital of St Jacob (established in 1414).
- In the suburbs: the Hospital of St Barbara (established in 1378), the Hospital of St Gertrud (established in 1342), the Smallpox Hospital with the so-called Lazaretto (end of the fifteenth Century, extended in 1542 by a Hospital for Mental Illness), the Hospital of Corpus Christi (established before 1385), the Hospital of All God's Angels (1380), and the Pestilence Hospital (1454).[11]

Altogether there were nine urban hospitals, each richly endowed with land and annuities. For instance St Jacob's Hospital owned large meadows at the outskirts of the city and several parcels of land in the city.[12] The Hospital of the Holy Spirit owned six villages, the St Elisabeth Hospital five to seven villages.[13] Besides plots of land in the countryside and parcels of land in the city, hospitals owned annuities and collected rents allotted to them in foundations and legacies made by town authorities, guild brotherhoods and individual rich burghers.[14] They also used casual alms collected by the hospital officers, sometimes by hospital lodgers themselves. In the middle of the sixteenth century a special institution called a Charity Board (*Spendeamt*) was established to seek alms and distribute the sums collected among individual beggars as well as among the hospitals.[15]

Hospitals, as can be seen from their accounts, had large sums of money at their disposal – thousands of Prussian Marks yearly.[16] No wonder that the office of hospital supervisor was regarded with envy as a very profitable business; that many conflicts occurred over who controlled hospitals; and accusations of fraud in hospital accounts were made throughout the sixteenth century.[17] As early as 1546, stricter control by the town council over hospitals was demanded and established.[18] At the beginning of the seventeenth century a new attempt was made to improve poor relief: in 1606 the financial arrangements as well as the administration of five main hospitals (St Elisabeth, the Holy Spirit, the Back Hospital, the Smallpox Hospital, and the Pestilence Hospital) were united and put under the closer supervision of the Charity Board. In 1610 the Board was given a new constitution which gave it better control over all the hospitals as well as over all the city's poor.[19]

In spite of the reform, the hospitals retained their twofold character as both poorhouses for old and invalid people, and simultaneously as infirmaries for the temporarily sick. The majority of Danzig's hospitals, however, were hospices, for instance St Jacob's Hospital (where old and crippled seamen were lodged),[20] or the Hospital of the Holy Spirit, the St Gertrud Hospital, the St Elisabeth, as well as the Corpus Christi Hospital. Only the Pestilence Hospital and the Smallpox Hospital with its Lazaretto had the character of infirmaries.

Although numerous, the hospitals were inadequate to the needs of a quickly expanding city. In spite of the fact that hospitals were rebuilt and extended during the sixteenth century, each of them

could accommodate only a few people. St Jacob's Hospital, for
instance, could keep only thirteen poor sailors, together with a
number of wealthier seamen who could pay for their stay in the
institution. Altogether in this hospital were lodged probably
between twenty and thirty people.[21] In the year 1545 in the
Hospital of St Elisabeth there were forty-five people accommodated,
while in the Holy Spirit there were twenty-eight.[22] It is estimated
that altogether Danzig's hospitals could house probably 300–400
people. This was very few considering the needs of the several
thousand resident poor.

There was great competition for getting a place in the hospitals
and it was certainly not the poorest individuals who were always the
winners. In the sixteenth- and seventeenth centuries the most
popular form of introduction into a hospital was by the purchase of
residence, an opportunity which arose only on the death of a
previous lodger. Between the end of the sixteenth century and the
beginning of the seventeenth (before the great devaluation of the
Prussian Mark in 1619–21) the price varied between twenty and
200 Prussian Marks.[23] These were rather substantial prices. The big
difference in them could serve as evidence of a significant material
differentiation among the hospitals' lodgers. Often they were not
really poor people and their probate inventories confirm such
suspicions. Among the hospitals' lodgers there were people who
owned some money which they used to lend to people in need;
besides cash and loan bills, inventories often list respectable people's
belongings, for instance good garments or even pieces of jewellery.
On 12 February 1641, the Hospital of Corpus Christi sold the
belongings of two of its dead lodgers for the not inconsiderable sum
of fifty-seven Prussian Marks.[24] At the beginning of the year 1612
the same hospital received 100 Prussian Marks due from debtors of
one of its lodgers.[25] In the year 1619 the Hospital of Corpus Christi
sold belongings of its dead lodgers for fifty-two Prussian Marks and
received 800 Prussian Marks as returned loans.[26]

The probate inventories of two women who died in the Pestilence
Hospital have been preserved. The wife of Hans Kuren, who died on
12 December 1608, left some garments (four shirts, two bonnets,
one towel, one napkin, five collars, one cap, one fur coat, one blue
dress of coarse cloth, one old coat), one brass cauldron, one tripod,
one shelf, one barrel, one pail and a few bedclothes (one featherbed,
one sheet – the second one 'she took with her to the grave' – one
pillow and one mattress). She left some debts to be paid, together

totalling fifty-eight Prussian Marks. Her funeral cost forty-eight Prussian Marks and six Pennies.[27] Before she was accepted into the hospital she had been ill at home for three months.

On 30 August 1609 a woman called Elisabeth (the last name is not mentioned) died in the same hospital. She left some modest garments and bedclothes as well as a small 'treasury' – a silver scale and silver belt both pawned for twenty Prussian Marks (the cash, however, was not found). She also owned five books, three painted glass vases, thirteen paintings, one 'painted letter to hang on the wall', one painting on wood and five small pictures printed on paper (woodcuts?). Her funeral cost fifty-three Prussian Marks.[28]

Both lists show some degree of wealth, in the second case the existence of objects associated with culture and education (books!). Both of the cited inventories are, however, not typical of our theme: they present the belongings not of a permanent hospital lodger, but only of a temporary one.

The conditions of life in a hospital were very much differentiated. They depended mostly on the route of admission to the hospital: the poor accepted without any fee had to be satisfied with modest conditions, while people who had bought their residence were offered some privileges. There were basic rooms where two or more people had to share one bed, but some lodgers were given their own bed or even their own private room.[29] The duty to work (cleaning, wood cutting, water carrying, helping in the kitchen) was also shared unequally. The same was the case with personal discipline (limited rights to invite guests, a prohibition on leaving the hospital premises without permission, prohibition on returning late at night, etc.). Each offence was punished by different penalties: reprimand, food deprivation or even expulsion from the institution.

All lodgers, without regard to their wealth and status in the hospital, were united in prayers and large religious ceremonies, which took up a great part of the daily routine in each hospital. Prohibitions on fighting, stealing, name-calling and abusing fellow inmates, which are included in all hospital ordinances, testify that life within the institution was not always harmonious.[30]

Meals were also differentiated, depending on the status of lodgers, despite the fact that food was mainly served in a common room. Hospital accounts list large sums spent on purchasing meat, fish, butter, peas and groats; farms owned by the hospitals produced milk and cheese, fruit and vegetables.[31] For drink, cheap beer was served.[32] It seems that food in the hospitals was varied and perhaps much better than that available to individual poor living on their own. At the end of the sixteenth- and on the threshold of the seventeenth century, in Corpus Christi Hospital on average 760 Prussian Marks were spent on food yearly.[33] Assuming that the hospital sheltered thirty-five people this would give twenty-two Prussian Marks per person, that is one penny daily, the same as a hard working journeyman received towards his food.[34] It means that food in hospitals was not scarce. The problem, however, was its distribution; probably the largest share went to the hospital officers and wealthy lodgers, while the poor had to be satisfied with leftovers. Hence the complaints from one side and the ban on rejecting food on the other, as well as the prohibitions on food stealing or taking food out and selling it outside the hospital.[35]

In cold seasons the hospitals were heated – the accounts usually list the expenses for firewood. Expenses for musicians and singers are also mentioned, probably connected with the religious ceremonies performed in these institutions.[36]

Hospitals were not the only institutions dedicated to poor relief. In the year 1542 a Home for Children was established close to St Elisabeth's Hospital; at first both establishments had a common administration and finances. The Home for Children was meant to solve one of the important problems of the quickly expanding maritime town: the care of numerous illegitimate children, of foundlings and orphans. The institution could, however, foster at most forty children, which seriously limited its role. In 1552, King Sigismund Augustus issued a special privilege giving to the charity boys and girls the same rights which the children of legal birth enjoyed.[37] The Home was directed by four supervisors appointed by the town council. Here also a fee for admission was required and sometimes a substantial one: from ten to 2,000 Polish Florins! We do not know the proportion of poor to more wealthy children accepted into the Home, but competition for admission was probably great. The majority of admitted children were infants (hence the several wet nurses on the staff), but older ones may also have been accepted. The nurslings were kept in the Home till their adolescence. They were taught to read, write and do some arithmetic as well as to perform some practical manual jobs; above all, however, they learned to pray and to sing religious songs and psalms.[38] We know very little about the conditions of life in the Home, but from casual evidence they were probably quite tolerable. Food and garments were largely provided by donations made by rich merchants.

Rising criminality, especially youth delinquency, resulted in 1629 in the establishment of a workhouse.[39] Here the men, women and children had to learn social discipline by hard work, prayers and hunger; all offences, even minor transgressions, were to be punished by confiscation of meals and floggings. It was a classical kind of workhouse, organised on the Dutch pattern (after the model of Amsterdam's workhouse), with men rasping Brazilian wood or weaving cloth, women spinning, and children combing wool. The working hours in summer were from four to nine o'clock, in winter from five to nine, and the food ration was extremely small. Only very efficient workers received some extra pay with which they were allowed to buy extra food.[40]

As we can see from this short survey, poor relief in Danzig encompassed several kinds of institutions: hospitals for adults, an orphanage and a workhouse. The purpose of all these institutions was not only to ease the life of the poor, but also to control them, and to limit the danger of poverty disturbing social stability or resulting in criminality. But in spite of considerable resources accorded to it, poor relief and the network of charity establishments were too weak to solve the problems of the rapidly increasing numbers who were in need of help. Admission to hospitals as well as to the orphanage constituted a field of bitter competition which resulted in the favouring of the upper strata of poverty; the very poor, those without any financial resources, had little chance of becoming hospital lodgers. Hence the great number of beggars in Danzig and the constant increase in numbers of the socially marginal, including thieves and prostitutes.

The inadequacy of institutional poor relief resulted in the survival of individual charity in spite of the new attitudes toward poverty introduced by the Reformation. Beggars, often invalid or sick, were visible in the streets, lying in front of churches and other buildings, seeking shelter within town gates or in the hollows in town walls. In cold weather it was not rare to find a dead person on the street. In spite of the Reformation's rejection of good works as expressed in charitable giving, rich merchants still eased their conscience by giving alms and donating large sums to poor people in their wills. In the year 1564 Conrad and Barbara von Suchten offered the city the capital of 15,000 Prussian Marks for a yearly rent of 1,000 Marks, from which 100 Marks were to be distributed among the poor, 100 Marks given to the orphans and 100 Marks to the Smallpox Hospital. Other wills were less generous, but amounts

XIII

from 1,000 to 1,500 Marks were often bequeathed to the poor, as well as garments and food. For instance in the second half of the sixteenth century a rich merchant, Anthony Ulrich, offered 1,500 Marks

> davon 60 Mrk Zinsen alle Jahr fallen, wofur man den elenden Kindern des Waisenhauses und den anderen personen auf den Tag Ulrici eine Mahlzeit anrichten soll: nemlich eine Tonne Bier, einen halben Ochsen, item Grutz mit Milch gekocht und einen Jedem einen Strutzel von 2 Groschen.[41]

Beggars and poor people were invited to funerals, and for their attendance and prayers were given food as well as small sums of money. All these donations were, however, insufficient and the expanding town had to cope with a growing margin of poverty and social discontent.

HEALTH CARE

As mentioned above, hospitals were above all poorhouses and not medical institutions. But they did supply certain medical services. The Smallpox Hospital had a medical doctor and a barber-surgeon among its personnel who attended sick people admitted to this institution. The Pestilence Hospital and Lazaretto were also institutions with medical functions. In other hospitals physicians and barbers were called in as required; in cases of need some medicines were distributed among the lodgers without charge.

As a large maritime city, Danzig had to cope with several diseases. The town's area of little more than 200 hectares was literally crammed with people. Sanitation facilities were inadequate. Only few rich houses had their own water supply, special bathrooms and well arranged privies. The level of personal hygiene was low. Most people lived close together: five or six to a room, sleeping two or three to a bed, sharing towels, eating from one bowl. As a result, contagious diseases were easily spread either by direct contact between individuals via the respiratory system, or by use of the same utensils, or transferred by insects such as fleas and lice. Venereal diseases spread rapidly mainly because of the influx to Danzig of large numbers of single men. The coastal climate of the city – cold and damp – as well as the insufficient heating and the use of cellars for housing the poor, resulted in a high frequency of rheumatic and pulmonary ailments. Dirt in kitchens, as well as stale food, must have caused a number of digestive troubles.

The frequency of bodily injuries resulted from the rough conditions of daily life as well as from the conditions of work on shipboard, at the harbour or in the workshops. Hard work, performed without suitable protection, caused numerous accidents. The typical diet of the poor inhabitants of Danzig was composed mostly of grain, and, lacking in vitamins and protein, resulted in anaemia, scurvy and a generally low individual resistance to contagious diseases. Over-nutrition – too much meat, animal fat, alcohol – caused heart and circulatory troubles among the wealthy burghers.[42]

Illness in the early modern period was primarily a family affair. The bedridden were attended by other family members, mostly women. But not everyone in Danzig had family around their sickbed. The number of single people in this large maritime city was growing throughout the period under consideration.[43] An even more complicated problem was posed by the influx of people coming to the city for a short stay, usually for some weeks only. Such visitors were especially numerous in summer, when the harbour was busy.

Since the Middle Ages guilds and journeymen brotherhoods had organised special 'sickrooms' in their inns, where ill wandering craftsmen (also local ones, but only those without family or their masters' support) could find bed and care.[44] In the sixteenth- and seventeenth centuries such sickrooms and dispensaries were organised by furriers, tawers, cartwrights, wheelwrights, coopers, pailmakers, carpenters, pewterers, nailmakers, gunsmiths, cutlers, blacksmiths, coppersmiths, butchers, ship carpenters, bricklayers, saddlers, beltmakers and potters.[45] At the beginning of the seventeenth century, carpenters tried to establish a sickroom for their journeymen in one of the municipal hospitals.[46] To take care of a sick person in such a room, a woman was usually hired, and sometimes other journeymen also gave their services to help sick colleagues.[47] The problem of taking care of sick journeymen was so important that it was the main reason why masters and town authorities allowed several journeymen's brotherhoods to be established in Danzig.[48]

But the journeymen's sickrooms and dispensaries solved the needs of one social group only. Danzig's influx of sailors and foreign merchants as well as people from the Polish hinterland (noblemen as well as their servants and craftsmen) resulted in complications if they were suddenly taken ill. The hospital of St Jacob was dedicated, as mentioned above, to the permanent care of old sailors, and could not offer any help to those seamen who came to Danzig for a short stay and fell ill.[49] St Barbara's Hospital in the suburbs should theoretically have taken care of Polish raftsmen,[50] but as a hospice it could not afford to admit the sick for a short stay and cure. The growing need to help sick visitors to the city resulted in the emergence of a network of inns providing them with a bed, meals appropriate to contemporary ideas of good diet (white bread, wine, nourishing soups) and the care of a doctor or a barber as well as of nursing women.[51] The level of services depended on a patient's means; in the event of death the innkeeper usually arranged the funeral, covering his expenses by selling the belongings of the departed.[52]

THE MENTAL AND MEDICAL RESPONSE TO ILLNESS

There were two characteristic responses to illness in early modern Danzig: one resulting from the pervasiveness of the Protestant faith on citizens' mentality, and the second resulting from the lively contacts between 'learned' and 'popular' culture. Both attitudes were fused into one system of beliefs which enabled individuals to cope with the terrifying phenomena of illness and death.

As faithful adherents of the Lutheran or Calvinist creed, the inhabitants of Danzig saw illness as God's punishment for their sins, and at the same time as an antechamber to death, the gateway leading to a better existence.[53] Their striving for a stoic response to suffering was linked to the idea of predestination, popular in Danzig not only among Calvinists. Pain was regarded as the inevitable path to redemption and eternity. It was, however, logical to conclude that an illness inflicted by God could not be cured without God's help and consent. Medical treatment was therefore accompanied by prayers, and some physicians were bold enough to claim that God was their special ally.[54]

Religious attitudes to illness were confirmed by some 'learned' theories in which health and illness were regarded as phenomena subordinated to astral influences. Renaissance medicine had fortified the traditional belief in the unity of nature, a unity that encompassed God and the stars at one extreme and humanity and the terrestrial world at the other; it therefore seemed reasonable to assume that the stars would influence human life and especially human health. In sixteenth- and seventeenth-century Danzig, many scholars and physicians, such as Bartholomew Wagner, Severin Goebel and Willem Misocacus, agreed that astral influences moulded the state of a person's physical condition. Such attitudes led inevitably to natural magic, which spread among the educated inhabitants of Danzig in the form of several 'learned' theories, as well as among other citizens as witchcraft practices pretending to cure every ailment. The gap between 'learned' and 'popular' issues was not very wide.

Danzig in the sixteenth- and seventeenth centuries was an important centre of medical knowledge.[55] The High School established in the town in the middle of the sixteenth century was of university standard; in the first half of the seventeenth century it obtained the title of Academic School. Danzig maintained lively relations with the best European universities. A great influence on medicine in Danzig had been the famous John Placetomus, who in the second half of the sixteenth century introduced new ideas about the functioning of the human body. The leading physicians in Danzig were Christopher Heyll, who translated and commented on the works of Galen, and Adrian Pauli who worked on problems of diet and personal hygiene. Knowledge of anatomy was advancing rapidly; the first public dissection of a human corpse in Danzig was performed in 1613 by Joachim Oelhaf.[56] In 1643 his son Dr Nicholas Oelhaf published a herbal enumerating 350 plants from the Danzig region and describing their medicinal properties. Laurentius Eichstadt, a professor of anatomy in the years 1645–60, author of an eminent book on osteology and an expert on blood circulation, also achieved some fame. In the 1660s another physician, John Schmidt, tried intravenous injection of medicine on his patients; and some modern theories of blood circulation were developed by Dr Israel Conradt.

How big was the gap between this learned pinnacle of the medical world and average medical practice in Danzig? At the beginning of the seventeenth century the daily treatment of patients was still based primarily on the ideas of the ancients Hippocrates and Galen. Structurally the medical community of Danzig was composed of five distinct layers:

1 physicians or *promoti doctores*, trained in foreign universities and well experienced;

2 mostly self-taught surgeons;
3 barber-surgeons;
4 apothecaries;
5 unlicensed or non-professional healers of all kinds.[57]

At the top was the highly trained elite, the physicians – limited by the municipal authorities to between ten and twenty in number. In about 1530 the post of chief doctor or 'town physician' was created; his duty was to supervise the medical activities conducted by his colleagues. Surgeons and apothecaries had to prove their skill before him in order to obtain a license. In 1636 a collective supervisory body was established: the *Collegium Medicum*. It was a kind of Chamber of Medicine with the power to control medical affairs in the city. Anyone who wanted to get into medical practice in Danzig was obliged to present himself and his diploma before the *Collegium* and to pass an examination; in 1677 the duty to deliver a public lecture was added to the requirements.

Regulations improved the level of medical services. Blood letting and purgations were still in popular use, but there were also attempts to make individual diagnoses. Patients were carefully examined, their urine tested, their pulse and temperature checked. Physicians used both dietary prescriptions as well as chemical or herbal remedies. The dense network of dispensaries offered easy access to a wide range of syrups, powders, ointments and pills. Danzig had two town apothecary shops, one in the Main Town and another in the Old Town, which were put out on lease to some learned people. In addition there were many small private establishments, controlled by the town's physicians.[58]

Alongside learned medicine, popular healing continued to be widely practised. It was based on traditional folklore as well as on belief in magic amulets, secret miraculous remedies and witchcraft. Such beliefs were also shared by members of enlightened circles, who often resorted to the help of unofficial healers. Quacks were numerous in spite of fierce protests from learned professionals.

Women played a considerable role in popular medicine. The task of attending the sick was traditionally a female duty which over the centuries had enabled women to acquire a substantial body of medical knowledge. Women attended not only members of their own families but also ailing neighbours or foreign visitors in need. Women traditionally held a monopoly on delivering babies. Only in the richest families had calling a doctor to childbed come into practice in the seventeenth century; middle-class women were attended by a professional midwife.[59] In 1610 Danzig had established an official post of 'town midwife' with an annual salary of 100 marks, to attend women of wealthier families as well as to supervise the activities of other professional midwives. She was also obliged to testify in the court of justice in cases where infanticide was suspected.[60]

Analysis of Danzig's records shows that the incidence of professional medical care by physicians and barbers was rising in the town, especially in the seventeenth century.[61] The sources also show that acute illness in the seventeenth century was usually of short duration in Danzig: of 162 cases studied, 105 (64 per cent) resulted in death within one week, twenty-nine (18 per cent) within one month, twenty (12 per cent) within two months; in seven cases (4 per cent) the illness lasted more than one year.[62]

One might assume that the lack of more sophisticated treatment did not allow sick people in a critical condition to stay alive longer than a few days or weeks. But another explanation is also possible: the records analysed mostly concern the poor, and these probably only sought professional help *in extremis*, in order to avoid the high cost of treatment for as long as possible. Unfortunately we do not possess any statistics concerning the duration of illness among the wealthier inhabitants of Danzig.

Because of the limited dimensions of this study it is not possible to include an assessment of the epidemics, which plagued sixteenth- and seventeenth-century Danzig with extraordinary frequency and high mortality. This needs to be investigated separately.

CONCLUSIONS

1 In spite of extensive provisions, poor relief in Danzig in the sixteenth- and first half of the seventeenth century did not meet the great needs of the expanding maritime city. It resulted in the survival of traditional forms of charity (individual alms-giving, the poor begging on the streets) along with the development of institutional forms such as hospitals, an orphanage and a workhouse.

2 Health care outside the family was organised in the form of several institutions: hospitals, guild dispensaries, private sickrooms. The existence of such establishments was important in a large port

where many visitors fell ill without family or friends to attend them.

3 Along with the learned, rather well developed medicine, popular healing, consisting of extensive use of traditional remedies including some witchcraft practices, also existed in Danzig. The gap between learned and popular medicine was narrow. Both regarded illness as a punishment inflicted by God which could not be cured without God's help. Pain should be met with patience and stoicism. But in spite of the popularity of such ideas, the inhabitants of Danzig were eager to try every wonder medicine that promised to cure them.

NOTES

1 Maria Bogucka, 'Danzig and der Wende zur Neuzeit: von der Aktivon Handelsstadt zum Stapel und Produktionszentrum', *Hansische Geschichtsblätter*, 102 Jg., 1984, 95.

2 *Historia Gdanska (History of Danzig)*, ed. Edmund Cieslak, vol. II, Danzig 1982, 552.

3 Maria Bogucka, 'Amsterdam and the Baltic in the First Half of the Seventeenth Century', *Economic History Review*, second series, XXVI, no. 3, 1973, 433–47.

4 Maria Bogucka, 'Przemiany Form Zycia w Gdansku u Progu Ery Nowo Zytnej' ('Changes in the Forms of Life in Danzig at the Threshold of Early Modern Times'), *Kwartalnik Historyczny* no. 4, 1982, 547 ff.; Zdzislaw Kropidlowski, *Formy Opieki nad Ubogimi w Gdansku od XVI do XVIII w. (Poor Relief in Danzig in the Sixteenth- to Eighteenth Centuries)*, Danzig 1992, *passim.*

5 Paul Simson, *Geschichte der Stadt Danzig*, vol. II, Danzig 1918, 77.

6 *ibid.*

7 *ibid.*

8 See Wolfram Fischer, *Stadtische Armut und Armenfürsorge im 15 und 16. Jh.*, Göttingen 1979, *passim.*

9 Bogucka, 'Przemiany', 548.

10 *ibid.*

11 See Reinhold Curicke, *Der Stadt Danzig Historische Beschreibung*, Amsterdam-Danzig 1689, 342 ff.

12 Maria Bogucka, *Gdanscy Ludzie Morza w XVI–XVIII w. (Seamen in Danzig in the Sixteenth- to Eighteenth Centuries)*, Danzig 1984, 101 ff.

13 Kropidlowski, *Formy Opieki*, 76 ff. Danzig Archives (hereafter AG) 300, 61/96; 300, R/Rr q 5.

14 Kropidlowski, *Formy Opieki*, 38 ff.

15 *ibid.*

16 See the accounts of the Holy Spirit and the St Elisabeth Hospitals for the years 1587–99, AG 300, R/Rr q 5; as well as Corpus Christi Hospital for the years 1609–19, AG 300, 61/96, 98, 104.

17 Kropidlowski, *Formy Opieki*, 48 ff.; Bogucka, *Gdanscy Ludzie Morza*, 103.
18 Simson, *Geschichte*, 187, 191, 390, 543.
19 Kropidlowski, *Formy Opieki*, 45 ff.
20 Bogucka, *Gdanscy Ludzie Morza*, 101–5.
21 Bogucka, *Gdanscy Ludzie Morza* 105.
22 Kropidlowski, *Formy Opieki*, 81.
23 AG 300, R/Rr q 5, 300, 61/96–104.
24 AG 300, 61/97.
25 AG 300, 61/98.
26 AG 300, 61/104.
27 AG 300, R/Vv 117, 232–23. Her husband was ill for six months, but had not died, *ibid.*
28 AG 300, R/Vv 117, 274–5.
29 Kropidlowski, *Formy Opieki*, 106. See also Ag 300, 61/104.
30 Bogucka, *Gdanscy Ludzie Morza*, 102; Kropidlowski, *Formy Opieki*, 103 ff. See also Chapter 8 of this volume.
31 Their own food was largely produced by, for instance, the St Jacobs, St Elisabeth and Holy Spirit Hospitals; see Maria Bogucka, *Organizacja Szpitalnictwa w Gdansku w XVI–XVII w.* (*Organisation of Hospitals in Danzig in the Sixteenth- to Seventeenth Centuries*), forthcoming.
32 *ibid.*
33 AG 300, 61/96–104.
34 *Historia Gdanska*, 554; Maria Bogucka, *Gdańsk Jako Osrodek Produkcyjny od XIV do XVII w* (*Danzig as Production Centre from the Fifteenth to the Seventeenth Century*), Warsaw 1962, 332 ff.
35 Kropidlowski, *Formy Opieki*, 104 ff.
36 *ibid.*, 94, 106.
37 *ibid.*, 116.
38 *ibid.*, 116.
39 Maria Bogucka, 'Les Origines de la Pensée Penitentiaire Moderne en Pologne du 17e s.', *Acta Poloniae Historica*, vol. 56, 1987, 19–28.
40 *ibid.*
41 Gottfried Loschin, *Beitraege zur Geschichte Danzigs und seiner Umgebung*, vol. II, Danzig 1837, 67.
42 Maria Bogucka, 'Illness and Death in a Maritime City: the case of Danzig in the seventeenth century', *The American Neptune*, vol. 51, no. 2, Spring 1991, 91–104.
43 Bogucka, 'Illness', 97.
44 Bogucka, *Gdansk Jako Osrodek Produkcyjny*, 352.
45 *ibid.*
46 AG 300, C/ 1766, 1770, 1772.
47 Bogucka, *Gdansk Jako Osrodek Produkcyjny*, 352.
48 *ibid.*
49 Bogucka, *Gdanscy Ludzie morza*, 103 ff.
50 Kropidlowski, *Formy Opieki*, 78.
51 Bogucka, *Gdanscy Ludzie Morza*, 103 ff.; *idem*, 'Illness', 97 ff.; *idem*, 'Smierc Niezamoznego Mieszkanca Miasta u Progu Ery Nowozytnej' ('Death of a Poor Towndweller on the Threshold of Modern Times'),

XIII

in Andrzej Wyrobisz and Michal Tymowski wiekach, eds, *Gzas-przestrzen-praca w dawnych wiekach*, Warsaw 1991, 285–9.
52 Bogucka, *Gdanscy Ludzie Morza*, 103 ff; *idem*, 'Illness', 97 ff.; *idem*, 'Smierc', 285 ff.; *idem*, 'Tod und Begrabnis der Armen. Ein Beitrag zu Danzigs Alltagsleben im 17. Jh.', *Zeitschrift für Ostforschung*, vol. 41, no. 3, 1992, 321 ff.
53 Maria Bogucka, 'Mentalität der Bürger von Danzig in 16–17. Jh.', *Studia Maritima*, vol. 1, 1978, 64–75.
54 Bogucka, 'Illness', 93
55 See Stanislaw Sokol, *Medycyna w Gdansku w Dobie Odrodzenia (Renaissance Medicine in Danzig)*, Wroclaw 1960, *passim*.
56 Kazimierz Kubik, Lech Mokrzecki, *Trzy Wieki Nauki Gdanskiej (Three Centuries of Science in Danzig)*, Danzig 1976, 139 ff.
57 Bogucka, 'Illness', 94–5.
58 Simson, *Geschichte*, 182.
59 Bogucka, 'Illness', 96.
60 *ibid.*
61 *ibid.*, 100.
62 *ibid.*

XIV

TOWN HALL AS SYMBOL OF POWER

Changes in the Political and Social Functions of Town Hall in
Gdańsk till the End of the 18th Century

The Polish name *ratusz* originates from the German *Rathaus* — "home of
the council", some times also called the "burghers' house" — *Bürgerhaus*.
The institution was strictly connected with the idea of a self–governing
urban centre endowed with special rights, that is with the early medieval
town. The oldest town halls came into being already in the 12th century,
bearing at first the name *domus consulum* (Soest 1120) or *domus civium*
(Cologne 1149). In Poland they appeared at least 100–150 years later. When
the necessity arose to call meetings at which to discuss the common interests
of burghers, it was at first sufficient to have a small room, usually on the
first floor above the market hall, in which the merchant laid out their goods
and drew up transactions, and in which also the town scales were arranged[1].
As the town court also at first had its seat in the town hall it was often called
the "court house" (German *Richthaus* order *Dinghaus*)[2]. Located in town
halls were also the archives with the most valuable and important urban
documents, town's office, seats of the town guards, sometime also the
prison, finally often an inn and pharmacy owned by the city. Apart from the
meetings of the town authorities, court hearings and commercial transactions, the town hall rooms (or square in front of the building) saw ceremonies
connected with important political events on the town– and countrywide
scale such as the rendering of homages, signing of treatises etc. It was here
also, in the town hall, that the social life of the rich towns people was
concentrated, festivities and banquets were held on the occasion of holidays,

---

[1] Cf. O. S t i e h l , *Das deutsche Rathaus im Mittelalter in seiner Entwicklung geschildert*,
Leipzig 1905, pp. 10 ff; J. S p i l l e , *Rathäuser im Rhein —Neckar —Raum bis 1800*. Quellen und
Forschungen zur hessichen Geschichte 62, Darmstadt und Marburg1985, pp. 18 ff.
[2] O. S t i e h l , *op. cit.*, p. 11.

weddings, funerals etc. Thus the town hall was the very centre of life and activities of the town, its main multifunctional headquarters, satisfying various requirements and needs of the burghers. It was not only building, but also, and perhaps even mainly an institution. It was precisely the town hall which fulfilled also an important symbolic function, being a visible sign of the town's autonomy, of its wealth and importance. Hence the situation in the very centre of the town, in the main market or in the main street, as well as the outstanding architecture of the town hall, usually surpassing in size and splendour other urban constructions. Alongside church towers, the town hall towers dominated the panorama of every town and it was here that the great clock was placed to measure time of daily existence, of work and leisure of the town's population.

As from mid–19th century Town Hall of Gdańsk Main City has boasted a wealth of literature, illustrating the interest it awoke[3]. Its past should, however, be considered against the town's history as a whole, and not just against the legal and political situation of the townspeople only, or against the history of the urban architecture. The past of the Town Hall in Gdańsk constitutes an important part of the urban socio–political history as well as a part of the history of the urban mentality, and it is from this point of view that it will be here analised.

Up to the close of the 18th century Gdańsk remained an exceptional town, both in the scale of the Polish Commonwealth as well as of the Baltic region, and thus of the whole North– Eastern Europe[4]. It was an extremely dynamic town, attaining a population of 70–1000,000 inhabitants in the first half of the 17th century, this figure being very considerable even in the scale of Western Europe at that time[5]. A great commercial metropolis, economically dominating over the huge Polish hinterland in the 16th– 17th centuries[6], the main partner of Amsterdam in its turnover with the Baltic until

[3] Cf. J. C. S c h u l t z , *Danzig und seine Bauwerk*, Danzig 1855; K. H o b u r g , *Geschichte und Beschreibung des Rathauses der Rechtstadt Danzig*, Danzig 1857; P. B r a n d t , *Das rechtstädtische Rathaus zu Danzig*, Danzig 1909; K. G r u b e r , *Zur Baugeschichte des Rechtstädtischen Rathauses* in: "Ostdeutsche Monatshefte". Vol. 9, 1928, N° 6; E. K e y s e r , *Die Baugeschichte der Stadt Danzig*, Köln–Wien 1972; T. D o m a g a ł a , *Ratusz Głównego Miasta w Gdańsku w latach 1327–1556*, in: *Sztuka pobrzeża Bałtyku (Art on the Baltic Coast)* Warszawa 1978.
[4] Cf. J e a n n i n , *L'Europe du Nord–Ouest et du Nord aux XVIIᵉ et XVIIIᵉ siècles*, Paris 1969, *passim*.
[5] Cf. M. B o g u c k a , *Danzig an der Wende zur Neuzeit*, "Hansische Geschichtsblätter", Jg. 102, 1984, p. 95.
[6] Cf. S. H o s z o w s k i , *The Polish Baltic Trade in the 15th–18th Centuries*, in: *Poland at the International Congress of Historical Sciences in Stockholm*, Warsaw 1960; M. B o g u c k a , *Handel zagraniczny Gdańska w pierwszej połowie XVII w. (Gdańsk's Foreign Trade in the First Half of 17th Century)*, Wrocław 1970.

at least the mid– 17th century[7], and playing the role of an important intermediary in Western Europe — trade[8], Gdańsk was simultaneously a great centre of industrial production and of handicrafts[9] as well as of credit operations[10] on a scale incomparable with other towns of the Baltic region as well as of the Polish–Lithuanian Commonwealth.

The ambitions of the Gdańsk burghers and particularly of the ruling elite were tremendous — shaped after the calibre of the town's economy and demography, maybe even surpassing it. Much was written already about Gdańsk's legal and political situation in early modern times. From this extensive literature I shall refer here to W. C z a p l i ń s k i 's observations, these probably best defining the character of the town, comparing it to a great feudal lord, to a magnate the typical for such one notions of himself and imperious aspirations[11]. It certainly had an impact on the structures of Gdańsk's Town Hall.

In the Middle Ages, before the arising of an uniform urban community, Gdańsk had not one but four town halls: alongside the Main and Old Town Halls there were two others: the Young City and Osiek Town Halls[12]. The latter two were abolished in the mid– 15th century as rival power centres for the Main Town. The Old Town retained, albeit to a limited extent, its municipal autonomy and thus conserved its seat — a separate Old Town's Hall[13]. Due to the Old Town Council subordination to the Main Town Council, its social and political role was, however, greatly restricted.

Since the mid– 15th century the Main Town Hall was the real centre of power as well as a symbol of the whole township of Gdańsk. The history of the building as well as the history of the institution (and in this study the interest will be focused on the Town Hall as an institution rather than as a building, the latter being a subject of research for the art historians) is, as mentioned, strictly related to the general history of the town and its ruling elite.

---

[7] A. E. C h r i s t e n s e n , *Dutch Trade to the Baltic about 1600*, The Hague 1941.

[8] Cf. E. C i e ś l a k , *Wybrane problemy handlu gdańskiego w okresie rozbiorów Polski*, "Rocznik Gdański", Vol. 33, 1973, Nº 1.

[9] M. B o g u c k a , *Gdańsk jako ośrodek produkcyjny od XIV do połowy XVII wieku (Gdańsk As a Production Centre from the 14th to the mid– 17th Century)*, Warszawa 1964.

[10] M. B o g u c k a , *Les lettres de change et le credit dans les echanges entre Gdańsk et Amsterdam dans la première moitié du XVIIe siècle* Actes du Cinquième Congres International d'Historie Economique, 1970, Moscow 1976, Vol. IV, pp. 31 ff.

[11] W. C z a p l i ń s k i , *Problem Gdańska w czasach Rzeczypospolitej szlacheckiej*, "Przegląd Historyczny", Vol. 43, 1952, Nº 2.

[12] R. C u r i c k e , *Der Stadt Danzig Historische Beschreibung*, Amsterdam–Danzig, 1688, p. 52.

[13] Cf. J. H a b e l a , *Ratusz staromiejski w Gdańsku (The Old City Town Hall in Gdańsk)*, Wrocław 1975.

30

The origin of the Main Town Hall reaches back to 13th century. T. D o m a g a ł a refers it to a document issued by Ladislaus Łokietek (The Elbow) in 1298, in which Łokietek permits the construction of a *pallatium* in Gdańsk, where merchants from Lubeck could store and sell their goods, and matters subject to the town's jurisdiction would be heard. The *pallatium* was also granted the privilege of asylum[14].

This oldest of the Gdańsk town halls, organized after West–European patterns and combining trade with judicial functions, survived the events of 1308 and was extended in 14th century. It worked also after 1346 as in Gdańsk the Lubeck law was replaced by that of Chełmno (the new *locatio* in 1378)[15]. The Town Hall in those times performed various socio–economic functions: in one part of its cellar bear was sold, in another the prison was arranged; the ground floor enclosed merchants' hall alongside with the town treasury and scales. On the first floor the Council's and court rooms were located, and in the corner called Great Christopher — the archives[16].

The changes in the town's legal system resulted in the restructurisation of the Town Hall. According to the Culm law, the juridical activities were now performed by a separate body — the Bench — for which it was necessary to build a special meeting room. This was carried out by demolishing the old skeleton structure of the first floor and building two new brick–built storeys. As from that time, the Town Hall was a two–storey building with the Council on the first floor and Benchers on the second.

The rapid development of the town demanded further expansion of the Town Hall, the original size of which was suited to the modest needs of a rather small urban community. In the second half of the 14th century Heinrich Ungeradin, master Tidemann and the carpenter Gruwel extended small building according to the instructions of the Council, by hightening — among other things — the formerly low Council's conference room and giving it a more imposing appearance. Most probably at that time the Town Hall got its first tower, this being an important symbolic sing of the growing ambitions of the town authorities.

The Thirteen–Years' War opened the way to a new, splendid period in the history of Gdańsk: the city became Poland's main export centre (about 80% of the Polish Commonwealth's seaborne trade)[17]. It enabled its inhabitants to accumulate considerable riches, such as no other town in Poland as

---

[14] T. D o m a g a ł a , *op. cit.*, p. 117.
[15] *Ibidem*, p. 125.
[16] *Ibidem*, p. 127.
[17] Cf. S. H o s z o w s k i , foot–note N⁰ 6.

well as in the Baltic region could even dream of[18]. Polish King Casimir Jagellon favoured Gdańsk with several large privileges[19]; they became the basis for the town's exceptional socio–political position in the 16th–18th centuries.

The Thirteen Years' War constituted also an important stage in the development of the Town Hall. As mentioned, the urban community in Gdańsk was united and two rival centres of power — Osiek and New Town — were abolished; the latter virtually ceased to exist. In the years 1454–1457 the Town Hall was made ready for a royal visit: Casimir Jagellon stayed there twice, 1.5.–7.6.1457 and 11.8.–7.8.1468[20]. As the royal residence the Town Hall was hightened by the third storey, in which the armoury was situated; also reconstructed and hightened was the tower, in 1466 crowned with a spire[21]. In the years 1486–88 the tower's wooden construction was replaced by a brick–built one, the whole being crowned in 1492 with a new slender spire built by Heinrich Hetzel and Michael Ekinger. T. Domagała connects all those improvements with the new special function of the Town Hall which was to house Polish monarchs[22]. Apart from Casimir Jagellon two Polish Kings: Alexander (25.5.–7.6.1504) and Sigismund "The Old" (17.4.–23.7.1526) also stayed here[23].

Housing of the Polish Kings was a highly important function, worthy of special note, as it illustrates the ties between Gdańsk and Poland's rulers. The residing of the King in the Town Hall was a symbolic gesture of exposing to the ruler the very "heart" and "brain" of the town, as well as demonstration of real subjection of Gdańsk's burghers towards their suzerain. The culminant points of this subjection were the homage paid to Casimir Jagellon by the townspeople of Gdańsk in 1457 as well as the trial of the participants of the urban revolt held by Sigismund "The Old" in 1526, both events unrolling in the front of the Town Hall[24]. The fact, that Sigismund August while visiting Gdańsk in 1552 (8.7.–1.9.) resided in the home of one of the prominent burghers instead in the Town Hall, was due not to

---

[18] Cf. M. B o g u c k a , *Z problematyki zysków w handlu bałtyckim. Handel Gdańsk —Europa Zachodnia 1550–1650 (The Profits in the Baltic Trade. Exchange Gdańsk — Western Europe 1550–1650)*, "Rocznik Gdański", Vol. 40, 1980, N⁰ 1.

[19] E. C i e ś l a k , *Przywileje Gdańska z okresu wojny trzynastoletniej na tle przywilejów niektórych miast bałtyckich (Gdańsk Privileges from the Times of Thirteen Years' War Against the Background of Privileges of Other Hanzeatic Towns)*, "Czasopismo Prawno — Historyczne", Vol. 6, 1954, N⁰ 1.

[20] I. F a b i a n i – M a d e y s k a , *Gdzie rezydowali w Gdańsku królowie polscy? (Where Did the Polish Kings Reside in Gdańsk)*, Wrocław — Gdańsk, 1976, pp. 8, 116.

[21] T. D o m a g a ł a , *op. cit.*, pp. 136–137.

[22] *Ibidem*, p. 140.

[23] I. F a b i a n i – M a d e y s k a , *op. cit.*, p. 116.

[24] *Historia Gdańska (The History of Gdańsk)*, Ed. E. C i e ś l a k , Vol. II, Gdańsk 1982, p. 245.

works being carried out in the rear of this building, as some historians try to explain. After Sigismund "The Old" no other Polish king ever held the residence in the Town Hall — and this has certainly a special significance. The aspirations of the Gdańsk's upper strata had grown to such an extent that from the mid– 16th century the relations between the town (or rather its Council) and the central authorities of the state began to be reshaped[25]. The disputes, often drastic clashes between the Kings Sigismund August, Stephen Batory, Ladislaus IV and Gdańsk constitute the best proof in this field. The fact, that the Town Hall from the mid– 16th century became reserved for the use of the town authorities only and was as jealously guarded by them as the power itself, could be seen as the symbol of their exuberantly growing ambitions.

It was during these years, however, that the Town Hall opened its doors, to a certain extent, to the representatives of the urban middle strata. The so–called "Third Order", established in 1526, was to meet in the Town Hall. This was, after all, the result of not so much the democratic changes in the town's political system, as the desire of the Council to maintain strict control over the newly formed body. It is enough to acquaint oneself with the formulations on the subject in the work by R. C u r i c k e [26] to get the impression that the members of the "Third Order" were to enter the Town Hall not as partners but as subjects of the Council. They were to be called there by the Council and controlled by it as members of the low ranking body; appointed by the Council, they could debate on proposals made by Council only[27]. Despite the restricted range of its activities (at least in the first stage of its existence) the Council preferred to keep an eye on the "Third Order", hence probably the decision to hold its meetings in the Town Hall.

Simultaneously the Town Hall doors were definitely closed to all commoners, who yet in the 15th century were able, without great difficulty, to enter this building on various occasions. The most symptomatic fact was the disappearance of any commercial accommodations from the Town Hall. Comparing the Town Hall of Gdańsk with the Town Hall of the neighbouring city of Toruń, a significant difference in their structures and functions can be noted. The impressive dimension of Toruń Town Hall (wings 13–14 m. deep, grouped around a courtyard of the size 28x19 m., a tower 40 m. high)[28] also expressed the considerable ambitions of the burghers there. It was, however, a Town Hall in which the ground floor was occupied by

[25] *Ibidem*, p. 579 ff.
[26] R. C u r i c k e , *op. cit.*, pp. 52, 123 ff.
[27] *Historia Gdańska (The History of Gdańsk)*, Vol. II, pp. 556 ff.
[28] O. S t i e h l , *op. cit.*, p. 108.

various shops, where one could buy almost everything needed for everyday use — from bread to hatbands; hence the townspeople entered the building daily and unceremoniously. It was here also that various social occasions were still celebrated in the 16th– 18th centuries, such as balls, wedding receptions, funeral banquets etc. Thus a characteristic feature of Toruń Town Hall in early modern times was the continuation of its multifunctionality typical of all European towns halls in the Middle Ages; it did not serve to create barriers between the town authorities and town inhabitants, but rather contributed to strengthen common social bonds and ties between them.

In Gdańsk the medieval multifunctional character of the Main City Town Hall was gradually limited in the 16th– 18th centuries. The barrier between the town authorities and common burghers was successfully erected by several material and psychological means. Not only did trade disappear from the Town Hall building; already in the mid– 15th century social life of the richer circles was transferred to the neighbouring (equally exclusive) the so–called Artus Court. The construction of a separate Arsenal at the turn of the 16th and 17th centuries resulted in the transfer of the arms stores from the Town Hall to this building; only some small stocks of arms remained in Town Hall for tactical and strategic reasons. The "everyday" judicial practice also disappeared from the Town Hall. As from about 1530 justice sittings of the Bench took place in the Artus Court, later (1549) the Council purchased a separate house near the Artus Court for this purpose[29]. In 1712 the Benchers moved to the new building adjoining Artus Court (Długi Targ no 43)[30]. The Town Hall prison was retained in rudimentary form only, probably for psychological reasons. Prisoners in the 16th– 18th centuries were put permanently in the so–called Prison Tower (near the High Gate) where also the pillory, removed from the Town Hall, was located in 1604[31].

According to the plans of the town authorities, the Town Hall was to be a "sacred space" of authority, almost a temple, the seat and symbol of the town's highest power. It is worth to recall that the Council of Gdańsk at that time began to call itself a Senate, according to old, distinguished Roman tradition. The limitation of old utilitarian functions and banishing from the Town Hall of all daily, "trivial" activities could, of course, as some old studies did, be explained by the shortage of space. It was, however, in the mid– 16th century, that two great fires (1550 and 1556) destroyed the old, cramped Gothic building and thus opened the possibility of rebuilding and

---

[29] P. S i m s o n , *Geschichte der Stadt Danzig*, Vol. II, Danzig 1918, p. 175.
[30] *Gdańsk, jego dzieje i kultura (Gdańsk, Its History and Culture)*, Warszawa 1969, p. 196.
[31] R. C u r i c k e , *op. cit.*, p. 60, P. S i m s o n , *op. cit.*, p. 528.

34

expanding the Town Hall in its new Renaissance shape. The architecture of the new Town Hall was consciously formed by Gdańsk authorities, who were able to spend for this purpose huge sums of money in order to design the construction according to their own wishes.

Famous architects and master–builders from the Netherlands e.g. Wilhelm van den Meer (Barth the Elder), Dirk Daniels, Anthony van Obberghen, were engaged in the construction of the new Renaissance Town Hall. Three new wings which formed an inner courtyard were built on the North side. The Eastern wall from the side of Długi Targ (Long Market) was crowned with an open–work attic and decorated with the coat–of–arms of Poland, Gdańsk and Royal Prussia. In the whole building the small Gothic windows were substituted by large rectangular Renaissance windows. The next centuries added but little to this decor. In the mid– 17th century the Town Hall gained a baroque portal, its annex — a second floor. A further storey to the annex was added in the 18th century. In the years 1766–1768 Daniel Eggert completed a new rococo–classicist portal of the main entrance, with coat–of–arms of Gdańsk and rich stonework decoration. This new, splendid Towns Hall constituted the dominating accent of the main street of Gdańsk — Long Street. Thanks to a bend of this street the building appeared in full view immediately after one's passing through the so–called Golden Gate — the main entrance to the city. The Town Hall was the most outstanding lay building in the town. Its tall, slim tower overlooked town architecture and was visible from the whole surrounding region. It was embellished by a clock (the measuring of the time was an important attribute of power)[32] and a carillon of 15 bells. The summit boasted a gilded figure of the Polish King Sigismund August. This constituted a bow on the part of the town Council to the powerful monarch, whose heavy hand had weighed over Gdańsk several times. It was this King who once imprisoned the Gdańsk mayors and considerably weakened town's position by incorporation of Prussia during the Diet at Lublin in 1569; he also sponsored both of the Karnkowski's Commissions and the so–called Karnkowski's Statutes. Sigismud August certainly knew how to inspire the respect in Gdańsk. His successors to the Polish throne up to August III did not have such achievements. Hence also many efforts were made in Gdańsk to forget that the figure on the Town Hall tower represented Sigismund August: in the second half of the 17th century Reinhold Curicke writes simply of the "gilded figure of a man" at the top of the Town Hall tower[33].

---

[32] Cf. J L e G o f f, *Au Moyen Age: Temps de l'Eglise et temps du marchand*, "Annales ECS", 15/1960 N° 3, pp. 417 ff.

[33] R. C u r i c k e, *op. cit.*, p. 53.

Despite the rebuilding of the Town Hall, its exterior was much more modest than the magnificence of its interior, and this was already noted by the contemporaries[34]. It is an interesting example of the mentality of the Gdańsk upper strata: with all their pride they disliked exhibiting the wealth. As a further example could serve the testaments of Gdańsk rich burghers, very laconic usually, without revealing the size of the left property and only disposing of the proportions according to which it was to be divided. In the opinion of the Gdańsk elites wealth was to ensure the owner a high standard of living, authority and power — but public manifestation of riches was considered unnecessary and even harmful. A small group of chosen people only were to enjoy the sight and use of luxury.

This principle affected the shaping of the Town Hall. Its site plan illustrates clearly the functions of the Town Hall in early modern times. The building accommodated the highest offices of the town: custom duties office, archives, cash box department, trade control office, and, of course, the conference rooms: the Great (so–called Summer or Red Chamber) and Small (Winter) Chambers of the Council, as well as the Chamber of the Bench. It was here that the most important decisions were made on matters concerning the internal life of the town as well as its external policies.

According to the ideas conceived by such famous mayors of Gdańsk as Constatin Ferber, Bartholomy Schachmann and John Speimann, Town Hall as institution was to perform two basic socio–political functions: to dominate over the town and to represent it. Both were connected to the demonstration of power and strength of the town's ruling elite. It was put into effect by dazzling all who crossed the threshold of the Town Hall with splendour and might. The scholars' controversy as to the extend to which the Town Hall in Gdańsk was designed after the Doges' Palace in Venice should not be considered solely from the point of view of the history of art; the problem belongs certainly to the history of mentality. Gdańsk Town Council, assuming the pose of the Roman or Venetian Senate desired without any doubt to make Gdańsk into a Venice of the North. Thus, after removal from the Town Hall of such utilitarian activities as trade, administration of justice and entertainments, only activities directly related to the displaying of power were left, such as meeting of town authorities (in particular Counicl's sessions) and mayors official workings with some technical services connected with them (chancellery, archives, finance offices, guardroom).

The interior of the Town Hall was splendidly furnished. Such famous artists as Jan Vredeman de Vries, Isaak van dem Blocke, Anthony Möller,

---

[34] *Ibidem*, p. 52.

36

had contributed to it. The works of the art accumulated here expressed the consistent, broadly developed ideological programme of the Gdańsk ruling elite at the high of its power; it was illustrated by themes of paintings and sculptures, by their composition, by emblems and inscriptions displaying the philosophy and hierarchy of values instructed on the mentality of Gdańsk rulers. On entering the entrance hall one was met with the Latin sentence: *Preacedit labor, sequitur honor* — "honours follow labour". Looking from the ceiling decorated with the coats of arms of same prominent Gdańsk families was the image of Concord. Thus work and harmony were to constitute the foundation of an ideal urban society. The ideas of the Gdańsk elite are reflected to the full in the painting on the ceiling of the Town Hall's main room — the Red Chamber[35]. It is worth to mention that the first decorations of the ceiling by Jan Vredeman were removed after barely a dozen or so years, as they failed to satisfy the prestige seeking demands of the Council. The work was entrusted — this time certainly after issuing detailed instructions — to Izaak van dem Blocke. As a result the ceiling of the Red Chamber was given a highly complicated and suggestive decoration, constituting a specific apotheosis of the Town Council and simultaneously illustrating its style of ruling, its practice of policies. None of the 25 ceiling paintings is of a fortuitous character, nothing here is superfluous, everything is arranged in accordance with the well thought–out socio–political system of views of the collective Maecenas — a group ruling the town in the 16th and 17th centuries, thus when the city of Gdańsk was at peak of its power and wealth. This system of views and values presented in scenes borrowed from the Bible and ancient history was perfectly legible to people of the Renaissance and Baroque, whose education was based on punctilious knowledge of the Bible and antiquity. Here the painting of "Helvidius Priscus and the emperor Vespasian" illustrates the defence of freedom as the main task of the town authorities in their relations with the central power (we must recall that these were the years following the fierce clash which the city had with King Stephen Batory and just before the great conflict with Ladislaus IV). The painting "Servilius and Appius" calling to mind the conflict between the patricians and plebs in ancient Rome, suggests that the idea of concord should unite citizens and prevail over particular interests. The painting "Atillus Regulus" postulates faithfulness to the town authorities and stamps it as an expression of the greatest patriotism. "Alexander the Great and Hephaestion" calls in mind the necessity to keep a secret (this postulate of discretion in matters of authority and policy is repeated in many

---

[35] Cf. on this subject the study by R. I w a n o y k o, *Apoteoza Gdańska (Gdańsk's Apotheosis)*, Gdańsk 1976.

works of arts in the Town Hall). Many painted allegories of a biblical and mythological character supplement and expand the programme with additional elements such as the idea of the divine origin of authority and wisdom ("David before the council of judges", "Solomon's prayer"), the warning against impiousness ("The fall of Jericho" below which the inscription warns: "When the Lord does not watch over a town, it is useless to guard it").

The central field of the ceiling of Red Chamber is occupied by a great composition frequently presented and analysed by many scholars: the "Allegory of Gdańsk Trade", or, as some would say: the "Apotheosis of Gdańsk Links with Poland"[36]. In this picture Gdańsk is represented as an ideal "God's city" — a town chosen by the Providence and given special opportunities. God Himself had founded the basis of Gdańsk's prosperity. This prosperity would be guaranteed by people's trust in Heavenly care and strong fidelity to the principles of faith. The programme of this picture reflects the ideas of the Protestantism with a Calvinist tinge quite clearly (and in the early 17th century Calvinists predominated among the members of the Council), strongly accenting the connection of Heaven and Earth as the foundation of town's power and of the well-being of its inhabitants.

The allegory, below a multicoloured rainbow, shows the Vistula river carrying on its waves barges and boats filled with grain as well as Long Market in Gdańsk with crowds of merchants, Polish noblemen, rafters, musicians. Coats-of-arms of Poland, Lithuania, Gdańsk, Royal Prussia, carved in wood by Simon Herle, a famous Gdańsk's sculptor, circle round the painting. Thus the apotheosis of the Town's Council authority is united with the apotheosis of the Gdańsk's trade and of Gdańsk's links with Poland. It is also expressed in the maxim below the rainbow: *Coelesti iungimur arcu* — "We are linked by Heaven". The delicate matter of Gdańsk's political subordination to Poland is not mentioned in the painting. The fierce disputes with Polish Kings did not prevent, however, the founders of the Town Hall to order for the White Chamber — one of the splendid rooms in the building — a portrait gallery of Polish monarchs.

Summing up: Gdańsk Main City Town Hall, gradually resigning from its multifunctional character and undergoing architectural transformations became at the end of the 16th– begin of the 17th centuries a specialized institution symbolizing towns' wealth and power as well as the great prestige and ambition of its ruling elite. The Town Hall interior with its magnificent painted and sculpted decorations was passing an important ideological and

---

[36] H. S i k o r s k a, *Apoteoza łączności Gdańska z Polską (Apotheosis of the Union Gdańsk and Poland)*, "Biul. Historii Sztuki" Vol. XXX, 1968, pp. 228 ff.

38

political message to visitors. According to the intentions of the Council, the mystery of power, inaccessible to outsiders and "laymen", full of well guarded secrets (the door to the Small Council Chamber, where winter meetings took place, bore the image of a man with a warning finger on his lips) was to be unrolled here. Even the period of the town's crisis and decline in the second half of the 17th and in the 18th centuries did not change the position of the Town Hall nor the basis of its conception. It was only on 7th May, 1793, when General Raumer entered the Town Hall to accept the homage of the cities of Gdańsk and Toruń on behalf of the King of Prussia, that the symbolic role of the Gdańsk's Town Hall as a civic institution and symbol of power collapsed, although the splendid walls of this building had to survive till the Second World War.

XV

MENTALITÄT DER BÜRGER VON GDAŃSK IM XVI. – XVII. JH.

Die Untersuchungen über die Mentalität, die sich in Frankreich seit einer Reihe von Jahren so intensiv entwickeln, in Polen dagegen kaum begonnen haben, sind hinsichtlich der besonders interessanten Region Pommerns überhaupt noch nicht in Angriff genommen worden. Indessen gehört dieses Problem nicht zu den bedeutungslosen. Auf dem Boden der entscheidenden Rolle der ökonomischen Basis in den geschichtlichen Prozessen stehend, dürfen wir nicht die Tatsache übersehen, daß die Sinnes- und Geistesart wie auch das Selbstbewußtsein gesellschaftlicher Gruppen einen wichtigen Faktor darstellen, der auf das Leben einer jeden Gemeinschaft einwirkt, und zwar sowohl heute, was von der Soziologie voll eingeschätzt wird, als auch in der Vergangenheit, die eine Domäne der Historiker ist. Der vorliegende Versuch, die Mentalität der Bürgerschaft im 16.-17.Jh. zu skizzieren, wird notwendigerweise kurz (wegen der zeitlichen Begrenzung des Referates) und bestimmt nicht vollständig sein (letzteres aus Mangel an eingehenden Untersuchungen). Es scheint jedoch, daß schon allein die Beschäftigung mit diesem Problem und die Erörterung gewisser seiner Aspekte sehr nutzbringend sein und den Ausgangspunkt für weitere Untersuchungen und Überlegungen bilden kann.

Auf der Suche nach den wichtigsten Faktoren, welche die Mentalität sowohl des Individuums wie auch einer Gruppe bestimmen, müssen nach meinem Erachten folgende an die Spitze gestellt werden: 1. Gesellschaftliches Milieu, 2. Die Zeit im Sinne der Epoche und des kulturpolitischen Klimas, 3. Allgemeiner Bildungsstand, der in großem Maß von den erstgenannten Faktoren abhängig ist.

Wir wollen uns zuerst mit dem dritten Faktor befassen, denn das Bildungsniveau hatte den stärksten unmittelbaren Einfluß auf die geistige Struktur des Individuums als auch der Gruppe. Die Handelstätigkeit, insbesondere im komplizierten Welthandel, erfordert Wissen; es ist auch bei der Führung eines größeren Produktionsunternehmens unentbehrlich. Der Kaufmann und Handwerker schätzte den Wert der Bildung und war bemüht, sie seiner Nachkommenschaft zu gewährleisten. Der Sohn eines begüterten Bürgers besuchte zuerst eine der sechs städtischen Elementarschulen, die aus den kirchlichen Gemeindeschulen des 15. Jh. hervorgegangen waren. Hier wurde neben dem Katechismus die Kunst des Lesens und Schreibens in deutscher Sprache und Latein unterrichtet; in den höheren Klassen machten sich die Jungen mit Werken der altertümlichen Schriftsteller (Cato, Terentius, Cicero

XV

u.a.) und der großen Humanisten (u.a. Erasmus) bekannt. Großes Gewicht wurde den musikalischen Übungen und dem Gesang beigemessen, und die Schüler wie auch Pädagogen waren verpflichtet, jeden Sonntag im Kirchenchor mitzuwirken [1]. Die größte Blüte der Elementarschulen in Gdańsk entfällt eben auf die Wende des 16. zum 17. Jh. In dieser Zeit eigneten sich diese Schüler tatsächlich viele und dabei solide, aber dennoch ziemlich einseitige Kenntnisse an. Die Elementarschule mit ihrem ausdrücklich humanistischen Profil war hauptsächlich für die Söhne der reichen Stadtbürger bestimmt. Es gab zwar die sog. Armenklassen (seit 1592 an der Marienschule und seit 1616 an der Johannisschule), doch diese wurden überwiegend von den naturgemäß nicht zahlreichen Stipendiaten besucht, die vom Rat oder von Privatpersonen gestiftete Geldbeihilfen erhielten. Die Elementarschule war übrigens als Vorstufe für die weitere Ausbildung gedacht, die sich allerdings nur die Jugend aus reichen Häusern leisten konnte. Eine für das praktische Leben notwendige Ergänzung der Elementarschule waren die in Kaufmannskreisen sehr verbreiteten Reisen der Jugend zu einem Praktikum, verbunden mit beruflicher Ausbildung (Warenkunde, Geographie, Wechselrecht) und Fremdsprachenunterricht in einer der pommerschen Städte (hier wurde Polnisch gelernt) oder weiter ins Ausland, nach England, Frankreich, die Niederlande oder Deutschland [2].

Neben den sechs städtischen Elementarschulen gab es in Gdańsk im 16. und 17. Jh. zahlreiche private Grundschulen verschiedenen Typs. Ihr Programm, in welchem die humanistischen Elemente nicht mehr überwogen, war auf das praktische Leben ausgerichtet und sollte zur beruflichen Arbeit auf verschiedenen Gebieten vorbereiten. Es gab demnach französische Schulen, in welchen größter Nachdruck auf den Unterricht dieser im Handel wichtigen Sprache gelegt wurde, ferner polnische Schulen, die nach demselben Prinzip organisiert und in den bürgerlichen Kreisen außerordentlich populär waren, die mit dem polnischen Adel und polnischen Flößern ständig in Berührung kamen. Außer Fremdsprachen lernten die Kinder in den privaten Schulen Lesen, Schreiben un Rechnen. Sie wurden auch in verschiedenen Handarbeiten unterwiesen. Schulen dieses Typs wurden von Jungen aus weniger begüterten Familien besucht, z. B. von Söhnen kleiner Kaufleute oder Handwerker, die an keine Weiterbildung dachten, sondern ziemlich früh die Berufsarbeit aufnehmen wollten. Die Privatschulen wurden auch von Mädchen aus mittleren Bürgerkreisen besucht. Sie lernten Lesen, Schreiben, Rechnen, übten Gesang, Sticken und Nähen. Die Töchter der reichen Familien und Patrizier wurden von Hauslehrern unterrichtet oder besuchten die Klosterschule der Brigitten; im Kloster der Prämonstratenserinnen in Żukowo hatten sie Gelegenheit, sich Hofmanieren anzueignen. Die Privatschulen zählten 10, 20, 30, manchmal 40−50 Schüler oder Schülerinnen unterschiedlichen Alters. Neben Schulen für 4−7-jährige Kinder gab es solche, die von über dreizehnjährigen Jungen und Mädchen besucht wurden.

---

[1] Siehe: M. B o g u c k a, *Życie codzienne w Gdańsku w XV−XVII w.*, Warszawa 1967, S. 159 ff.; W. F a b e r, *Die Johannisschule in Danzig*, Danzig 1925, S. 11−61; Th. H i r s c h, *Die Oberpfarrkirche von St. Marien in Danzig*, Danzig 1843, S. 56 ff.

[2] M. B o g u c k a, a.a.O., S. 160.

Im Jahre 1663 haben die vom Rat beauftragten Visitatorem in Gdańsk allein in der Rechtsstadt 33 Privatschulen mit 842 Schülern (darunter 120 Schülerinnen) notiert. Laut Berechnungen des Rektors der Marienschule, der die Konkurrenz der Privatschulen beklagte, stieg die Zahl dieser Schulen im 17. Jh. auf 56 an[3]. Es läßt sich schwer feststellen, was für ein Prozentsatz der Schuljugend in Gdańsk die verschiedenen Grundschulen besucht hat. Nichtsdestoweniger scheint die Kunst zu lesen und zu schreiben an der Wende vom 16. zum 17. Jh. in Kreisen des mittleren Bürgertums (ganz abgesehen vom Patriziat) sehr verbreitet gewesen zu sein. Die gelegentliche Erklärung eines Handwerkers von Ende des 16. Jh., daß er des Lesens und des Schreibens unkundig sei, wurde von den Behörden mißtrauisch aufgenommen und ihm wenig Glauben geschenkt[4]. Die Anfang des 17. Jh. in Gdańsk sehr verbreiteten Glückwunschkarten für Kinder und Jugendliche setzen als selbstverständlich voraus, daß jeder Junge und jedes Mädchen lesen und schreiben lernt[5]. Die Inventare armer Einwohner der Stadt und der Vorstädte aus dieser Zeit enthalten zahlreiche Erwähnungen über Bücher; Bibeln, Sammlungen von Psalmen oder erbaulichen Geschichten kann man in dieser Zeit im Nachlaß bescheidener Handwerksgesellen und Spinnerinnen finden[6]. Ein bedeutender Prozentsatz der Stadtbürger erlangte auch Ober- und Hochschulbildung, vor allem in dem seit Mitte des 16. Jh. in Gdańsk bestehenden Gymnasiums, das den Ehrentitel eines Akademischen Gymnasiums erhielt[7], außerdem in den Gymnasien in Toruń und Elbląg und auf den Universitäten in Kraków und in Królewiec, in Deutschland, den Niederlanden, Italien usw.[8] In Kreisen des Patriziates waren die Universitätsstudien die Regel; zu den Universitätsstudien drängte auch der mittlere Bürgerstand, ja

[3] K. Kubik, *Polska szkoła prywatna w dawnym Gdańsku*, Gdańsk 1963; W. Faber, *Zur Geschichte des Danziger Winkelschulwesens*, „Mitteilungen des Westpreußischen Geschichtsvereins", H. 2, 1930, S. 19—26; M. Pelczar, *Nauka i kultura w Gdańsku*, [in:] *Gdańsk, jego dzieje i kultura*, Warszawa 1968, S. 514 ff.; P. Simson, *Französische Schulen in Danzig*, „Mitteilungen des Westpreußischen Geschichtsvereins", H. 3, 1903, S. 46—49.

[4] Staatliches Archiv in Gdańsk, 300, 1/31, S. 71, 300, 1/62, S. 303.

[5] M. Bogucka, *W kręgu mentalności mieszczanina gdańskiego w XVII w.*; *notatnik Michała Hancke*, [in:] *Ars Historica*, Poznań 1976, S. 617—633.

[6] M. Bogucka, *Książka jako element kultury masowej w Gdańsku w XVII w.*, [in:] *Szkice z dziejów kultury polskiej*, Warszawa 1972, S. 267—76.

[7] Siehe: *Księga wpisów uczniów Gimnazjum Gdańskiego 1580—1814*, hrsg. Z. Nowak, P. Szafran, Warszawa—Poznań 1974, *passim*.

[8] H. Barycz, *Związki intelektualne Pomorza z Uniwersytetem Krakowskim w XIV—XVII w.*, „Przegląd Zachodni", 1955, H. 1—2; H. Freytag, *Die Beziehungen Danzigs zu Wittenberg in der Zeit der Reformation*, „Zeitschrift des Westpreußischen Geschichtsvereins", H. 38, 1898; Ders., *Die Beziehungen der Universität Leipzig zu Preußen von ihrer Gründung bis zur Reformation*, „Zeitschrift des Westpreußischen Geschichtsvereins", H. 44, 1902; Ders., *Die Preußen auf der Universität Wittenberg und die nichtpreußischen Schüler Wittenbergs in Preußen von 1502—1602*, Leipzig 1902; G. Müller, *Die preußische Nation auf der Universität Leipzig*, „Neue Jahrbücher für Philologie und Pädagogie", Bd. CL, 1894; B. Nadolski, *Wyjazdy młodzieży gdańskiej na studia zagraniczne w XVII w.*, „Rocznik Gdański", Bd. XXIV; Z. Nowak, *Młodzież Prus Królewskich i Książęcych na Uniwersytecie Krakowskim w latach 1526—1772*, „Zapiski Historyczne", Bd. XXIX, 1964, H. 2; D. Rotscheider, *Ost- und Westpreußische Studenten in Utrecht*, „Altpreußische Geschlechterurkunde", Bd. V, 1931; J. Schultz, *Zur Geschichte der deutsch-*

XV

sogar ärmere junge Leute, und zwar dank den von der Stadt und von Privatpersonen gestifteten Stipendien. Es wäre interessant, das Profil der von den Bürgern in dieser Zeit gewählten Studienrichtungen zu analysieren; anscheinend wurde praktischen Studien, wie Jurisprudenz, Naturkunde und Medizin, der Vorrang gegeben, obwohl das Interesse für Theologie und humanistische Fächer (Philologie, Geschichte usw.) natürlich auch sehr stark war.

Ein entscheidendes Gepräge gab der Mentalität der Bürger – neben der Bildung – das Leben in einem großen Hafen, dessen Rückgrat die schnell anwachsende städtische Agglomeration bildete, die immer deutlicher einen neuzeitlichen Charakter gewann. Der politische und geographische Horizont der Einwohner eines solchen Mittelpunktes mußte besonders ausgedehnt sein; im alltäglichen Leben kamen sie mit Ankömmlingen aus der großen Welt in Berührung, sahen die aus West- und Ostindien eingeführten exotischen Waren, hörten Berichte über neu entdeckte Erdteile und die dort wohnenden Völker, und zwar von direkten Augenzeugen, den Schiffern und Seeleuten. Die Inventare der Bürger nennen zahlreiche „Souvenirs" aus fernen Reisen: Teller und Tassen – Lackarbeiten aus China und Japan – orientalische Diwandecken, Figürchen usw. In den Wohnungen nicht nur der Patrizier sondern auch der mittelmäßig begüterten und ärmeren Bürger befanden sich Ansichten fremder Städte, Landkarten u.dgl.[9] Die Kenntnis der Welt wurde durch häufige Auslandsreisen erweitert, sei es zu Studienzwecken, zur Besichtigung, oder um Fachwissen zu gewinnen und in verschiedenen politischen und Handelsgeschäften[10]. Auch die armen Stadtbewohner reisten: Handwerksgesellen wanderten nach fremden Städten und Ländern, die Schiffer und Matrosen steuerten ferne Häfen an. Die ausgedehnten Beziehungen wurden durch den lebhaften Briefwechsel von Gdańsk und seiner Einwohner mit der ganzen damaligen Welt gefördert, desgleichen durch den Zustrom von Büchern und Publikationen in verschiedenen Sprachen und über verschiedene Themen, die bei zahlreichen Verkäufern und Krämern, auch im Straßenhandel zu haben waren[11]. Das alles begünstigte die Herausbildung einer aufgeschlossenen geistigen Haltung der Bürger von Gdańsk, die sich leicht Neuheiten aller Art aneigneten, gleichzeitig jedoch zu ihrer kritischen Beurteilung durch Vergleiche und Analogien bereit waren.

Der Weltanschauung der Bürger von Gdańsk und ihren Sitten drückte der Protestantismus ein starkes Gepräge auf. Er hemmte die Fröhlichkeit der Bürger, die gelegentlich von Feiertagen oder Familienfesten auszubrechen pflegte, und er zensurierte unerbittlich den Inhalt der Theaterstücke, Drucksachen und Bilder. Tiefe Religiosität in lutherischer oder kalvinischer Fassung durchdrang sehr stark die

---

polnischen Beziehungen. Studenten aus Polen an der Universität Jena 1548–1795, „Wissenschaftliche Zeitschrift der Karl-Marx-Universität", Bd. VI, 1956/57, Serie I, H. 4; O. V o i g t, Preußische Studenten auf niederländischen Hochschulen im XVII. Jh., „Ekkehard", Bd. XV, H. 2–3.

    [9] M. B o g u c k a, Z problematyki form życia „marginesu mieszczańskiego" w Gdańsku pierwszej połowy XVII w., „Zapiski Historyczne", Bd. XXXVIII, 1973, H. 4, S. 55–79.

    [10] Siehe: Eine Reisebeschreibung von Ratsherr G. Schröder, Bibliothek der Polnischen Akademie der Wissenschaften zu Gdańsk, Manuscripten, MS 925a.

    [11] M. B o g u c k a, Życie codzienne..., S. 88.

Mentalität sowohl des Patriziats als auch weiter Bürgerkreise. Und doch waren die Bürger dermaßen nüchtern, daß sie, wenn nötig, die religiösen Fragen den Anforderungen der Politik und Wirtschaft unterordneten. Daraus resultierte eine der Vorbedingungen für die aufschlußreiche Tatsache, daß in der Zeit der „schwedischen Sintflut", als das ganze ultrakatholische Polen dem protestantischen König Karl XII. zu Füßen lag, das konfessionell mit Schweden verwandte Gdańsk dem Angreifer mit eiserner Konsequenz Widerstand leistete.

Obgleich nicht fanatisch, waren die Bürger doch auf ihre Weise sehr fromm. Der Atheismus, eine damals sehr seltene Erscheinung, war von Amts wegen verdammt. Im Jahre 1639 beschlossen die Stadtbehörden, daß die Begräbnisse von Personen, die sich an keine Kirche halten, „ohne Ansprachen und Zeremonie" stattzufinden haben[12]. Das war also schon ein soziales Problem. Strenge Strafen wurden auch gegen Gotteslästerer angewandt[13]. Andererseits haben Buchhändler in Gdańsk ganz frei Bücher verkauft, die den Geist des religiösen Skeptizismus verbreiteten. Im Jahre 1669 notiert der Ratsherr Georg Schröder in seinem Tagebuch, daß er bei einem Holländer auf dem Marktplatz das Buch eines gewissen Adrian Kurbach gesehen habe, das in den Niederlanden wegen Verbreitung des Atheismus verbrannt und der Autor mit Gefängnis bestraft worden sei[14]. Man muß es den Bürgern hoch anrechnen, daß in ihrer Stadt solche Bücher verbreitet und offen zum Verkauf angeboten werden durften, doch ist dies kein Beweis, daß hier absolute Religionsfreiheit herrschte. Das ganze 16. und 17. Jh. lang lagen die Katholiken mit den Lutheranern im Streit, und die Lutheraner und Kalvinisten bekämpften sich verbissen. Daß die Bürger sich lebhaft für Glaubensfragen interessierten folgt aus dem Bestand ihrer Hausbibliotheken[15], aus privaten Notizen und Tagebüchern[16]. Die städtische Gesetzgebung war zweifellos weniger tolerant als die einzelnen Bürger oder die stillschweigende Praxis der Behörden; theoretisch wurde den Antitrinitariern und Mennoniten alle Rechte abgesprochen (ihre Tätigkeit in der Stadt jedoch geduldet), den Juden der Aufenthalt im Gebiet der städtischen Gerichtsbarkeit verboten (wiederum nur in der Theorie, praktisch wurde dieses Verbot vielfach mißachtet), und nur für die Zeit des Dominikmarktes waren Ausnahmen zugelassen. Man kann also schwerlich von einer vollen, jedenfalls offiziellen und rechtlich geschützten

---

[12] G. Löschin, *Geschichte Danzigs von der ältesten bis zur neusten Zeit*, Danzig 1828, Bd. II, S. 375.

[13] M. Bogucka, *Życie codzienne...*, S. 211.

[14] Bibliothek der Polnischen Akademie der Wissenschaften zu Gdańsk, MS 673, S. 112b—113a.

[15] Siehe: J. Bellwon, *Księgozbiór Ludwika Ajchlera zachowany w zbiorach Biblioteki Gdańskiej*, „Libri Gedanenses", II/III, 1968/69, S. 5—32; S. Sokół, M. Pelczarowa, *Księgozbiór gdańskich lekarzy Krzysztofa i Henryka Heyllów*, Gdańsk 1963; P. Szafran, *Die historische Werkstatt der Danziger Geschichtsschreiber des XVII. Jh. Reinhold Curicke im Lichte seiner Bibliothek*, „Libri Gedanenses", Bd. II/III 1968/69, S. 87—127; Ders., *Z problematyki badawczej studiów nad mieszczańskimi księgozbiorami prywatnymi w Gdańsku XVII—XVIII w.*, „Rocznik Gdański", Bd. XXXI, 1971, H. 1, S. 73—92.

[16] Z. B. *Tagebuch von Michael Hancke*, Bibliothek der Polnischen Akademie der Wissenschaften in Gdańsk, MS 915.

XV

Toleranz in Gdańsk sprechen. Im übrigen fand dieser Begriff, der Nachsicht und Achtung gegenüber fremden und andersartigen Überzeugungen bedeutete, in der geistigen Struktur dieser alten Stadt keinen Platz. Das Leben verlief hier in dem strengen, noch vom mittelalterlichen Zunfts- und Korporationssystem überlieferten Rahmen, in welchem es für den Individualismus, für die Eigenart von Einzelpersonen oder ganzer Gruppen an Platz mangelte. Nur ausnehmend großer Reichtum oder größte Armut erlaubten es, sich aus diesem System der Gemeinschaften loszu- lösen und zu befreien, die in diesem unabänderlichen organisatorisch-juristischen Schema eingeschlossen waren. Der Grund für diese Erscheinungen lag in der noch im Mittelalter erwachsenen und aus seinen typischen Entbehrungen und der schwa- chen wirtschaftlichen Entwicklung fließenden Angst vor allem Neuen, die Besorgnis um die Erhaltung der vorhandenen Sachlage, mit einem Wort — die Furcht vor der Konkurrenz im weitesten Sinne dieses Wortes. Unzweifelhaft nicht aus inbrün- stiger Frömmigkeit, sondern aus Angst vor der Konkurrenz wurden den Mennoniten in Gdańsk die Stadtrechte vorenthalten, denn diese öffneten gut florierende Werk- stätten und führten umfangreiche Handels- und Finanzgeschäfte durch, die das Tätigkeitsfeld der lokalen Kapitalbesitzer einschränkten[17]. Aus ähnlichen Gründen wurden in Gdańsk die Quäker und Juden diskriminiert. Die verbissenen lutherisch- kalvinistischen Auseinandersetzungen hatten zu einem großen Teil ihren Grund in dem Kampf um den Zugang zu städtischen Ämtern, in dem Streit darum, welche Gruppe die Macht in der Stadt übernehmen soll. Der Bürger drückte gern ein Auge zu wenn es sich um Dogmen handelte, er bestand nicht darauf, daß alle seine Kon- fession als die beste anerkennen[18], trat aber energisch zum Kampf an, wenn das materielle oder gesellschaftliche Interesse, sein eigenes oder der Gruppe, welcher er angehörte, bedroht war und drapierte sich bei dieser Gelegenheit gern mit dem Gewand eines Glaubenskämpfers.

Die Gruppensolidarität war in Gdańsk außerordentlich stark entwickelt, sie manifestierte sich in den sehr starken Bindungen zwischen den Mitgliedern derselben Gesellschaftsschichten (insbesondere des Patriziats, wie auch der gemeinen Bürger- schaft, die als „dritte Ordnung" ein stark ausgeprägtes Selbstbewußtsein besaß) und den Mitgliedern einzelner Gruppen (Zünfte und Gilden, Artushof). Die höchste Stufe dieser Solidarität war das Gefühl der Verbundenheit sämtlicher Einwohner von Gdańsk, die hier Bürgerrechte besaßen, ohne Rücksicht auf Nationalität und Sprache. Gdańsk, das vornehmlich den Charakter einer Hafenstadt hatte, bildete in nationaler Hinsicht ein außerordentlich farbenreiches Mosaik. Neben der altein- gesessenen Bevölkerung polnischer wie auch deutscher Herkunft, lebten hier Hunderte Holländer, Schweden, Dänen, Engländer, Flamen und siedelten sich zahlreiche Einwanderer aus Deutschland und Frankreich an. In sprachlicher Hinsicht war die Stadt ebenfalls kein Monolith; die Patrizier und die reicheren Bevölkerungs- schichten sprachen überwiegend Deutsch, das auch die Amtssprache der Stadt war. In den ärmeren Schichten war die polnische Sprache sehr verbreitet, so daß der

---

[17] Siehe: M. B o g u c k a, *Obcy kupcy osiadli w Gdańsku w pierwszej połowie XVII w.*, „Zapiski Historyczne", Bd. XXXVII, 1972, H. 2, S. 59—82.

[18] Siehe: *Tagebuch von Michael Hancke*, S. 17.

Stadtrat manche Verordnungen in Polnisch herausgeben mußte [19]. Der in der zweiten
Hälfte des 17. Jh. in Gdańsk weilende französische Diplomat Charles Ogier erwähnt
mehrfach in seinen Tagebüchern polnische Andachten und Predigten, die in verschiedenen Kirchen abgehalten wurden; über die Vesperandachten schreibt er, daß „zu
ihrem Schluß das Volk polnische Choräle gesungen hat" [20]. Am Akademischer
Gymnasium wirkte übrigens ein Lektorat der polnischen Sprache, und die Söhne
von Kaufleuten — wie bereits oben erwähnt — lernten emsig die polnische Sprache,
um sich leichter mit dem Adel verständigen zu können [21]. In dieser vielsprachigen
Stadt waren die Unterschiede in der Herkunft nicht wichtig. Wie in einem großen
Tiegel verschmolzen hier verschiedene Nationalitäten und aus ihren Sitten und
Gebräuchen entstand ein gemeinsamer Lebensstil, und Kultur. Wenn also ein
Einwohner von Gdańsk vom Vaterland sprach, dann dachte er in erster Reihe an
die Stadt und erst danach an Preußen und ganz Polen [22].

Der stark entwickelte lokale Patriotismus und das Gefühl der Zugehörigkeit
zu einer konkreten städtischen Gemeinschaft wie auch die Anhänglichkeit für ihre
Gesetze, die übrigens im Empfinden der Bürger die Grundlage seiner eigenen
individuellen Wohlhabenheit bildeten, — waren die charakteristischen Merkmale
der Mentalität der Einwohner von Gdańsk im 16. — 17. Jh. Damit ging ein starkes
Interesse für Geschichte und Politik einher. Das Interesse für Geschichte, das sich
u.a. im Profil der in Privatbibliotheken angesammelten Bücher, im Inhalt der in
Memoiren und Tagebüchern verzeichneten Notizen und in der Thematik der Bilder
widerspiegelte, welche die Wohnungen nicht nur der Patrizier, sondern auch weniger
begüterter Bürger schmückten [23], war nicht nur ein Ergebnis der in Gdańsk verbreiteten humanistischen Ideen, also ein eigenartiges *signum temporis*, sondern ver-
knüpfte sich in konkreten praktisch-didaktischen Zielen mit der Tradition der
Vergangenheit zur Festigung der aktuellen Position der Stadt, ihres Ruhms und ihrer
Macht. Die Anknüpfung an die siegreichen Kämpfe gegen den Deutschen Ritter-
orden, die Unterstreichung der engen Beziehungen zu Polen und die Hervorhebung
der zahlreichen Privilegien, die Gdańsk von den polnischen Königen erhalten hatte,
das sind die ständig wiederkehrenden Motive im künstlerischen Schaffen in Gdańsk
im 16. und 17. Jh., das hinsichtlich seines ideologischen Gehaltes von den Mäzenen
und Abnehmern, also vom Patriziat und reichem Bürgertum richtungsweisend zu
dem Zweck gefördert wurde, um sowohl die Vergangenheit als auch die Gegenwart
der Stadt zu verherrlichen. Das Interesse für Geschichte verband sich eng mit dem
Interesse für Politik, dem alle in der Stadt, von den Ratsherren bis zu den Hafenarbei-
tern leidenschaftlich ergeben waren. Im Artushof kommentierten die reichen Kauf-

---

[19] Z. B. für Träger, Kornmesser, Tagelöhner usw. Siehe: Cz. Biernat, *Życie portowe
Gdańska w XVII—XVIII w.*, [in:] *Szkice z dziejów Pomorza*, Bd. II, Warszawa 1959, S. 261—62.
[20] Ch. Ogier, *Dziennik podróży po Polsce*, Bd. II, Gdańsk 1952, S. 75, 109, 115.
[21] W. Faber, *Die polnische Sprache im Danziger Schul- und Kirchenwesen*, „Zeitschrift
des Westpreusischen Geschichtsvereins", H. 70, 1930, S. 89—131.
[22] St. Herbst, *Świadomość narodowa na ziemiach pruskich w XV—XVII w.*, „Komunikaty
Mazursko-Warmińskie", 1962/1, S. 3—10.
[23] M. Bogucka, *Z problematyki form życia...*, S. 73 ff.

herren und Schiffer alltäglich die wichtigeren Ereignisse in Polen und im Ausland[24]. Dieselben Themen wurden in Privathäusern und Zünften, in Gaststätten und Schenken oder direkt auf der Straße diskutiert; die Politik nahm viel Raum in privaten Briefen und Tagebüchern ein. In der Stadt der Kaufherren und Seefahrer, die einen großen Ehrgeiz und dazu die Möglichkeit, ihn zu erfüllen, besaß, war dies nicht nur ein gewöhnliches Hobby. Jeder Einwohner von Gdańsk wußte, daß von der internationalen Situation in beträchtlichem Maße die Konjunktur im Handel abhängig ist, diese wiederum ist für die pünktliche Ankunft der holländischen Flotte wie auch für die Getreidelieferungen aus Polen, also für die Existenz der Stadt entscheidend. Kein Wunder, daß schon sehr früh, noch im 16. Jh. hier offizielle Informatoren über die Ereignisse in der ganzen Welt — also Zeitungen — erschienen, die zunächst in der Form von Flugblättern, blad aber als umfangreiche Wochenschriften regelmäßig herauskamen[25].

Neben den politischen Ereignissen interessierte den Bürger fast in gleichem Maße — das Wetter. Wir können es heute kaum begreifen, wie sehr das Leben des damaligen Menschen (und zwar nicht nur des Bauern auf dem Land, sondern auch des Städters) mit der Natur und ihren Kapricen verflochten war, welche atavistische und auch reale Angstzustände (Feuergefahr, Überschwemmung, Schiffbruch) die Stürme, heftigen Winde und Gewitterentladungen weckten. Die Folgen dieser Erscheinungen desorganisierten häufig das Leben nicht nur von Einzelpersonen, sondern ganzer Städte, kein Wunder, daß sie ihre Bewohner so sehr beschäftigten[26]. All das durch Naturgewalten hervorgerufene Unheil wurde als eine Strafe Gottes füt die Sünden und Verschulden der Menschen angesehen. Dieser Glauben half übrigens dem damaligen Menschen die Verluste zu ertragen, besänftigte gewissermaßen seine Angst, erklärte ihm auf diese eigenartige Weise die Natur des Unglücks und dessen Ursachen und erfüllte ihn mit der Hoffnung, daß durch Buße alles Unheil abgewendet oder wenigstens sein Verlauf gemildert werden könne. Das war im übrigen nicht nur mit der Frömmigkeit des damaligen Menschen verbunden, sondern auch mit dem besonders für das 16.—17. Jh. charakteristischen Aberglauben, dem Glauben an übernatürliche Vorgänge, an Magie und Zauberei[27]. Die in Gdańsk sehr populären zahlreichen Voraussagen und astrologischen Kalender und die auch in gebildeten Kreisen kolportierten entsetzenerregenden Geschichten über Hexen und Zauberer, über die ständige Ingerenz des Satans im Leben der Menschen, zeugen davon, daß der Bürger von Gdańsk in dieser Hinsicht ein typischer Repräsentant seiner Epoche war.

Ein interessantes aber schwieriges Problem sind das Wertsystem und die Vorbilder im Leben, wie auch das Weltbild und die Lebensphilosophie, die zum Bestand

---

[24] H. K. Gspann, *Die Anfänge der periodischen Presse in Danzig*, „Zeitschrift des Westpreußischen Geschichtsvereins", 1923, J. 64, S. 43—82.

[25] *Wie oben.*

[26] Siehe: *Tagebuch von Hancke*, S. 101—102; *Tagebuch von Ernest van der Linde*, Staatliches Archiv in Gdańsk, 300, R/LI 69, S. 2b, 3b, 6a usw.

[27] M. Bogucka, *Życie codzienne...*, S. 209—210; K. Kubik, *Kalendarze gdańskie w XVI—XVII w.*, „Rocznik Gdański", Bd. XXXII, H. 2, S. 107—156.

der Mentalität der damaligen Einwohner von Gdańsk gehören. Sie waren ein Produkt des Milieus, das eine Ausnahmestellung im damaligen Königreich Polen einnahm (große starke Stadt, die sich ihrer Rechte und Bedeutung bewußt war), haben sich aber auch unter dem Einfluß der Epoche: Renaissance, die allmählich in den Barock übergeht, herausgebildet. Wenn wir zu dem privaten Notizbuch des Stadtschreibers Michael Hancke greifen, das dieser in der ersten Hälfte des 17. Jh. geführt hat und das als repräsentativ für den durchschnittlichen, mittelmäßig begüterten Bürger gelten kann, dann fällt am stärksten das Gefühl der Unsicherheit auf, die über dem Weltbild und Schicksal des Menschen lastet. Möglicherweise sind hier die Kriegsjahre 1627 - 29, die Geldkrise 1619 − 21 und die Erschütterung des bürgerlichen Wohlstands als erste Anzeichen von Wandlungen in der für Gdańsk im ganzen 16. Jh. so günstigen Wirtschaftskonjunktur nicht ohne Einfluß geblieben [28]. Die Anfänge des Barocks, einer Epoche voller Konflikte, Zerrissenheit, Unruhe und Enttäuschung, mußten in Gdańsk besonders dramatisch verlaufen, denn die neue Epoche bedeutete eine ausnehmend starke Zunahme der Spannungen. Die alltägliche Erfahrung lehrte, daß in der Welt nichts sicher sei: das Geld verlor von Tag zu Tag an Wert, größere und kleinere Firmen machten bankrott und stürzten ihre Gläubiger ins Unglück. Der Erfolg balanciert wie auf einem runden, glitschigen Apfel; Glück und Unglück grüßen den Bürger täglich schon beim Frühstück. Die einzige Zuflucht ist der Glaube an die Vorsehung, die die Geschicke des Menschen lenkt; somit ist die göttliche Approbation bei jeder Unternehmung unentbehrlich [29]. Das führte natürlich zu einer Art Fatalismus, der einerseits das Ergebnis der kalvinistischen Lehre von der Prädestination, andererseits eine Selbstverteidigung angesicht der Unsicherheit dessen, was das Morgen bringt, war. Unter diesen Umständen konnte das Bild des Gesellschaftssystems keine Merkmale der Stabilität aufweisen, die z.B. für die früheren, mittelalterlichen Vorstellungen so charakteristisch war; es dominierte die Vorstellung vom wechselhaften, launischen Glück, das die Reichen zu Armen macht und umgekehrt den fleißigen und rührigen Armen in die Höhe erhebt. An die Spitze der Tugenden wurden Bescheidenheit und Mäßigung gestellt. Derjenige, der mehr an sich raffen will, als „sein Pflug zu beackern vermag", wird zur Strafe unfehlbar alles verlieren, behauptet Hancke (hier sei auf die Verwendung der charakteristischen Metapher vom Pflug hingewiesen, die Hancke aus landwirtschaftlichen, dörflichen Begriffen schöpft und die somit im bürgerlichen Milieu lebendig waren!). Der Stadtbewohner soll fromm und fleißig sein, er soll ehrlich und tugendhaft leben, keine Schulden machen, nicht als Bürge anderer Schuldner auftreten, Anleihen sehr vorsichtig erteilen, um keine Einbuße am Vermögen zu erleiden; Mißtrauen und Vorsicht sind seine zweite Natur. Das ist zwar ein ehrbares aber doch schwungloses Programm, typisch für den kleinen, ängstlichen Kaufmann, der aus Angst vor dem Risiko keine neuen Initiativen aufnimmt und sich lieber mit kleinerem Gewinn

---

[28] Siehe: M. B o g u c k a, *Zur Problematik der Münzkrise in Danzig in der ersten Hälfte des XVII. Jh.,* „Studia Historiae Oeconomicae", 1971, vol. 2, S. 65 ff.; D e r s., *The Monetary Crisis of the XVIIth Century and its Social and Psychological Consequences in Poland,* „The Journal of European Economic History", 1975/1, S. 137 − 152.

[29] *Tagebuch von Michael Hancke,* S. 3 − 4.

zufriedengibt, als sich in den Strudel großer Projekte und kühner Spekulationen zu stürzen. Eine solche Atmosphäre muß tatsächlich in der Stadt Gdańsk geherrscht haben, und damit auch lassen sich in beträchtlichem Maße der Rückzug der Bürger aus dem aktiven Überseehandel, die Rückkehr zu den alten, mittelalterlichen Methoden des Handelsaustausches im Hafen usw. wie überhaupt die in dieser Zeit in der Stadt auftretenden Erscheinungen erklären.

Mäßigkeit und Vorsicht, diese Devise wirkte nicht nur in der Sphäre des wirtschaftlichen und beruflichen, sondern auch im persönlichen und gesellschaftlichen Leben. Eine sehr geschätzte Fähigkeit war das zeit- und ortsgemäße Benehmen, entsprechend der sozialen Position und den Anforderungen des Augenblicks. Daher die unzählbaren Formeln in Briefen, Glückwunschschreiben, Einladungen und die gereimten (um sie besser im Gedächtnis zu behalten) Anweisungen über das Benehmen bei Tisch, in der Gaststätte usw.[30] Rührend ist die Pedanterie aller dieser Rezepte und die vom damaligen Stadtbürger unternommenen Anstrengungen, um ja nur ein Niveau zu erreichen, das bei jeder Gelegenheit als „vorbildlich" gelten kann. Gleichzeitig muß man hier aber im Auge behalten, daß diese Dokumente von einer Formalisierung des persönlichen und des Gesellschaftslebens zeugen, von der Unfähigkeit, die eigenen Gefühle und Gedanken individuell zum Ausdruck zu bringen, sie sind somit der Beweis eines gewissen geistigen Primitivismus und Schematismus.

Das protestantische Modell der bescheidenen sittlichen Lebensführung regt zum Lernen und zur Arbeit, zur Sparsamkeit, zur Vermeidung von Luxus in der Kleidung, zur Mäßigkeit bei Tisch usw. an. So jedenfalls war es in der bürgerlichen Kultur im Westen Europas, wo in jener Zeit sich ein besonderer Lebensstil herausgebildet hat, dessen Elemente bis heute überdauert haben. Auf die Mentalität der Bürger wirkte jedoch der in ganz Polen verbreitete aufwendige Lebensstil des Adels ein, der mit seinem ganzen farbenreichen Prunk und Luxus vom Bürgertum übernommen wurde[31]. Die zahlreichen Verordnungen der Stadtbehörden im 16. und 17. Jh., die den Pomp in der Kleidung, bei Empfängen usw. einschränkten, wurden in der Regel nicht befolgt. Beispielgebend in der Entfaltung von Prunk und Luxus war das Patriziat, das im Laufe des 16. Jh. immer deutlicher den Lebensstil der Feudalherren übernahm (Aufnahme in den Adelsstand und Niederlassung in ländlichen Residenzen, die nach dem Vorbild der Landsitze des reichen Adels, ja sogar der Paläste der Magnaten eingerichtet waren); dieselben Vorbilder wurden auch von den mittelmäßig begüterten und sogar ärmeren Einwohnern der Stadt angestrebt.

Zu interessanten Schlüssen führt eine Analyse der oben erwähnten, in Gdańsk verbreiteten Glückwunschformulare, und zwar weniger unter dem Gesichtspunkt der Sitten, als der von den damaligen Bürger anerkannten Rangordnung der Werte. An erster Stelle werden Glück und Frieden sowie Wohlstand (nicht Reichtum!) also irdische Werte gewünscht; Seelenheil und ein Platz im Himmel rangieren im

---

[30] *Wie oben*, S. 76—77.

[31] M. B o g u c k a, *L'attrait de la culture nobiliaire? Sarmatisation de la bourgeoisie polonaise au XVIIe s.*, „Acta Poloniae Historica", XXXIII, 1976, S. 23—42.

Prinzip niedriger, was immerhin von der Verweltlichung der Mentalität, jedenfalls im Vergleich zu den früheren Epochen, zeugt. Damit ging ein außerordentlich starkes, für den Barock typisches Gefühl der Vergänglichkeit einher, das ständig bewußte unerbittliche Herannahen des Endes aller irdischen Freuden und schließlich des Todes. Wenn man den damaligen Briefen und vor allem dem Notizbuch von Hancke Glauben schenkt, dann war der Zeitbegriff des Bürgers von Gdańsk im 17. Jh. schon gänzlich verweltlicht und den Fesseln der Kirche entwachsen [32]. Die Uhren maßen sehr präzis (auch in Viertelstunden) den Tagesrhythmus der ganzen Stadt und ihrer einzelnen Einwohner ab, dies um so mehr als die Uhr ein sehr populäres Gerät auch in weniger bemittelten Häusern war. Das Bewußtsein der technisch-praktischen Zeit verbindet sich jedoch bei Hancke mit einem sehr ausgebauten Gefühl für die biologisch-philosophische Zeit, die auf unerbittliche Weise das ganze menschliche Leben erfaßt; die Fragen der Vergänglichkeit, des Alterns und Todes kehren auf den Seiten seines Notizbuches immer wieder fast zwangsläufig zurück. Diese trübselige Stimmung fand in den schweren Seuchen, die Gdańsk besonders in den Anfängen des 17. Jh. heimsuchten, einen zusätzlichen Nährboden. In Hanckes Notizbuch nivelliert der Tod, gleichsam wie in einem mittelalterlichen *Danse macabre*, jegliche Standesunterschiede und reißt den Menschen aus dem Gewirr des Lebens heraus zu einem Zeitpunkt, an dem er am wenigsten erwartet wird. Zeit und Tod, das sind die zwei großen Kräfte, welche die Welt regieren, doch diese Erkenntnis wird nicht mehr durch die mittelalterliche Ergebung in die göttlichen Pläne gemildert. Für den Bürger des 16. – 17. Jh. war der Tod ein rein körperlicher, brutaler und sämtlicher mystischer Gewänder entkleideter Akt und das war schon eine völlig neuzeitliche Auffassung vom Ende alles Zeitlichen.

Das letzte Problem, das ich hier erörtern möchte, ist die Einstellung zur Kunst und das Schönheitsgefühl. Gdańsk war im 16. – 17. Jh. ein starker künstlerischer Mittelpunkt, hier entstanden herrliche Bauwerke der Renaissance und des Barocks, hier entwickelte sich die Bildhauerkunst und Malerei, dank dem Mäzenatentum der Stadtbewohner. Die Interieurs der Patrizier und auch anderer Gesellschaftsschichten waren nicht selten mit ganzen Sammlungen von Kunstwerken angefüllt. Wie jedoch wird die Schönheit vom damaligen Bürgern aufgefaßt, der sich im Alltag unter so herrlichen Kunstwerken bewegt? Ganze zwei Seiten widmet Hancke in seinem Notizbuch dem Stolz eines jeden Stadtbewohners – der Marienkirche; er berechnet genau ihre Bauzeit, notiert Angaben, die die Abmessungen des Bauwerks, die Zahl der Altäre, Fenster, Türme usw. betreffen, informiert peinlich genau über den Wert der einzelnen Elemente ihrer Ausstattung. In summa erinnert diese Beschreibung des herrlichen Denkmals der Architektur an die nüchternen Seiten eines Handelsbuches. Ähnlich sehen die Beschreibungen der von den damaligen Bürgern auf ihren Auslandsreisen besuchten berühmten Bauwerke Londons, Antwerpens usw. aus [33]. Es unterliegt keinem Zweifel, daß für den Stadtbürger (und nicht nur

---

[32] Siehe: J. Le Goff, *Au Moyen Age: Temps de l'Eglise et temps de marchands*, „Annales, Histoire, Economies, Societes", XV, 1960, 3, S. 417–33.

[33] Z. B. *Reisebeschreibung von G. Schröder*, Bibliothek der Polnischen Akademie der Wissenschaften zu Gdańsk, MS 925 a.

XV

für diesen, ähnlich sehen in jener Epoche die Reiseberichte des Adels aus) die Schönheit sich auf direkte Weise mit dem materiellen Wert der Sache verband. Kostspieligkeit erhöhte den Wert eines Kunstwerks und war dessen solider, handgreiflicher Wertmesser. Von der Kostspieligkeit eines Bauwerks zeugten die benötigte Bauzeit, seine Ausmaße, der für die einzelnen Elemente der Ausstattung bezahlte Preis. Anstelle allgemeiner Eindrücke werden dieser Art Informationen notiert, die als bester Ausdruck der ästhetischen Bewunderung und Verehrung für die Herrlichkeit der Kunstwerke galten. Die Trennung des Begriffs der Schönheit von ihrem materiellen Untergrund mußte viel später erfolgen. Bei dieser Gelegenheit sei auch erwähnt, daß der durchschnittliche Stadtbewohner, der kein Kunstmaler war, in jener Zeit die Natur in Kategorien ästhetischer Eindrücke nicht aufzunehmen vermag. Hier will ich mich wieder auf Hancke berufen, bei dem das Wetter, Gewitter usw. sehr viel Platz einnehmen. Gleichzeitig findet sich jedoch nirgends eine Spur von Gemütsbewegung im Zusammenhang mit dem Landschaftsbild (sie treten z.B. in den Memoiren des französischen Diplomaten Ogier auf); die Jahreszeiten werden nie in einem anderen Kontext, denn als nüchterne Bemerkungen über Kälte und Hitze, über die Möglichkeiten der Schiffahrt etc. erwähnt. Das ist ein kennzeichnender Zug der Mentalität bei Hancke und wohl auch der Mehrheit der damaligen Stadtbewohner; für sie war die Natur weiterhin ein zu gefahrdrohendes Element (Feuersbrünste, Überschwemmungen, Schiffbrüche usw.) um auf sie mit den Augen eines Ästheten zu schauen, was die allerdings noch wenig zahlreichen Künstler bereits taten.

Die hier vorgestellten Bemerkungen sind natürlich − wie bereits bemerkt − unvollständig und diskutabel. Sie sollen als Einleitung weiterer umfangreicher Untersuchungen über die Mentalität der Bewohner von Pommern und des ganzen Ostseeraums in den einzelnen Epochen dienen. Die Analyse des Mechanismus der Mentalität von Einzelpersonen und ganzen Gesellschaftsgruppen als eines der im Rahmen des geschichtlichen Prozesses wirkenden Faktoren, hat große Bedeutung bei der Rekonstruktion des vollständigen Bildes dieses Prozesses und Klärung seines Verlaufs. Die Geschichte von Gdańsk, wo sich im 16.−17. Jh. ein seiner Macht bewußtes, gebildetes Bürgertum entwickelt hat, welches eine spezifische Einstellung zu vielen wichtigen Lebensfragen hatte und zweifellos auch den Einflüssen der „sarmatischen" Denkart unterlag, ist hier das beste Beispiel.

Übersetzt von Bruno Heinrich

XVI

LE GESTE DANS LA VIE DE LA NOBLESSE POLONAISE
AUX XVI° - XVIII° SIECLES

Le geste dans la culture, tant sous le rapport des manifestations du phénomène que de ses fonctions, n'avait pas été jusque-là
étudié dans l'historiographie polonaise. L'unique étude parue jusqu'à ce jour sur ce sujet est l'article de P. Sczaniecki sur le geste
de la prière dans le bas Moyen Age [1]. Le mot geste vient du latin ;
d'après le dictionnaire de la langue polonaise contemporaine, il
désigne un mouvement du corps accompagnant la parole pour en
souligner le contenu, parfois il la remplace [2]. La plupart des ency-
clopédies polonaises omettent cet article. Le *Larousse* informe
cependant qu'il s'agit d'un mouvement du corps, surtout de la
main ou des bras (d'où gesticulation), éventuellement d'une action
d'éclat (d'où la chanson de geste médiévale) [3]. Cette ambiguïté n'est
sans doute pas un fait du hasard. Le rôle du geste était, à n'en pas
douter, beaucoup plus considérable dans les anciennes cultures
qu'aujourd'hui. Selon J. Huizinga, « Quand le monde était de cinq
siècles plus jeune qu'aujourd'hui, les événements de la vie se déta-
chaient avec des contours plus marqués [...] Chaque acte, chaque
événement était entouré de formes fixes et expressives, élevé à la
dignité d'un rituel. Les choses capitales, naissance, mariage et
mort, se trouvaient plongées, par le sacrement, dans le rayonne-
ment du divin mystère ; les événements de moindre importance,
eux aussi, voyage, tâche ou visite, étaient accompagnés d'un mil-

---

[1] P. S c z a n i e c k i, *Gest modlitewny w późnym średniowieczu.* [*Le geste de la prière dans le bas Moyen Age*], in : *Kultura elitarna a kultura masowa w Polsce późnego średniowiecza*, sous la dir. de B. G e r e m e k, Wrocław 1978, pp. 41 - 51.
[2] *Mały słownik języka polskiego* [*Petit dictionnaire de la langue polo-naise*], Warszawa 1968, p. 193.
[3] *Nouveau Petit Larousse*, Paris 1952, p. 448.

lier de bénédictions, de cérémonies et de formules » [4]. Le geste
semble remplir au Moyen Age, puis aux XVIᵉ - XVIIᵉ siècles, une
triple fonction, tout en étant un moyen : 1° de communication,
2° d'expression particulière des sentiments, et 3° un signe d'appartenance à un milieu socio-culturel défini. Il était d'autant plus
important, plus chichement intervenaient les autres moyens de
communication, plus grande était la tendance à l'expressionnisme
(son apogée correspond à l'époque du baroque), plus urgent enfin
était le besoin de définir par des marques extérieures la place de
l'individu dans la hiérarchie (en famille ou dans la vie de société).
L'importance et la place du geste dans la culture nobiliaire de
l'ancienne Pologne étaient en outre déterminées par les goûts
spécifiques formés au point de contact de deux aires culturelles :
occidentale et orientale. De là venait la prédilection particulière
pour le faste et l'expression non seulement dans la sphère du
costume ou du mobilier mais aussi dans la façon d'être. Celle-ci
à son tour devait mettre en relief la place occupée sur l'échelle
de la hiérarchie sociale, distinguant très nettement ceux « d'ex-
traction noble » des plébéiens (qui, d'ailleurs, mettaient beaucoup
de zèle à imiter cette manière d'être). Dans cette façon d'apparaî-
tre, le geste était quelque chose d'également important que le port
du costume noble ou la coupe « à la façon noble » des cheveux ;
plus même, tout comme le costume ou la chevelure, il subissait
les variations de la mode qui, à l'époque, était une course aux
modèles non encore popularisés ou adoptés par des gens de position ou de fortune inférieure, voire par les imitateurs plébéiens.
« Ce que je me souviens de mode différente dans les vêtements,
les coiffures, les bottes, les sabres, les harnais et tout équipement
militaire ou domestique, même dans les toupets, les gestes, la
démarche et les salutations, Grand Dieu, on ne saurait le trans-
crire sur dix peaux de boeufs », avouait le mémorialiste du XVIIᵉ
siècle, Jan Chryzostom Pasek [5].

Notre propos, nécessairement très abrégé, s'articulera en trois
points où nous traiterons du geste successivement : 1° dans la vie

---

[4] J. H u i z i n g a, *Le déclin du Moyen Age*, Paris 1948, p. 9.
[5] J. P a s e k, *Pamiętniki* [*Mémoires*], éd. W. C z a p l i ń s k i, Wrocław
1968, p. 93.

religieuse de la noblesse, 2° dans sa vie de famille et de société, 3° dans la vie politique et publique.

Nous laisserons hors de nos considérations le geste sur le forum judiciaire et le geste attaché aux us et coutumes militaires ; l'élargissement des dépouillements des sources permettra certainement dans l'avenir de présenter également ces domaines importants de la vie où le geste jouait un rôle marquant.

Une question essentielle qui, malheureusement, ne peut être définitivement résolue dans le cadre de cette étude par manque de littérature comparée, est le problème de savoir ce qui, dans le geste de l'ancienne Pologne, était exclusivement indigène, original, et ce qui était partagé en commun avec la convention des autres pays aux XVIᵉ - XVIIIᵉ siècles. Une « unification » considérable en la matière était favorisée par les sources communes de la tradition antique (qui attribuait un rôle important à la symbolique du geste) et du geste liturgique pratiqué dans l'Eglise catholique. L'iconographie polonaise et étrangère présente justement en abondance ce geste « international », caractéristique des époques de la Renaissance et du baroque dans toute l'Europe. Particulièrement typiques sont ici les gestes de soumission et d'obéissance (la tête inclinée, les mains croisées sur la poitrine ou la main sur le coeur) se répétant par exemple dans les scènes de l'annonciation et de l'adoration, le geste de la prière (les mains jointes, la tête inclinée ou levée), les gestes de désespoir (les mains tordues ou levées au-dessus de la tête), fréquents dans les scènes où l'on pleure les morts, etc. Dans la présente esquisse, nous nous efforcerons d'analyser non pas tant cette convention internationale du geste généralisée dans toute l'Europe occidentale et centrale aux XVIᵉ - XVIIᵉ siècles que plutôt ce qui, à notre sens, peut être considéré comme spécifiquement polonais en ce temps-là, quoiqu'il ne soit pas toujours possible à l'étape actuelle des recherches de dégager cette spécificité.

1° Le rôle du geste de la prière dans le bas Moyen Age polonais a été présenté par P. Sczaniecki déjà cité, qui en relève l'abondance et la synchronisation avec les paroles de la prière [6].

---

[6] P. S c z a n i e c k i, op. cit., p. 42.

L'accroissement général du rôle du geste dans la liturgie romaine à partir du déclin du XV° siècle était relevé récemment par W. Tatarkiewicz qui rappelle par exemple que l'agenouillement pendant l'Elévation ne date que d'environ 1488 [7]. Dans la liturgie et la religiosité baroque de la Contre-Réforme, qui se plaisait particulièrement dans les effets théâtraux, le geste avait connu dans toute l'Europe une carrière colossale ; la chaire surtout était le lieu où la verbalisation dramatique ne pouvait se passer du geste amplificateur du prédicateur. L'aire culturelle spécifique qu'était la Pologne des XVI° - XVIII° siècles, était le berceau d'un catholicisme aux teintes régionales fortement marquées et d'un rituel souvent exotique pour les voyageurs venus de l'étranger [8], ce rituel se ressentant entre autres des influences de l'Eglise orthodoxe et des autres cultes librement pratiqués dans la Pologne multinationale et multiconfessionnelle. On rencontrait rarement dans les églises polonaises le genre de prière contemplative ; la piété s'y exprimait d'une manière égale par la parole comme par le geste qui accompagnait généralement la prière et parfois même la remplaçait. Charles Ogier, le secrétaire de l'ambassadeur français Claude de Mesmes d'Avaux, qui avait fait un séjour en Poméranie en 1635 - 1636, note dans ses mémoires son étonnement à la vue des signes de dévotion typiquement polonais pendant la messe : « Quand le prêtre élève le Corps du Seigneur, ils se frappent fortement à la bouche, au front, aux joues et à la poitrine et se prosternent jusqu'à terre » [9]. Particulièrement grand était le rôle du geste au cours des multiples manifestations de la piété collective à l'époque du baroque. Le Vendredi Saint, Ogier avait été témoin de toute une pantomime dramatique, de l'auto-flagellation qui, comme tous les ans, avait lieu dans les églises polonaises. « Quand, vers le soir — écrit-il —, nous étions revenus chez nos Dominicains, j'ai été témoin d'un spectacle que je n'avais jamais vu encore. Il s'était notamment formé, vers sept heures du soir, une procession de pénitents vêtus de manteaux rouges, qui,

[7] W. Tatarkiewicz, *O sztuce polskiej XVII i XVIII w.* [*De l'art polonais des XVII° et XVIII° s.*], Warszawa 1966, p. 433.

[8] J. Tazbir, *Kultura szlachecka w Polsce* [*La culture nobiliaire en Pologne*], Warszawa 1978, pp. 104 sqq.

[9] *Karola Ogiera dziennik podróży do Polski. 1635 - 1636* [*Caroli Ogerii ephemerides sive iter...*], vol. I, éd. W. Czapliński, Gdańsk 1950, p. 75.

en chantant des chants polonais, faisaient le tour de l'église, s'arrêtaient, tombaient à terre devant le Corps du Seigneur et se flagellaient [...] Et quand, après cent coups ou plus, ils ont cessé au signe de leur chef qui marquait le rythme avec son bâton, et sont restés à terre, j'ai cru que c'en était fini. Cependant quand le chef, immédiatement après, eut recommencé à marquer le rythme, ils ont repris le spectacle avec plus de violence encore [...] Il paraît qu'en Pologne nombre de gens de la noblesse ont l'habitude en ces jours [le Carême — M. B.] de se torturer et flageller ainsi, soit publiquement, soit en privé »[10]. La même coutume a été décrite d'une manière non moins pittoresque cent ans plus tard par le mémorialiste polonais J. Kitowicz[11]. Le Carême n'était pas le seul à fournir une occasion de spectacles dramatiques à l'église. Se prosterner les bras en croix sur le pavement de l'église était une pratique journalière et une manifestation massive de la piété, d'ailleurs pas seulement en Pologne mais aussi en Europe occidentale[12]. Un usage typiquement polonais, en revanche, était de tirer le sabre du fourreau au moment de l'Evangile pendant la messe (pour marquer qu'on était prêt à défendre la foi), ou bien d'entendre la messe en pleine armure et le sabre levé en pénitence pour ses péchés[13]. Les pratiques de ce type illustraient visuellement l'identification des notions, si caractéristiques du XVII° siècle : Polonais — catholique — défenseur de la foi.

Le rôle du geste était spécial dans les processions eucharistiques, dont le nombre et la popularité s'accroissaient si considérablement aux XVI° - XVIII° siècles, ainsi que pendant les offices de la Passion et les rites de Noël[14] au cours desquels des acteurs mimaient les rôles du Christ, de Marie, de st Joseph, des soldats romains, d'Hérode. Aux cérémonies funèbres prenaient part dès le XVI° siècle ce que l'on appelle les archimimes. Tout d'abord

---

[10] *Ibidem*, vol. II, p. 71.
[11] J. K i t o w i c z, *Opis obyczajów za panowania Augusta III* [*Description des coutumes polonaises sous le règne d'Auguste III*], 3° éd., éd. R. P o l l a k, Wrocław 1970, pp. 43 - 44.
[12] K. O g i e r dit que l'ambassadeur français Claude d'Avaux pratiquait aussi l'usage « de se prosterner les bras en croix » (*op. cit.*, vol. II, p. 69).
[13] J. P a s e k, *Pamiętniki...*, p. 120.
[14] *Kościół w Polsce. Wieki XVI - XVIII* [*L'Eglise en Pologne. XVI° - XVIII° s.*], sous la dir. de J. K ł o c z o w s k i, vol. II, Kraków 1969, p. 465 ; J. K i t o w i c z, *Opis obyczajów...*, pp. 43 - 52.

aux enterrements des rois, puis, sur le même modèle, aux enterrements solennels des soldats, était jouée la scène de la mort
consistant à s'effondrer sur le pavement ou à tomber de cheval
près du catafalque. Un élément stable de la *pompa funebris* des
XVI° - XVIII° siècles était de briser ostensiblement les insignes
du pouvoir (le sceptre royal, le bâton de l'hetman, le bâton de
maréchal) ou de casser les armes et les sceaux ayant appartenu au
défunt si celui-ci n'était pas parvenu aux dignités supérieures [15].

Ainsi donc, tout au long des XVI° - XVII° siècles, l'église se
transformait en un grand théâtre sur la scène duquel se jouait
une incessante pantomime à laquelle participaient fidèles et clergé.
En effet, les acteurs de la scène de l'église étaient non seulement
les ecclésiastiques exécutant les gestes liturgiques traditionnels et
amplifiant au moyen du geste l'éloquence de la chaire ; c'étaient
aussi les participants laïcs des offices et des rites. Par le geste
individuel et collectif ils manifestaient leurs sentiments religieux
avec plus de force peut-être qu'au moyen de la prière orale, et ils
considéraient à coup sûr le geste qui accompagnait celle-ci comme
une partie intégrale de la piété manifestée.

2° Quand on parcourt les carnets appelés *silva rerum* du XVII°
siècle, ces compendiums authentiques du savoir du noble polonais,
on est étonné par la quantité des formules et des exemples qu'ils
recèlent : discours, lettres, salutations, adieux pour toutes les
circonstances différents, suivant les situations, adaptés à l'état,
à l'âge, au sexe, etc. La vie de famille et de société de la noblesse
polonaise se déroulait d'après certaines règles que tout noble
devait connaître ; à ce savoir justement on reconnaissait les gens
« nobles de race », alors que l'ignorance en la matière trahis-
sait le plébéien [16]. En plus des capacités oratoires, le noble devait
posséder un savoir-vivre particulier, au sens de la connaissance de
tout un cérémonial de gestes accompagnant les paroles aux
diverses occasions. Les observations notées par les voyageurs
visitant la Pologne aux XVI° - XVIII° siècles, sont unanimes à re-

---

[15] J. C h r ó ś c i c k i, *Pompa funebris*, Warszawa 1974, p. 52.
[16] Selon l'écrivain polonais du XVII° s., Walerian Nekanda T r e p k a
(*Liber Chamorum*, éd. W. D w o r z a c z e k, J. B a r t y ś, Z. K u c h o w i c z,
Wrocław 1958, vol. I, pp. 8, 101, 151, 181, 336, 468, 567, 641, 1144, 1874, 2098,
2327, 2465).

lever la prolifération du geste dans les moeurs polonaises. Il se peut d'ailleurs que la prédilection manifestée pour les spectacles de toutes sortes et la popularité considérable du théâtre dès la Renaissance, portée à son apogée à l'époque du baroque, y aient joué leur rôle. Les gens du baroque identifiaient en toute conscience la vie à la scène (« *vita est scenae similis* »). Le rôle du geste dans la vie de famille et de société venait de ce qu'il fonctionnait en ce temps dans deux sphères : a) en tant qu'élément déterminant la position sociale de l'individu — c'était donc un guide spécifique des degrés au sein de la famille et des systèmes hiérarchiques dans la société, b) en tant qu'expression particulière des états émotionnels.

Un des attributs indispensables du noble était de savoir se déplacer et agir « dignement », conformément aux circonstances et à sa propre condition. Un rôle particulier dans la formation de la jeunesse en la matière était sans doute incombé aux écoles jésuites. Les jésuites passaient pour des connaisseurs exceptionnels de ce savoir-vivre mimique non écrit, de vigueur dans certains milieux ; eux-mêmes d'ailleurs ils y attachaient une grande importance dans leur façon d'être, surtout sur la chaire. J. Kitowicz nous dit qu'ils exerçaient les novices « dans les gestes, la parole, la démarche ; dans chaque mouvement du corps transparaissait une formation particulière » [17].

La posture et la démarche du noble devaient être empreintes de gravité et de dignité. C'est la main appuyée sur le pommeau de l'indispensable sabre long ou court, la masse d'armes ou le bâton de commandement à la main, ou encore la main à la hanche, dans une attitude respirant l'orgueil et le sentiment d'appartenance au groupe privilégié, que le représentent les portraits du XVII⁰ ou du XVIII⁰ siècle [18] et les nombreuses gravures du XVIII⁰ siècle, d'Orłowski, Chodowiecki, Norblin. Quand Jeremiasz Falck, qui préparait la page du titre des *Mowy* (*Discours*) de Jerzy Ossoliński, y a présenté l'auteur agenouillé, le magnat offensé a ordonné d'acheter et de détruire tout le tirage. Dans l'édition suivante, on

---

[17] J. K i t o w i c z, *Opis obyczajów...*, p. 110.
[18] *Portret polski XVII i XVIII w.* [*Le portrait polonais aux XVII⁰ et XVIII⁰ s.*], Katalog Wystawy Muzeum Narodowego w Warszawie, Warszawa 1977.

n'osa plus le représenter autrement que debout. C'était un sentiment de dignité étroitement attaché à la hiérarchie sociale et à l'âge, d'où l'obligation strictement respectée de céder le pas au plus digne ou au plus âgé dans les occasions les plus diverses : le cortège, le passage de la porte, la danse, à table. Et cela s'accompagnait de révérences cérémonieuses et de gestes d'invitation dont ne pouvait se passer aucune rencontre. La démarche, à elle seule, du noble attestait sa condition. « Ils avancent majestueusement, la masse d'armes à la main et le sabre au côté, dont ils ne se séparent qu'au moment d'aller se reposer », écrit un voyageur du XVII° siècle [19]. De cette manière de marcher, pleine de dignité et marquée de fréquentes révérences, tirait son origine la danse caractéristique de la noblesse : la polonaise, dite danse « marchée » ou « grande danse », qui faisait aussi une forte impression sur les étrangers [20]. Cet attachement à la majestée manifestée jusqu'aux divertissements a fait peut-être que la noblesse traitait avec mépris tous jeux mobiles, surtout la balle [21]. On considérait en revanche comme un sport digne des « bien nés » uniquement l'équitation et la chasse qui en était inséparable [22].

Un protocole gestuel particulièrement développé présidait aux salutations et aux adieux : toutes sortes de révérences, la main tendue ou, dans des circonstances plus cordiales, le baiser à l'épaule au cas d'une position identique dans la hiérarchie sociale, l'inflexion du genou, le baiser de la main, ou encore l'embrassement des genoux ou des jambes des personnes avancées en âge ou situées plus haut sur l'échelle sociale. Il s'est conservé sur ce sujet de nombreuses mentions dans les mémoires et des témoignages iconographiques [23]. « Les hommes s'embrassent à l'épaule et se traitent fraternellement quand ils sont d'égale condition, mais

---

[19] *Relation historique de la Pologne... par le Sieur de Hauteville*, Paris 1657, pp. 229 - 235.

[20] J. S. B y s t r o ń, *Dzieje obyczajów w dawnej Polsce. Wiek XVI - XVIII* [*Histoire des moeurs dans l'ancienne Pologne. XVI° - XVIII° s.*], vol. I, Warszawa 1976, p. 215.

[21] V. le mépris de la noblesse pour le roi Sigismond III à cause de son attachement au jeu de balle.

[22] J. S. B y s t r o ń, *Dzieje obyczajów...*, vol. II, pp. 199 sqq.

[23] *Cudzoziemcy o Polsce. Relacje i opinie* [*Les étrangers sur la Pologne. Relations et opinions*], élab. par J. G i n t e l, Kraków 1971, vol. I, pp. 201 - 205, 297 ; vol. II, p. 93.

quand il n'y a pas d'égalité entre les personnes en présence, la plus basse dans la hiérarchie tombe aux pieds de la plus élevée, embrasse les pieds ou enlace ses bras autour des genoux, ou tout simplement fait un geste de déférence en proférant la formule : « Je tombe à vos pieds »[24]. Les cérémonies de salutation étaient souvent préparées à l'avance : un serviteur était envoyé prévenir les hôtes de l'arrivée de l'invité pour que le maître du logis puisse l'accueillir sur le pas de la porte ou même partir à sa rencontre ; dans certaines gentilhommières, on tenait toujours quelqu'un aux aguets pour qu'il observe si personne n'approche. Les salutations s'exprimaient par un échange abondant de révérences et d'embrassements pendant que l'invité était conduit dans la maison, le maître de céans accompagnant l'homme, et la maîtresse de maison, son épouse. Le passage de la porte fournissait une nouvelle ocassion de cérémonie à qui céderait le pas, la même chose se répétant au moment de l'occupation des sièges. « On n'en finissait pas de se complimenter, de faire des façons au passage de la porte et au moment de s'asseoir », dit le mémorialiste. « Ensuite le maître de céans invitait debout à déceindre l'épée, et là non plus ne manquaient pas les longs échanges de politesses et de prétendus refus ; finalement, cédant aux instances réitérées, le nouveau venu enlevait son arme et, accompagné de l'hôte, la déposait dans un coin du salon. Sur ces entrefaites entrait un domestique portant sur un plateau plusieurs bouteilles et [...] un verre ; celui-ci [...] était vidé avec des embrassades réciproques »[25].

Les révérences jouaient un rôle particulier dans la vie de la société. On les répétait maintes fois[26], exagérant dès le XVII° siècle leur profondeur, ôtant le couvre-chef avec lequel on balayait presque le plancher ou le gazon[27] ; certaines occasions, en revanche, n'exigeaient que de soulever la coiffure[28]. En ôtant le couvrechef, on manifestait en effet un respect particulier ; la personne jeune, située plus bas dans la société ou obligée, ôtait la première

---

[24] *L'observateur en Pologne*, par H. V a u t r i n, Paris 1807, pp. 242 - 243.
[25] J. S. B y s t r o ń, *Dzieje obyczajów...*, vol. II, p. 162.
[26] J. P a s e k, *Pamiętniki...*, p. 244 ; *Cudzoziemcy o Polsce...*, vol. I, pp. 202, 205.
[27] On en trouve beaucoup de preuves dans l'iconographie de l'époque.
[28] J. P a s e k, *Pamiętniki...*, p. 431.

sa coiffure. Les égaux enlevaient leurs coiffures simultanément[29]. On soulevait aussi la coiffure et on se levait en lisant une lettre d'une personne de haute condition à laquelle il convenait de manifester du respect ; d'une manière analogue était parfois ostensiblement manifesté le respect en prononçant le nom d'une personne particulièrement digne[30].

Au cours des XVII° et XVIII° siècles, du fait des transformations sociales et culturelles (entre autres, la dépendance plus grande de la noblesse vis-à-vis des magnats et la démoralisation de la clientèle des grands), les marques d'humble soumission commencèrent à se multiplier, adoptant des formes de plus en plus expansives. On embrasse les protecteurs non plus seulement sur la main, mais aussi sur la poitrine, le ventre, les genoux, les pieds, on se jette devant eux à plat ventre[31]. Des gestes nombreux accompagnent aussi tous les événements de famille, surtout la cour faite aux demoiselles et les demandes en mariage (qu'il s'agisse de jeune fille ou de veuve) qui s'accompagnent toujours d'agenouillements empressés aux pieds des parents ou des tuteurs, les cérémonies nuptiales (là aussi, on se jette aux pieds), les enterrements (il en a été question ci-dessus). Tout comme les salutations, un rituel particulier de gestes accompagne les adieux, surtout des fils envoyés aux écoles ou à la guerre. L'un des gestes d'adieu les plus populaires était le génouflexion devant la personne à laquelle on faisait ses adieux, celle-ci serrant la tête du partant[32]. Ce même geste d'ailleurs se retrouve aussi à l'époque comme une expression de cordialité familière manifestée à la personne agenouillée, de condition inférieure (p. ex. le roi à l'encontre d'un courtisan, l'évêque ou le moine à l'encontre d'un laïque)[33].

Le baiser joue dans la vie de société des XVII° et XVIII° siècles un rôle de plus en plus important. Au XVI° siècle, à l'époque des influences assez fortes des moeurs occidentales, italiennes surtout, il n'était pas pratiqué fréquemment et était considéré comme une coutume plébéienne.

[29] J. S. B y s t r o ń, Dzieje obyczajów..., vol. II, p. 164.
[30] Cudzoziemcy o Polsce..., vol. I, pp. 201 - 202.
[31] Cudzoziemcy o Polsce..., vol. I, p. 297 ; W. Ł o z i ń s k i, Życie polskie w dawnych wiekach [La vie dans l'ancienne Pologne], Kraków 1958, p. 192.
[32] J. P a s e k, Pamiętniki..., pp. 25, 103, 243, 244, 251, 297 ; Cudzoziemcy o Polsce..., vol. I, p. 201.
[33] J. P a s e k, Pamiętniki..., p. 197.

« Aujourd'hui cet usage a presque disparu chez les Polonais,
Et ne s'est guère conservé que chez les Ruthènes vulgaires
Qui s'embrassent volontiers en se saluant »
écrivait Jan Protasowicz [34]. A l'époque où l'emprise occidentale
a commencé à faiblir et la dignité réservée de la Renaissance
a commencé à céder le pas à l'exagération baroque dans le manifestation des sentiments, intensifiée encore par les influences
orientales, le baiser est devenu un élément indispensable des contacts de société. « Généralement, les Polonais ont l'habitude de
s'embrasser en se saluant (ce que les autres nations n'ont pas
coutume de faire, même s'ils ont des liens de parenté) pour manifester par cette cérémonie extérieure leur sentiment amical réci-
proque », nous dit Starowolski dans la *Reformacja* [35]. On embrassait les mains des membres âgés de la famille et toutes les personnes de condition sociale supérieure. Les paysans embrassaient les
mains des seigneurs et des membres de leurs familles, y compris
les enfants ; de même le hobereau embrassait aux XVIIᵉ et XVIIIᵉ
siècles la main du magnat — chose impensable encore au XVIᵉ
siècle. On embrassait aussi les mains des femmes mariées, et même
des jeunes filles ; les jeunes femmes s'inclinaient en baisant les
mains des matrones. Les enfants avaient l'obligation d'embrasser
les pieds de leurs parents quel qu'ait été leur âge, dans des circonstances particulières : départ de la maison ou retour, bénédiction
au moment de la prise d'une décision importante, par exemple le
mariage, l'entrée au monastère ou au couvent, le départ en pèle-
rinage, etc.

Au XVIIᵉ siècle, où la noblesse tombait sous une dépendance de
plus en plus grande vis-à-vis des magnats, s'est généralisée la
pratique de se jeter aux pieds des grands protecteurs pour de-
mander une faveur ou remercier pour quelque bienfait. Mais surtout on s'agenouillait devant ses parents.

« Le fils sur un genou, la fille sur les deux
Rend hommage à sa mère »
écrivait Wespazjan Kochowski [36]. Les femmes se jetaient à genoux non seulement devant leurs parents mais aussi devant les

---

[34] J. S. B y s t r o ń, *Dzieje obyczajów...*, vol. II, pp. 166 - 168.
[35] *Ibidem.*
[36] *Ibidem.*

membres plus âgés de la famille et même leurs frères. Les garçons se jetaient aux pieds des jeunes filles. Cet usage s'était tellement généralisé au XVIII° siècle qu'il commença à susciter des inquiétudes chez le ecclésiastiques qui considéraient que trop d'honneur manifesté aux hommes portait atteinte au respect dû à Dieu. *Le recueil général de tous les péchés* paru en 1776, destiné à aider à faire l'examen de conscience avant la confession, renferme les questions : « Est-ce que tu t'es agenouillé devant les jeunes filles ? Est-ce que tu te mets à genoux devant les personnes [laïques — *M. B.*] ? » [37].

Les gestes ne servaient pas uniquement à manifester le respect ; on pouvait aussi par ce moyen exprimer le mépris, par exemple par « le retrait de la main », c'est-à-dire le refus de tendre la main [38], en faisant la figue à quelqu'un [39], en giflant de la main ou avec un gant, enfin en frappant du plat du sabre [40]. On manifestait la colère en montrant le blanc de l'oeil, en grinçant des dents, en tirant ou mordillant la moustache [41], par le cliquetis du sabre ou en jetant le bonnet à terre [42] ; le contentement en revanche, en relevant la moustache ou en jetant le bonnet en l'air [43]. Certains gesticulaient si violemment à toute occasion qu'ils donnaient l'impression de mener un jeu d'acteur exagéré ; ceci s'appelait *wydwarzanie*.

Le geste, comme en témoigne l'iconographie, jouait un rôle important pendant les festins qui occupaient beaucoup de place dans la vie de société de la noblesse [44]. Les convives étaient placés dans l'ordre de leur dignité et de l'âge [45] ; si quelqu'un était insatisfait du voisinage, il fendait la nappe devant lui, abolissant ainsi symboliquement la communauté de la table [46]. Au XVII° siècle

---

[37] *Ibidem*, p. 168.
[38] J. P a s e k, *Pamiętniki...*, p. 176 ; J. O s s o l i ń s k i, *Pamiętnik [Mémoires]*, élab. par W. C z a p l i ń s k i, Warszawa 1976, p. 55.
[39] J. S. B y s t r o ń, *Dzieje obyczajów...*, vol. II, pp. 168 - 170.
[40] J. P a s e k, *Pamiętniki...*, p. 119.
[41] *Ibidem*, p. 256.
[42] *Ibidem*, p. 316.
[43] Le geste est très souvent souligné par l'iconographie (Norblin, Orłowski).
[44] W. Ł o z i ń s k i, *Życie polskie...*, pp. 190, 204.
[45] J. P a s e k, *Pamiętniki...*, pp. 15, 103 ; J. O s s o l i ń s k i, *Pamiętnik...*, p. 48.
[46] J. S. B y s t r o ń, *Dzieje obyczajów...*, vol. II, pp. 180 - 181.

encore et au début du XVIII°, on se mettait à table la tête couverte et on ne la découvrait qu'au moment des toasts : à cette
occasion on se levait aussi des chaises, se conformant au dicton
du XVII° siècle :

> « L'hôte fait cette obligation [que]
> qui boit enlève son bonnet et en buvant se lève » [47].

L'habitude de se lever pendant les festins était déjà raillée
par Kochanowski [48], et l'Italien Jean-Paul Mucante s'en plaignait
vers la fin du XVI° siècle [49], s'en plaignait aussi le Français Hubert
Vautrin au XVIII° siècle : « Ainsi, en portant les toasts, il faut se
lever et s'asseoir, s'asseoir et se lever à nouveau, et ainsi jusqu'à
la fin du festin » [50]. Les toasts les plus importants étaient chaque
fois portés dans des verres différents ; l'amphitryon avait de ce
fait l'habitude de ranger devant lui toute une collection de coupes,
gobelets et verres de formes différentes, « tantôt un carré, tantôt
un triangulaire, tantôt une figure longue et tantôt un ronde »,
écrivait Beauplan au XVII° siècle [51]. La personne qui portait le
toast levait le verre et en vidait le contenu, après quoi on faisait
circuler ce même verre, le remplissant et le vidant au fur et
à mesure. L'amphitryon poli buvait ainsi à la santé non seulement
du commensal le plus digne, mais aussi de chacun des présents ;
la maîtresse de maison faisait de même, sauf qu'elle ne vidait pas
son verre mais, l'ayant porté à ses lèvres, le passait à l'invité que
le toast devait honorer. Assez souvent après l'avoir vidé, l'invité
ainsi distingué jetait le verre à terre pour indiquer que personne
plus n'était digne d'en boire à l'avenir. Les commensaux plus
zélés ou grisés cassaient les verres contre leur tête. Un incident
célèbre de ce type avait eu lieu au début du XVII° siècle à To-
łoczyn : l'hetman Chodkiewicz avait brisé sur son crâne le verre
que lui avait tendu le roi Sigismond III. « J'ai cassé le verre sur
ma tête », écrivait l'hetman à sa femme, « et le roi a dit : Aimable
hetman, ne casse donc pas ta tête ; nous y tenons énormément » [52].
Un autre épisode pittoresque du même genre avait été noté cent

---

[47] W. Ł o z i ń s k i, Życie polskie..., p. 209.
[48] J. S. B y s t r o ń, Dzieje obyczajów..., vol. II, p. 186.
[49] Cudzoziemcy o Polsce..., vol. I, p. 195.
[50] Cf. note 24.
[51] W. Ł o z i ń s k i, Życie polskie..., p. 210.
[52] Ibidem, p. 211.

62

ans plus tard (1740) par le mémorialiste Marcin Matuszewicz :
la demoiselle Szamowska, une noble de Mazovie, ayant mouillé
ses lèvres dans la coupe de l'étrier, la passa au jeune Sollohub
qui était déjà à cheval. Celui-ci, ayant bu le vin, mit le verre en
éclats d'un coup de pistolet et, ayant mis pied à terre, se jeta
à plat ventre devant le père de la jeune fille, lui demandant la
main de celle-ci [53]. Voilà bien un tableau caractéristique, montrant
dans toute son évidence le rôle du geste dans la vie quotidienne
de la noblesse polonaise de ce temps-là.

3° Le geste, ce facteur si important dans la sphère familiale
et dans la vie de société, devait avoir une non moindre signification dans l'arène publique. Là d'ailleurs aussi nous observons aux
XVII° et XVIII° siècles une expansion de la gesticulation plus
grande qu'au XVI°. Au milieu de ce siècle, en effet, on relevait
comme une chose extraordinaire le fait que les députés suppliaient
à genoux Sigismond-Auguste de renoncer au mariage avec Barbara Radziwiłł, impopulaire parmi la noblesse [54]. Cent ou cent
cinquante ans plus tard, cette scène n'aurait plus étonné personne-
ne : la position à genoux, les prostrations ou la position à plat
ventre, les bras en croix étant devenues extrêmement fréquentes
sur le terrain officiel [55]. Un rôle particulièrement important incom-
bait à la gesticulation pendant les discours publics : la modération
en la matière ne faisait pas bonne impression sur les auditeurs.
L'ambassadeur suédois qui tenait un discours à Varsovie, en automne 1632, à la Diète, les bras croisés (« plicatisque brachiis »),
obtint le surnom de rustre [56]. Aux diétines, pendant les Diètes et
les élections souvent orageuses, le geste devenait d'ailleurs une
nécessité puisque dans le brouhaha général on n'entendait pas les
paroles. Au XVI° siècle déjà, on abolissait à coups de sabre les
projets de lois et les privilèges qui n'allaient pas dans les goûts
des députés. Le piétinement deux cents ans plus tard (1780) du
code de lois de A. Zamoyski était donc le résultat non seulement

---

[53] *Ibidem.*
[54] *Diariusz sejmu piotrkowskiego w r. 1548* [*Journal de la Diète tenue
à Piotrków en 1548*], in : *Scriptores Rerum Polonicarum*, vol. I, éd. J. S z u j -
s k i, Kraków 1872, pp. 178 - 207.
[55] J. S. B y s t r o ń, *Dzieje obyczajów...*, vol. II, p. 167.
[56] *Karola Ogiera dziennik podróży...*, vol. II, pp. 127 - 129.

de tempéraments enfiévrés, mais aussi une démonstration visuelle de certaines attitudes, inscrite dans la tradition. L'attachement au rituel gestuel s'exprimait entre autres dans la cérémonie, célébrée avec une onction particulière, du baiser de la main royale, qui avait lieu immédiatement après l'élection et était répétée à chaque Diète. Pendant les débats, les députés n'enlevaient pas leurs bonnets et ne quittaient pas leurs armes [57], ce qui pouvait devenir dangereux pendant les échanges d'opinions plus violents. « A n'importe quel mot cliquetis des sabres, brandissement des masses d'armes », écrit Pasek [58]. La violence de la gesticulation aux diétines et aux Diètes est attestée tant par l'iconographie [59] que par les chroniqueurs [60]. Au XVIIIᵉ siècle, les choses étaient allées si loin que, pendant les débats de la Diète, on mangeait et buvait ouvertement (des vendeurs de bière, de friandises, etc. circulaient parmi les députés), on bavardait en gesticulant, alors que les arbitres lançaient du haut de la galerie contre les orateurs impopulaires des pommes et des poires dures [61]. La fin du XVIIIᵉ siècle seulement mit fin à ces excès, enrichissant l'histoire du geste sur le forum du Parlement de la tragique intervention du député de la terre de Nowogród, Tadeusz Rejtan, qui, ayant déchiré ses vêtements et s'étant jeté à terre, protestait de la sorte contre la légalisation du premier partage de la Pologne.

La question de la tête couverte ou découverte occupe une place particulière dans l'histoire de la vie publique et de la diplomatie polonaises. Le costume polonais d'apparat exigeait que l'on se produisît en public la tête couverte, d'où, comme on l'a vu, l'usage de festoyer, de débattre à la Diète, etc. la tête couverte. Garder le chef découvert ou enlever la coiffure en la présence de quelqu'un, était une marque de respect particulier et cette question était l'objet de disputes même dans les appartements royaux [62]. Au moyen des bonnets on manifestait son appui aux magnats pendant les assemblées des nobles. Couvrir la tête ou la découvrir

---

[57] D'après l'iconographie.
[58] J. P a s e k, Pamiętniki..., p. 453.
[59] Cf. les dessins de Norblin ou le tableau de B. Canaletto représentant l'élection du roi Stanislas-Auguste (Musée National à Varsovie).
[60] J. K i t o w i c z, Opis obyczajów..., pp. 577 sqq. ; Cudzoziemcy o Polsce..., vol. I, pp. 342 - 343, vol. II, pp. 31, 66 - 68.
[61] Ibidem.
[62] J. S. B y s t r o ń, Dzieje obyczajów..., vol. II, p. 165.

avait aussi une signification particulière dans la vie diplomatique ; surtout pendant les députations à l'étranger, le rituel des gestes acquérait les dimensions d'une affaire d'Etat. Dans les instructions écrites pour les ambassadeurs en 1601, nous lisons : « [Leurs — M. B.] gestes doivent être virils, pondérés selon les besoins, et non pas efféminés, ni enfantins, ni peureux, ni honteux, ni coléreux, ni craintifs, ni étourdis, ni mortifiés [...] Dans l'exercice de l'ambassade, se tenir tel un pieu, regarder devant soi. Puis, porter les yeux sur celui auprès duquel on est ambassadeur. Sans faire de mouvement. Sans regarder à droite ou à gauche. Sans hocher la tête. Tenant les mains tranquilles, sans gesticuler. Ne pas tirer sa barbe. S'abstenir de tousser, de cracher et de se moucher. Sans se gratter la tête ni nulle part. Sans mettre le doigt dans le nez ou dans l'oreille. Sans mâchonner » [63]. Les instructions du roi pour les ambassadeurs envoyés le 30 mai 1667 auprès du tsar, recommandaient qu'ils se conduisent « selon les usages anciens sans se découvrir » et qu'ils saluent le tsar « à la polonaise » [64]. On lit dans la relation de cette ambassade que les courtisans du tsar sommaient les ambassadeurs se rendant en audience qu'ils enlèvent leurs bonnets, mais « messieurs les ambassadeurs n'en voulaient rien faire ». Des tractations assez longues s'ensuivirent et, finalement, le tsar lui-même consentit que les Polonais entrent dans la salle en bonnets et qu'ils ne se découvrent que « in conspectum le tsar Sa Majesté assis in maiestate ». Peu après cependant, ils se couvrirent à nouveau, expliquant que de cette façon « ils gardent la dignité de leur souverain et de l'Etat polonais ». Selon les idées de ce temps-là, il n'était en revanche pas contraire à la dignité d'ambassadeur d'embrasser la main du tsar et du tsarévitch [65].

Rien d'étonnant donc qu'au déclin du XVIIᵉ siècle, l'incident touchant le port de la coiffure pendant la présentation par Jean III Sobieski de son fils à l'empereur Léopold après la délivrance de Vienne, avait si fortement bouleversé la partie polonaise, très

---

[63] *Dyplomaci w dawnych czasach. Relacje staropolskie z XVI - XVIII stulecia* [*Les diplomates aux temps anciens. Relations des XVIᵉ - XVIIIᵉ s.*], élab. par A. Przyboś et R. Zelewski, Kraków 1959, pp. 170 - 171.
[64] *Ibidem*, pp. 339 - 340.
[65] *Ibidem*, p. 345.

sensible à ce geste [66]. L'affaire fut envenimée par le fait que, répondant à la révérence des colonels polonais, l'empereur s'était contenté de faire un signe de tête sans soulever son chapeau. En représailles, l'hetman Sieniawski ne fit que baisser devant lui son bâton de commandement et non pas l'étendard, comme c'était de coutume. Ayant appris de quoi il s'agissait, Léopold s'efforça, quoique tard, de réparer sa maladresse et, depuis ce moment « où qu'il rencontrât un étendard, il tendait vers lui son chapeau — écrit un mémorialiste — rendant ces honneurs même aux étendards valaques et tartares après l'admonition » [67]. Encore à l'époque saxonne, quand l'ambassadeur turc venait à la cour de Pologne, l'entourage du roi qui s'habillait alors à l'allemande et ne couvrait jamais les perruques du chapeau, mettait spécialement pour cette circonstance les couvre-chef dès que l'ambassadeur pénétrait en turban dans la salle [68].

Devant les étendards militaires il était absolument obligatoire de lever son couvre-chef. D'autre part, l'étendard incliné était une marque d'hommage et de respect ; le geste de la victoire était de jeter les étendards et insignes conquis aux pieds de l'hetman ou, pendant le triomphe, aux pieds du roi. Cette cérémonie cependant n'était pas une spécificité polonaise [69].

Notre propos n'est certainement pas complet. On peut toutefois en déduire la thèse sur la grande importance accordée au geste dans la culture nobiliaire en Pologne. Cette importance augmentait surtout au cours des XVIIᵉ et XVIIIᵉ siècles quand l'expressivité baroque se fût alliée à la fascination exercée par les civilisations de l'Orient. Le rituel développé du geste dans différents domaines de la vie était, à n'en pas douter, un des éléments importants, jusque-là, semble-t-il, insuffisamment apprécié, de la spécificité des moeurs sarmates dont des vestiges se sont prolongés jusqu'au XIXᵉ siècle [70].

---

[66] Jan S o b i e s k i, *Listy do Marysieńki* [Jean III S o b i e s k i, *Lettres à sa femme « Marysieńka »*], élab. par L. K u k u l s k i, Warszawa 1962, p. 527.

[67] J. S. B y s t r o ń, *Dzieje obyczajów...*, vol. II, p. 165.

[68] *Ibidem*, pp. 165 - 166.

[69] La problématique du geste militaire mérite une analyse bien plus approfondie.

[70] J. T a z b i r, *Kultura szlachecka...*, pp. 179 sqq.

Le geste symbolisait et en même temps protégeait la dignité du noble, du dignitaire, du roi ; dans la diplomatie, de la Pologne tout entière. Il exprimait aussi les états d'âme : les liens émotionnels unissant la famille, renforçant les relations d'amitié entre connaissances et voisins, les actes de piété à l'égard de Dieu. Il était plus facile et plus suggestif à la fois d'exprimer ces sentiments par les gestes que par les paroles (dont d'ailleurs on était très prolixe à l'époque).

L'expressivité semble disparaître avec les éléments spontanés et ludiques dans la culture, comme le souligne J. Huizinga dans son ouvrage déjà classique *Homo ludens.* La chose est d'ailleurs compréhensible, car justement le ludisme spontané et toute sorte de « jeu », caractéristiques tant du Moyen Age que des XVIe - XVIIIe siècles, devaient mettre en relief le geste sous ses formes les plus diverses. Des vestiges de ces phénomènes ne se retrouvent plus aujourd'hui que dans le folklore populaire en rapide régression.

(Traduit par Lucjan Grobelak)

XVII

SOCIAL STRUCTURES AND CUSTOM
IN EARLY MODERN POLAND

Custom can be no worse a guardian of the existing social structures and hierarchies than a legal system. What is more, if the legal system — and also the state apparatus — are weak, custom takes over a large part of the controlling functions by producing what is known as case–law and by determining everyday patterns of behaviour in all spheres of life. The nobility and the Church, the two dominant forces in old Polish society, found in custom an important instrument for defining their position and subordinating individuals and entire social groups to themselves.

The Noblemen's Commonwealth took its name from the estate of the nobility which though accounting for only about 10% of the Polish society, was, according to the then prevailing views, the salt of the earth, the group which not only held the highest position in the social structure of the country, but was simply identified with the Polish nation. The legends which added lustre to the genealogy of the nobility by tracing its origin back to the ancient Sarmatians strengthened the conviction that noble birth was the prerequisite of virtue, courage and patriotism. "Genuine nobility is a peculiar power and a genuine nest of virtue, fame, dignity and integrity", wrote Rej[1]. "Nobility soars up high with the eagles" and "it would be a wonder if anybody found an owl or a common sparrow in a falcon's nest", he remarked in another place[2]. He was echoed later by Sęp–Szarzyński: "The valiant female eagle does not give birth to pigeons"[3], and by other poets of the Baroque period. In his *Diary*, Pasek included a poem which said: "People are attached to their likes, an owl does not trade with an eagle"[4]. 17th century *silva rerum* — records kept by nobles — abound in formulations, poems, sayings and proverbs which glorify the nobility as an estate generating virtues and good qualities. This self–adoration left a heavy imprint on the nobility's attitude to other social groups.

---

[1] M. Rej, *Zwierciadło (The Mirror)*, ed. by J. Czubek and J. Łoś, Kraków 1914, vol. I, p. 159.

[2] *Ibidem*, vol. II, pp. 238, 383.

[3] M. Sęp–Szarzyński, *Poezje wybrane (Selected Poems)*, selected and edited by J. Z. Lichański, Warszawa 1976, p. 17.

[4] J. Ch. Pasek, *Pamiętniki (Diary)*, ed. by W. Czapliński, Wrocław 1968, p. 519.

Already in the 15th century the landowning nobility complained about the "lazy and loath" peasant who did not work properly on his master's land. An interesting paraphrase of the medieval satire on the peasants' laziness was written in the middle of the 16th century; it was entitled *The Description of the Peasants' Artful and Cunning Nature against Their Masters*[5]. Already at the beginning of the 17th century it was given a reply in the form of countless *Peasant Laments* about the Lords and epigrams which called the Polish–Lithuanian Commonwealth *infernus rusticorum*; they were willingly included in the pages of *silva rerum*, which shows that many owners of manorial estates did not have a completely clear conscience as far as their serfs were concerned. "Nobody has exploited its serfs more than our Poland has", jotted down Stanisław Albrycht Radziwiłł in 1649[6]. Nevertheless, there was not much pity for the peasants in the theory and literature of Sarmatism, though expressions of compassion can be found there, too (Szymon Zimorowic's *Idylls*).

It should not, however, be forgotten that in practice the nobility was linked with the peasants by the rural way of life; the two groups formed a certain community based on mutual benefits and duties. A nobleman had to take care of the peasants in his own interest. A serf tilled the master's land, but the manor succoured him in the event of bad crops, fire or sickness. "It was a hard year [1757 — M. B.] and there was hunger in the spring. The serfs were continuously coming with sacks for bread to the manor", wrote Matuszewicz and added that finally, irritated by the distribution of grain, he decided to make use of the help–seekers and told them "to work in the garden"[7] in return for food and some payment. In spite of the chasm separating them, the nobility and the peasants formed part of the same agricultural world, they lived in the same rhythm. The town and its inhabitants were outside the confines of this rural world.

The noblemen's contempt for the townsmen was therefore as a rule as deep as that for the "ignorant and lazy" peasants, if not even more so, since the noblemen questioned the urban occupations from the ethical point of view. According to the writers of noble birth, who expressed opinions common among the nobility, engaging in urban occupations was shameful and dishonest by their very nature. "A shopkeeper living on toil forgets the truth and the faith", wrote S. Orzechowski in the 16th century, trying to prove at the same time that "the nature of those crafts is such that they are obscene and stinking"[8]. Rej argued that the art of trade consisted in hoodwinking the client:

---

[5] A. B r ü c k n e r, *Źródła do dziejów literatury i oświaty polskiej* (*Sources to the History of Polish Literature and Education*), V. *Wiersze polskiego średniowiecza* (*Polish Medieval Poems*), «Biblioteka Warszawska», 1893, vol. I, pp. 260–261.

[6] A. S. R a d z i w i ł ł, *Pamiętnik o dziejach w Polsce* (*Diary on Events in Poland*), ed. by A. P r z y b o ś and R. Ż e l e w s k i, Warszawa 1980, vol. III, p. 218.

[7] M. M a t u s z e w i c z, *Diariusz życia mego* (*The Diary of My Life*), ed. and prefaced by B. K r ó l i k o w s k i, Warszawa 1986, vol. I. p. 819.

[8] Quoted after M. B o g u c k a, *Miejsce mieszczanina w społeczeństwie szlacheckim* (*The Place of the Townsman in the Noblemen's Society*), in: *Społeczeństwo staropolskie*, vol. I, Warszawa 1976, p. 187.

He who is called a shopkeeper
Is never a silly weeper.
To sell cloth below full measure
And give short weight is his pleasure[9].

The only Polish poem glorifying non agricultural work is *Officina ferraria* or *The Ironworks and Smithies for the Noble Work in Iron* written by Walenty Rozdzieński, a poet ironworker, in 1612. Sebastian Fabian Klonowic's *The Raftsman*, a poem about the rafting of goods down the Vistula, written in 1595 and frequently quoted in this context, is more a poem glorifying the occupations of a landowning nobleman than one about the townsman. What is more, Klonowic, who was a townsman himself, rather frowns upon urban occupations, complains about the depravation brought about by the lust for profit and asserts that "the ship has been invented by sheer greediness". For Klonowic, a shopkeeper is a despicable creature who "weighs his health for profit" and fears "a sudden loss", while a nobleman when he "has stacked up his corn" and "sits down by a pine fire with a salubrious drink, need not envy the townsmen their shopkeeping, need not envy the Gdańsk merchants their riches"[10]. In the 17th century, as the economic crisis increased, as monetary disturbances grew sharper and the living standards fell (because of the increase in the prices of industrial goods and the stagnation and even a drop in the income from manorial estates), anti–urban moods grew in force rapidly. An anonymous treatise of 1611 described merchants as extortionists and swindlers and attributed the existing difficulties to their "tricks"[11]. In 1622 Wojciech Gostkowski reviled against "the cunning people and merchants" who were enriching themselves at the expense of the honest nobility[12]. In 1623 Stanisław Zaremba accused merchants not only of demoralising society by the import of luxury goods but also of "tricks and intolerable profits", of raising prices, engaging in money speculation and unbearable usury; "the merchants, like keen bloodhounds and pointers, have designs on our purses", he said. Broad ranks of the nobility were becoming more and more convinced that every townsman was an enemy and a fraud engaged in speculation, sponging on other social groups and ruining the country. "They are destroying and impoverishing Poland and robbing her of wealth while enriching foreign countries and themselves", wrote Zaremba[13].

---

[9] M. Rej, *Zwierciadło (The Mirror)*, vol. II, p. 288.

[10] S. F. Klonowic, *Flis (The Raftsman)*, ed. by S. Hrabec, Wrocław 1951, pp. 28, 32, 43, 47.

[11] *Traktat rycerstwu koronnemu, z której przyczyny się tak fałszywej monety namnożyło i czemu towary wszelakie co dzień w większą drogość przychodzą na uważanie i przestrogę przez szlachcica polskiego de Armis Roża wydany (Treatise offered by the Polish nobleman, de Armis Roża to the Polish Knighthood for their warning and consideration and showing why false money has so multiplied and why all goods are from day to day becoming more expensive)*, in: *Rozprawy o pieniądzu w Polsce pierwszej połowy XVII w.*, ed. by Z. Sadowski, Warszawa 1959, pp. 85ff.

[12] Quoted after J. Górski, E. Lipiński, *Merkantylistyczna myśl ekonomiczna w Polsce XVI i XVII w. Wybór pism (The Mercantilistic Economic Thought in Poland in the 16th and 17th Centuries. Selected Works)*, Warszawa 1958, pp. 129ff.

[13] *Ibidem*, pp. 257ff, 263.

Opinions of this kind were frequently expressed in records kept by noblemen in the form of short pieces of poetry, fragments of treatises, puzzles and replies.

Attempts to bring the estates closer together evoked violent protests from the nobility, which jealously protected its privileges and manifested its superiority in various ways. Particularly great importance was attached to protecting the nobleman's way of life which was linked with the manor house. The prohibition against townsmen owning landed estates, issued as early as 1496, was repeated in 1538 (it made it obligatory on the townsmen possessing landed estates to sell them by 1543). In practice, this regulation was never fully observed, but it was more sternly exacted in the 17th century. The Act of 1611 stated: "Since the *plebei passim...* are infiltrating the worthy Polish nobility, *nullis meritis*, but by buying noblemen's estates, and are thus diminishing the estate of the nobility and curtailing the prerogatives of this noble jewel, we decide hereby that all the towns and their inhabitants in all Polish territories and Prussian lands may *sub omissione bonorum* no longer buy noblemen's estates. And as regards those which have already been bought and given up we give *propinquioribus* the powers to claim and vindicate them *iure refractatus*"[14].

Even the slightest attempt to put a townsman on equal footing with a nobleman always irritated and hurt people of "noble birth". Stanisław Albrycht Radziwiłł noted in his *Diary* that on February 7, 1633 after the coronation in Cracow, Władysław IV "dubbed knights of the Golden Spur" beginning with noblemen, among whom were members of illustrious houses; when the turn came for townsmen, clergymen and lawyers (to distinguish them from the nobility the king touched them with his sword once or twice, while the noblemen were touched three times), some felt insulted by this conduct, especially the starosta of Ejszysze, Krzycki (Adam — M. B.), a noble man, "who became angry at this simultaneous dubbing"[15]. The awarding of the title of Knight of the Golden Spur to townsmen, conceived as a kind of ennoblement, of bringing the townsmen's social status closer to that of the nobility, was repeatedly attacked by the advocates of Sarmatian ideology, who associated this chivalrous custom only with people of "noble birth".

The nobility's main prerogative was freedom, which already in the 17th century was frequently defined as "golden" and called the apple of the nobility's eye. Already in the 17th century it frequently degenerated into wantonness, and from there there was only a step to anarchy. "The root of evil lies in excessive freedom or rather wantonness", says an anonymous author in his *silva rerum*[16]. "It is difficult to shut the mouth of freedom", said Stanisław Albrycht Radziwiłł to Queen Cecylia Renata, and in another place he wrote: "We must tame our freedom or rather its abuse"[17]. A Frenchman who visited Poland about the year 1660 wrote that the Polish nobleman "fully succumbs to his inclinations and

---

[14] *Volumina Legum*, vol. III, p. 11.
[15] A. S. Radziwiłł, *Pamiętnik (Diary)*, vol. I, p. 283.
[16] The Czartoryski Library in Cracow, MSS 377, Mf 11652, p. 637.
[17] A. S. Radziwiłł, *Pamiętnik (Diary)*, vol. II, p. 309 and vol. III, p 220.

does not recognize any other master but freedom"[18]. This was an apt observation if Marcin Błażowski had already written at the beginning of the 17th century:

> Freedom means to live securely as one wants to in one's home,
> To have no master but God, the laws and the courts o'er one's dome[19].

Reformers, moralists and preachers sounded the tocsin and warned against the degeneration of this love of freedom into wantonness and various abuses. "It cannot be called freedom if somebody lives according to his inclination; true freedom and liberty means to live according to the law", warned Łukasz Górnicki in his *Dworzanin (The Courtier)*[20]. "Everybody defends himself by the nobleman's freedom, everybody puts this coat on his crimes and turns the good golden freedom into disobedience and dissipation", pointed out Piotr Skarga in his *Sermons to the Sejm*[21]. Probably the most severe opinion of the nobility was expressed in *Reformacja obyczajów (The Reformation of Customs)* by Starowolski, who said: "This is a hapless Polish freedom if one may do what is improper"[22].

In addition to freedom, the chief prerogative of the nobility and its most popular slogan was equality. The nobility furiously opposed the use of all titles, whether of a prince or a count (Stanisław Albrycht Radziwiłł described the passionate rows over this question in reporting the debates of the 1638 Sejm[23]), and torpedoed Władysław IV's proposal to set up a fraternity of knights on the model of the Order of the Golden Fleece of the Netherlands. In spite of the fact that the king linked his idea with the cult of the Virgin Mary, extremely popular in Poland (this was to be the Order of the Immaculate Conception), the proposal could not be put into effect. The senators, fearing to lose popularity, refused to accept the decoration, and leaflets against "the cavalry", as the members of the fraternity were called, circulated around the country. The king had to put off his idea *ad calendas Graecas*. How greatly this matter perturbed the noblemen is testified to by the countless references to "the cavalry" in *silva rerum*; they were usually accompanied by outpourings about the danger of "absolutum dominium" in Poland.

An outward expression of the noblemen's equality was their habit of addressing one another as "my lord brother". Even the magnates, wishing to win popularity among the noblemen, used this expression emphasising the nobility's joint origin when addressing their clients from among the medium and petty nobility. As the clients' dependence on their patrons spread and increased, the noblemen became even more determined to keep up this illusion

---

[18] *Cudzoziemcy o Polsce. Relacje i opinie (Foreigners on Poland. Accounts and Opinions)*, compiled and edited by J. Gintel, Kraków 1971, vol. I, p. 275.

[19] Quoted after J. S. Bystroń, *Dzieje obyczajów w dawnej Polsce (A History of Customs in Old Poland)*, Warszawa 1976, vol. I, p. 148.

[20] Ł. Górnicki, *Dworzanin Polski (The Polish Courtier)*, Kraków 1928, p. 37.

[21] P. Skarga, *Kazania sejmowe (Sermons to the Sejm)*, ed. by J. Tazbir with the collaboration of M. Korolko, Wrocław 1972, p. 11.

[22] Quoted after J. S. Bystroń, *Dzieje obyczajów (A History of Customs)*, Wrocław 1976, vol. I, p. 149.

[23] A. S. Radziwiłł, *Pamiętnik (Diary)*, vol. II, pp. 89–90.

104

of fraternity. Though kowtowing to a magnate when seeking a post in his house for themselves or their sons, they consoled themselves by repeating that "a nobleman on his farm is equal to a voivode".

The noblemen's constant worry was not only the threat posed by the magnates. Even though the social structure was in keeping with the privileges they had won through the centuries, the noblemen were aware of the society's great mobility. Throughout the 16th century and even in the 17th, more ambitious and enterprising persons of plebeian origin frequently joined the estate of the nobility through marriage, the purchase of a landed estate, military service, practising at the bar or work at a magnate's court. This induced the noblemen to constantly define and enforce the border between their own group and members of other social strata. Custom was an important instrument in this constant struggle. The best reflection of this state of affairs is Walerian Nekanda Trepka's notorious *Liber chamorum*, a furious denunciation of "plebeians aspiring to the rank of the nobility", written in the first half of the 17th century. The author, a nobleman from Little Poland, soured and impoverished after the loss of his landed estate, settled in Cracow in 1630. A litigant and brawler, he filled his time travelling by easy stages from one fair to another, from one dietine to another, nosing about and collecting information and gossip about misalliances, persons born out of wedlock, about peasants, townsmen and Jews endeavouring to conceal their origin and pass for persons of noble birth. Like the majority of the nobility, Trepka did not recognize ennoblement, especially if granted by the king. The king "may offer a village", wrote Trepka, "but he cannot recreate, for he is not God. He would have to put the man back into the mother's womb"[24]. This extremely naturalistic, physical treatment of nobility was intended to drastically restrict the number of "the chosen". If the king issued an ennobling privilege, "let the man be *nobilis* only for the king, and a peasant for the entire nobility as long as he lives", argued Trepka[25].

Trepka's boundless hatred of the peasants sounds pathological. "The Wyżłowie [surname meaning pointers — M. B.] and the Kusiowie [surname meaning the skimpy ones — M. B.] must not turn themselves into noblemen; the Wyżłowie should line up like dogs and the Kusiowie should go to the peasants", he wrote[26]. He noted with indignation that a certain Brodecki had given his orphaned ward in marriage to a "landless peasant's son", hoping that the latter would let him retain the bride's village, Rudna. But he miscalculated. What upset Trepka was not the guardian's greed but the fact that "by doggish, roguish cheating a peasant without property has got a wife of noble birth as well as a village... A paltry peasant is unworthy of noble blood, which in addition has been seasoned with a village and wealth for this penniless filthy peasant..."[27]. Trepka even approved of a crime and rejoiced at it, if an ambitious

[24] W. N. Trepka, *Liber generations plebeanorum. Liber chamorum*, ed. by W. Dworzaczek, J. Bartyś, Z. Kuchowicz, Wrocław 1958, vol. I, p. 165, no. 548.

[25] *Ibidem*, vol. I, p. 86, no. 245.

[26] *Ibidem*, vol. I, p. 628, no. 2374.

plebeian was a victim. Stanisław Piorunowski "was killed with a stick on garbage behind the Mikołajska portcullis beyond the wall [in Cracow — M. B.] anno 1626. *Deposit Deus plebeum superbum de sede* [God has deposed the vain plebeian from his seat]", stated Trepka with satisfaction[28].

The carrying out of certain occupations was regarded as proof of a mean character, for this was forbidden by successive acts (1550, 1633, 1677). According to Trepka, Suchodolski's "low nature came to light" for he married a peasant woman and took an inn on lease[29]. The widow of a certain Ulański leased a brewery. This is Trepka's comment: "If she were a woman of noble birth, she would not be attracted by things which are proper to *penitus plebeis* and are forbidden to a nobleman by laws, as improper for him"[30]. Trepka was very rigouristic in this respect: "The noblemen who ally themselves by marriage with peasants should forfeit their nobility", for "he who combines a fine thing with a foul one becomes foul himself". According to Trepka, marriage with a townswoman also led to the offspring being plebeian: "a corn cockle, too, even if sown on good soil does not become wheat"[31].

But how was a true nobleman to be distinguished from a plebeian who pretended to be of noble birth? According to Trepka this was very simple: a man of a low status was betrayed by everything, by his appearance, speech, custom. For instance, Walenty Szymborski, a scribe from the Lublin district, was a "*plebeus*, for both his complexion and his habits are unlike those of a nobleman". "Pińczowski was betrayed by his peasant language, even though he tried hard to be taken for a nobleman; he spoke with a Mazovian lisp like a peasant and blabbered about his noble birth; if someone, wishing to flatter him, addressed him as a nobleman, he would ceaselessly regale him with wine. And so others, wanting to drink wine free... would flatter him and call him a nobleman". Smiglecki "courted Miss Gosławska in the Sandomierz region, but they spotted the peasant in him for he lisped like a peasant and had boorish habits". Stork from Silesia sent Miss Morawiecka "garlands on a platter covered with another one", which unmasked him at once as a peasant and he was rebuffed. The Żarczyńskis, too, were unmasked, for they did not know how to behave in society: "They were unmasked by their peasant nature, they could neither converse nor talk with the nobility, they hid and shunned [society]". Stanisław Zbijewski, the leaseholder of Uszwa, protegé of bishop Tylicki, was a simpleton who did not know how to receive guests properly. "This peasant adopts a haughty demeanour", wrote Trepka. "He decks himself out in rich garments so as to be taken for a nobleman. When he has somebody to dinner he says: 'eat, my Lord, you wouldn't have this at home'. However large the number of guests, he will get up from the table and say

---

27 *Ibidem*, vol. I, pp. 629–630, no. 2379.
28 *Ibidem*, vol. I, pp. 405–406, no. 1535.
29 *Ibidem*, vol. I, p. 523, no. 1197.
30 *Ibidem*, vol. I, p. 577, no. 2187.
31 *Ibidem*, vol. I, p. 9.

'I need to go somewhere', to get them off his hands"[32]. Violation of the noblemen's principles of hospitality invariably betrayed a plebeian.

The denial of nobility — sometimes applied deliberately as a means of confirming one's possession of this jewel following a simulated rebuke — could however greatly complicate life. Matuszewicz's diary shows that accusations of this kind were taken extremely seriously; the accused person always vehemently rebuked them, to cleanse himself and his progeny of even the slightest suspicion of plebeian origin[33]. Matuszewicz, who with passion and stubborness prosecuted a "slanderer–hag", was not an exception. It is not surprising, therefore, that Trepka did not dare to publish the data he was collecting; this would have been too great a risk; maniacal as he was, he had to take into account the revenge of the attacked and defamed people.

Alongside good, polished manners, that is familiarity with the nobility's savoir vivre, education, too, distinguished a nobleman from a plebeian, according to Trepka. Adam Bronicki was "an idiot, who could neither read nor write, an ordinary peasant", stated the author of *Liber chamorum*[34]. Paradoxically, latest research has shown that the townsmen were for a long time better educated, though this is not what the public believed. According to W. Urban's research, townsmen held the dominant position in primary education in the 16th century: 70% of the patricians and 40% of the plebeians in the towns of Little Poland could write, while only 31% of the nobility of the Cracow province had that skill[35]. It seems that the results of this research can also be applied to other regions of the country. As regards secondary and higher education, the townsmen may also have been superior, in any case nothing indicates that they were on a lower level in this respect. As late as the end of the 16th century and the beginning of the 17th, townsmen accounted for some 40% of all students at the University of Cracow, and for nearly 90% of the pupils at the academic schools of Gdańsk, Elbląg and Toruń[36]. It was probably only in the second quarter of the 17th century that the level of education in towns lowered, and this, together with the development of Jesuit schools catering mostly for noblemen's sons and with the drop in young townsmen's departures for studies abroad, led to the clear victory of the nobility in this field in the second half of the 17th century. Of course, in the countryside representatives of the nobility and the clergy were the only educated persons in the entire period of interest to us; the peasants, but for a few exceptions, were illiterate.

---

[32] *Ibidem*, vol. I, p. 472, no. 1785; p. 404, no. 1531; p. 497, no. 1887; p. 645, no. 2433; p. 655, no. 2466.

[33] Cf. M. Matuszewicz, *Diariusz (Diary)*, vol. I, pp. 473ff.

[34] W. N. Trepka, *Liber chamorum*, vol. I, p. 69, no. 181.

[35] W. Urban, *Umiejętność pisania w Małopolsce w drugiej połowie XVI w. (The Skill of Writing in Little Poland in the Second Half of the 16th Century)*, „Przegląd Historyczny", 1977, No. 2, p. 251.

[36] Cf. M. Bogucka, H. Samsonowicz, *Dzieje miast i mieszczaństwa w Polsce przedrozbiorowej (The History of Towns and Townsmen in Pre–Partition Poland)*, Wrocław 1986, p. 555.

Nevertheless, it is a fact that the nobility thought highly of education. Rej, who in his youth did not willingly apply himself to books, set a high value on "honest learning and constant exercises" in his *Life of an Honest Man*, but he understood these more as reading and free conversations than as specific studies of, for instance, grammar "which only teaches to prattle and twist obscene words" or logic "which only teaches how to quibble". What was useful in Rej's opinion was to adopt virtues and acquire general wisdom which in his view meant common sense and not a theoretical knowledge of individual fields of learning. "What will be the use of refined grammar–painted words if the truth and effect depart far from them... Or of what help will geometry be, when a person has learned to measure the world or other people's land, if he is unable to evaluate himself honestly?... Or of what use will it be to a person to learn astronomy, that is, to be able to [discover] impending things, and not to be able to use and recognize those he has in front of his eyes?"[37] (It is interesting that Rej identified astronomy with astrology.) This practical sense in the field of education was typical also of the generation following Rej. "It is a bad thing in the world to be a simpleton, and such a man cannot have a worthy place among wise men, nor will he attain any dignity. What I need is that you should not neglect the German language, for not only is it needed in foreign countries but also here, at the court of the king, our Lord; he who is at the court can by no means do without it", wrote Aleksander Ługowski in July 1639 to his son studying abroad[38]. The school, especially the Jesuit colleges, taught a young nobleman Latin and elements of history, and acquainted him with classics; the point was to give the young nobleman a humanistic polish, to prepare him for appearances at dietines and in parliament (hence the important role played by oratory), to awaken his civic spirit, as it was understood by the noble estate. Many of these young noblemen also gained some experience in magnates' courts where they attained polish and learned good manners, but unfortunately also acquired the ambition of getting on in life and servilism, as was noticed by Simon Maritius, a pedagogue from Pilzno, already in the first half of the 16th century. The sons of magnates and prosperous nobility also travelled abroad. These travels gave them the knowledge of the world and foreign languages (praised by all foreigners visiting Poland), but often yielded no fruit as regards solid studies in a specific field. A young Pole usually enrolled for a semester or two at a famous university in Italy, the Netherlands, Germany or France, attended about a dozen lectures by some celebrity, met a few people and went on. Very few men, among these especially townsmen, decided to undertake thorough studies and gained academic titles. The noblemen were more interested in sight–seeing, in the course of which they acquainted themselves with architecture, in particular with fortifications, with the art of war and historic

---

[37] M. R e j, *Zwierciadło (The Mirror)*, vol. I, p. 59–62.

[38] *Jasia Muszyńskiego podróże do szkół w cudzych krajach 1639–1643 (Jaś Muszyński's Journeys to Schools in Foreign Countries 1639–1643)*, ed. and prefaced by K. M u s z y ń s k a, Warszawa 1974, pp. 102–103.

monuments which expanded their humanistic knowledge of the Antique. These study travels were more like tourist peregrinations and they were frequently combined with pilgrimages to holy places.

Travels were inscribed in the world of ideals and patterns forming part of the Polish nobility's mentality. Rej had already warned against an excessive fondness of home life: "Try not to be too encumbered by home life", and he encouraged noblemen: "And when the young master grows up... it would not be amiss for him to visit foreign countries now and again, especially those where the people are reliable, sound, moral, where they are guided by reason and are engaged in honest learning"[39]. Conversance and familiarity with foreign countries were part of the nobility's custom, although until the middle of the 17th century townsmen were not inferior to the nobility in this respect.

But travels were only one side of the nobility's life pattern. Its most eulogised base was rural life, a landowner's life in the bosom of his family and among friends, a life comprising multifarious farming occupations. Rej had already praised the joys and benefits of a landowner's foresight, and this theme was taken up by many Renaissance and Baroque poets and writers from Jan Kochanowski to the two Morsztyns, to Twardowski and Zbylitowski. Entire volumes have been written about the patterns of a landowner's life; let us emphasise but two characteristic traits. First of all, this was a practical approach: the pleasure derived from living in the country, from cultivating one's garden, from attending field work was linked with the crops reaped, with a well stocked larder and a table groaning with food, with an almost sensual delight of consumption. Secondly, this ideal rural life also meant moderation, modest requirements; excessive ambitions were condemned in favour of a secure existence, of contentment with the little field–patch inherited from one's ancestors. Many scholars regard this as a dangerous tendency towards quietism and inertia. On the other hand, if we take a look at the records of the law courts, we see that they are full of court cases over bequests, dowries, grabbed acres, that they are swollen with information on forays, neighbours' squabbles over a piece of forest, a field, a meadow, and we come to the conclusion that the road from the ideal of moderation, from modesty in one's requirements to its implementation in everyday life was very long.

In the nobility's ideology, the pattern of a good landowner was closely linked with that of a good citizen and soldier. An ideal nobleman was expected to participate in the country's political life, attend dietines and elections and if elected a deputy, take an active part in the work of the Sejm. The noblemen were genuinely interested in political life as is testified to by the records kept by them, 70% of the contents of which consist of notes and entries connected with political events (copies of speeches delivered in parliaments and at the meetings of dietines, deputies' instructions, letters concerning political matters, poems and songs connected with political events, etc.). The nobility, which in

---

[39] M. Rej, *Zwierciadło (The Mirror)*, vol. I, pp. 120, 68.

the 16th century was constructing the model of a noblemen's state and in the 17th feared all the time for its golden freedom, was really the most politicised group of old Polish society, a group highly interested in public matters. It was not only its numerical strength, but also the degree of its politicisation that distinguished it from the nobility of other European countries.

The nobility's privileges were attributed to its chivalry, to its duty to shed blood in defence of the country. A landowner was always to be ready to become a soldier, to exchange the plough for the sword, as the ancient Cincinnatus had done. Courage was regarded as an inborn trait of every nobleman, who was said to be a descendant of the militant Sarmatians. The 16th century, a period so rare in her history when Poland enjoyed peace, provided few opportunities for testing the noblemen's martial virtues; only in the eastern borderlands did the noblemen have to be constantly ready to fight and seal their nobility with their blood nearly every day. The inhabitants of the safe centre of the country were at that time exchanging their helmets for straw hats, replacing their armour by comfortable garments and unlearning the hardships of soldiering. It was the 17th century which with its ominous threat to not only the frontiers but even the very existence of the Polish–Lithuanian Commonwealth reminded the nobility of its soldierly duty. The noblemen fulfilled this duty sometimes better, sometimes worse; they gave proof of greatest courage and self–sacrifice, but there were also cowards and persons avoiding all effort among them. Nevertheless, the ideal of the defender of the motherland and the Catholic faith (the invaders were mainly people of other religions — Swedes, Turks, Tartars) was inscribed in the canon of Sarmatism as its main watchword.

As Sarmatism adorned the nobility's genealogy with increasingly splendid colours, eulogised its real and imagined virtues, its way of life and political role, making it the only representative of the nation, the townsman was being pushed ever more clearly to the fringe of social life. The weak urban population was unable to produce its own ideology and custom which could have successfully competed with those of the nobility. Urban literature with a plebeian tinge (Biernat of Lublin, Sebastian Petrycy of Pilzno and others), rich even as late as the 16th century, weakened visibly in the 17th. The output of Władysławiusz, Jan of Kijany, Roździeński and various anonymous minstrels and epigramists was but a margin of the main current of the 17th century literature proclaiming the victorious world outlook of the nobility. Already in the 16th century some townsmen had gone over to the nobility's camp. Łukasz Górnicki, a townsman by birth, demonstrated the superiority of the nobility over the other estates in his *Courtier.* "And this is why it nearly always happens that in a battle or a place where people can win respect, a nobleman manages better and is more prominent than a man of another descent; for nature has into everything sown this hidden seed which has the property and power taken from the first seed and it transfers these to the seed it generates and makes it the same as it is. We see this not only in the herds of horses and other animals but also in trees, the branches of which are always similar... to the trunk..."[40]. From the end of the 16th century writers began to express the nobility's ideology and opinions ever more strongly to the exclusion of other views: they glorified the government system of the Commonwealth, extolled the ancient origin of the Sarmatians, shaped the pattern of the hero, presenting him as a knight from the borderlands defending his country and his faith, and praised the joys of life in a manor house. This was done by writers of both noble and urban origin. "Even townsmen when they reached for the pen, put on a nobleman's mask", wrote A. Brückner[41]. At the beginning of the 17th century, Jan Jurkowski, a teacher from Pilzno in Little Poland, included by some scholars in the plebeian current (because he demanded the strengthening of royal power), sang the glory of the old Sarmatians, thus glorifying the nobility in spite of some criticism, extolled the nobility's virtues and courage and even took over the xenophobia characteristic of the nobility. He was fascinated by the vision of the knight defending his country and faith and colonising the borderlands, and approved of the nobility's social programme, keeping the soldierly occupations for people of noble birth, leaving the tilling of land to the peasants, and exertions over profits to the merchants and Jews. In *Chorągiew Wandalinowa* (*Wandaline Banner*) Jurkowski says:

> *It's the gentry's craft to engage in soldiery*
> *And leave crops to boors addicted to drudgery*
> *Let yeomen till land, grow wheat for the daily bread*
> *Let women count profits from spinning a fine thread*
> *Let merchants have gold, let the Jew count his treasure*
> *You stick to the soldier's prize, your only measure,*
> *But not at home...*[42]

Józef Bartłomiej Zimorowic, the son of a bricklayer from Lwów and later mayor of the town and owner of an estate in its neighbourhood, glorified the nobility's bravery in the battle of Chocim, praised gardening and land cultivation and adopted the nobility's point of view in condemning the peasants' rebellions[43]. Such examples can be multiplied.

An important role in the adoption of the Sarmatian ideology by townspeople was undoubtedly played by their Polonisation, which was very rapid in the 17th century. The German, Armenian and Italian nationality groups, losing their distinctiveness and fusing together, adopted what was the fullest expression of Polishness, namely, the culture and custom created by the nobility. At that time the nobility not only identified itself with the nation; it was indeed the leading section of society, a section which was the most awake and therefore fit to take a conscious, mature part in national life. In these conditions, Poloni-

---

[40] Ł. Górnicki, *Dworzanin* (*The Courtier*), ed. by K. J. Turowski, Kraków 1858, pp. 35–36.
[41] In the preface to K. Badecki's *Literatura mieszczańska* (*Townsmen's Literature*), Lwów 1925, p. IX.
[42] Quoted after M. Bogucka, *Miejsce mieszczanina* (*The Place of the Townsman*), p. 189.
[43] *Ibidem*.

sation naturally meant subordination to the nobility's custom and culture and acceptance of Sarmatism. This was usually accompanied by the consolidation of the influence of Catholicism and the Counter–Reformation. It is worth pointing out that only the circles which retained their ethnic and religious distinctiveness were resistant to Sarmatism and its patterns in ideology and custom. A characteristic example in this respect was provided by the Jews who in the 16th and 17th centuries constituted large groups in many towns and villages and were hermetically closed to other cultures, customs and religions. Pomeranian townspeople are an even more characteristic example. Because of their size, prosperity and weak Polonisation (a result of their Lutheran or Calvinist religion and their close contacts with Dutch and German towns), the towns of Royal Prussia were culture–forming centres with specific original characteristics. The Prussian townspeople always displayed great independence, also in ideology, which manifested itself in their frequent criticism of the nobility and its socio–political programme. This was reflected in the well known *Tragedy about the Rich Man and Lazarus* with its bold anti–nobility and anti–magnatial undertones. Researchers (T. Witczak) have lately expressed the opinion that the *Tragedy* was written by Marcin Gremboszewski, a musician and poet in the service of the Gdańsk council. One should not, however, forget that the same Prussian urban milieu also created dozens of historical and political poems, eulogies and incidental verses tinged with the ideology and emotional tones of Sarmatism and frequently dedicated to individual magnates and rulers. Thus, even the culture of Royal Prussia, an exceptionally urbanised area for Polish conditions and different from the rest of Poland in its social and nationality structure and customs, combined elements characteristic of townsmen's culture with those of the nobility's culture, so that one can hardly speak of the formation and functioning of two equal cultural models; this was rather a model which was an interesting symbiosis of various elements.

At the end of the 16th century, the townspeople, especially the upper strata, being unable to create their own model, began to succumb to the influence of the nobility's culture and customs. This was connected with their fascination in the lustre of the noblemen's treasure and their aspiration not so much to level the estate barriers (which was evident as late as the first half of the 16th century) as to find themselves on the other, "better" side of these barriers. This was sought by the entire city of Cracow which by virtue of the privilege of 1493, confirmed in 1513, acquired the nobility's rights; as a result, its deputies participated in the debates of the dietines and the Sejm (with a vote only on urban matters), took part in elections, and the inhabitants of Cracow had the right to purchase and own landed estates. Similar rights were acquired by Wilno in 1568 and Lwów in 1658 (Poznań and Warsaw tried hard to acquire them). In practice also the largest Prussian towns, Gdańsk, Toruń and Elbląg, had the status of the nobility, though not quite formally (participation in dietines, the right to own land, the right to send representatives to the Sejm with the status of observers). Ennoblement was the life ideal of the individual townsman. It meant not only social but also cultural promotion and was the condition *sine qua non* for gaining social esteem in one's own eyes and in the eyes of others. Those who failed to be ennobled tried to at least imitate the noblemen's customs, regarding them as a better, ennobling style of behaviour. The result was that the nobility's code of conduct, custom and mentality penetrated into towns. It was, above all, the upper, prosperous strata of the inhabitants of towns which spurred by ambition, tried to become similar to the nobility in various ways; they were the only urban strata which could afford this.

The interesting and extremely important question of peasant culture in old Poland is still to a large extent a puzzle. The simplified picture of exploitation and poverty presented by economic historians in the 1950s has already been largely corrected. In the 16th and even in the first half of the 17th century, the Polish village seems to have still been relatively rich, especially as regards its upper strata, the rich farmers. The degree of this prosperity depended on the region. The records of law courts present peasants as active, enterprising economic activists who bought and sold land, buildings and cattle, divided their property, extended loans, owned large amounts of cash, to say nothing of cattle and grain, drew up their last wills, ensured the future of their wives and children in the event of their death, etc. A drastic impoverishment and the consequent reduction of the peasants' economic activity and mobility seems to have occurred on a larger scale in the second half of the 17th century, as a result of wars and the elementary disasters linked with them (fires, epidemics).

Nor were the serfs reduced to the role of passive working animals and deprived of all traits of human dignity. Flogging is no proof for in those years it was a generally accepted educative means also among the nobility and the magnates, and was not regarded as a specially humiliating punishment. An important role in the life of villages was played by the self–government, which was still in operation. Although restricted in its rights and dependent on the landowner, it fortified the dignity of the peasant community as a whole and developed its internal solidarity. It also allowed its richer and more energetic members to take part in a kind of public life. The village self–government was headed by the *wójt* or *sołtys* (lat. *scultetus*; this was frequently a hereditary post) and assessors (the so–called jurors); a village usually had six assessors and they were either elected by the community or appointed by the landowner. They held their functions for several and sometimes even several dozen years. The assessors were chosen from among the more prosperous farmers who enjoyed authority in the village and the confidence of the manor house; sometimes the sacristian, the inn–keeper or the miller became an assessor. The function frequently passed from father to son. This led to the emergence of a group of village "dignitaries" and to the establishment of not only a financial but also a social and consequently a cultural hierarchy. When taking over office, the assessors took an oath; this was to ensure their honesty and enhance their authority; the assessor was obliged to maintain the dignity of his position so as to set an example to the entire village; in case of a misdeed, he faced severe punishment[44]. The assessors were not only to set an example; they also took an active part in shaping the moral pattern binding on the village; the self–government was empowered to pass judgment for misdemeanours and watch over all the affairs of the village, that is, take care of orphans, secure bequests, appoint guardians, settle all matters concerning property, such as division of property, inheritance and marriage contracts, and also collect money for the construction or repair of the church, collect the poll–tax, etc. The existence of the self–government with the entire ritual of its functioning could not but exert a great influence on the development of cultural life and custom in villages.

To what extent was this development spontaneous and independent and to what extent was it shaped by the manor house? There is no doubt that the peasantry, oppressed by serf–labour and hardly having the time or strength to work in their own fields and their own farmyards, did not have enough strength to create independent cultural values on a large scale. They also found it difficult to continue the tradition inherited from the previous epochs. Nevertheless, the villages were not a cultural and moral desert. We have stressed above that life within the same agricultural rhythm created a certain community between the nobility and the peasants, in spite of all the differences between them. The manor house to which the peasant went for advice, for help in case of sickness or in the event of a disaster, was not something abstract for him; it was of necessity the source of various inspirations and sometimes even a model to follow in some respects. On the other hand, the way of life of the noble small holders who tilled their land themselves (a very numerous class in Mazovia but one which also existed in other regions) did not differ much in practice from that of the peasants. This means that culture and custom flowed not only from the top down but also in the other direction. Besides, with all their contempt for the peasants, the inhabitants of even rich manor houses did not demur from making use of folk medicine or peasant recipes against pests, and sometimes, though in great secrecy, they would send for a peasant woman skilled in the use of magic.

The influence from the top was naturally more varied and stronger, playing the dominant role in shaping village customs. This was in keeping with the inborn instincts governing imitation processes and with the natural inclination to seek ways of social promotion. It was at that time that the nobleman's manor, eulogised by poets and writers of different backgrounds, became in a way the centre of cultural life in Poland. It provided the patterns of conduct, opinions, customs and even fashions which were accepted and imitated by all the other social groups. The townspeople and peasants, dominated by the nobility and unable to create their own independent culture, imitated the patterns set by the nobility zealously, to the best of their ability. This is how a uniform custom arose in old Poland despite deep social differences and the nobility's endeavours to turn custom into a guardian of social hierarchy. This helped to diminish

---

[44] Cf. *Księgi wiejskie sądowe klucza jazowskiego 1663–1808* (*Village Court Records of the Jazow Demesne 1663–1808*), ed. by S. G r o d z i s k i, Wrocław 1967, pp. 44, 73, 108.

regional and even ethnic differences. The unification of customs was favoured by the Church, which was playing an increasingly important role in cultural life as the Counter–Reformation developed, and which regarded custom as an important controller and guarantor of the implementation of the commands and interdictions of religion (sexual life, the rules of consumption, etc.). The old Polish customs were thus a result of frequently contradictory actions, a manifestation of the differentiation of society, though at the same time they were the foundation of its unity, for they strengthened the links between the estates and the regions.

The best proof of the triumph achieved by the manor house in the field of culture and customs was the adoption of the noblemen's pattern by magnates and even the monarch. The court of John III Sobieski at the king's favourite residence at Jaworów, where no strict ceremonial was observed, was, in fact, an enlarged replica of the seat of a typical Polish medium–rank nobleman: in behaviour, tastes and way of life, the Sarmatian king was well within the canons of the noblemen's manor houses.

(Translated by *Janina Dorosz*)

XVIII

Work, Time Perception and Leisure in an Agricultural Society: The Case of Poland in the Sixteenth and Seventeenth Centuries.

Two main factors shaped attitudes toward work, time and leisure in Poland on the threshold of modern times: 1.- the agricultural character of the Polish society, 2. - the weak and short-lived impact of the Reformation, which only slightly touched the gentry as well as a part of the urban population, but did not penetrate into the masses of peasantry.[1]

The agricultural character of the Polish society was determined by the fact, that in the sixteenth and seventeenth centuries urban population should be estimated at 20% of the total. Moreover, Polish urbanization was of a specific character, with only a few large (over 10,000 inhabitants) towns of western type. Most urban centres were small - between 500 and 1,000 inhabitants and had wooden houses scattered amidst the gardens and plots cultivated by the burghers. So it can be assumed that over 90% of the population of the country was linked to the agriculture and livestock breeding and lived according to the natural rhythm of seasons.[2]

The agricultural character of the society resulted in its special mentality e.g. in its specific conception of time, which was more cyclic than linear. It resulted from the fact, that the people's whole existence was determined by the changes of the seasons, that is by the cycle of Nature. This cyclic perception of time was strengthened because of the domination of religious ways of thinking, typical of the Middle Ages but still vivid in the sixteenth and seventeenth centuries; in Christianity. sacral time is, to a large extent cyclic, as is manifest in the liturgical year

---

[1] Bogucka, M., "Towns in Poland and the Reformation. Analogies and Differences with Other Countries", *Acta Poloniae Historica*, LX (1979), passim.

[2] Bogucka, M., " Space and Time as Factors Shaping Polish Mentality From the 16th until the 17th Century" *Acta Poloniae Historica*, LXVI (1992), p. 42; Wyrobisz, A., "Economic Landscapes: Poland from the 14th to the 17th century" in *East - Central Europe in Transition from the 14th to the 17th Century* (eds.),Maczak, A., Samsonowicz, H. and Burke, P. (Cambridge 1985), pp.36 ff.

46

of religious holy days, marking the mystic recurrence of events from Christ's life: His Birth, His Death, His Resurrection, His Ascension. The liturgical year, intermingling with the changing seasons, forced a cycle into which work as well as leisure - in sum the whole human life was woven. Such perception of time and such perception of human life are typical for all agricultural societies.[3]

The break in the cyclic perception of time and the emergence of its linear conception requires a certain level of civilisation connected with the urbanisation and progress in productive techniques. The appearance of mechanical clocks on the towers of Polish town halls brought a real revolution in this respect; very rare in the fourteenth and fifteenth centuries. they became popular in the sixteenth and especially in the seventeenth century and could be seen not only in the largest towns (Cracow, Poznan, Gdansk) but also in those of medium size (e.g. Gniezno, Przemysl). Even more important was the appearance and popularization of household clocks and pocket watches. They were used in the homes of prosperous noblemen and rich burghers as early as the sixteenth century and became very popular in the seventeenth century. Probate inventories of that century frequently mention several clocks and watches even among belongings of not very rich persons. The use of watches contributed to making the perception of time more precise, to isolating it from the cycle of Nature as well as from the conception of sacrum and to turning it into a socio-economic value.

The rapidly developing western countries discovered the economic value of time at a very early date and already attached great importance to it in the fifteenth century (Leo Battista Alberti and others). In Poland, a country in which in spite of the development of towns, agriculture still predominated, people (especially the gentry) were never short of time; this is why these ideas developed much more slowly even in the sixteenth and seventeenth centuries. The typical time of a husbandman - a noble as well as a peasant - was conditioned by an instinctive sense of the time of day and the seasons: he lived in accordance with sunrise and sunset and with the rhythm of the changing seasons and church holy days but had rather a poor notion of the days of the week (except for Sundays) as well as of the individual years (unless they were marked by some unusual events such as : flood, fire, plague, war), and did not envisage haste, with the exception of the short periods of sowing and harvesting.[4]

Conformity to the requirements of time was encountered much more frequently in towns where many people were employed as hired

[3] Bogucka, M., " Space and Time", pp. 43 ff.
[4] Ibidem, pp. 48 ff.

labourers, receiving payment for some defined period of time (a day, a week, a month a half year or year). In this context it is worth drawing attention to the fact that the statutes of journeymen in the sixteenth century more and more frequently established work time in hours, sometimes even specifying the length of breaks for a meal.[5] Similar provisions could also be encountered, though more rarely, in the sixteenth century regulations for peasants working in the fields belonging to the gentry. Usually, they were met with resistance. In the seventeenth century poem of Syzmon Szymonowic "The Harvesters" a young peasant girl sings a beautiful song: "Sun, you pretty eye of the beautiful day", in which sun symbolizes the laws of Nature; the evil official of a lord tries to break them and to interpose his own artificial, unjust rules.

What contributed to a more accurate definition of time was the development of credit and monetary operations in the sixteenth and seventeenth centuries (the growth of usury, the popularization of bills of exchange) since the rate of interest depended on the length of the loan and the debt had to be paid back on time. Larger towns also witnessed an increase in the number of rentiers - people actually "living on time" i.e. from rents they received for having invested their capital in various enterprises, mortgages etc. The floating of agricultural products down the Vistula river to Gdansk, a practice which was growing in Poland in the sixteenth and seventeenth centuries, drew an increasing number of noblemen, burghers and even peasants into the market economy[6] and thereby strengthened their sense of time. The price obtained depended on how quickly the product was delivered to the market. Since many contracts were made for standing corn which was to be supplied to Gdansk later and since there were fines for late deliveries, every week or even day of delay could be assessed in terms of money. The development of the courts of law and parliamentary practice also required a more precise sense of time among broad social circles. The various courts had a more or less strictly observed schedule of cases, as well as rules on when entries in real-estate registers and appeals should be made. It seems, however, that in this respect punctuality was a virtue of the burghers rather than the gentry, as can also be seen in parliamentary practice. Deputies frequently arrived late for the Sejms, as a result of which the opening of the debates was often postponed for even as

[5] Ibidem, pp. 33 ff.
[6] Zytkowicz, I., "Trends of Agrarian Economy of Poland, Bohemia and Hungary from the Middle of the 15th to the Middle of the 17th Century" ,in *East - Central Europe in Transition from the 14th to the 17th Century* (eds.), Maczak, A., Samsonowicz, H. and Burke, P. (Cambridge 1985), pp. 64 ff .

much as few days. It shows that the Polish gentry was still inclined to treat time with disregard and did not realized fully its value. On the contrary the debates of the urban authorities started in the sixteenth century more punctually.[7]

In general it should be stressed that the attitude toward time in sixteenth and seventeenth century Poland was rather vague, despite some progress made in this direction in comparison to the Middle Ages. The easy introduction of the Georgian Calendar in the year 1582, indeed serves as a proof for the existence of a still rather cyclic, not very precise perception of time. The elimination of ten days caused by the calendar reform resulted in serious social disturbances in several advanced Western countries. In Poland, however, it passed almost unnoticed.[8]

The traditional perception of time as well as the weak impact of the Reformation on the society could not but have serious consequences for attitudes toward work and leisure. Together with the deterioration of the townspeople's position in the Commonwealth of the Gentry[9] some types of work were banned and perceived as a taboo by the nobles (trade, usury, crafts all urban occupations), while other types of work were idealized (agricultural pursuits). Work in itself was not so highly praised as it was in the contemporary Protestant thought of the early modern western urban society. Polish writers and moralists agreed generally that "without work no bread could be made" and "work produces riches and glory" (Mikolaj Rej, sixteenth century). The famous reformer of the Polish state in the sixteenth century, Andrzej Frycz Modrzewski, advised that poor men be forced to do some useful work instead of begging ("who is not working according to his ability, should not eat"). At the beginning of the seventeenth century in the well developed urban centres of Royal Prussia (Gdansk, Elbing, Torun) workhouses were established to discipline the members of the lower stratas of the urban population.[10] The idea of work as a main factor shaping the whole of human life was, however, rather strange to the Polish nobility.

Although already Mikolaj Rej criticized a man who "wants to gorge himself, drink to excess, idle his time away and with his mouth

---

[7] Bogucka, M., " Space and Time", pp. 49 ff.

[8] Ibidem, pp. 50-55.

[9] Maczak, A., "The Structure of Power in the Commonwealth of the 16th and 17th centuries" in *Republic of Nobles. Studies in Polish History to 1864* (ed.), Fedorowicz, J. K. (Cambridge 1982), pp.115 ff.

[10] Bogucka, M., "Les origines de la penseé pénitentiaire moderne en Pologne du 17ᵉ siècle" *Acta Poloniae Historica*, LVI (1987), passim.

open lie flat as an ox so that the flies get into it" and scolded those who "frivol their time away", although Piotr Skarga at the beginning of the seventeenth century condemned sluggards who "spend all their time on drinking, hunting, carousing and dissipation", the contrary current, stressing one's need for free time which should be protected as a time of rest, of detachment from everyday occupations, a time of reflection and prayer, seems to have been much stronger. Preachers emphasized that it was wrong "to work day and night" for this was a sign of greed (K. Janicki, M.Bialobrzeski). The lively social life of the gentry, a fact stressed by many researchers indicates that Polish nobles reserved much free time for themselves and did not liked the excessive preoccupation with work.

Only a few authors stated that time should be used efficiently, that it should be well organized, and that unused time was wasted time. The whole structure - social as well as economic - of the country contributed to a contempt for work rather than an idealisation of it, despite the official cult regarding agricultural pursuits, which impregnated Polish literature especially in the seventeenth century. The noblemen, in their letters, testaments and instructions, advised their sons to be industrious and not to waste time, especially when they sent them abroad, for neglect of their studies in this instance would have meant a waste of money, but those admonitions were often forgotten in adult life. Even if we assume, that a typical "leisure class" did not emerge in Poland and Polish noblemen actually worked, managing their manors and taking part in public life, work was not appreciated very highly. The greatest part of society, the peasants, reduced to the position of serfs, hated the compulsory labour services and tried to work as slowly and inefficiently as possible. The town dwellers dreamed of abandoning their urban occupations and of leading a life without effort, patterned upon the life of the nobility. Work was perceived as an unnoble burden, not as a blessing.

The attitude toward work was in some way determined also by the fact that in the sixteenth and seventeenth centuries labour was usually very hard; it required great physical effort because of the low level of techniques and the use of primitive tools. On the other hand, work seems have been somehow less exhaustive in early modern times than it is today. One did one's chores mostly without haste (except during periods of intensive agricultural pursuits such as sowing or harvesting), some times with consideration. Work usually constituted a social affair, linked with conversation, joking and singing. A slow development of techniques, the fact that the process of work did not change from generation to generation, resulted in the repetition of the same behavioural patterns and gestures; a ritual of work which had been established during previous centuries, was typical of most agricultural and even most urban activities.[11] In some urban centres (craftsmen, tradesmen) a professional pride in well-done work was a common phenomenon. In the countryside the existence of the serfdom did not allowed the development of such feelings on a larger scale among peasants, but they could be traced among the noblemen.

Working hours - especially for common people - were long in the countryside as well as in towns - from sunrise to the sunset, that is according to the cycle of Nature. Practically, weekdays were wholly sacrificed to work: after work one was supposed to get a meal and go to bed for the night rest, which lasted till dawn, thus depending strongly on the season (8-12 hours in the winter, 4-6 hours in the summer). In this respect there was not a great difference between work in the cities and in the countryside, as the day-night cycle constituted the general frame for human activities.

Thus work was long-lasting even if slow and not too intensive. Vacations, free Saturdays, dispensations because of illness etc. were unknown. The intensity of work was linked to the seasons: winters constituted periods of lower activity, summers periods of higher activity and greater efforts in the countryside as well as in urban centres. Holidays were numerous in both seasons, breaking every now and again the monotony of workdays; they ensured the possibility of physical as well as psychological relaxation to the whole population including commoners. According to some researchers holidays (together with Sundays) comprised about a third of the year, the same in the Middle Ages. The impact of the Reformation was in Poland too weak, and the needs of an economy based on agriculture to small to bring greater changes in this sphere.

Nevertheless exhortations to cut the excessive number of holidays were not exceptional in Polish writings of the sixteenth and seventeenth centuries. An antitrinitarian thinker, Grzegorz Pawel from Brzeziny, called too many holidays " an Anti-Christ invention", the famous preacher Piotr Skarga stated that "lazy and idle people love holidays", and that such an inclination resulted in sin. The moralists were, however, less worried by the number of festivities, than by the growing practice of working during them, especially the attempts made by lords to force the peasants to work instead of attending Holy Mass and Church celebrations. The admonitions against greedy lords, warning them not to make peasants till the fields on Sundays, were repeated more and

[11] Bogucka, M., *Obycza je staropolskie w 16-18 wieku* (in print).

more often from the end of the sixteenth century.[12] The life story of St. Isidore, the ploughman, very popular in the seventeenth century Poland, emphasised that every day he had prayed in church for an hour or two, and criticized his lord for having tried to punish him for this. It was an admonition addressed to all Polish noblemen, who already at the beginning of the seventeenth century forced their serfs to work 3, 4 and even 5 days a week on their manors,[13] a practice which resulted in the growing use of Sundays for work.

Time of leisure, which was perceived by moralists and preachers as time for prayer, time for reflection and union with God, was practically used in all social stratas as time for distraction and enjoyment. But prayer and religious practices were linked in those centuries to enjoyment, especially by some traditional customary ways of using leisure. The Catholic Church's main framework for such activities consisted of the cyclic ritual of the liturgical year, composed of the celebration of holy days, but at the same time linked strongly to the old pagan customs and popular rites of the passing seasons and changes in Nature, so dear and important to every agricultural society.[14] Festal observances and customs such as those pertaining to Christmas, Carnival, Lent, Easter, Whitsun, Corpus Christi, St. John's Eve, harvest celebration at 15th August (the Ascension of St.Mary), fiest of sowing at 8th September (the days of St. Mary, Patroness of sowing), in the countryside as well as in towns were connected with colourful spectacles, processions, rituals stemming mostly from old agricultural beliefs and traditions. They were deeply rooted in the needs of farming, aiming to protect crops and livestock and to assure good harvest and abundance of food. The Counter - Reformation contributed greatly to the development of those celebrations, using many Baroque techniques to enrich the Church festivities and thus to connect more strongly piety and enjoyment.

Church holidays and festivities, accessible to all groups of society, shaped basic forms of leisure for the whole population. It should be stressed, however, that leisure, as much as work, was also stamped by social differences and social prejudices. Polish Carnival, for instance, did not include in its plays, as in the West, the general "upside-down" masquerade. It was a custom at the Royal Court for the King, the Queen and the courtiers to dress up as peasants, but it was impossible for a peasant to dress up as his lord; the Polish gentry would not tolerate such a reversal of the social rules even for the short period of Carnival.

[12] Ibidem.
[13] Zytkowicz, l., "Trends of Agrarian Economy", pp. 6 ff.
[14] Bogucka, M., *Obycza je staropolskie* (in print).

The leisure of a nobleman should have been dignified; hunting and riding was only reserved for him and not allowed to the members of the lower social stratas. Reading and writing (letters, diaries, poems etc.) was also regarded as an occupation worthy of a person of a noble birth, as long as it was executed for pleasure, and not as a professional job. On the contrary all physical play (except dance and, of course, riding), especially playing ball, was treated with contempt as a leisure activity of youngsters and town-dwellers. The nobility criticized sharply King Sigismund III, Vasa, because of his fondness of playing ball.

As a very popular enjoyment should be mentioned attendance at theatrical shows: sophisticated spectacles at the Royal Court or the theatre organized by Jesuits, as well as paratheatrical spectacles such as the entrances of the kings and magnates to the cities, public performances on occasion of hommages, royal funerals and weddings, as well as funerals and weddings of magnates. In towns, the urban authorities and guilds organized also more or less rich spectacles. The most popular shows were in towns, as in the country side, performed by strolling players alongside rather morbid spectacles on the occasion of public punishments of criminals. The fascination with theatrical shows was shared by the whole society, but the possibility of attending them, as well as the kind of performance depended on social status.

The most cherished past-time of the Polish gentry involved a lively social round: mutual visits, long hours of eating and drinking in company, telling anecdotes and jokes. Family celebrations such as christenings, betrothals, weddings and funerals provided special occasions for gathering and meetings friends, as well as Carnival which was spent in dancing and sleighing parties. There also existed, however, such more private enjoyments as long walks in the fields, enjoying trees and flowers in the carefully cultivated gardens. Polish writers and poets of the sixteenth and seventeenth centuries (M. Rej, J.Kochanowski, and others), praising the beauty of Nature and extolling life close to it in "the quiet and happy village", disclose the fondness of the whole Polish nobility for the rural existence on their manors.

Town-dwellers, especially the rich ones, tried to adopt the leisure customs of the nobility, shaping their family celebrations as well as their social life on the habits of the gentry, buying, against law, landed estates, they wanted to live like the nobles in their country homes. The medieval urban traditions of leisure, were kept only in larger centres (entertainments organised by town authorities and guilds such as common suppers with music and dancing, contest for young burghers to prove their physical ability, procession and shows etc.). The peasants, whose leisure was strongly affected by the growth of the compulsory labour, beside enjoyments offered by Catholic Church, had rather small choice: their free time was consecrated mostly to sleeping and drinking, playing cards and dicing with the occasional opportunity to dine-out in local inns, with common music and singing.

To sum up: work as well as leisure were in Poland strongly stamped by the agricultural character of the society, the agrarian, cyclic time, marking working hours by sunrise and sunset, and denoting years by the ever returning cycle of seasons, to which the procession of religious holy days was linked formed a general shape for existence, into which human life was woven. Attitudes to hard work and leisure were impregnated by the gentry's likings and beliefs. Some types of work were regarded as taboo, while others, linked to agricultural pursuits, were highly praised. Excessive work was regarded as a sign of greed, but at the same time the owners of the manors tried to force their serfs to deliver more unpaid labour even by making them to work during holy days. Patterns of leisure were linked to social status; some of the forms of enjoyment and relaxation were reserved only to landowners (hunting, riding, sleighing parties). Only the celebration of religious festivities were accessible to all groups in society; in the same time they were strongly linked to the old agrarian customs, stemming from the needs of farming and livestock breeding.

XIX

GENDER IN THE ECONOMY OF A TRADITIONAL
AGRARIAN SOCIETY: THE CASE OF POLAND
IN THE 16th–17th CENTURIES[1]

In this study the term gender will be perceived as a form of social relationship, both affecting the economic change as well as resulting from it. The
last decades have shown the necessity of rewriting the history from the
perspective of social gender interaction. It could not be done without the
analysis of the economic situation and its changes in the context of gender
as an important factor shaping social structures.

The case of Poland in the 16th–17th centuries could offer an especially
interesting field of research because of some characteristic traits of its
development. The urbanization of Western Europe in the early modern times
resulted in the quick rise of demand for food on international markets.
Poland, an agricultural country, ruled by grain producing nobles became in
the 16th–first half of the 17th century a granary of Europe. The market
economy and the new methods of capitalistic production, however, had not
emerged on a larger scale in Poland. Polish towns, although numerous, were
small in size and weak; because the noble manor needed labour to produce
food for export, peasants were forced into second serfdom. On the threshold
to modern times Poland — a peripheral area of the European world economy
— remained a traditionally agricultural country with manorial system based
on serf labour and with hierarchical society dominated by the gentry[2]. The

[1] The study was prepared thanks to the grant from KBN (State Committee for Scientific
Research).
[2] See: J. T o p o l s k i , *Sixteenth Century Poland and the Turning Point in European Economic
Development*, in: *A Republic of Nobles. Studies in Polish History to 1864*, ed. J. K. F e d o r o w i c z ,
Cambridge 1982, pp. 70–90; I. W a l l e r s t e i n , *The Modern World System*, vol. I, New York
1974, esp. pp. 300 ff., vol. II, New York 1980, esp. pp. 128 ff; A. W y r o b i s z , *Economic
Landscapes. Poland From the Fourteenth to the Seventeenth Century*, in: *East–Central Europe in
Transition. From the Fourteenth to the Seventeenth Century*, ed. A. M ą c z a k , H. S a m s o n o -
w i c z , P. B u r k e , Cambridge 1985, pp. 36–46; L. Ż y t k o w i c z , *Trends of Agrarian Economy
in Poland, Bohemia and Hungary from the Middle of the Seventeenth Century*, ibidem, pp. 59–83.

great role of the family as production unit remained unchallenged till the end of the 18th century.

The great movement for religious reform had touched Poland in the middle of the 16th century only for a short period. Poland remained a catholic country, with convents (the alternative to the marriage offering to some women the possibility of escaping life under male dominancy and of constant childbearing), with the veneration of many female saints and with the great cult of Virgin Mary who in the middle of the 17th century was proclaimed Queen of Poland. All this affected the gender relations in Poland and was at the favour of woman's image in the mass–scale mentality. The ambivalent results of Reformation on women's situation are underlined by recent studies[3]; older works, however, expressed rather opposite views, affirming that the positive evaluation of marriage and of women as wives as well as the doctrine of the priesterhood of all believers improved women's status[4]. Poland's experience supports rather the hypothesis that Counter — Reformation, in spite of the subordinate position of women in the Catholic church, resulted to some extent in the development of female prestige.

Patriarchalism, however, was the foundation of the old Polish world structure[5]. The family, dominated by father and husband was the basic social unit in all social groups. It is not easy to define the woman's position in the Polish family as well as in general — in the old Polish society. The conclusions drawn from old Polish literature may be misleading, for this literature was strongly permeated with misogyny. The Renaissance emancipation movement then in progress in the whole of Europe, was barely noticeable in Poland. The exception was Andrzej G l a b e r, who demanded that women be given access to education, arguing that intellectually they were not on a lower level than men. This writer from Great Poland asserted in the 1530s that men were afraid "lest women should overtake them with brain power" and were therefore against educating them. "But why should these poor creatures be spurned and treated as more ignoble creatures than men?", asked Glaber. According to him, on the contrary, "the girls' constitution is very subtle and their ability to learn and understand all things is sharp and quick"[6]. But another writer, more famous, Andrzej F r y c z –

---

[3] See: Lyndal R o p e r, *The Holy Household. Women and Morals in Reformation Augsburg*, Oxford 1989, *passim*.

[4] R. B a i n t o n, *Women of the Reformation in Germany and Italy*, Minneapolis 1971; S. O z m e n t, *When Fathers ruled: Family Life in Reformation Europe*, Cambridge, Mass., 1983.

[5] M. B o g u c k a, *The Foundations of the Old Polish World: Patriarchalism and the Family. Introduction into the Problem*, "Acta Poloniae Historica", vol. 69, 1994, pp. 37–53.

[6] Quoted after M. B o g u c k a, *Nicholas Copernicus. The Country and Times*, Wrocław 1973, p. 142.

—M o d r z e w s k i, declared himself as determined anti–feminist. Chapter XXI of the book *On Customs* in his work *On the Improvement of the Republic* (*De Republica Emendanda*) has the significant title: "Women should not meddle in public affairs". This is a brief but terse chapter. "It should be brought about that women, whom God has put under the rule of men, are not admitted to public affairs" — says Frycz. "Shame on those men who, while regarding themselves worthy of public dignities, never do anything but at the suggestion of women... There is no doubt that women are born for the spindle and he who has painted Venus trampling a tortoise indicated thereby that they should be vested with concern for household matters, not public ones"[7]. Polish nobles, whose way of thinking was similar to that of Frycz's, sincerely hated the queens who like Bona in the 16th century and Marie–Louise in the 17th, instead of carrying charitable works and absorbing themselves in prayers, as tradition would dictate, wanted to push through reforms of the state and interfered in politics in order to strenghten royal power. The fact that both queens were foreigners (Italian and French) naturally only increased the nobility's dislike. The last representant of Jagiellonian dynasty, Anna, was elected in 1575 King of Poland only when she promised to renounce all her family estates to the Republic and decided to marry Stephen Bathory, who was to rule the country. Her own role in the government was never envisaged.

Marriages were usually contracted without the girl concerned being asked for consent; it was not until she was a widow that a woman acquired a sufficiently independent status to take decisions concerning her fate. The noble woman as a widow was becoming the ruler of her deceased husband's fortune as well as the guardian of the children till their maturity[8].

The wife's situation depended to a great extent on the dowry (the marital dot or the so–called portion) she had brought into her husband's house and on the family she was descended from (preference was given to marriages between persons from the same social strata)[9]. The only daughters of rich families were in great demand on the matrimonial market for they often brought their husbands large landed estates. Women's right to inherit landed property was, however, not clear enough in the Middle Ages[10]. In the early modern period the rights of daughters were limited to 1/4 of the immobilien

[7] A. F r y c z – M o d r z e w s k i, *O poprawie Rzeczypospolitej* (*On the Improvement of the Republic*) Warszawa 1953 (first published Cracoviae 1551), p. 193.

[8] J. B a r d a c h, *Historia państwa i prawa Polski* (*The History of Polish Law and State*), vol. I, Warszawa 1966, pp. 282, 285.

[9] M. B o g u c k a, *The Foundations*, p. 43.

[10] See M. K o c z e r s k a, *Rodzina szlachecka w Polsce późnego średniowiecza* (*Noble Family in Poland in the Late Middle Ages*), Warszawa 1975, pp. 42 ff.

inheritance, while 3/4 were reserved for sons[11]. As a rule therefore the son or sons were given most of immovables, while the daughters received smaller or larger dowries consisting mostly of movables[12]. These comprised cash and silver, jewellery, clothing, bed and table linen, furniture. This was the practice not only in noblemen's but also in urban families (the son usually received the house and allotments, while daughter cash and various movables), and in peasant families, in which the dowry usually consisted of livestock (a cow, a calf, a pig, sheep, hens etc.) as well as clothes and various household utensils. As if in return for the dowry the husband offered the newly–wed wife a counter–gift (Lat.: *dotalicium*). In richer circles the *dotalicium* (sometimes called also morning gift, Polish: *wiano*) was secured by the settlement of some of the husband's property on the wife as the so–called jointure (Lat.: *reformatio*). Often it was listed in a document entered into the court records as a safeguard again later dispute. After the husband's death his widow was entitled to take over this part of her deceased man property before the settlement of other inheritance claims.

The situation of a married woman was better in noble circles than in urban milieu. Noble woman had the right to rule her estates as well as to take the legal steps before the court; in the 16th–17th centuries, however, her ability to proceed before the court in her husband's absence became in some counties limited. To sell her landed estate a wife had to have her husband's consent; on the other hand in most cases husbands selling their property made this act endorsed by wife too[13]. In towns the situation of women depended on the kind of law enjoyed by the city. In towns under Chełmno law the marriage was based on the principle of full community of possessions, what meant that wives were more subjected to their husbands, who managed to hold their power over the whole of the conjugal fortune. *Ius municipale Magdeburgense* seemed to be more kind to women. Especially the rights of a woman to her goods and valuables brought to the future husband's home (dowry) were protected. The dowry could, for instance, not be seized for the debts made by husband and after his death would return without any harm to the widow[14].

[11] J. B a r d a c h , *Historia*, vol. II, p. 274.

[12] *Ibidem*, vol. I, pp. 282, 285, 343, 491.

[13] *Ibidem*.

[14] M. S ę d e k , *Instytucje i praktyka prawa chełmińskiego w Warszawie w XV w. (Institutions and Practice of the Chełmno Law in Warsaw in the 15th Century)*, in: *Warszawa Średniowieczna*, vol. 2, Warszawa 1975, pp. 227–234; i b i d e m , *Czy uprawnienia majątkowe kobiet w Starej Warszawie odpowiadały zasadom prawa chełmińskiego? (Did the Actual Economic Power of Women Correspond to the Chełmno Law in Old Warsaw?)*, in: *Warszawa Średniowieczna*, vol. I, Warszawa 1971, pp. 135–148.

However, it was not only the material and legal situation that determined a woman's position in marriage and in the family. Much depended on the husband's character, and especially on the character, energy and wisdom of the woman herself, on the role which she succeeded to win in the family. The result varied very much. There were many marriages ill — matched because of age difference (young girls married to old men) or character discord. In records one could find many cases of wives being maltreated by their brutal, sadistic husbands, wives who were too weak to resist such practices[15]. But there were also scolds and drinking women who were a plague to their husbands and made married life a nuisance[16].

The type of woman known in all Europe as *virago* or *femme forte* or *mujer varonil*[17] emerged also in Poland. This type has many representatives especially in the 17th century, like the famous Mrs. Dorota Chrzanowska, who defended the fortress at Trembowla against the Turks or Mrs. Teofila Chmielecka, who fought bravely against the Tartars at the side of her husband[18]. The old Polish society respected and loved strong, courageous, energetic women. This is what the diarist Marcin M a t u s z e w i c z wrote with admiration in the 18th century of Helena Ogińska, the Wilno voivode's daughter:"a beautiful and wise lady, of such great strength that she was able to break a horseshoe with her hands"[19]. Many husbands asked their wive's opinion before taking a decision and some not only respected their spouses but were ven a little afraid of them. In the house of the famous hetman Jan Karol Chodkiewicz (early 17th century) it was his energetic spouse who held sway while the old soldier, as is evident in his letters to her, did his best not to offend or anger his dearest Sophie[20]. The most common kind of relationship in a marriage, however, seems to have been in old Poland a partnership, based on mutual respect and trust[21].

Theoretically, it was housekeeping, care of the pantry and the dairy production, the poultry–house and the garden that was the woman's domain. The women's traditional occupations also included spinning, weaving, sewing and adorning clothes, bed linen and table–cloths with embroidery. But in fact, a woman's world was not so restrained in practice.

---

[15] M. B o g u c k a , *The Foundations*, pp. 40–41.
[16] *Ibidem.*
[17] See M.Mc K e n d r i c k , *Women and Society in the Spanish Drama of the Golden Age. A Study of the "Mujer Varonil"*, Cambridge 1974.
[18] M. B o g u c k a , *The Foundations*, p. 41.
[19] M. M a t u s z e w i c z , *Diariusz życia mego (The Diary of My Life)*, ed. B. K r ó l i k o w s k i , Warszawa 1986, vol. II, p. 315.
[20] M. B o g u c k a , *The Foundations*, p. 42.
[21] *Ibidem.*

The woman's main occupation was the upbringing of children; women were expected not only to look after them but also to shape their character and mind. The mother brought up not only her daughters but also sons; it was not a custom (as it had been in the early Middle Ages) to put the boys under the father's exclusive rule and care when they were seven years old. Despite the patriarchal structure of the family, mother's influence on the children was great in the old Polish home. It was the mother who was their first teacher; it was she who indicated and explained the secrets of life to them, formulated interdictions and commands, and introduced them into the world of norms and priciples governing the society. The noble woman also played an important role in contacts between the gentry's manor house and the peasant; she was the person to whom they came for help and advice, she looked after them when they were ill, she taught them and settled small disputes, and she was frequently an intermediary between the serfs and their lord.

A serious handicap for women was a rather difficult access to education. Only girls from the most privilegded noble and urban families were attended by a private tutor, while others have to be satisfied with their mother's teaching. A small part of girls were fortunate enough to attend a convent school or a private school for girls existing in some larger cities. The result was the great share of illiteracy among women. According to the recent studies in the years 1575–1580 in the city of Cracow 50–67 per cent of men but only about 20 per cent of women were able to sign a document[22]. In the 30's of the 17th century the number of literate women went, however, in Cracow up to 36 per cent or even more[23]. More literate were probably women from the noble strata, but the lack of research does not allow to give some more detailed estimation. We do know, however, that many of noble women conducted quite a large correspondence (letters of women from the 16th and 17th have survived). Their mental horizons were of course limited, with matters of the household, the family and the neighbours playing the dominant role, but they were also interested in the outside world and felt the need to gather information on it or even managed to travel (visits to relatives, pilgrimages).

It should be stressed however, that women's position in the Polish early modern society was shaped before all by economic factors. Paradoxically it was the backwardness of the Polish economy, its lagging behind the new

---

[22] W. U r b a n , *Umiejętność pisania w Małopolsce w II połowie 16 w. (The Knowledge of Writing in the Little Poland in the Second Half of the 16th Century)*, "Przegląd Historyczny", 1977, no 2., p. 245.
[23] *Ibidem*, p. 247.

forms and trends developing in Western Europe, that resulted in the large possibilities of women's economic activity. In her famous book on working women Alice C l a r k underlines the bad effects of the development of the early capitalism on women's situation[24]. The shift from the household as a productive unit to manufacture and factory as well as the professionalization of work resulted in the marginalisation of female labour and in the decline of the female ability to support the family with some substantial income. The survival of the wife and children began to depend exclusively on the earnings of husband and father, what resulted in the growing contempt for woman's unpaid work in the household.

The book of Alice Clark was very much discussed and criticized in last decades, but some of recent studies confirm her observations[25]. The work of A. Clark throw also a light upon Polish situation in the 16th–17th centuries, the situation which could be perceived as an antimodel of the capitalistic development. In the agricultural country (almost 90 per cent of the population of Poland were people engaged in agricultural pursuits, because even town–dwellers owned gardens and cultivated fields), with traditional system of production focused on the household, with weak market economy and the overwhelming role of unpaid serf labour, the gender relations were shaped to the great degree by the traditional economy. It is after all not only the case of Poland. Almost 20 years ago S. C. R o g e r s found some interesting traits of development of male–female relationship in a traditional agrarian society in France. She namely found, that the division of labour and tasks in peasant households is more functional than hierarchical or connected to the prestige and that women have here great influence on decisions and control of family matters[26]. Similar observations were made by M. S e g a l e n [27] who stressed an equipollence in division and distribution of roles and tasks between males and females in French peasant households, which seem to be organized on the principle of the partnership rather than on the subordination.

---

[24] A. C l a r k , *Working Life of Women in the 17th Century*, London 1919.

[25] See C. U l b r i c h , *Unartige Weiber. Präsenz und Penitenz von Frauen in frühneuzeitlichen Deutschland*, in: R.van D ü l m e n (ed.), *Arbeit, Frommigkeit und Eigensinn. Studien zur historischen Kulturforschung II*, Frankfurt a.M. 1990, pp. 29 ff.

[26] S. C. R o g e r s , *Female Forms of Power and the Myth of Male Dominance: A Model of Female/Male Interaction in Peasant Society*, "American Ethnologist", 2 (1975), pp. 727 ff.

[27] M. S e g a l e n , *Mari et femme dans la société paysanne*, Paris 1980.

In early modern Poland the backwardness of the economy resulted in the still central role of the household as a productive unit, in the countryside (both in the noble manor as in the peasant farm) as well as in towns (close connections between the household and workshop or a trade enterprise)[28]. In this situation the female work was of great importance in many fields. The serfdom, which dominated the countryside, meant that unpaid labour performed both by male as well as by female serfs was the basic factor for the noble manor existence and its productive ability. The average population density was in Poland barely 6–7 persons per 1 sq.km and its increase was rather slow. Therefore every pair of hands, especially in the situation of low techniqual level of agriculture, had a great value. Because of lack of research we do not know how was shaped the sex ratio in the Polish countryside in the 16th–17th centuries. But it seems, that because of the lesser female mobility as well as longer life expectancy a slight surplus of women could be expected (in spite of their great mortality during childbearing). Especially after wars and Cosack's uprisings in the middle of the 17th century this surplus should have been more accentuated. The big demand for workers and the great importance of female labour could be used as one of explanations for the lack of mass–scale witch–hunting and witch persecution in Poland. On the contrary to the neighbouring countries e.g. Germany, only very few witch trials took place in early modern Poland[29].

The old Polish literature[30] describes largerly the female tasks in running farms and manors. Those tasks differed according to the social status (noble woman, peasant woman) as well as according to the civil status (unmarried girl, wife, widow). Mistress of the manor had under her full control servants, especially female ones; she was responsible for cattle breeding (especially cows) and poultry rising, as well as for the manufacturing of the dairy products. The selling of milk, cheese, cream, butter as well as of chicken and eggs, often very profitable business, was entirely in female hands[31]. The gardens and orchards, including the growing of medicine herbs, was also the female responsibility, as well as the first aid and help in the case of illness. The housekeeping — cleaning, washing, making preserves (very

[28] M. B o g u c k a , *Die städtische Familie in Polen während des 16. und 17. Jhs*, in: *Ehe, Liebe, Tod*, ed. P. B o r s c h e i d , H. J. T e u t e b e r g , Münster 1993, pp. 233–244.

[29] J. T a z b i r , *Hexenprozesse in Polen*, Archiv für Reformationsgeschichte, vol. 71, 1980, pp. 280–307.

[30] J. K. H a u r , *Białogłowskiego gospodarstwa powinności (Female Household's Duties)*, in: *Staropolska poezja ziemiańska. Antologia*, ed. J. G r u c h a ł a , S. G r z e s z c z u k , Warszawa 1988, pp. 305–306.

[31] A. I z y d o r c z y k – K a m l e r , A. W y c z a ń s k i , *La femme et l'économie rurale en Pologne aux XVIe et XVIIe siècles*, in: *La donna nell'economia secc. XIII–XVIII*, ed. S. C a v a - c i o c c h i , Prato 1990, pp. 275–282.

important task because it provided the family for the winter), cooking meals — traditionally constituted the female domain. The type of involvement in all those works depended on social status enjoyed by woman. Women of petty gentry had to work in person, while the mistress of big manor in the middle class gentry or in rich nobles' milieu would control only the work done by servants and supervise their activities.

Very often noble women transgressed and enlarged those traditional fields of female activity and took over the whole of the running of manorial estates. It was the case of widows as well as of those wives, whose husbands were sickly, or drunkards, or too much involved in public affairs. Such involvement resulted in frequent man's absences from home in order to attend the regional gatherings of nobles (dietines), the General Seyms, the courts of justice (to carry out own actions as well as to take part in sessions as member of courts and tribunals). Many nobles travelled eagerly abroad or simply enjoyed social life visiting distant family members or friends. In the rich milieus they were hired managers (economs) who took the responsibility of running the estate in absence of its lord. In the middle class and among poor gentry it was usually the wife who took over the general management of manor and became a real head of the family, responsible for its existence and prosperity. In most middle and poor families women had therefore great influence on settling family matters. The field of action depended on the woman's social and financial status, beeing usually enlarged on the bottom of the nobility's hierarchical ladder[32].

Women's economic activities among peasants were very large too. Not only did the peasant woman the housework, attended the garden, took care of cattle and poultry, brew beer, gathered herbs, wild fruits as well as dry twigs, but she should spin wool and linen, weave them into cloth, make dresses for the whole family[33]. Often it was she who attended weekly market in the closest township in order to sell eggs, chickens, butter, cheese, home made yarn. It means, that cash for peasant's household was in great part provided by women. The task of women was also to produce a significant part of the rent in kind due to the lord of the village. Peasant women worked also alongside men on the fields, especially during harvest times[34]. They had to share the work due from each peasant farm to the manor; as it was often the obligation of three, four or even more working days weekly, not only

---

[32] M. B o g u c k a, *The Foundations*, p. 44 ff.

[33] M. B o g u c k a, *Staropolskie obyczaje w XVI–XVII w. (Polish Customs in the 16th–17th Centuries)*, Warszawa 1994, pp. 136 ff.

[34] *Ibidem.*

men but also the women of the family had to participate in it[35]. The common serf's harsh fate contributed to the blurring of gender's differences.

There is a great deal of evidence in sources that countryside women — probably widows — acted often as heads of the peasant farms and could keep such a position for many years[36]. Often they developed large economic activities leasing fields, meadows and lakes, borrowing and lending money, keeping mills and inns etc.[37]

The scale of the use of hired labour was in the Polish countryside rather small, but they were paid workers and paid servants both in the noble manors as well as in rich peasant farms; among those hired hands women are estimated as one half[38]. They were mostly young girls from the region, trying to earn some money and to save them before getting married. As their wages they received food and shelter (60–80 per cent of the earnings) but also some clothes and cash. We have data concerning wages paid in Polish *grosz* (penny) to female servants (young girls or older women, probably widows) in royal manors in Cracow and Sandomierz districts in the Little Poland[39].

Cracow district

Years	1530–1549	1560–1588	1611–1636
Cook	—	40	37
Servant	36	41	66
Manager	66	100	88

Sandomierz district

Years	1529–1546	1564–1569	1611–1629
Cook	23	28	16
Servant	31	42	52
Manager	48	65	130

Some rise of wages resulted from the inflation and deterioration of *grosz* (decrease of the silver contents in coins)[40] therefore is not of interest to us. More significant for our topic would be the comparison of the level of female

---

[35] *Historia chłopów polskich (The History of Polish Peasants)*, vol. I, Warszawa 1970, pp. 264 ff.

[36] A. Izydorczyk, A. Wyczański, *La femme*, p. 278. See also A. Wyczański, *Uwarstwienie społeczne w Polsce XVI w. (Social Stratification in Poland in the 16th Century)*, Wrocław 1977, pp. 183–191.

[37] *Ibidem.*

[38] A. Izydorczyk–Kamler, A. Wyczański, *La femme*, p. 279.

[39] *Ibidem*, pp. 280–281.

[40] *From 0,695 gramm in 1580 to 0,27 in 1630*, see J. Pelc, *Ceny w Gdańsku (Prices in Gdańsk)*, Lwów 1937, pp. 2–4.

wages with the wages of male workers — the difference is estimated at 20–30 per cent in average to the women's detriment[41]. Female manor's managers received usually only 1/2 of the male wages[42]. It shows that in this sector of economy, which was shaped by the free market and hired labour principles the female discrimination was more accentuated than in the traditional serfdom economy.

Female workers, especially female managers of manors — were appreciated by employers. In Sieradz district (Great Poland) in the middle of the 16th century there was a rise in number of female managers ruling whole manors[43]. In the year 1541 from 10 manors under research 3 were run by women, in 1543 from 12 manors — 4, in 1546 from 8 manors 5 were run by women, in 1565 from 12 manors 9 were run by women[44]. Probably economic effects were better when a woman was taking care of a manor than when a man was managing it. Women were often developing cattle breeding and dairy manufacturing on a larger scale than men. In the same time female wages were, as we had seen, lesser than male wages[45]. Therefore the best Polish expert on agriculture in the 16th century, Anselm G o s t o m - s k i, advised to hire an experienced female rather than a male manager for running a manor[46].

Similar active economically were women in towns. Here too we have to look at the sex ratio first as an important factor shaping gender relations. This ratio is rather difficult to establish because of the lack of demographic research. The older scholars supposed that a surplus of women existed in big cities during the Middle Age as well as in the 16th–17th centuries[47]. Some recent studies however, put it in doubt[48]. We could risk a supposition that in the big city of Danzig, an extremely active harbour with a constant influx of immigrants[49] the male population would exceed in number the female group. The question is more difficult to answer for Polish capitals — Warsaw and Cracow. The high death rate among young women giving birth (some scholars think it resulted in the shorter life expectancy for

---

[41] A. I z y d o r c z y k – K a m l e r, A. W y c z a ń s k i, *La femme*, p. 81.

[42] *Ibidem.*

[43] A. W y c z a ń s k i, *Kobiety kierowniczki folwarków w starostwie sieradzkim w XVI w. (Women Managers of Manors in Sieradz District in the 16th Century)*, "Zapiski Historyczne" vol. XLI, 1976 no 3, pp. 41–49.

[44] *Ibidem.*

[45] *Ibidem.*

[46] A. G o s t o m s k i, *Gospodarstwo (The Housekeeping)*, ed. S. I n g l o t, Wrocław 1951, p. 94.

[47] See E. E n n e n, *Frauen im Mittelalter*, München 1984, pp. 141–147.

[48] *Ibidem.*

[49] S. G i e r s z e w s k i, *Obywatele miast Polski przedrozbiorowej (Citizens in Polish Cities Before Partitions)*, Warszawa 1973, p. 55.

females than males in those times[50]) as well as the high number of *clerus* among town's population[51] allow us to assume rather superior number of men in Warsaw[52] and in Cracow. But in small towns the situation could have been quite different.

Another factor moulding women's situation was the level of the economic development of the city. The average earnings as well as the demand for labour on the city market were shaping the situation of many women from lower strata of the urban society, either allowing them to stay at home to perform household duties only or pushing them to seek some work outside. In Danzig e.g. where in result of the spectacular growth of trade and crafts and the development of the early capitalism[53] the household as production unit began to loose its monopoly and the demand for hired workers was expanding, the woman's work outside the household became in the 16th–17th centuries a necessity[54]. In other Polish big cities, in Warsaw and Cracow, the request for woman's labour outside home was limited because of the weaker development of local industry and trade[55]. Similarly looked the situation in small towns.

The lack of education as well as an inferior legal position (in Polish towns women were regarded as persons without full civic rights and could not act unaided in courts of justice[56]) were a serious handicap to women as the big trade and banking are concerned. Very few women were engaged in the large international exchange as well as in big credit operations; I have found almost no traces of female foreign trade in Danzig or in Warsaw[57]. Some widows seem to run their late husband's affaires in Cracow, but probably on a rather modest scale[58]. On the contrary — the petty trade and all sorts of peddlery seem to be the predilected territory of female merchants and

[50] See U. M. Cowgill, *Life and Death in the Sixteenth Century in the City of York*, "Population Studies", vol. 21, 1967, pp. 61–62.

[51] See M. Bogucka, *Warszawa w latach 1526–1720 (Warsaw in the years 1526–1720)*, in: *Warszawa w latach 1526–1795*, ed. A. Zahorski, Warszawa 1984, pp. 15, 192; J. Bieniarzówna, J. M. Małecki, *Dzieje Krakowa. Kraków w wiekach XVI–XVIII (History of Cracow. The City in the 16th–18th Centuries)*, Kraków 1984, pp. 262 ff.

[52] See C. Kuklo, *Rodzina w osiemnastowiecznej Warszawie (The Family in the City of Warsaw in the 18th Century)*, Białystok 1991, p. 73.

[53] M. Bogucka, *Gdańsk jako ośrodek produkcyjny w XIV–XVII w. (Danzig as a Centre of Production in the 14th–17th Centuries)*, Warszawa 1962, pp. 7–165.

[54] See M. Bogucka, *Women and Economic Life in the Polish Cities During the 16th–17th Centuries*, in: *La donna*, pp. 185–ff.

[55] *Ibidem.*

[56] *Ibidem.*

[57] *Ibidem.*

[58] *Ibidem.*

hawkers, what resulted in the female domination of this field of exchange[59]. Especially the selling of food such as poultry, eggs, butter, fish, flour, grits, vegetable, fruits, was almost a monopoly of women, who because of their household keeping experience were experts on those goods[60].

The same could be said about the small credit operations and usury. Many women from the middle or even poor strata of the urban population were specialist in various forms of lending small sums of money, acting mostly as pawnbrokers[61]. They were single women — widows, as well as wives of small merchants and craftsmen, who tried to provide their families with some additional income[62].

Women's activities played also an important role in the development of crafts. It was a long medieval tradition that in many workshops master's wife as well as his daughters worked as part– or full–time helpers; on the verge to modern times in big urban centres it became a necessity because of the quickly rising demand for manufactured goods. The guild's attitude toward women remained, however, ambivalent. On the one hand the guild's authorities were keen to help artisans to improve their productivity without breaking old rules on the size of workshop (that is using wife's or daughter's help instead of hired labour), on the other hand cheap women's work was regarded as competition for men. Therefore the large rights of wives and daughters of bookbinders in Cracow allowing them to work in workshops of their fathers and husbands and even to be employed by other masters were little by little limited in the 17th century[63]. The articles of weaver's guild in Cracow already in 1532 prohibited to use in workshops wife's help[64].

Yet only few guilds were openly denying the membership to women; it was, however, usually reserved for wives of late masters as a sort of providing for bereaved families. A woman who was not a widow of the late master and yet belonged to a guild was in most Polish cities an uncommon phenomenon. We have, however, some proofs, before all from Danzig, where the economic growth generated a special conjoncture for industrial activities, that same guilds (butchers, basketmakers) were accepting female members[65]. Articles of the shoemaker's guild from Danzig (1580) let us

---

[59] A. Karpiński, *The Woman on the Market Place. The Scale of Feminization of Retail Trade in Polish Towns in the Second Half of the 16th and in the 17th Century*, in: *La donna*, pp. 283–292.

[60] *Ibidem.*

[61] M. Bogucka, *Women and Economic Life*, pp. 190–191.

[62] *Ibidem.*

[63] J. Pachoński, *Zmierzch sławetnych (The Twilight of the Old Burghers)*, Kraków 1956, pp. 161–162.

[64] M. Bogucka, *Women and Economic Life*, p. 191.

[65] *Ibidem*, p. 192.

suppose that a daughter of a master could became a member of the corporation[66]. Articles of the hammersmith's guild also from Danzig (1576) stated that a woman could be a member of the fraternity on the condition that she will marry a hammersmith[67]. In some small towns the practice to allow women to obtain guild's membership was probably more frequent. In the small town of Ostrołęka in Mazovia the membership of the guild of merchants and brewers was open to both men and women; the guild's charter stated (1622) that all members of the guild, without any regard to sex difference could trade, brew beer and sell alcoholic drinks; the only condition was to be a married person. Only "rascals" of both sexes were to be excluded from the fraternity[68].

In many guilds (Danzig, Cracow, Warsaw as well as small towns) widows were allowed to run the workshop after their husbands' death two, three or even more years (sometimes till the majority of the children or until the second marriage)[69]. It resulted from the guild's natural concern about the welfare of the dead members' families.

The reluctant attitude toward women does not mean that female work was not appreciated and used in the industrial production. We had already mentioned the help usually delivered by wives and daughters in many workshops in Danzig, Warsaw, Cracow. The female strangers were also hired because one could pay them less than men were to be paid and because manpower in some cities was not easy to find. The textile industry in Danzig in the 16th–17th centuries was based to great extent on women's labour[70]. Women were working also in the dressmaking, in breweries, bakeries and other food–producing shops[71]. Many women worked in Danzig very hard as extra hands in the building– and transport–trade, in metal workshops as well as in woodworker's shops[72]. The carpenter's ordinance from the 15th century forbade to use females except for help by woodsawing (!) as well as by giving a coat of paint or of varnish[73].

---

[66] *Ibidem.*

[67] *Ibidem.*

[68] Z. N i e d z i a ł k o w s k a, *Ostrołęka. Dzieje miasta (Ostrołęka, the History of a Town)*, Wrocław 1967, pp. 68–69.

[69] M. B o g u c k a, *Women and Economic Life*, pp. 192–193.

[70] *Ibidem.*

[71] *Ibidem.*

[72] *Ibidem.*

[73] *Ibidem.*

The large field of female activity in both large as well as small cities were the production and retail of alcoholic drinks and the innkeeping. Domestic service was also in towns in 80–90 per cent a female occupation[74], because it was cheaper to have a servant woman and the supply of females was higher than supply of male servants[75].

Conclusions:

Because of the traditional structure of the Polish economy in the 16th–17th centuries women had large possibilities to be economically active in many directions. Their opportunities for action seem to have been especially large in the countryside. In order to survive in the conditions of serfdom, gender relations among peasants had to lean more on solidary collaboration than to be shaped by struggle for domination. Probably more competitive were the gender relations among nobles, but even here the role of female work and initiative in running manors resulted in the importance of women's position in many families. The most complicated was the situation in towns, especially large ones, where the development of early capitalism and of free market economy resulted in the sharpening of the male–female competition in the several spheres of economic life.

---

[74] A. Karpiński, *Żeńska służba domowa w miastach polskich w XVI i XVII w. (Female Domestic Servants in Polish Towns in the 16th and 17th Centuries)*, in: *Nędza i dostatek na ziemiach polskich od średniowiecza po wiek XX*, ed. J. Sztetyłło, Warszawa 1992, pp. 41–61.
[75] *Ibidem.*

XX

The Destruction of Towns by Natural Disaster, as reported in Early Modern Newspapers

This study is based on a review of 300 German and 43 French non-periodical newspapers or pamphlets (German: *Flugschriften*)[1] published between 1530 and 1630. Made in hundreds of copies, very short (mostly 2–4 pages in 8°), and cheaply sold at fairs and inns or on the street, they were a source of information for the masses on current political, religious and economic, as well as sensational, incidents. As well as entertaining their audience, the authors aimed also to instruct them and to provide moral exemplars.

Out of 343 newspapers, 26 (about 8%) deal with the destruction of towns: 4 by fire (Magdeburg 1613, Amsterdam 1618, Paris 1621, Breslau 1628),[2] 6 by earthquake (6 towns in Arabia 1580, Vienna 1581, Vienna again, but also Prague and other Czech towns 1590, Reval 1592, 6 towns in Northern Italy 1627, Mekka 1630),[3] 8 by flood (Rome 1530, Antwerp 1530, several towns in the Netherlands 1570, Antwerp 1570, suburb St. Marcel in Paris 1579, Weimar 1613, Warsaw 1625),[4] 8 by terrific tempests and storms (Oels, Silesia 1535, Malines, Solothurn, Lecce 1546, Freyberg, Meissen 1559, Malines 1564, Annaberg, Meissen 1565, Troppau, Silesia 1574, Reinberg, Moravia 1622, Wolleschaw (probably Wohlau), Silesia 1625).[5]

Most of the newspapers under review were Protestant writings, and only a few (the French ones) represented a Catholic point of view. All of them, however, coped with the problem of natural disasters in a similar way, characterising them as admonitions from God and as His warning of the coming Last Judgement.

People in early modern times lived in constant fear: of God, of the Devil, of sin and of powers of Nature. Those fears focused on disasters. People felt weak and helpless in the face of both natural and supernatural forces. Life in town was no more secure than in the countryside. Despite town walls, communal arrangements for combating fire and flood, and the mutual help which could be more effective in a well-peopled settlement than in an isolated spot, townspeople were as vulnerable at moments of danger as countryside dwellers. They were perhaps perceived to be vulnerable, even more since towns were characterised as centres of evil and sin. According to medieval and early modern views, the scourge of God had, since the time of Sodom and Gomorrah been directed against whole towns as well as against their individual inhabitants. The natural disasters which led to the destruction of towns were therefore seen as the outcome of supernatural forces, meant to convey a revival message, and to call people to repent and to reform.

Most of the newspapers under review were printed in Germany (5 in Nürnberg, but also in Augsburg, München, Frankfurt/O, Schmalkalden), some in France (2 in Paris, 2 in Lyon) as well as in Bohemia (Prague, Olomouc); in 9 cases the place of printing is not known. It is noteworthy, however, that they present news from the whole of Europe – from Paris to Rome, from Antwerp to Reval and even include the Arabian countries. This demonstrates that the geographical scope of interest was already very large.

In this study I try to analyse the newspapers as a mirror of attitudes rather than as a source for the history of natural disasters. Therefore I will not discuss the degree to which the details given were factually correct. Furthermore, I am convinced that the accounts comprise both descriptions of real facts and imaginative and theological constructions. It should be, however, said that more exact and detailed information concerns the centre of Europe in Wallerstein's sense of this term. When a pamphlet deals with Arab towns[6] or even the Polish city of Warsaw[7] the description is stereotypical and vague; the most detailed and factual reports concern German and French cities. Factual precision is also linked to the form of the pamphlet: those made as songs and ballads (in our study 4 pamphlets) and therefore designed more for oral presentation before a wide audience than for silent individual reading in private, are more superficial and stereotypical, probably according to the principle of *licentia poetica*.[8]

Ten of the pamphlets – that is about 38 % – are decorated with woodcuts.[9] That seems to be a fairly high rate. The woodcuts are rough, naive drawings which underline the text, add details to the story and picture people's behaviour during the disaster, simply to make greater impression on reader.

The descriptions of town's destruction by natural disasters are mostly anonymously written. Those few with a signature appear to have been composed by local pastors or teachers.[10] In two cases in order to make the whole story more serious, a text by a well-known theologian is printed as an introduction.[11]

The accounts of natural disasters have an uniform structure. They are divided in three parts: an introduction explaining the causes of the catastrophe; a description of the catastrophe; a conclusion stating the moral readers should draw from the catastrophe.

The causes of the catastrophes are clear: they always arise from the breach of the contract between God and man. The newspapers claim that especially in recent times, the sins of people have become great: murder, prostitution, incest, stealing, gluttony, drunkeness are daily events. The God is so much irritated by sin that his patience is coming to an end. God's great kindness, however, does not allow him to punish the people without giving them time to repent. Therefore He sends the catastrophes to remain human beings that they should reform their lives.[12]

This does not mean that the authors fail to identify some natural causes of disasters. Heavy rain and storm are often described as the cause of flood.[13] Fire is easily caused by a forgotten candle or clumsy tampering with hay.[14] There were also some attempts to explain earthquakes by natural causes. Some leaflets derive arguments from ancient writers, citing the most famous earthquakes known from ancient and medieval history. They state that the humidity of earth combined with underground fire under the influence of the stars or of the weather could cause movements within the earth and crack its surface.[15] Some incorporate within this rational approach, itself a manifestation of humanistic culture, a touch of popular beliefs: it could be also that in an earthquake some underground spirits are at work.[16] But behind all these natural and supernatural factors is always God's will and God's power.[17] He uses the forces of Nature to accomplish his own plans. Sometimes He does not deign to use the intermediary of Nature and goes into the action himself. Irritated by sins, He stamps his foot and the earth trembles and sags under his heavy walk.[18] Angered by the obstinacy and hypocrisy of Anabaptists of Amsterdam, for instance, who in spite of His admonitions and warnings had not returned to the true (that is Catholic) creed, He had sent in 1618 «twelve men of fire» («douze hommes de feu»), who burned in the city of Amsterdam 22 houses known to be Anabaptist meeting places.[19] Sometimes not only God, but also the Devil in person is active in the disaster.[20] But his activities are limited by God's will: much as he may want to damage people, he could do nothing without God's permission and therefore is only an instrument in His hands.[21]

It is interesting that among causes of catastrophes, the activities of witches are never mentioned, in spite of the newspapers under review coming from times of witch-craze in Germany as well as in France. To see disasters as being caused by witches would probably undermine a theological explanation of them as God's signs destined to bring salvation to people.

The descriptions of disasters are cruel and terrifying. Nothing has spared the reader, since the main aim of the texts was not so much accuracy of information as a moral exhortation to repentence. They usually underline the contrast between peaceful, but also sinful, daily life and the catastrophe. The disaster comes unexpectedly, falls upon unprepared people who sleep in their beds, or who – worse – sit in some inn playing cards, drinking alcohol, and whoring.[22] Within a few moments the sky becomes black, lightning strikes, it pours in buckets (the rain is often described as mixed with stones, perhaps with hail?), it is thundering, the wind rips the roofs off and tears out the windows and doors. Security is destroyed; furniture, barrels, carriages roll on the streets,[23] houses collapse by dozens.[24] A woman who dared to thrust out her head out from the window is struck by the lightening and her head is cut from her body.[25] The people in their terror believe that Doomsday is already coming. For many of them that is really true, because the storm always results in some deaths, which our newspaper accounts describe in full, possibly with many details (number of victims, and sometimes their names).[26]

A heavy storm results often in fire or flood or both. The newspapers describe water flowing on the streets while at the same time many houses with the people inside are burned. Such a horrible account is well developed in the description of Malines' destruction in 1546; here the disaster had probably really great dimensions because a lightning struck the city's Armory and caused great explosion of powder supplies.[27] Usually, however, the results of a catastrophe are probably overestimated in order to make a greater impression on the reader.[28]

Fire is another catastrophe which often plagues the town. The French leaflet on the destruction of the whole quarter of Paris in October 1621 supplies one of the most drastic pictures of this calamity.[29] The fire broke out at night in the vicinity of the Pont-aux-Oiseaux and the Pont-au-Change and spread immediately. Within few moments it was as bright as by the daylight in the whole town. The writer describes the cries and groans («les cris, les hurlements épouvantables») of poor people surprised by fire in their beds and burnt alive («les pauvres corps surpris dans le lit et cruellement brulés»). Nobody could help much the wretched people caught in the centre of disaster, enclosed by walls of fire, trying in vain to escape «tout nus ou en chemise pour le plus: hommes, femmes, jeunes et vieux».

To this horrible spectacle the sad thought is linked that the fire consumed also the riches accumulated by inhabitants of Paris. «Que de moyens furent engloutis par la flamme en peu de temps!» – says the writer – «Combien de belles et admirables pièces d'orfèvrerie élaborées avec une infinité de curiosités! Combien de pierres et autres semblables! Combien de perles orientales! Combien de chaînes, carcans, fermails, vases, basins et autres pièces! Enfin, l'on ne saurait estimer la perte qui s'y est faite».[30] The houses of several streets were totally destroyed before the fire at last died down.

Flood was another natural catastrophe which brought death and destruction to many towns. In newspapers it is always depicted with pathos and awe. The writers describe how the water is rising higher and higher taking in its possession, floor by floor, of the buildings in the town. People caught in the accident – whole families with children and servants – try to escape by climbing roofs and trees. The woodcuts attached to the leaflets describing floods show men and women, children and animals trying desperately to keep their heads above water just before drowning. Sometimes a baby is depicted floating perilously in its wooden cradle. The cries of people and animals can almost be heard. The anger of God seems to be as pitiless as the obstinacy of men in sinning.

Flood is always depicted as a symbolic repetition of the biblical Deluge, which was sent by God to punish the sons of Abraham for their sins. The woodcuts thus often depict Noah's Ark among the destroyed houses and drowning people.[31] As in the case of fire, the leaflets record the numbers of destroyed buildings and of drowned people and animals. Those numbers, going often into several hundreds, are probably overestimated. To make the story more convincing, some writers provide the names and occupations of the more well-known victims, whose terrible experiences before drowning are included in the texts.

In contrast to realistic, drastic descriptions of misery and suffering caused by the catastrophe there are also some imaginary prayers and dialogues incorporated in the text. They serve to underline the eschatological perspective of the horror. Children close to death by drowning ask their parents if they are surely going to heaven and will meet the God himself. Parents promise children salvation, and adults as well as youngsters go quietly under the water praying or singing religious songs.[32] Naive as they are, such dialogues in articulo mortis show that the authors' aim was not only information but also moral exhortation. In some leaflets such time-less theological and didactic message seems to be more important than conveying news about the event.

The texts concerning earthquakes generally fit the same pattern; their authors, however, seem to be more inclined to use biblical and classical examples as well as to be more interested in the natural causes of the cat-astrophe. That probably is connected with psychological aspects of the earthquake. To the people who believed in the solid, immobile nature of earth as the centre of the cosmic hierarchy the spectacle of an earthquake must have been the most terrifying experience. The descriptions of ruin and terrible suffering is therefore especially drastic in the case of earth-quake.[33] The number of supposed victims is also much higher than in other catastrophes – it is estimated at thousands of persons, for instance in 1627 at 70,000 persons in 6 Italian towns.[34] It could, however, be true that earthquakes caused more deaths than other natural disasters.

There are few mentions of the social response to natural disasters. Perhaps they did not fit well into the mostly theological narrative pre-sented in newspapers. Some remarks on the city's fire-fighting forces can be found in the description of fire in Paris (1621). This probably did not reflect the more secular attitude of the French author, but rather the greater development of precautions against and responses to fire in a me-tropolis such as Paris. There are some mentions on the help resulting from neighbourly and family ties such as neighbours temporarily sharing hous-es spared by disaster, husbands helping wives from floods or parents keep-ing children above water, trying desperately to prolong their life if only for a few moments more. It could serve as an argument in the discussion on supposed coldness of parents toward small children and the supposed in-difference of adults in the face of child's death in the early modern times, as presented in the works of Philipp Ariès, Laurence Stone and Peter Laslett.

In general, however, people of the early modern times seem to have been totally helpless when confronted with natural disaster. It seems that they had very limited prospects of support from social solidarity and in-stitutions. The technical possibilities of the times were limited too. Each human being depicted in the newspapers under review faces the catastro-phe alone, in the same way in which he or she will face God at the Last

Judgement. It supports the general conception of natural disaster as a fore-runner of the End of the World.

Some descriptions include stories about miraculous escapes from death. This usually concern a small innocent child, and sometimes an old man or woman, who was probably less guilty of sin and more religious as others, praying vigorously and therefore spared by God.[35] The contrast be-tween the horror of the general loss and the escape of individuals makes the whole story more exciting and in the same time impresses better on the mind of the reader an important didactic message: only prayer and re-pentance could save people from the terrible anger of God.

The newspapers of the 16th and 17th centuries fulfilled, it seems, three functions. First, they conveyed news about important events, spiced with sensational details in order to arise as wide as interest as possible. Phenomena such as the destruction of towns by natural catastrophes were sufficiently important and picturesque to discuss before large audience. Secondly, being written mostly by theologians they conveyed not only in-formation but also a religious, didactic message concerning the relation-ship between God and men. Drawing from learned sophisticated culture examples of biblical and ancient towns such as Niniveh, Sodom, Gomor-rah and Jerusalem, which were destroyed by God because of the sins of their inhabitants, the newspapers connected them with popular early-modern beliefs about towns, which were perceived by large groups of so-ciety as centres of evil and vice. It meant that their destruction resulted from God's will and should be regarded as a serious warning before com-ing of real punishment at the Last Judgement. Thirdly, it seems that this theological presentation of disasters served as a religious explanation of the misery resulting from them, and so enabled early-modern people to cope with terrifying news and helped them to control their fears. Modern psychology calls such phenomena «catharsis by horrors», a process of affirming one's own security by looking at the misfortunes of others. Twentieth-century newspapers, as well as TV, use similar tricks in show-ing us pictures of bomb attacks, drastic details of wars in distant coun-tries, African babies dying of hunger etc. Those modern presentations, however, lack the theological dimension. Even with that limitation one may say that we are much closer to the early modern men than we usual-ly think.

XX

1 The German ones come from the collection of Herzog-August-Library at Wolfenbüttel, researched by the author of the study in the years 1992–1993 thanks to the grant received from this Library. The French ones are printed by LEVER, Maurice, *Canards sanglants. Naissance du fait divers*, Paris 1993. From the general rich literature on early modern newspapers here should be cited two recent works: DAVIES, Marie-Hélène, *Life, Tought and Religion Mirrored in Illustrated Pamphlets 1535–1640*, Allison Park, Pennsylv. 1986; WATT, Tessa, *Cheap Print and Popular Piety 1550–1640*, Cambridge 1991. On the terminology see: KÖHLER, Hans-Joachim, «Die Flugschriften. Versuch der Präzisierung eines geläufigen Begriffs», in *Festgabe für Ernst Walter Zeeden zum 60. Geburtstag am 14. Mai 1976*, hrsg. von Horst Rabe, Hans-Georg Molitor und Hans-Christoph Rublack, Münster 1976, 36–61; SEGUIN, Jean-Pierre, «L'Information en France avant le périodique. 500 canards imprimés entre 1529 et 1631», in *Arts et Tradition Populaires* 11 (1963), esp. 20–22.

2 Herzog-August-Library [later HAB] 198.14/62 and T. 369 Helmst. 4°(17); LEVER, *Canards* (see note 1), 227–231, 295–299.

3 HAB 198.14 Hist. (6,84); 218.13 Quodl. (28, 56, 88); 170.15 Hi. (7).

4 HAB T 570 Helmst. 4° (26); 240.84 Quodl. (7); 240.61 Quodl. (11, 12); 253.1 Quodl. (6, 10); 223.1 Quodl. (18); 240.64 Quodl. (14).

5 HAB 198.14 (36, 159); 108.17 Quodl. (13); 218.13 Quodl. (75); 170.15 Hist. (5); 125.34 Quodl. (19); 253.1 Quodl. (11); T 570 Helmst. 4° (26).

6 HAB 218.13 Quodl. (22).

7 HAB T 570 Helmst. 4° (26).

8 As songs and ballads are made the stories about the storm in Wohlau, Silesia 1625 HAB 198.14 (159) and in Reinberg 1622 HAB 198.14 (36) as well as about the fire in Breslau 1628 HAB 198.14 (62) and flood in Warsaw 1625 T. 570 Helmst. 4° (26).

9 Earthquake in Prague and Vienna 1590, HAB 218.13 Quodl. (56), earthquake in Reval 1590, HAB 198.14 Hist. (6), storm in Troppau 1574, HAB 170.15 Hist. (5), earthquake in Vienna 1581 HAB 170.15 Hist. (7), flood in Weimar 1613 HAB 240.84 Quodl. (7), flood in the Netherlands 1570 HAB 240.64 Quodl. (14), flood in Verona 1567 HAB 223.1 Quodl. (18), Flood in Annaberg 1565 HAB 253.1 Quodl. (5), flood in Paris 1579, LEVER, *Canards* (see note 1), 221, fire in Amsterdam 1618, LEVER, *Canards* (see note 1), 295.

10 The news on tempest in Freyberg 1559 are signed by Johannes Schütz parson in St. Petrus Church in this city, HAB 253.1 Quodl. (11). The description of flood in Annaberg 1565 was made by local parson Philipp Wagner, HAB 253.1 Quodl. (6). The earthquake in Vienna in 1581 was depicted by Johan Rasch, author of religious songs, in the form of a letter to the publisher Adam Berg in München, HAB 170.15 Hi (7). The news about flood in Weimar, 1613, were composed – according to the publisher Wolffgang Ketzeln in Schmalkalden – on the base of informations collected from pastors of this city's region, HAB 240.84 Quodl. (7). The description of the earthquake in 1615 which was felt in Austria, Hungary and Böhmen was made by a parson in Reheberg, small township near Krems in Austria, HAB 267.6 Quodl. (14). A ballad about catastrophic flood in Poland (with the destruction of Warsaw), Liffland, Sweden, Denmark, Pomerania and a great part of Germany in 1625 was «zugestellt» by Michael Zezius, a school servant in Penkun (or Benkun), a small town in Pomerania on the river Randow, HAB T 570 Helmst. 4° (26). The leaflet written in the form of a letter sent from Reval to Danzig in November 1590 with news about the earthquake does not have any signature, HAB 198.14 Hist. (6).

11 In the case of Freyberg in 1559 it is a theologian Dr. Hieronim Meller who introduced the subject to the reader, HAB 253.1 Quodl. (11). In the case of Oels, 1535, it is a letter of Luther himself written 1531 to Ambrosius Moibamius, *Prediger* at St. Elisabeth in Breslau, in which Luther mentions the troublesome weather in Silesia and explains it as God's warning for the people, HAB 125.34 Quodl. (19).

12 «Es sind vil erschröckliche wunderzeychen hin und wider in kürz geschehen ... davon vil geschriben und gedrückt. Aber der meyste teil der menschen achtet solche for lügen» – says a Lutheran writer describing the storm over Malines in Brabant, 1546 – «und verachtet es, welch doch wol zu glauben, denn der Herr ist barmherzig und lest solche zey-

chen geschehen der menschen sünden halb...». HAB 108.18 Quodl. (13). In connection to earthquake in Vienna and Prague an other Lutheran writer tells: «Da durch Gott der all-mechtige sonderlich seinen grossen Zorn sehen lest und uns sündige Menschen zu einer waren buss vermanet, wo wir nicht ablassen wollen von sünden, seine straffe etlicher massen weisen und zeiten wil», HAB 218.13 Quodl. (56). «Nous pouvons dire que Dieu est extrêmement irrité contre France et que l'énormité de nos vices a surpassé les bornes de sa patience» – we read in a Catholic French newspaper about the fire in Paris in 1621, LEVER, *Canards* (see note 1), 227.

13 HAB 198.14 (159); T 570 Helmst. 4° (26).
14 HAB T 369 Helmst. 4° (17); 223.1 Quodl. (20).
15 HAB 218.13 Quodl. (88); 267.6 Quodl. (14); 288.2 Hist.
16 «Bergmännlein» HAB 170.15 Hi (7).
17 «Gott allein sey die wirckend Ursach aller Erdbeben» HAB 267.6 Quodl. (14).
18 HAB 218.13 Quodl. (18).
19 LEVER, *Canards* (see note 1), 295–299.
20 HAB 108.17 Quodl. (13).
21 HAB 253.1 Quodl. (11).
22 See the description of a storm in Malines in 1546: «auff die selbigen Zeyt is ein wirthaus gewest in der Stadt Mecheln auff dem Eck des Hoffs Bernhardts, der wirt war bey den leuthen Croes genant, daselbst sind noch etliche geste gesessen, die haben getruncken und mit Karten gespilt. Die weil aber die wirtin nach hier in Keller gegangen ist, geschah ein solcher donnerschlag das dasselbige haus ganz verworffen ist worden und die geste sind alle todt funden, der von etliche die Karten bletter in den henden gehalten, die wir-tin allein im Keller behütet worden» HAB 108.17 Quodl. (13).
23 See HAB 253.1 Quodl. (11); 125.34 Quodl. (19).
24 For instance a storm in 1546 destroyed in Solothurn 16 buildings, HAB 218.13 Quodl. (75), in Lezzo in the same year 400 houses, HAB 218.13 Quodl. (75).
25 «Item in der Blockstrasse ist eine fraw aus irem bett gestigen auff das sie ire fenster zu that, und der Kopff ist ihr so nahent abgeschlagen worden, das es nur noch an ein klein hewtlein ist hangen gebliben», HAB 108.17 Quodl. (13).
26 See HAB 138.17 (159); 198.14 Hist. (36).
27 «Durch hilff des bösen feindtes der ymmer sein böses sehet hatt der donner und plitz ge-schlagen in das hauss das man hayst Sandtthor. In welchen hauss Kriegsrüstung gelegen. Fürnemblich aber eine grosse menge fesser mit pulver. In welche der böse feindt der Teuf-fel durch sein falsche und listige Practick das ungewitter, donner und plitz gefüret das da-von das gantze Stadt und vil umbeliegende örter gezittert und eyn solcher yammer ent-standen des gleichen in den Niederlanden nie geschehen oder gehört. Denn kein stein ist auff dem anderen gebliben, Ja auch fundament des Sand thurms oder Zeughauses ist gar auss und hingeworfen von den grossen erschröklichen schlag», HAB 108.17 (Quodl. (13).
28 For instance the storm in Reinberg (April 1622) has killed 200 persons because of the stones which poured from the sky, HAB 198.14 Hist. (36).
29 LEVER, *Canards* (see note 1), 227–231.
30 Ibidem.
31 See descriptions of flood on suburbs of Paris in 1579, LEVER, *Canards* (see note 1), 221–226 as well als of flood in Weimar 1613, HAB 240.84 (7) and Verona, 1567, HAB 223.1 Quodl. (8).
32 Ibidem.
33 For instance Vienna in 1581, HAB 175.15 Hi (7), Prague and Vienna in 1590, HAB 218.13 Quodl. (56), Verona and other Italian cities on the Adige river in 1567, HAB 223.1 Quodl. (18), in the region of Apulia in 1627, HAB 218.13 Quodl. (88).
34 Ibidem.
35 See HAB 240.84 Quodl. (7).

INDEX

Russia: I 441, 442, 447, II 137, IV 11,
15, 17, 18, VI 22, VII 59
Ruthenia: I 443, III 297, IX 106, X
329, 330, 335, XVI 59
Rydzyna: VIII 157, X 334

sailor: I 443, 446, V 114, 115, VI 19,
XIII 204, 206, 207, 212, 213,
XV 67, 71
salt: I 437–443, 445–447, III 294,
296–300, 303–305, IV 20, V
113, 116, VII 60, IX 103,
XVII 99
San Lucas de Barrameda: I 438, III
303, 306
Sandomierz: VII 59, IX 99, X 327,
328, 330, 332, XI 76, XIX 14
sarmatism: VIII 165–169, XI 80, XVI
65, XVII 99, 100, 102, 109–
111, 114
Sącz: X 327, 330, 332
Scandinavia: II 293, V 109, 113, 118,
120, VIII 166, IX 102
Schachmann Bartholomy: XIV 35
Schmalkalden: XX 312
Schmidt John: XIII 214
scholars: IV 17, VIII 154, 159, XII 50,
51, XIII 213
school: VIII 158–160, IX 98, X 336,
XI 73, 76, 77, 80, 91, XII 50,
51, XIII 214, XV 64–67, 70,
XVII 106, 107, XIX 10
Schröder Georg: XV 68
Schultz Daniel: VIII 157
science: VIII 158–160, 168, X 336, XI
80, XIII 214, XV 67
Scotland: V 110, 111
sculpture: XI 80, XII 50, XIV 36, 37,
74
serfs: IX 101, XI 90, XVII 100, 112,
XVIII 49–51, 53, XIX 5, 10–
14, 19
Setubal: 438, 439, III 303
Seville: II 291, 305, XV 8
Sęp-Szarzyński Mikołaj: XVII 99
ship: I 433, 434, 436–438, 440–447,
III 290–294, 296, 300–304,
306, 307, IV 10, 17, V 109,
110, 112–116, 119, VI 19, 27,

VII 60, X 332, XIII 212, XV
71, XVII 101
shipbuilding: IX 103, X 332, 333, XI
88
shipowner: I 433, 442, 443, III 303, V
116
shipmaster: I 433, 434, 436, 437, 440,
442, 443, 445, 446, III 290,
292, 293, 300, 303, IV 17, V
109, 114–116, 119, IX 104,
XV 67
Sibiu: IX 98
Sicily: I 438, IV 8
Siebeneicher Jakub: VIII 163
Sieniawski Mikołaj Hieronim: XVI 65
Sigismund I, King of Poland: VII 65,
XI 79, 80, XIV 32, 32
Sigismund II August, King of Poland:
VII 65, XI 80, 86, XIII 209,
XIV 31, 32, 34, XVI 62
Sigismund III Vasa, King of Poland:
XI 80, XVI 61, XVIII 52
Sieradz: IX 103, X 330, 335, XIX 15
Sieraków: VIII 158, X 336
Silesia: II 140, 143, 144, 150, VI 20,
30, VII 56, 59, IX 98, 99, 102,
103, 105, XI 87, XX 311
silver: I 437, 439, 446, II 137, 139,
141, 143, 145, 149, III 300,
305, 306, IV 6, 12, 13, 15, VI
25, 27, 28, 30–32, VII 60, IX
104, 105, XII 51, XIII 208,
XIX 8, 14
Skarga Piotr: XVII 103, XVIII 49, 50
Sochaczew: X 327, 330
social conflicts: II 137, 141, 146, 152,
VII 56, 57, 67, 68, 70, IX 108,
XIV 31, XV 69, XVII 110,
XVIII 48
Solothurn: XX 311
Sopron: IX 98
Sound: I 434, 436, 440, III 290, 292,
293, IV 8, 9, 12, 20, V 112, VI
25
South: II 145, III 304, IV 6–8, 10, XI
78
Spain: I 438, 439, III 289–291, 293,
294, 296–300, 302–306, IV 7,
8, 12
Speimann John: XIV 35

For Product Safety Concerns and Information please contact
our EU representative GPSR@taylorandfrancis.com Taylor & Francis
Verlag GmbH, Kaufingerstraße 24, 80331 München, Germany

T - #0028 - 230425 - C0 - 224/150/18 [20] - CB - 9780860789093 - Gloss Lamination